Jefferson Davis: Private Letters

1823–1889

Jefferson Davis at forty-five, when he was Secretary of War

JEFFERSON DAVIS

PRIVATE LETTERS

1823–1889

SELECTED AND EDITED BY

HUDSON STRODE

DA CAPO PRESS • NEW YORK

Library of Congress Cataloging in Publication Data

Davis, Jefferson, 1808-1889.
  Private letters, 1823-1889 / Jefferson Davis: selected and edited by
Hudson Strode.
    p.   cm.
  Originally published: New York: Harcourt, Brace & World, 1966.
  Includes index.
  ISBN 0-306-80638-X
  1. Davis, Jefferson, 1808-1889–Correspondence. 2. Statesmen–United
States–Correspondence. 3. Presidents–Confederate States of America–Cor-
respondence. I. Strode, Hudson, 1892-1976. II. Title.
E664.D28A4 1995
973.7'13'092–dc20
[B]   94-47997
                                                                           CIP

First Da Capo Press edition 1995

This Da Capo Press paperback edition of *Jefferson Davis: Private Letters* is
an unabridged republication of the edition first published in New York
in 1966. It is reprinted by arrangement with Mark Hudson Mabry.

Published by Da Capo Press, Inc.
A Subsidiary of Plenum Publishing Corporation
233 Spring Street, New York, N.Y. 10013

Manufactured in the United States of America

For two valued friends in two hemispheres
Count Lennart Bernadotte
and
Ernest Going Williams

Man does not live by experience alone, but by transcending experience. To dwell in the wide house of the world; to stand in true attitude therein; to walk in the wide path of men; in success, to share one's principles with the people; in failure, to live them out alone; to be incorruptible by riches or honors, unchangeable by poverty, unmoved by perils or power—these I call the qualities of a great man.

MENCIUS, 371?–288? B.C.

CONTENTS

Introduction   xi

PART I

Earliest Extant Letters   5

The Love Letters   17

First Years of Second Marriage · To Washington and Mexico   29

First Years in the Senate   53

Secretary of War   71

In the Senate Again · Secession Looms   87

The War Comes   119

Evacuation of Richmond · Surrender at Appomattox ·
  Flight and Capture   147

The Prison Letters, 1865   165

The Prison Letters, 1866   223

The Prison Letters, 1867   261

PART II

Refuge in Canada · The Treason Trial Postponed   281

Welcoming Arms Abroad   293

Return to America and a Different Kind of Presidency   317

Family Reunion	337
The Panic Year of 1873	361
Again Across the Ocean · Brierfield Litigation	375
Speechmaking and a New Undertaking	407
Northern Animosity Lingers · Winnie in Carlsruhe	433
A Haven without Encumbrances	445
Varina Helps with the Book—from a Distance	467
Pestilence, Bereavement, and a Blessed Legacy	487
Publication, Last Trip to Europe, and the Shadow of J.E.J.	503
Plantation Harassments, Visitors, and a Fitting Memorial	531
The Last Three Years	547
Acknowledgments	565
Index	569

INTRODUCTION

IN PRESENTING THE intimate letters of Jefferson Davis I have the hope of illuminating further the character of this unique historic figure. From these letters, which were never intended for publication and some of which were dashed off under peculiar stress, there emerges a new dimension of the man. After thirteen years of probing into the reality of Davis and writing three volumes on his life in its historical setting, I came to realize that a selection of his private letters would give off further glints of "the rainbow intangibility of personality."

As the web of life is spun out of common things, these personal letters deal for the most part with the elemental, the detailed, the familiar. They reveal Jefferson Davis in diverse aspects: on the softer side of domestic daily living, at dramatic heights of statesmanship, in grief over four dead sons, through the humiliations of a tortured imprisonment, in the post-prison search for positions to provide means for his large family, in the rural quiet of the Gulf Coast, and amidst the tumultuous public acclaim in his last years. The letters give a composite picture of Davis in love, Davis as war hero, Davis in house slippers, Davis as revered by blood-kin and in-laws, Davis as an adoring parent, Davis as a pestered planter beset by floods of the unruly Mississippi.

Of almost equal value in filling out and highlighting the portrait of Jefferson Davis are the letters written *to* him. The truth about Jefferson Davis is etched in hundreds of letters he received—from his offspring, from churchmen, from Mrs. Robert E. Lee, from Franklin Pierce, from his first father-in-law, Zachary Taylor, from nieces and brothers-in-law, from admirers on both sides of the

Atlantic (including the devoted Judah P. Benjamin in never-before-published letters about Davis to his wife) and most importantly, from his vibrant wife, Varina.

Though Davis lived under the most taxing tensions for years on end, in character he is remarkably consistent. In reality he was a simple man, ruled by common sense and a good heart, with a penetrating mind, unfaltering courage, incorruptible integrity, widespread generosity, and a defined religious faith. Because of the consistency of his convictions, however, he was not always a conciliatory man in his manner. His superior mind and his inviolate composure sometimes gave him an assured air that made him resented by ambitious inferiors, but the more esteemed by understanding friends. Even when he himself was obsessed by ominous doubts he could hearten spirits individually and en masse.

In his prison cell, tormented by a lamp shining on his weakened eyes all night and by the ceaseless tramp of two roughshod guards within his casemate, Davis came to find an extraordinary consolation in Christian resignation. In the 1960's it may seem strange that Jefferson Davis was so sustained by a surety in God's ultimate kind intentions. He came to possess, as it were, a kind of mystic spirituality. Indeed, Davis's triumph in his last quarter-century was almost wholly spiritual, displayed against a "text of tribulations."

During the nerve-searing prison experience, in sequent letters to his agitated wife, he not only urged patience to cool her raging resentment, but also the solace of prayer. Varina, though something more than a conventional believer, was not so easily assuaged. In February, 1866, she wrote: "I find myself all unconsciously making conditions with God—Give me my Husband, and I will bow to everything else."

The large proportion of the letters between husband and wife during the imprisonment are included here because they divulge the essential natures of the two protagonists, even though both wrote within the restrictions of censorship. Davis's sympathetic prison physician, Dr. John Craven, ruminating over Davis's character traits and continually remarking how he bore the harshness of prison while suffering the agonies of *tic douloureux* or erysipelas, concluded that "self-control" was his most dominant attribute.

Canard will persist in history. Those historians who portray Davis as cold, aloof, unapproachable, have simply not read deeply enough into the records or have merely re-etched stereotypes originated by hostile critics. In good part because he served a failed cause, Davis had some peculiarly vicious enemies. Yet he possessed a rare gift for inspiring friendship, and his friends loved him with an ardor uncommon among men. Several bishops, who knew him long and well, unabashedly wrote to him not only of their love but of their veneration.

Obstinacy is a charge repeatedly made against Davis. Only in three instances in a thousand private letters have I found trace of it. Once, when James Murray Mason jokingly chides him for terminating a visit to him in Niagara, Canada (June, 1867), just before the herring fishing got really good, and urges an immediate return visit: "Ah! what you have lost by the perverse habit of having your own way." James Lyons, the noted Richmond attorney, remonstrated with Davis for not requesting amnesty from the United States Government so that he could again take his place in the Senate, but from a sense of honor and in deference to his supporters in the Confederacy, Davis could not ask for pardon when he was convinced that he had done nothing wrong. As the elected head of a defeated people, he preferred to spend his last years as a man without a country. A third time, in Paris, Davis at seventy-three declines his wife's request that he take a French physician's new medicine which purported "to rejuvenate old men." He said he had "rather die a natural death than an experimental one."

Doubtless there is truth in Allen Tate's opinion that "all Davis's thoughts ran on a considerably higher plane than the reality of human conduct." He was disappointed to find men moved by expediency rather than principle. He was not himself basically an ambitious man. History pursued him. High offices were presented him by compatriots. Only after persistent appeals did his close friend Franklin Pierce persuade him to join his Cabinet. In his first year as Secretary of War, a position in which he surpassed, Davis wrote that he "was paying dearly for public honors, worn out by excessive boring, and separated from all which brings freshness to my heart." Against his expressed will, and in his absence, the first Confederate Congress unanimously chose him to be President of the newborn nation. No man in American public life was less of a demagogue than Jefferson Davis; he was zealous only in the pursuit of duty.

Davis suffered deeply over the miseries of his countrymen after the war, yet there is no bewailing of his own lost occupation—

statesmanship. In June, 1888, following his eightieth birthday, his wife wrote a friend that her husband "did not altogether suffer from the sense of having no place 'among men that be'"; however, she could not help but add sorrowfully, "It is a frightful thing to drop out of one's place and never find it again." Considering Varina's love of "the world," one suspects that she minded far more than he. He was distressed by his inability to provide for her the place in the world for which he knew her eminently fitted. But he himself had an attunement with the rhythms of nature that drew him to the quiet countryside. The routine of a remote plantation—when the river behaved seemly—and the quiet life at Beauvoir were to him blessed dispensations of Providence. Though he seemed to most contemporaries a straight-backed man of action, who liked soldiering, statesmanship, and planting about equally, Davis had a secret side that could happily indulge in a *via contemplativa*. It may be recalled that after the death of his first bride, Sarah Knox Taylor, he lived for seven years in virtual seclusion.

In one aspect this volume of letters may be considered the record of a marriage, a union of strong attraction between two persons of high mental caliber, who more or less complemented each other, but who were at such variance temperamentally that they seemed mismated.

Varina Davis is a fascinating personality, as complex and contradictory as her husband is simple and consistent. A woman of intense feeling and strong prejudices, she was proud, brave, generous, and fiercely loyal to those she loved. She was also extremely possessive and jealous, and always demanded a demonstrative return of her displays of affection. She possessed a sophisticated Irish wit, and she could sometimes cut deep with her barbed witticisms, though she was not by nature unkind. She had a ready sense of the ridiculous and loved a good laugh; no one was better "company" than Varina when she was "in the mood." She enjoyed people in society and the bustle of cities, feeling herself made for the world. At eighteen, without any perceptible effort, she could attract and hold the attention of famous men, as she did John C. Calhoun one evening in Vicksburg, to the fury of other women seeking his interest. She was but eighteen when she captured the thirty-six-year-old widower Jefferson Davis for a husband. As a matron, Varina's charm was warm and glowing, her humor rich and quick. Up to the year of her death, at eighty, she could fascinate young people.

But from childhood Varina was obsessed with a restless discontent and an exasperating waywardness. When she did not get her way she was subject to neurotic vapors, and she could be lachrymose on a sagalike scale. She would display her feelings so dramatically to the household, and sometimes with such unconscious dissembling, that even her husband was fooled, though he generally managed to keep his composure. In a letter of September 6, 1844, to his youthful fiancée, Davis wrote a peculiarly significant line: "Some day I hope it will be mine always to be with you and then I shall possess increased powers to allay your nervous excitement. Until then may God and your good sense preserve you."

Even when she was middle-aged and alone, Varina's emotional disturbances could be tempestuous. In a letter of January 12, 1866, she related to her husband how a newspaper piece had upset her: "I walked until I could walk no more and then I cried and walked again. You have seen me so often troubled, I need not explain to you." Three weeks later, she wrote him: "My mind is so tossed, so tumultuously beats my heart from evening until morning, from morning to evening again." Varina frankly admitted that it was "difficult to extract me from trouble." Her husband excused her vagaries as "the defect of a sensitive and generous temper." In letter after letter to his daughters he urges them to keep their mother from agitation. By Varina's own written testimony her husband, though he was born with a high temper, would never quarrel with her, however provoking she might be. And never did he voice criticism of her, nor would he tolerate others to censure her.

However much Varina exasperated her husband, she never ceased to fascinate him, to hold his love, and to sustain him in crises. While she had a struggle to exercise control over her emotions, conversely she was most effective in rallying other's flagging spirits. She fought a formidable and skillful battle in helping to get her husband released from prison. Like Emilia in *Othello*, Varina would stand up to the devil himself. Even her husband's hated jailer, brash young General Miles, was once so overawed in a heated argument with her that he backed away in astonishment. Joseph Davis, Jefferson's senior brother by twenty-three years and a patriarch to the family, quickly found that he could not control his brother's young bride, whose will matched his own.

Jefferson himself was in no sense dominated by Varina. A relative who is now past eighty, "blood-kin" to both Mr. and Mrs. Davis, wrote me: "Only a strong man could have commanded as ardent and powerful a nature as Aunt Varina's and keep her love and loyalty. Never would she have followed a man she could dominate." And this family pronouncement seems to be borne out in the intimate letters. However tactful and gentle, Jefferson Davis was the master in his marriage and in his house. That Varina was aware of her dependence on her husband is exemplified in a letter of December, 1865: "I always knew where the glory and pride of my house lay, but never until now how entirely the strength was in your possession. Twenty-one years of happy dependence upon the wisdom and love of another so much better and wiser does not fit one to stand alone."

Varina was closely bound to her own family and was invariably and unfailingly the most dutiful and affectionate of daughters. Whoever married Varina was marrying the large Howell family. Joseph Davis, just before the marriage, decided that he had no liking for the match, for he foresaw the drain the Howells might make upon his youngest brother. But Jefferson Davis was a man of enormous generosity. It was his suggestion that he help educate his wife's brothers, William and Becket. He seemed pleased to adopt and educate her little sister Margaret, whom he supported until she married in her late twenties. His youngest brother-in-law and namesake, Jeffy D. Howell, he reared and loved as a son. It was not only his wife's kin, however, that Davis was drawn to help. He was often called upon by various nieces to pay the taxes on their farms and advance them money, which he could ill afford and which they could never pay back.

During his last years, with typical philanthropic extravagance, Davis provided education for several poor children in the neighborhood of Beauvoir. An elderly lady who was born and reared in Biloxi, wrote me: "In the 1880's there was a scarcity of money in the South. I remember my father (once principal of the little Gulf Coast College at Handsboro) telling me that Jefferson Davis 'impoverished himself to help educate young people.' They kept coming to him for guidance and financial help." Matt Tom Green of New Orleans related to me Mr. Davis's kind generosity to his grandmother, Elizabeth Tillman, whom he found destitute at the age of five in 1879 and virtually adopted, supporting and educating her.

Another drain on the family income in Davis's last decade was the stream of visitors and house guests at Beauvoir, not only persons of note, like Oscar Wilde, Joseph Pulitzer, and young Walter Hines Page, but reporters, penniless old soldiers, sincere admirers, and mere curious time-wasters.

Although often in most straitened circumstances, Jefferson Davis, whose needs were always simple, managed to live with modest satisfactions until well into his eighty-second year. Since tranquillity is more or less the good ordering of the mind, he came to possess a stoical serenity. And on his deathbed in December, 1889, he confessed that he still retained a pleasant savor for living. If these letters have a lesson for the present generation it seems to be that a man can endure a multitude of troubles, beyond the general wear and tear of life, and yet retain an inner harmony.

Not since 1923 has an edition of Jefferson Davis letters appeared. That monumental undertaking of 1923 by Dunbar Rowland, entitled *Jefferson Davis: Constitutionalist*, comprised ten large volumes of letters by Davis and to Davis, as well as his public addresses, proclamations, and impromptu speeches reprinted from newspaper reportage. The first two volumes, consisting of some 1200 pages, were filled largely with official Davis papers as Representative, Senator, and Secretary of War. Rowland's extremely valuable work was released in a very small printing, and has been examined by few other than historians.

This present work is conceived on an entirely different scale from the compilation of Dr. Rowland. I have had the rare advantage of access to some thousand personal letters of Jefferson Davis, which no one except a few family members has seen besides myself. They largely belonged to Jefferson Hayes-Davis, the only living grandson of the Confederate President and a banker in Colorado Springs. Other collateral relatives from Newark, New York, to Pass Christian, Mississippi, gave me of their smaller store. Descendants of nineteenth-century friends of the Davises—in Pittsburg, Denver, St. Louis, New Orleans, and elsewhere—have also sent me many occasional letters, of which a few seemed worthy of preserving. Numbers of pertinent personal letters of the Davises are in the collections at the University of Alabama, Transylvania College, the University of North Carolina, Duke University, the University of Virginia, the Howard Tilton Library of Tulane University, the New York Public

Library, the Library of Congress, The New-York Historical Society, and the Confederate Museum of Richmond, Virginia.

Jefferson Davis's letters to and from his wife form the bulk of this work. Because the man was so overwhelmed with the nation's affairs from 1846 to 1861, and because most of this time his wife was with him, there are comparatively few intimate letters written by him during this period. But as a commentary on his days and doings, I have selected many of Mrs. Davis's perceptive and realistic letters to her parents to reveal his month-to-month career. Some of these incidentally give a unique view of the plantation life and the diplomatic society of the times. For Varina went to Washington as a bride of nineteen in 1845, and she lived in and out of the national capital until 1861, as Davis was successively Representative, Senator, Secretary of War, and again Senator.

Because letters of the war years, 1861–1865, have already been printed in Rowland's collection, as well as in the *Official Records,* and many have appeared in both my biography of Davis and other biographies, only a few of the wartime letters are reproduced in this volume, and then chiefly for the sake of continuity. But I have concentrated on the emotion-charged notes and letters that passed between husband and wife after the evacuation of Richmond on April 2, 1865, before he overtook his wife in flight in early May of that year.

Davis's letters to his wife from prison and her replies have never before been reproduced except in excerpts. His prison letters, a gift of Jefferson Hayes-Davis, are now owned by Transylvania College. Varina's letters to him in prison have been given by Mr. Hayes-Davis to the University of Alabama.

Short extracts from some of the various letters to Davis have been quoted in my biography. But very few of the letters have before appeared in print in their entirety; a large proportion of them are wholly new. Several—like that of Varina Davis describing the death of Zachary Taylor—have come to my notice since the last volume of my biography was published in 1964.

Except in the case of a few letters, like Davis's extraordinary one of confidence to Lee when the disheartened General offered to resign following Gettysburg, these selected letters for the most part belong to the genre of "family letters." Those of both Jefferson and Varina Davis are entirely spontaneous. As a rule, Davis simply fulfills the chief purpose of a letter, which is to relate what the writer has done and thought since he last wrote. Varina's letters are also *en famille*, but those from Washington and London may serve as a social document. While Davis himself is generally chary of details, he enjoyed his wife's "running on" as good company to cheer his solitude. He found her a most talented and vivid letter writer, as did Joseph Pulitzer, and a score of others.

When one considers the various removals of the Davises, it is phenomenal that so many private letters have survived. Back and forth they went from their Mississippi plantation to Washington. Then came the residences in Montgomery and in Richmond, and the flight after Appomattox. During Davis's imprisonment Mrs. Davis moved about in Georgia and on to New Orleans, to New York, and to Canada. After his release from prison in 1867 several domiciles in Canada followed. Then there were four different sojourns of the Davises in Europe and a transatlantic trip for him alone, and settling and resettling in Memphis, before the final retirement to Beauvoir. Yet hundreds of letters have survived intact in their envelopes; only a few are torn or have missing pages.

All the letters written by Davis as schoolboy at St. Thomas's in Kentucky and all but one written from Transylvania College have been lost, as have the letters from West Point and Wisconsin Territory. These early letters were stored in an attic near Bolton, Mississippi, but Grant's soldiers found them and they were supposedly sent to the War Department in Washington. A decade later when Davis asked for the return of these letters, which included those of his parents and sisters to him, no record of them could be found in the archives. So they seem to be hopelessly lost, though it is possible, of course, that like Boswell's laid-by manuscripts in the Malahide croquet box, they may yet be brought to light.

In regard to the text of the letters as here printed, I have made numerous deletions. For instance, in Mrs. Davis's letters I have omitted long gossipy paragraphs about persons of no continuous significance in the Davis's lives, as well as routine reports on the health of herself, her children, relatives, and acquaintances. And I have struck out occasional trivial repetitions. For the reader's convenience, I have eschewed the marks of ellipsis.

Mrs. Davis, with her impetuous nature, plunges on with headlong immediacy in her composition unhampered by editorial rule. I have often broken into paragraphs pages of precipitate writing. The dash is her favorite punctuation mark (as it was with Judah P. Benjamin and other nineteenth-century Americans). I have changed numerous dashes to periods. Commas drop helter-skelter in Mrs. Davis's letters and I have put many in their proper places. Occasional lapses of grammar, like "don't" for "doesn't," are more or less Southern custom sifted down from the Regency colloquialisms. In the case of the children's letters, I have left the spelling exactly as it appears, even when in the same letter Maggie spells "beautiful" correctly in one line and "butiful" in another. Winnie, as a school girl, was quite a law unto herself as a speller, but her odd misspelling, I think, adds a piquancy to the subject matter.

Because there is occasionally a variant spelling of the names of towns and villages I have generally substituted the more accepted one. For instance, the little town of Handsboro, Mississippi, is often spelled by Mrs. Davis without an "s." But Natchez was also spelt Natches in the nineteenth century and I leave these spellings as they come.

The Southern custom of nicknames can be confusing, to say the least. The last-born Davis child was christened Varina Anne Davis, but she was first called "Pie Cake," then "Li' Pie," then "Winanne," and finally she became known as "Winnie" like her mother. The elder daughter, christened Margaret Howell Davis, was called "Pollie" and "Maggie." Why Mrs. Davis called her husband "Banny" none of the descendants venture to guess. Davis often wrote to her as "Waafe," an endearment for "Wife."

This collection of letters is not intended to explain Jefferson Davis's political philosophy. My purpose in editing these letters was quite different from that in writing the biography of Davis. Nothing here, however, contradicts its statement of Jefferson Davis's belief as a Jeffersonian Democrat dedicated to State Rights under a strict construction of the Constitution. From this position, which he had shared with his father who fought in the Revolution of 1776, he never varied in his long life.

It is hoped that the household intimacy afforded by reading and seeing Davis "in his habit as he lived" will increase understanding of and sympathy for the man whose statues in marble and in bronze stand larger than life in many Southern states. This edition of letters with their nineteenth-century accents may be accepted, not only as a supplementary biography, but as a biography in itself that "lays open the fine network of the heart and the brain" and emerges from personal into universal significance.

At the time of Davis's death, when hundreds of tributes were launched in both Europe and America, two from Virginia came near to expressing the truth about the real man. One from the gallant General Dabney Maury, who often visited the Davises, appeared in the Richmond *Dispatch:* "Dauntless courage was the foundation of that great character which so long guided our struggles for nationality. When riding along the victorious armies at Manassas, when manacled in his cell, when confronted by his accusers, Jefferson Davis was ever the same calm, lofty leader of a great cause and a great people. Great and daring as he was in war and in council, he was even greater in his home." The other appeared in joint resolutions of the two houses of the Virginia Legislature at a memorial service decreed by Governor Fitzhugh Lee: "In every position of life, whether on the field of battle, in the councils of the nation, or as Chief of the Southern Confederacy, Mr. Davis was distinguished for his fidelity to principle, lofty patriotism, and loyalty to the trusts imposed upon him. The people of the South are honored in his pure record and stainless life. His name is inseparably connected with the history of our country, and the historian of the future, when passion and strife have cleared, will assign to this hero of the Lost Cause a place among the wise and good men of all ages."

HUDSON STRODE

49 Cherokee Road
Tuscaloosa, Alabama
June 3, 1966

PART I

EARLIEST EXTANT LETTERS

SAMUEL, THE FATHER of Jefferson Davis, was the only son of Welsh-descended Evan Davis, who had been born in Philadelphia but moved to Georgia and married after he was fifty. As a young man Samuel, born in 1756, had fought in the Revolutionary War and then settled on a farm near Augusta. He married Jane Cook, a South Carolinian of Scotch ancestry. After the birth of five children, the Davises moved to southwest Kentucky, where five more children came, Jefferson being the tenth and last, born on June 3, 1808. His father, who admired the democratic and State Rights principles of the current President, Thomas Jefferson, named his last child for his political idol. When Jefferson was three the family moved a final time to Woodville, in southwest Mississippi, where at Rosemont Samuel raised cotton with the help of six slaves. In 1823, after some monetary setback, Samuel journeyed to Philadelphia to try to reclaim the property of his father. Realizing the value of formal education, which had been denied him, and believing in the rare potentialities of his youngest son, Samuel had sent him to an excellent Catholic boys' school in Kentucky for two years, and then when he was thirteen to Transylvania University in Lexington. When Jefferson received this only extant and touching letter from his father, he was a Junior at Transylvania and had just passed his fifteenth birthday.

Samuel Emory Davis to Jefferson Davis

James Pemberton is a colored boy given to Jefferson at his birth. He is to become his devoted body servant and later his plantation over-

5

seer. David Bradford is married to Jefferson's sister Amanda.

Samuel's lack of formal education is manifest in his syntax and lack of punctuation.

Philadelphia, June 25 1823

My dear Son Jefferson

I have a few minutes past taken your letter out of the Post Office which has afforded me inexpressible satisfaction it being the only information which I have received since I left the Mississippi Country 'tho I have wrote often and from various places. my Journey has been unpleasant and expensive I have been delayed of necessity about seven Weeks only arrived here last Thursday noon in bad health and continue much the same I have left James & my horses at a little Village called Harford in Maryland seventy two miles from here from there I came in Mail Stages to Wilmington where I took I took [sic] passage in a Steam boat to this place which is the most beautiful City I ever saw the place where my father drew his first breath & the place if I had applied some thirty years ago I might now have been immensely rich but I fear all is lost here by the lapse of time yet I shall continue to search everything to the extent before I leave here which will likely be late in Aug or early in Sept as such you can write me again before I leave here. I am much pleased to find that you are at College perhaps on my return Voyage I may come thro Kentucky if so I shall call and see you but if otherways I know where you are and shall frequently write to you while my hand can hold a pen let me be where I may which is very uncertain I had frequently applyed at this Post Office got Nothing before your letter and got that broke open which had been done by a man of my name. Whenever I leave here or before I shall write you that you that [sic] may not send any thing to be broken open after I am gone if any discovery should be made favorable to my interest I shall be sure to let you know in due time & should I never return to see you any more your fathers pra [sic] I have notifyed you where I have left your boy James he is in the care of a Davis Malsby in the Village aforenamed I have also Written the same to David Bradford—

Remember the short lessons of instruction offered you before our parting. Use every possible means to acquire useful knowledge as knowledge is power, the want of which has brought mischief and misery on your father in old age— That you may be happy and shine in society when your father is beyond the reach of harm is the most ardent wish of his heart.

Adieu my Son Jefferson
your father
Saml Davis

Jefferson Davis to Susannah Davis

Susannah is the wife of his brother Isaac.

Written on extra-heavy stationery, this is the earliest extant letter of Jefferson Davis. Just turned sixteen, he was a Junior at Transylvania University, when he learned of the sudden death of his father, Samuel Davis. He is the more deeply moved because his youngest sister, Mary, only two years older than himself and his childhood companion, had recently died. Jefferson had accepted an appointment to the United States Military Academy reluctantly, for he had desired to study law at the new University of Virginia.

Lexington, August 2, 1824

Dear Sister:

It is gratifying to hear from a friend, especially one whom I had not heard from so long as yourself; but the intelligence contained in yours was more than sufficient to mar the satisfaction of hearing from any one. You must imagine, I cannot describe, the shock my feelings sustained at the sad intelligence. In my father I lost a parent ever dear to me, but rendered more so (if possible) by the disasters that attended his declining years. When I saw him last he told me that we would probably never see each other again. Yet I still hoped to meet him once more; Heaven has refused my wish. This is the second time I have been doomed to receive the heart-rending intelligence of the death of a friend. God only knows whether or not it will be the last. If all the dear friends of my childhood are to be torn from me I care not how soon I follow.

I leave in a short time for West Point, State of New York, where it will always give me pleasure to hear from you. Kiss the children for Uncle Jeff. Present me affectionately to brother Isaac; tell him I would be happy to hear from him; and to yourself the sincere regard of

Your brother,
Jefferson

Florida Davis McCaleb to Jefferson Davis

Jefferson Davis had graduated from West Point in 1828 and as a lieutenant had been assigned frontier duty in Wisconsin Territory where he served under Colonel Zachary Taylor and took part in the Black Hawk War. On his way to new duties in the Arkansas back country he has stopped at Jefferson Barracks in St. Louis. Among the few family letters of this period which have survived is this one from his niece, sixteen-year-old Florida McCaleb, the eldest daughter of Joseph Davis. Her father had given her a plantation called Diamond Place when she married David McCaleb. Florida was deeply devoted to her Uncle Jeff, whom she often addresses as Brother, for she was only nine years younger than he. Woodville is the little southwest Mississippi town where Jefferson Davis was reared on his father's plantation, Rosemont.

Rocky Spring, Miss.
July 5, 1833

Once more, my dearest Uncle, I enter on my long cherished employment. Yet so lately have I arisen from a sick bed, that I fear I shall send you but a poor and incoherent letter. Illness takes from our hearts too much of their buoyancy, and enfeebles our constitutions too much, to render us even tolerably agreeable even to our dearest friends. Fever and very unkind inflammation in the eyes have kept me shut up, nearly all the Spring—and dull, very dull and cheerless does every object appear when viewed with the eyes of sorrow and ill health.

My employments since your absence have been as usual. My music when I am able to see the keys, is still a source of inexhaustible amusement.

You are, I fear, in the midst of a disease which has proved melancholy in its effects in our own land. Thank God, we are still untouched by its destructive hand. Do you take care of yourself, my dear Uncle? I have my fears! But surely one, with high hopes and bright prospects, might be persuaded to shield himself from the evil day—and, if *he* did not, why should the miserable and obscure seek to prolong suffering?

July 6—I commenced this, yesterday, and have been so unwell all the morning, that I have not been able to finish it. My eyes, are growing worse and, I know not when my general health will be restored.

You think me very forgetful, Dear Uncle, that I have not written to you, before, but my heart must be cold indeed, when I remember you no more. Indeed I have cause to complain of you, for all your friends have been favoured with some mark of remembrance but myself—not a word, not a line to tell me you were well, but I trust you have more agreeable pastimes. I am too dull and common-place, too unwearied in my perseverance, to be highly appreciated, and you have grown weary of receiving the stupid letters of a very stupid friend. So I am wishing much in sending you another. Throw it aside, if too long, but do not let me know of it when I see you— I cannot hope for an answer.

I am on a visit to the Hurricane for some days, as Papa leaves to-morrow for Jackson and I have promised to remain with Mama, until he returns. She speaks of you frequently, and with affection and says, she would write to you, but thinks you would not care for her letters.

I anticipate a visit to Woodville in a few weeks, if my health will allow me to accomplish the trip. You are not here to go with us now—will we ever meet again? If not, I know my Dear Uncle too well to think he will forget me, even though the world should smile fondly on him, and his country hold out fair rewards to his ambitions.

You will never forget me, and I know that you will desire to see me again. Cherish ambition, cherish pride, and run from excitement to excitement, it will prevent that ever-preying upon melancholy, it will blunt your sensibilities, and cause you to be unmarred —armoured amidst all afflictions. You have cause to look for happiness, and that you may gather its sweet blossoms to your bosom at last, do I fondly pray. But—I, who am the very type of all obscurity, whose life has been but a tissue of misfortunes from my very birth. Your Sister Florida

David Bradford to Jefferson Davis

Lieutenant Davis is now stationed at Fort Gibson, Arkansas. Bradford was married to Jefferson's sister Amanda. James (Jim) Pemberton is

Davis's colored body servant who is with him in Arkansas. Jim's wife remains at Rosemont, the family place near Woodville, Mississippi.

April 18 '34

To Lieut Jefferson Davis,
Fort Gibson, Arkansas.

Dear Brother—
Mother is greatly afflicted with grief by the death of Sister Matilda Vaughn and wishes to see you above all things and to hear from you frequently if you cannot come to see her before another summer.

Amanda is about to lay in, and I hope to have to open this letter to inform you you have a young namesake in my family, which might occur before the closing of the mail.

I have little time for scientific or literary reading. I have a volume of Jacotal's *Enseignement Universel* with which I am greatly taken.

Mother says Jim's wife is in good health.

Your affectionate brother
David Bradford

Jefferson Davis to Sarah Knox Taylor

At Prairie du Chien Lieutenant Davis, on the staff of Colonel Zachary Taylor, had fallen in love with his commander's second daughter, Sarah Knox. Taylor had opposed the match, partly because he did not want any of his three daughters to go through the hardships of a soldier's life in the rude military outposts of the 1830's. But despite parental opposition Davis and Sarah Knox became engaged and purposed to marry eventually with or without her father's blessing. This letter, confiscated by Private Spillman White of the Thirty-third Illinois Regiment during Federal occupancy, is apparently the only extant letter of Jefferson Davis to his fiancée and first wife. Sarah Knox's letters to Jefferson are lost, though they were once hidden in an attic near Bolton, Mississippi, and taken during the Grant-Sherman occupancy of Mississippi.

Fort Gibson, Arkansas
Dec. 16, 1834

'Tis strange how superstitions sometimes affect us, but stranger still what aids chance sometimes bring to support our superstitions.

Dreams, my dear Sarah, we will agree, are our weakest thoughts, and yet by my dreams I have been lately almost crazed, for they were of you, and the sleeping imagination painted you not as I felt you, not such as I could live and see you, for you seemed a sacrifice to your parents' desire, the bride of a wretch that your pride and sense equally compelled you to despise. A creature here, telling the news of the day in St. Louis, said you were about to be married to a Doctor McLarin, a poor devil, who served with the battalion of rangers. Possibly you may have seen him. But last night the vision was changed. You were at the house of an uncle in Kentucky. Captain McCree was walking with you. When I met you he left you and you told me of your father and of yourself, almost the same that I have read in your letter tonight. Kind, dear letter; I have kissed it often, and it has driven away mad notions from my brain.

Sarah, whatever I may be hereafter, neglected by you I should have been worse than nothing, and if the few good qualities I possess shall, under your smiles yield fruit, it shall be yours, as the grain is the husbandman's. It has been a source productive of regret with me that our union must separate you from your earliest and best friend. I am prepared to expect all that intellect and dignified pride brings. The question, as it has occurred to you, is truly startling. Your own answer is the most gratifying to me; is that which I should have expected from you, for you are the first with whom I ever sought to cast my fortune, so you are the last from whom I would expect desertion. When I wrote to you I supposed you did not intend soon to return to Kentucky. I approve entirely of your preference to a meeting elsewhere than at Prairie du Chien, and your desire to avoid any embarrassments which might widen the breach made already cannot be greater than my own. Did I know when you would be at St. Louis I could meet you there. At all events, we will meet in Kentucky. Shall we not soon meet, Sarah, to part no more? Often I long to lay my head upon that breast which beats in unison with my own, to turn from the sickening sights of worldly duplicity and look in those eyes, so eloquent of purity and love.

Do you remember the heart's-ease you gave me? It is as bright as ever. How very gravely you ask leave to ask me a question. My dear girl, I have no secrets from you. You have a right to ask me any question without apology. Miss Bullitt did not give me a guard for a watch, but if she had do you suppose I would have given it to Captain McCree? But I'll tell you what she did give me—a most beautiful and lengthy lecture on your and my dreams once upon an evening at a fair in Louisville. I have left you to guess what besides a resistibility to your charms, constitutes my offense.

Pray, what manner of message could La Belle Florine have sent you concerning me? I hope no attempt to destroy harmony. I laughed at her demonstration against the attachment of dragoons; but that, between you and me, is not fair gains; it is robbing to make another poor. But, no, she is too discerning to attempt a thing so difficult and in which success would be valueless. I hope you find in the society of the Prairie enough to amuse, if not to please. The griefs over which we weep are not those to be dreaded; it is the little pains, the constant falling of the drops of care, which wear away the heart.

Since I wrote you we abandoned the position in the Creek nation and are constructing quarters at Fort Gibson. My lines, like the beggar's day, are dwindling to the shortest span.

Write to me immediately, my dear Sarah, my betrothed; no formality between us. Adieu, ma chère, très chère amie.

Jeff.

Jane Davis to Jefferson Davis

Jefferson Davis resigned his commission in the United States Army in June, 1835, to marry Sarah Knox Taylor. The ceremony was performed at the home of Zachary Taylor's sister in Louisville, Kentucky. Jefferson took Sarah Knox by riverboat to the Mississippi Delta to begin a new life as a cotton planter on virgin land given him by his eldest brother, Joseph, twenty-three years his senior. But three months after the marriage his bride died of malarial fever. At the time of her death they were visiting Jefferson Davis's sister Anna Smith at her plantation Locust Grove in St. Francisville, Louisiana. Sarah Knox was buried in the family cemetery and her tomb may be seen there today. The stricken husband was so grieved that he retired to his plantation where he lived more or less a recluse.

This letter from Jefferson Davis's mother is the only one extant. The children referred to are the two daughters of Mary Davis Davis, the youngest Davis daughter who married a South Carolinian, Robert Davis,

no relation, and died at eighteen. Jefferson's second sister Lucinda first
married Hugh Davis and then William Stamps.

Artomish, Mississippi
April 8th 1836

My dear Son

I received your kind letter by the girls and your kind favor was
joyfully accepted by your Mother. I am very anxious to see you
indeed and hope I shall have that pleasure before long or as soon
as you find it convenient. My children are gone to school, when
they return I shall bring them up to see you, as they are desirous
of so doing, and spend some time with you.

I have planted a small crop of corn and have a fine stock of Cattle.
I have Charles employed in cutting cord wood.

As regards your kind offer we will arrange it when I visit in the
fall. This summer I intend spending the most of my time with my
Daughters Anne and Amanda, I will stay here until it gets warm
and disagreeable. Mr. Stamps and Lucinda are as kind to me as
children could be and were they in a better situation themselves I
should be better contented. They are very well, their children are
all at school. As to my own health it is as I could expect at my time
of life. I must conclude this short letter, with the sincere love of
your affectionate mother,

Jane Davis

Florida McCaleb to Jefferson Davis

Jefferson Davis is now learning to be a planter at Brierfield, his plantation. Ever since Davis's military service in the Wisconsin wilds, when
he was almost blinded by the sun on glittering snow, his eyes were weak
and he eventually lost the sight of one eye. The youthful Jefferson had
done his utmost to be kind and attentive to the little girl Florida, who
was sometimes called Ida.

Diamond Place, Oct 15th, 1837

If you were not my uncle Jeff, I should not write to you to-day,
for I have a very weak eye, which makes me cross; knowing you

to be subject to the like infirmity, and that nothing increases the disease so much as waiting for an answer to a letter, I do give me credit for my consideration, hasten to thank you for your remembrance of me. I know you love me very much, Uncle Jeff, and have always done so; and you know that I am not forgetful of such kindness—so few bestow such kindness on me, that I cherish it perhaps more fondly, for that reason. You were always too kind to my faults, and too flattering to my few virtues. I remember always "the olden times, when we were still friends and schoolmates and then, our golden youth and then, the unwearied affection of after years." Do not believe I shall ever forget, a word kindly spoken, a look of encouragement, on the reproval of a fault—I am not changeful, not ungrateful; then always believe me your truest friend, and most affectionate

Ida

Can't you come up to see me? I think you might. When you do so I will return with you— Now do not come only to oblige me, for then I shall not be pleased to go—

THE LOVE LETTERS

WHEN JEFFERSON DAVIS first met the seventeen-year-old Varina Howell at his brother Joseph's plantation, Hurricane, during the Christmas season of 1843, he was thirty-five and had been a widower for eight years. His grief over the death of his bride Sarah Knox Taylor in September, 1835, had lingered long. He had lived more or less in seclusion, carving out of Delta virgin land a cotton plantation known as Brierfield. He spent his leisure hours reading in his brother's excellent library at Hurricane. His chief companion was the colored man James Pemberton, who had been his body servant throughout his army service and who was now both valet and overseer. Joseph, believing in his youngest brother's talent for public affairs, had tried to interest him in politics and hoped that he would come out of his seclusion. To make Christmas the gayer for his numerous nieces who lived at Hurricane and for Jefferson, Joseph had invited Varina, the eldest daughter of his onetime intimate friend, William Burr Howell, for a prolonged Christmas visit.

Varina had a remarkably bright mind and she had been tutored by Massachusetts-born Judge George Winchester, who lived with the Howells. Jefferson Davis fell in love with the striking dark-eyed girl, and before her six weeks' visit ended they were virtually engaged.

In the light of present-day style, these mid-nineteenth-century "love letters" seem stilted. It was the custom of the day to be formal in written expression.

There are six extant love letters of Jefferson Davis to Varina Howell written between March 8 and December 11, 1844. These six were carefully preserved by Mrs. Davis and tied in a little bundle with a thin white ribbon, soiled by the years. Under the ribbon was a card in Mrs. Davis's handwriting: "These letters from my dear husband were last read by me on May 26, 1890." This editor untied the ribbon and copied the letters on the sun porch of the grandson Jefferson Hayes-Davis in Colorado Springs.

There are no letters of this period from Varina. In one letter she had requested that Jefferson destroy all her missives to him, but at the time he did not do so. It is the belief of this editor that Varina later destroyed her own letters to her fiancé.

Jefferson Davis to Varina Howell

March 8, 1844

My own dearest Varina,

I cannot express to you my gratitude for your kind letter; when the "Concordia" put out the letters and I looked in vain in the package for one from you by which I might hear *of you* for I did not expect you would write *to me,* my heart sank within me. My fears painted you sick, unable to write. Some hours afterwards Sister Eliza handed me your letter. It was more than I had hoped for, it was what I wished, it came to dispel my gloomy apprehensions, to answer the longings of a love so selfish that it wished you to overcome your unwillingness to write to me, in other words to struggle against your own opinions to gratify my feelings.

When the weak cord is stretched it breaks, the strength of the strong one is proved by the trial. Ephemeral passion, or accidental preference, is withered by separation; sincere affection is sufficient for it's own support, by absence it is not cast down, neither is it heightened, the latter will, however, often seem to be the effect because in losing that which is essential to our happiness we are brought most actively to realize it's value. Your letter is proof that absence has thus acted on you, when we parted you did not (I believe) intend to write to me. You are always such as I wish you.

I am truly obliged by the defence put in for me by my friend the Judge. Yet it is no more than I expected from him. He would have a poor opinion, I doubt not, of any man who having an opportunity to know you would not love you, and this narrows my case down to the circumstances under which the avowal was made, quand on commence à raisonner, on cesse à sentir. I take the converse of the proposition, and here rest the case for the judgement of all except yourself. To you are known all the circumstances, how they led me from my design of visiting you after you had returned home, to make my declaration there, you whose good opinion I would have forfeited had I attempted to draw you into an engagement to me to be fulfilled despite a parental opposition, can judge me best and if to you I am justified then am I more content than if deprived of this I had the justification of the world beside.

But why shall I not come to see you? In addition to the desire I have to be with you every day and all day, it seems to me but proper and necessary to justify my writing to you that I should announce to your parents my wish to marry you. If you had not interdicted me, I should have answered your letter in person and let me ask you to reconsider your position. I am willing in this matter to be guided by you, although your reason may if you so wish not be given. How did you happen to call your Father by my name? Was it a mistake of language, if it so may be called to think of one thing and speak of another, or have you, my dear child, been sick again?

I wished myself so earnestly on the Boat that was bearing you off that had you called me when you were on the "guard" or could I have found any other excuse for going back I should have substituted your feeling of desolation with either surprise, annoyance or confusion. In your next letter, which make as long you can, please make the period of my prohibition as short as you can.

Since you left I have found the house [Hurricane] particularly dull. I believe everybody thinks of you as soon as they see me, or it may be only that when I enter any of the rooms in which we have been together I think of you, and thus suspect in others what alone exists in myself. If I have time I will write this better, i.e. with less scratching. Pray don't read at night, or punish your angel eyes by keeping a light in your chamber all night. In all things be careful of your health, otherwise what pain shall I not suffer to know that you are sick, suffering, and that I cannot be with you, then since you are always so good as to think last of yourself, for my sake take care of your health.

> Bon soir, mon cher ange, je suis votre
> Jeffn. Davis

Jefferson Davis to Varina Howell

Judge David Bradford, husband of Davis's sister Amanda, was ambushed and killed on the road from Washington, Mississippi, where he had been holding court, to his plantation. The assassin was angered because Judge Bradford had decided against him in a lawsuit. Jefferson Davis had brought his sister and her seven children back to Hurricane to live. After arranging his affairs at Brierfield, Jefferson Davis shortly presented himself at the Howell home in Natchez. Mr. and Mrs. Howell had met him in 1823 when he was a cadet at West Point and they had gone North with Joseph Davis. In fact, Mrs. Howell was carrying Varina at the time, and she was born in May of the next year.

All the family was delighted with him now and the betrothal was figuratively sealed. But no date was set for the wedding, for Jefferson Davis found himself thrust into politics as a delegate to the Democratic State Convention. And because he was naturally an eloquent speaker, he was soon traveling all about the state speaking for the Democratic Presidential nominee, James Knox Polk, and trying to defeat the Whig candidate, Henry Clay.

Van Benthuysen is the brother of Eliza (Mrs. Joseph) Davis.

> Hurricane Mi.
> 15th March 1844

My dearest, my own one,

I have just returned from the performance of a most painful and melancholy duty. My Brother-in-law was assassinated day before yesterday. I went out to his late residence yesterday and returned today bringing with me my sister and her Children.

In such gloom nothing could give me pleasure unless it were a part of you. Your letter, all that I could have of you, was waiting my arrival, and deeply do I thank you for it.

It had been my intention, if you did not further interdict me, to have gone down tonight by the "Concordia" to be seen of you, not to see you, because I do that notwithstanding the space that divides us; but your own heart will tell you of reasons enough to prevent my going away under the existing circumstances.

Two things in your letter are very gratifying to me, that your Mother had ceased from opposing the course of your love, and that *you are in good health,* the latter, which is to me the cause of constant hopes and fears, you seem almost to have forgotten to tell me. Again I entreat you take care of my wife.

You surely did not think how much it would cost me when you asked me to burn your letters, if the house was on fire those letters with the flowers you have made sacred by wearing and the lock of your hair, would be the first thing I should think of saving. I have not the ability to comply with that request without more pain than I can believe you would willingly inflict upon me. I therefore hope you will recall it, indeed I expect you will do so. You need not fear that anybody will see them unless my death should justify the opening of their present place of deposit. Now as that is a contingency which I have no reason to expect for many years, and as it would debar the discoverer from making any light use of the discovery, so do I think your request as far as it is founded on that fear, should be withdrawn.

You were equally wrong to blame and scold me for having neglected to write to you and then when you went to the other extreme and concluded I must have the small-pox as I had not written. If after the unlimited declarations I have made to you of my love I could neglect you, it would not become you to give me another thought, at least not to confess that you did, and on the other hand a sprained wrist, a hurt eye, a severe headache, many other things greatly short of small-pox might prevent even your own Jeff. from writing to his dearest Varina. Since you have given your consent and I do "wish to see" you face to face I will visit you as soon as I can possibly do so. Until then be assured my spirit is always with you.

I will ask Mr. V. Benthuysen to deliver this to you and though generally I would expect his visits to be somewhat dull to you, I suppose his ability to answer questions about us here may render him tolerable, and if he bears an answer from you his coming will be to me most agreeable.

Adieu, au revoir, ma chère, très chère, plus très chère Varina. Dieu te benisse. I commenced with no expectation of being able to write one page. I have nearly filled three with I know not what and haven't time to examine. Ever and entirely I am your

Jeffn. Davis

To My Varina

Jefferson Davis to Varina Howell

Jefferson Davis, campaigning for James Knox Polk, is taking his obligations seriously and Varina realizes that she cannot be his all-in-all.

"Hurricane"
22d June 1844

My dearest Varina,

Finding that I could best serve the cause in which I am engaged by so doing I agreed to meet the people at Port Gibson on the first of July, made my appearance at Vicksburg on Monday last and being engaged on that board for one day only, came here to attend to those interests more intimately connected with myself, and found as many have done before me, that whilst attending to the public, my private affairs had got much out of joint.

Whether I shall leave here immediately or not depends upon my political friends who have been authorized to call for me if needed. Please answer this by "Concordia," direct to this place.

Have been at work all day, and have too little time left to write you as fully as I wish. If you understood the necessity of the engagements which kept me out, you would not complain that I did not come in earlier. I have taken as a seal for my letters to you a German V— Farewell my own love, and again I pray you take care of yourself. Present my regards to your parents. A Dieu au récrire,

Votre mari
Jeffn. Davis

Jefferson Davis to Varina Howell

Even as a teen-age girl Varina gave undue attention to the state of her health, and at eighteen she was suffering from "nervous excitement," mentioned by Davis in this September, 1844, letter, in which he expresses the hope that God and her own good sense may preserve her.

Davis never did enjoy speaking in public, as many politicians or statesmen do. He did it when it was necessary, however, and he was remarkably good at it.

As a girl Varina was aware of her own wayward, high-strung, sensitive nature and even warned Davis of her faults before her marriage. Varina was excessively eager for admiration and she often imagined slights that were never intended.

Hurricane
6th Sept. 1844

My dearest Varina,

After writing to you yesterday I had the good and unexpected fortune to receive your kind letter of the 1st inst. which whilst it relieved a portion of the anxiety I felt concerning you increased if possible the desire I had previously to see you. Circumstances, which to be understood would have to be related at wearisome length, prevented me from visiting you as I intended when I wrote to you at Ripley. Some day I hope it will be mine always to be with you and then I shall possess increased power to allay your nervous excitement. Until then may God and your good sense preserve you. Pray never again allow a Whig report to affect you.

You find me changed in the matter of "speaking to Ladies," but, remember, you were not among them, and further that as public speaking was a new thing to me a change was to be expected and in more particulars than one has no doubt occurred. "How little do we know that which we are," but it is as far from being agreeable or desirable to me as ever.

If I were half as good as you believe me surely such little faults as you suppose you may commit could never disturb the harmony of our lives, and if I be no worse than I believe myself they could not. There is but one species of error of which an honorable woman is capable that could distress me if committed by my wife—e.g. such love of admiration, or excess of politeness as might induce one to fear that ridicule or even detractive remarks were secretly made. But of this as a morbid feeling in its extent I have long since informed you as one of my many weaknesses.

Eliza sends you "The Rose of Thistle Island." I send you my deepest, truest, purest love, and hope soon in person to give you renewed assurances of that which you cannot doubt, the reluctance with which I am ever apart from you. Farewell, my dearest, and may all that your husband wishes for you still be yours. Once more my dearest

Farewell
Jeffn. Davis

Jefferson Davis to Varina Howell

Varina was going to have to live at Brierfield, a rude domicile Jefferson had constructed for himself, about a mile from Hurricane House. Joseph Davis was a sort of patriarch. He had not yet put Jefferson in absolute possession of the Brierfield plantation and, in fact, he never did by law, though both considered it as belonging to Jefferson by gift from Joseph in 1835. Apparently Joseph is not enthusiastic about the wedding, which was planned for December. As William Howell has been remarkably unsuccessful in his business ventures, Joseph fears that the Howell family will be a drain on his brother's resources.

Hurricane
22d Nov 1844

Dearest Varina, your letter by *Concordia* arrived yesterday, and as you understand my feelings & wishes so fully that to speak of either must be to you the tedium of a twice told tale, I will spare you this until viva voce I may inflict it upon a drowsy cat, when like the tinklings of that bell, it may lull to sleep.

Brother Joe answered to your inquiry that he thought it probable he would attend at the ceremony of our union, but that he had not previously thought of it.

Should your mother be willing to write to Brother Joe & Eliza on the subject I would be glad that she would do so. I write in the midst of much noise and frequent interruption.

Were my will to decide where and how we should live, your preferences and judgement should certainly exercise great influence on that will, but if you will recall a small part of all that I have said to you on that subject you will not fail to perceive that we are controlled by a master not likely to regard either your wishes or mine, but I doubt not you will be fully competent to meet the exigencies and yield to the necessities our fortune imposes. It is well however to be prepared for the worst which is within the range of probabilities, as blessed are they who expect nothing, for surely they shall not be disappointed—e.g. I didn't expect of this pen with which I am writing *much,* therefore my disappointment is not *great.*

I am sorry I did not see your Father (as I expected when we parted) in Natches before leaving, I suppose however in all the places where I looked for him he had found an insufferable smell of sulphur, and retired to places of which I knew not. Mary Jane Bradford had gone to Mr. McCaleb's before my return and is still absent—Brother Joe is in better health (I think) than when I left him to visit you.

Farewell my own sweet Wife.

Ever your
Jeffn. Davis

Jefferson Davis to Varina Howell

After the November 22 letter, following Davis's visit to Varina in Natchez, something went wrong. In the letter from the riverboat *Ambassador,* the loverlike tone has definitely changed and there is a strong hint that the wedding is off. Since Varina's letters of this period are destroyed, it is impossible to know what actually was happening. In any case, "Dearest Varina" is now mere "Dear Varina." Jefferson implies in formal phraseology that he is prepared to leave her or take her—whatever is the dispensation of heaven. And he gives her no address to which she may write him. It seems as if Varina came near to losing Jefferson. How they were reconciled is unknown. But during an illness in the next February she may have sent for him wherever he was. They were hastily married on a few days' notice at The Briars in Natchez on February 26, 1845.

Steamboat Ambassador
11th Dec. 1844

Dear Varina,

I am on my way to New Orleans and thence my course is not quite certain, probably to the bayous southwest of the city.

In a letter addressed to you a few days since I wrote more at length than present circumstances enable me to do now, but Brother Joe who will probably see you can tell you all that I could write beyond what you know as well as myself.

May God grant you a speedy restoration to health, and secure to you that happiness for which he has so highly qualified you— & this granted I am equal to any dispensation which may be confirmatory thereof.

With my kind remembrances to your parents, I am as ever your
Jeffn. Davis

FIRST YEARS OF SECOND MARRIAGE

TO WASHINGTON AND MEXICO

Jefferson Davis to His Mother-in-law, Margaret Howell

After a honeymoon at the St. Charles Hotel in New Orleans, Jefferson and Varina are settled in the routine of a planter's life. It is significant that Jefferson reassures her mother that Varina "grows calmer, discreeter, happier." He is not pleased that his mother-in-law had been reading his so-called "love letters" to Varina. Sister Maggie Howell was a little girl at this time. Davis later "adopted" her, educated, and completely supported her.

Brierfield
25th April 1845

My dear Mamma,

Varina showed me this morning a portion of your letter in which you speak affectionately of me and request that I should write to you, playfully alluding to my former reluctance for your perusal of the letters written to Varina. Did you ever write a love letter? Or has it been so long that you have forgotten the feeling with which you sent it forth? As for myself though past the age of boyish fondness before I wrote the letters to which you referred, my reason had not yet gained the control of my sensibility, and my practice in that species of composition had been so small that I was no doubt sometimes obscure, without the obscurity being an ingredient of the sublime, and this alone might have justified me in wishing those letters restricted to her who had the key for their construction. But being now the head of a family I can better appreciate the necessity for the caution used in supervising your daughter's correspondence & will be willing for you to read all the letters I write to Sister Maggy.

Varina has not been entirely well for many days together, though she says her health has been better than heretofore, she is much thinner than when she left you and appears sometimes very languid, which latter effect might be well ascribed to the company she habitually keeps, being your corresponding son and a mongrel puppy, in both of whom by a power of vision peculiarly her own she sees highly valuable and loveable qualities; but unless (which you will hardly believe to be possible) she is inclined to coquetry, your son has the honor of being first among her present visitors whilst she avows the puppy to be second.

We are living so humbly that we may well expect great happiness if it be true that it springs from a condition which changes for the better. In the meantime Varina seems as much occupied with the flowers and vines she is raising as though our situation was permanent, and we should not probably be more happy if the walls of a castle sheltered us, than we are beneath the protection of our rugged hut.

Varina has written to you fully and I should probably repeat what she has said if I were to say much about her and as time presses will only add, that I think she grows calmer, discreeter, happier & lovelier with each passing day, that my relations hereabouts have been quite as attentive as I expected and they harmonize together better than I had hoped. With my best wishes for yourself, with my sympathies for the late accident of Mr. Howell and my kindest regards for him always, and with my love to the young folks, I am very truly,

Jeffn. Davis

Varina Davis to Her Mother

One of the first extant letters of Varina to her mother since her marriage in February. Mrs. Howell, who bore eleven children, is already anticipating Varina's pregnancy. But Varina was not to have her first baby until 1852. Jinny is the youngest Howell girl, who eventually married a grandson of President John Tyler. Varina's letters are full of details about women's affairs like dressmaking; but most of these references have been deleted in this collection. At nineteen she was a talented seamstress, and she took pride in her needlework.

Brierfield
July, 1845

My dearest Mother,

I have just received your affectionate letter, and know not which of us was the most delighted with our letters, Jeff or I.

I cannot affect to misunderstand your scratch under *"comfortable,"* but my dear Mother I do not need a "comfortable" dress, and think I shall probably never *require* one. Jeff has a great abhorrence to loose gowns, and does not wish me to wear one. So I don't wear them. That we both regret our being condemned to live in *single blessedness* it would be mock modesty to deny, but we will get over it—and—things.

We had a hurricane here this week. The vein of wind did not strike this house, but it blew down a favorite tree of Jeff's and mine, over in the cotton field—an enormous elm—twisted several very large trees off close by the roots. You may judge how strong the wind was when they had not a leaf nor branch on them. My vines come on beautifully. The cypress vines are beginning to run, but the Madeira vine is not so flourishing. Jeff laughs at me a great deal about it. I said it would grow a foot in a night, and it has grown very little and put out no runners yet. You know how the one grew that was choked by the Bermuda grass—well, this looks just like it, according very ill with my boast, but I live in hopes.

I should have begun my bulletin this week, but have two chills and my *usual pains* unusually severe. I am better this evening. I was at Sister Eliza's all day to-day—passed quite an agreeable day. I am very glad you like Mag's dress. Jinny's will be the prettiest though, I expect, for mine is much prettier than the pink. I made the backs exactly bias, and am the only one I ever saw who could make them fit close to the muslin and not bag. The dress fits me most beautifully. You ought to see how pretty my figure looks in it. Jeff says "wife has improved in personal appearance very much."

I began this letter last night, and had proceeded so far, when I felt too tired and went to bed. This morning I have been busy helping Jeff with the distribution of the negro clothes. I am so tired I can scarcely sit up. Please accept the sincerely affectionate kiss of "Son Jeff," through me. He is over "head and years" in business.

I have given up wearing night caps altogether—I do not wear anything on my head. With a kiss to all the little ones, love to dear Father, and the Judge, Brother and Billy, a howdy to the servants at large, I am obliged to stop. I am as ever,

My dear Mother, you most affectionate

Varina

Varina Davis to Her Mother

Varina has taken up the duties of plantation life with a will. Her eldest brother, Joseph Davis Howell, whom she called "Brother" and "Josy," is staying with her. He is a charming, well-read young man, six feet six, but idling at twenty-one. William is the brother born next after her. Varina is making pantaloons for "the hands." Hagar is a valuable Negro slave. Jefferson Davis has been persuaded to stand for United States Representative from Mississippi and is campaigning. Already six months after her marriage Varina is sending "supplies" to her family with the large brood of children: "a barrel of meat, a quantity of eggs." Jefferson seemed pleased to add to the Howell family larder.

Brierfield
September 5, 1845

My dear Mother,

Jeffy has left, and Josy and I are at what Judge Downes would call our "domiciliary residence." You would be astonished to see the work I have got through—25 pairs of pantaloons since Monday, and only two women to sew, fortunately for me there are a great many helpless ones, and they spin. Hagar has a baby, and has named it for you, Margaret. Jeffy intended writing to you before leaving, but was so harassed in different ways that he went off without it. I received a letter from him dated from Vicksburg on the first. He said he would start for Jackson next morning. God only knows when we will meet again.

I got wringing wet going up to Uncle Joe's, spoilt my bonnet completely, so I sent it down to New Orleans to have it cleaned, lined, and handsomely trimmed. When it comes, I will come down, and spend a week, as I cannot spare more time from the clothes.

Brother's health is much better than it was. He is at present reading the life of the Duke of Wellington.

I took the liberty to get a fashionable calico for you dear Mother, but it is not very costly or very pretty. I have not, you know, the power of choosing. I also send Bill 6 pairs of socks. I am trying to get a barrel of meat, and a quantity of eggs for you.

Brother and I often talk of the little ones and wish we only could see them for one minute, but we will be down probably next week, or the week after. I have several letters to write, orders and so forth, so I must stop much sooner than I am willing to do so. The negroes require constant attention, and that with the cotton book keeps me very busy. Please give my love to Pa, and Judge also and dear little Bill. With love to all I am as ever

Your affectionate daughter
V B H Davis

Joseph Davis Howell to His Mother

In early November Jefferson Davis was elected a Representative. The nineteen-year-old Varina is going to Washington as the wife of a Congressman. John C. Calhoun is one of Davis's political idols, though Davis never believed in nullification. Mary Jane Bradford, called Malie, Davis's twenty-year-old niece, accompanied the couple. William M. Gwin later became a United States Senator from California and entertained lavishly.

Brierfield, November 21st 1845

Dear Mother,

I was much surprised and disappointed at not receiving a letter from you yesterday, but comforted myself with the hope that you certainly had not neglected to write. I will now speak of something which I know you would like to have the full particulars of, it is sister's departure for Washington City.

We, (that is Mr & Mrs Jeff Davis, Miss Mary Bradford and myself) left here on Monday. Mr Davis going up on horseback, the ladies and I in the *Yazoo City*, the reason for which arrangement was that as Mr Calhoun was expected in Vicksburg on Tuesday, Mr Davis was compelled (being appointed to address him) to be there as soon as possible on the aforesaid day, and as the boat we expected to go up on did not arrive in time, he was obliged to go and leave me to take charge of the ladies. The *Yazoo City* arrived about 4 o'clock in the evening, a small, dirty, good-for-nothing little board, but as sister was very anxious to get to Vicksburg as soon as possible we took passage on her for the said town, where we arrived about 1 o'clock at night. The next day every one was anxiously expecting the arrival of J. C. Calhoun, cannon firing and drums beating all day, the whole town was in a commotion, every body seemed excited, some with liquor, others with politics, among the most conspicuous of whom was my Brother Jeff. The streets were crowded to an excess. With men, horses and carriages, I don't think I ever saw just such another crowd and all to no purpose, for the great man did not make his appearance until ten o'clock that night, when he was received by several gentlemen of a committee and conducted by them to the ball room at the Prentiss House, where, before a large company of ladies and gentlemen assembled in honor of his arrival he was welcomed by Mr Davis in a beautiful and appropriate address, in which Mr Davis attempted to bring Mr Calhoun out upon certain political subjects, which he wished him to address the people upon, which Mr C declined doing, merely giving as an apology that he was not accustomed to speak before a promiscuous crowd. He was evidently fearful of giving offence, as he had been made to believe that two-thirds of the people present were Whigs, whereas not more than 20 out of the three or four hundred in the room, were of that order of benighted politicians.

Well, after the reception and presentation to the ladies of Mr C—, the dancing commenced and such dancing I have not seen for a long time, none of your sliding and bending, but real old fashioned steps, the girls looked as they had some life in them, and they danced more gracefully than any set of ladies I ever saw. Sister, of course, did not dance; but she was honored with the entire attention of Calhoun, who did not leave her a instant during his stay in the room, which was about three hours. He told me just before he left that I should be proud of my brother and sister, that he was a man whose talents were of the highest order, and that, although she was so young, he had never met a lady with whose manners he was more pleased or of whose talents he had a higher opinion. The old man indeed seemed quite struck with her; he walked with no one else, talked with no one else and seemed to have no use for his eyes except to look at her and Mr Davis, thereby rendering Mrs Dr Gwin so jealous, that I believe she would have fainted had she had a fair opportunity.

Speaking of Mrs Gwin I will endeavor to give you some idea of her appearance, she was dressed in a black velvet cut so low in the neck that it was absolutely indecent, no sleeves to her dress, neck and arms perfectly bare, every movement of her body exposing more of her person than I should have thought any *lady* would care about, so much of it indeed, that I could not look at her without blushing and feeling ashamed, she seemed to think though that the dress was not low enough and did all in her power by drawing her shoulders out of the dress while waltzing with young Calhoun to expose as much of her person as possible to his view— looking at him all the while with such a licentious, languishing look that it made my blood run cold, and I felt like kicking both of them out of the room for daring to conduct themselves in such a manner before innocent young girls. Mr Davis says that by Mr Calhoun's attending to Sister more than Mrs Gwin made an enemy of her for life. I think it would be better for any lady to have Mrs Gwin for an enemy than for a friend— Well—to go on—the ball was kept up till . . . [*The rest is lost.*]

Varina Davis to Her Mother

The Davises had arrived at the Capital in early December, 1845, and Jefferson Davis at the age of thirty-seven had been sworn in as a member of the Twenty-ninth Congress. In those days in Washington congenial Senators and Representatives, unless they were quite affluent, lived in high-class boardinghouses, which they called Congressional messes. The following letter is one of Varina's earliest gossipy epistles, which delighted her mother. James Knox Polk is President. Varina, by nature critical, can be caustic.

Washington, Jan 30th 1846

My dearest Mother,

I had intended going with our mess to hear a celebrated juggler, and see him perform last night, but as Jeff had a bad ear ache I staid at home, and you may imagine I was not sorry for having done so when your letter came. It looks as if it had gone through the wars it was worn through. You seem to feel a very unnecessary anxiety about my health. It is true I have not been as well as usual but I think as spring comes on I shall feel much better, certainly my health is not so bad as to cause you any uneasiness.

Now let me tell you all the news I can think of. About two weeks since, I went to the President's to dine—Mrs Polk's entertainments consisting entirely of dinner parties, and levées. She is a strict Presbyterian you know. Well, I wore my black watered silk and a white polka dress made of bobbinet, and trimmed with my wedding lace—a white japonica in my hair. Mrs. P came up dressed to death. She is a very handsome woman, is too entertaining for my liking—talks too much à la President's wife—is too anxious to please. Polk is an insignificant-looking little man. I don't like his manners or anything else. We had about fifty courses it seemed to me.

Shortly after we gave a little hop here. I invited some sweet looking girls, some intelligent looking young men, and the other ladies did the same. We had quite a delightful time of it I assure you. At least every body but me had. You will know I did not when I tell you that Jeff had the hottest fever I ever felt in the next room to where it was all going on. I danced twice, and then went to him—but could not persuade myself to leave him again. I don't know which acted worst his dear head or my heart. You know how patiently Jeffy always bears suffering. I don't know Ma how it is that I cannot feel like telling any one but you how I feel towards Jeff. I feel so fearful—so uneasy—he has not been well since we arrived here. He sits up until two or three o'clock at night writing—until his eyes even lose their beauty to *me*, they look so red and painful. I feel as if he would not stand it another year. I had fearful enough anticipations of what a public life would be but they were nothing like the reality. Jeff is not away from me, but he is not so happy as he used to be. His mind wants rest.

I can tell you nothing comparatively speaking of politics here. Indeed from all I can hear there is nothing to be told. I hear nothing but Oregon—war resignations of the Secretarys, members of the Cabinet, etc. I have not been to the Senate yet, consequently have never seen Mr. Webster or any of the very great men, except Jeffy!!! I go to the House quite often—but always heretofore have heard nothing but empty vapouring about our abilities, or power to whip England. [*The rest is lost.*]

Varina Davis to Her Mother

In this letter Varina regards herself critically and notes her husband's charming effect upon people. Jacob Thompson was a Representative from Mississippi. Richard and Joseph Howell were Northern uncles of Varina's. They did not approve of their brother's business ventures and schemes, which always went awry. Davis used his power of logic and eloquence in the House to avoid a war with Britain over Oregon territory. Mrs. William H. Emory, born a Bache and a great-granddaughter of Benjamin Franklin, was Varina's best friend in Washington. Their friendship continued throughout the war though General Emory fought against the South.

> Washington, District C.
> April 3d, 1846

My dear Mother,

It has been a long time since I received one word from home, it seems to me all the world has forgotten me, and you too.

Mrs Jacob Thompson has just returned from Philadelphia—I gave her a letter to Uncle Richard Howell, he never noticed them in the least, and sent me no answer. So as I was not willing to force myself upon him, I did not write a second time. I should have liked to have seen him, because he looks so very like Pa. I intend writing to Uncle Joe—I know he will answer me.

Webster speaks Monday morning, and I am going to hear him. I will write you a separate letter to say what I think of him.

Have you got Jeff's Oregon speech? What does Pa, Judge, you, every body think of it? I do want to know so much. I think it was *great* of *course*. But seriously I think it is well written. I will send you his latest upon the harbor bill, also the corps of mounted rifle men. It is said the latter is excellent. I always keep away when I know he is to speak, for it is so trying to the feelings to hear remarks which those around make to each other.

Day before yesterday Mrs Emory sent me word that she and a belle from Baltimore would spend the evening with us. I had a desperate headache, but I sent up a note to the House to tell Jeffy to invite her beau, Mr Beddinger. I laid down, and thought no more of it—at night one after another they dropped in. I kept congratulating them on dropping in by chance so opportunely.

Malie had invited them, and so ferociously coupled them that every girl had her favorite beau. I sat down immediately and wrote a most despairing note to my confectioner—he sent me just enough—and I smoothed up my head which had not been combed that day, and went out in my silk wrapper. In about half an hour, gentlemen began to come in, several came without knowing anything was going on—there was an average of three to a girl. I played cotillions until I was tired, then Mrs Emory relieved me. Jeff flirted to his heart's content, I assure you. I had character, you must know, of giving the most delightful little hops of the season. That very thing helped them to be entertained, they thought if they were not so, it must be their own stupidity, not mine. However, my manners are much improved. Without the desire for any admiration but Jeffy's I have lost a great deal of that embarrassed, angry-looking manner which made me show to so much disadvantage.

I never more rejoiced in Jeff's elegant manner than last night. Wherever he went he left a smiling face.

God bless you, my own dearest Mother. Give dear Father my best love, kiss all the dear little ones, howdye to the servants, and receive again the blessing of

Your affectionate daughter
Varina B H Davis

Varina Davis to Her Mother

On May 11, 1846, President Polk announced to Congress that Mexicans had "shed American blood on American soil" and that war existed. A regiment of volunteers was formed in Mississippi and elected Jefferson Davis its Colonel. He has decided that it is his duty to accept the command. Varina, who has just passed her twentieth birthday in May, is in such a state of nerves that her husband wrongly thinks she must be pregnant.

Washington
June 6th 1846

My dear Mother, my best dearest friend,

To-day I am so miserable I feel as if I could lay down my life to be near to you and Father. It has been some time a struggle between Jeff and me, which should overcome the other in the matter of his volunteering, and though it was carried on in love between us, it is not the less bitter. Jeff promised me he would not volunteer, but he could not help it I suppose and you have by this time seen *The Sentinel* in which it is published.

The last remaining hope I have is that the President may not accept the regiment, in which case he will not go. If it comes to the worst, I *can* bear it, but God only knows how bitter it is to me. If he goes no earthly power shall persuade me to live with any one else but you. If I must lose my only treasure, I *will* be with those *equally* dear to me. He also has such great confidence in you, is so certain of my being happier with you than any one else that he will be anxious to leave me with you. He speaks of it as a matter of course.

I found out last night accidentally that he had committed himself about going. I have cried until I am stupid, but you know there is "no use crying, better luck next time." Jeff thinks there is *something* the matter with me, but I *know* there is not. Do pray, Ma, don't show this letter to any one, it is so deplorably below par. If Jeff was a cross bad husband, old, ugly, or stupid, I could better bear for him to go on a year's campaign, but he is so tender and good that I feel like he ought never to leave me—I won't weigh you down with my troubles.

Jeff is such a dear good fellow. I might quarrel a month and he would not get mad. It seems to me that Miller's prophecy is coming true that the end of the world is coming—there are so many catastrophes happening every day. You asked me, my dear Mother, if I attend church—I am not often well enough to sit up all day, my health is very bad. I am in hopes it will be better very soon. I am never dangerously sick.

I am so glad you and Judge liked my Jeffy's speech. A kiss to all and every one—God bless you my own dear Mother, and Father—

Your ever affectionate daughter
Varina Davis

P.S. Jeff says he must come in for a share of kisses.

Jefferson Davis to Lucinda Davis Stamps

Davis's favorite sister, Lucinda, lived at the old family place at Woodville, Mississippi.

Steam Boat, 8th July, 1846
Near Cincinnati

My dear Sister

I am on my way to Vicksburg as Colonel of the Regiment raised in Mississippi for the Mexican War. This movement was unexpected, though I hope not unnecessary, at least it was felt by me as a real compliment to be thus chosen over a field of competitors when absent, and if occasion offers it may be that I will return with a reputation over which you will rejoice as my Mother would have done. Varina and Mary Jane are with me—Mary Jane in fine health, Varina far from well. I wished to leave her in the North this summer, but she would not consent. If circumstances warranted it I would send her to you. To you and your family alone of all the world could I entrust her and rest assured that no waywardness would ever lessen kindness. She regrets very much that she can not see you all, and has never ceased to remember the kindness of yourself and the girls and Brother Stamps.

She will probably stay with her Mother most of the time during which I will be absent. With Eliza she could not be contented, nor would their residing together increase their good feeling for each other. This distresses me as you will readily imagine, but if you ever have an opportunity to understand Varina's character, you will see the propriety of the conclusion, and I feel that you will love her too much to take heed of the weaknesses which spring from a sensitive and generous temper. My dear Sister, I do not know how it is that I have not written to you often, God knows and I trust you believe there is nothing which I love better.

I intended and perhaps promised to write to little Netty. Kiss her for me and tell her she must permit her Aunt Varina to become fully acquainted with her. She must judge her uncle's wife by observation and not evade the kindest feeling of a warm heart. Remember me affectionately to Brother Stamps and the girls. I will write again. The boat shakes so this is I fear illegible. Farewell, my beloved Sister—

Your brother
Jeffn Davis

General Zachary Taylor to Jefferson Davis

> Headqrs. Ary. of Occupation or Invasion
> Matamoras Mexico Augt. 3d, 1846

My dear Col.

I heard with much pleasure of your safe arrival at Brazos Island, with your excellent Regt. of Mississippi Volunteers, & very much regret I cannot at once order you with your Comd. to Camargo. I can assure you I am more than anxious to take you by the hand, & to have you & your command with or near me.

I expect to leave by the first boat which reaches here from below on her way to Camargo, & should have been highly gratified could I have seen you before my departure for that place, but trust it will not be long before I shall have that pleasure. Wishing you continued health & prosperity I remain

> Truly & sincerely
> Your Friend
> Z. Taylor

Col. Jefferson Davis
   Comdg. Mississippi Vols.
    Brazos Island

Jefferson Davis to Varina Davis

In this letter is the only evidence of Davis's use of profanity, which he doubtless gave up. While not a member of any church until he was President of the Confederacy, Davis had a definite religious faith, which he acquired when he was a schoolboy at St. Thomas's Catholic school in Kentucky and in college under the ordained Unitarian President Horace Holley at Transylvania. Fully aware of his young wife's difficult temperament, he admonishes her to pray, as a father might a daughter.

> Mouth of Rio Grande
> 16th Aug 1846

Dear Wife,

I am here daily expecting boats to ascend the River, much chafed by delay, but in good health. Your Brother Joe is in good health,

though from change of diet and water we have had very many on
our sick report. The future has an aspect as peaceful as you desire,
and sorely to the disappointment of the Missi. patriots we can hear
nothing of warlike preparations by the Mexicans.

I have remembered your request on the subject of profanity and
have improved— Have you remembered mine on the subject of
prayer, and a steady reliance on the justice of one who sees through
the veil of conduct to the motives of the heart. Be pious, be calm,
be useful, and charitable and temperate in all things.

My love to our family and believe me to think the balance of
two sheets at least which I would like to write to my sweet Winnie.
Farewell wife

Your Husband

Joseph E. Davis to Jefferson Davis

Jefferson has proved one of the daring heroes in the Battle of Monterey.
James Pemberton, his colored body servant, is overseeing the Brierfield
plantation while Davis is at war.

Joseph Davis's second daughter Mary, married to Dr. Charles Mitchell,
had become a Catholic after attending a convent school. She is the
mother of "Lise" who remained with her grandfather until he died in
1870 in his eighty-sixth year.

Hurricane
Sept. 7th, 1846

My dear Brother

Yesterday we read accounts of the Battle of Monterrey. You may
easily imagine the feeling of intense anxiety with which the news
was read & listened to by all parties. I came to the list of killed &
wounded, here my eyes failed me, my voice grew tremulous. But
Heaven be praised you were not in the list. When the family assembled at breakfast I read it again, and never had so attentive an
audience. Yet much as I rejoice at this victory I am constrained to
think it barren of the fruits that such an expenditure of blood should
have produced. All accounts are imperfect and all the circumstances
should be known to form a just opinion, but scant as the means of
judging are, the enquiry forces itself why after forcing them into
the narrow streets under circumstances that compelled a surrender
unconditionally, were such terms accepted. Such an opportunity

will surely never occur again and then the *Armistice of eight weeks,* this is worse than all the rest. I feel that I am dealing with a subject that I do not understand. I hope to hear your opinion & such other matters as may shed more light upon the matter.

I have looked for some speedy termination of the war, and have therefore withheld your resignation from Congress. I have talked with some of your friends who seem very much opposed to your resignation.

Of domestic affairs, no new features since I wrote to you. James informed me the night before last that he had one hundred & seventy thousand pounds picked. He still holds the opinion that he will make three hundred bales—this will be near as much as the Hurricane crop. The health of the people pretty good. The health of the family not so well. Poor Mary was visited by the priest, who administered to the Sacrament & extreme unction.

I feel inclined to wait for your answer to this before sending in your resignation, and in the mean time some new facts may be developed.

Some complaints have been uttered against you for severity of training, but the battle I suppose will silence all murmurings, and the grumblers will hide their heads. We are anxious to hear more, to see the list of the killed, etc. I told Lise you had the Mexicans penned and let them go again, she wanted to know why you let them go, this I could not give a satisfactory reason for but promised you would tell her when you come home, for which she is not alone in expressing & feeling a strong desire.

Yr Brother

Col. Jeff. Davis
Army of Invasion

Joseph Davis Howell to His Mother

Private Joe Howell of the Mississippi Volunteers writes to his mother of the soldiers' admiration for their commanding officer, Jefferson Davis, her son-in-law.

Camp Allen, near Monterey, October 13, 1846

Dear Mother,

I am very much afraid that the hope expressed in my former letter, that we would shortly return home, was ill founded. I see no prospects of it at present; in fact everything that I can see or learn has a warlike tendency. There is a proclamation now in the camp, by Santa Anna, or at least it is attributed to him, which is anything but peaceful. It declares his intentions to prosecute the war to the utmost extremity; to use his own words, "he will gather the laurels for the Mexican Government by planting his flag upon the banks of the Sabine." Now, so far as his boast is concerned it is worthy of very little consideration, except as an evidence of the warlike animosity still existing in the minds of the Mexican people against the United States.

If the time of our regiment expires, and our Colonel, Jeff Davis, even then thinks that we could be useful, there is not a man in his regiment who would not sacrifice his life to obey him, so much has his gallant conduct raised him in their estimation. The degree of power his coolness, courage, and discretion have acquired for him in the army generally would hardly be believed at home. Everything difficult of decision is left to him, and I verily believe that if he should tell his men to jump into a cannon's mouth they would think it all right, and would all say, "Colonel Jeff," as they call him, "knows best, so hurrah, boys, let's go ahead." He is always in front of his men, and ready to be the first to expose himself; and moreover, he has taken them into so many tight places, and got them out safely, that they begin to think if they follow him they will be sure to succeed, and they think so, too, with some reason, for during the conflict we attacked, and several times took places and fortifications from which regular troops, greatly outnumbering us, had been three times repulsed by the Mexicans with considerable loss of life. I never wish to be commanded by a truer soldier than Colonel Davis.

> Love to everybody
> Your loving son, Joe

Varina Davis to Her Mother

Jefferson had returned from the war on furlough for a fortnight's stay at Brierfield. While there he and Varina had discussed plans for their new house. After his departure for Mexico Varina stayed on at Brierfield.

Jefferson Davis had offered to educate Varina's brother William.

Jesse Speight was a Senator from Mississippi who was to die in the summer, and whose place was given to Jefferson Davis.

Brierfield
January 3, 1847

My dear Mother,

Jeff has always intended to educate Billy—*he wishes me* to send him to school. Of course he did not expect me *to choose the school,* but he feels very anxious about him—and has spoken to me of him repeatedly. Now *do you think* it *is right and just* to him to allow your prejudice *to interfere with his welfare?* Do you think you are right in refusing to let him "go to school in Natchez"? Will it make any difference to him when he is grown *where* he has gone to school?

The money is my own. I have refused a piano because I wanted to apply the $450 to a better use. Don't consider it as anything from Jeff, and even if it were from him, he would send it with a son's affection. Please don't send me a refusal. Studying at home is the dreariest, the most disagreeable of all tasks, and makes a child hate the very sight of books—I *speak* from long *experience,* you know. Please, my dear Parents, call on me next week for the first quarter's tuition. Don't fail to find him a school.

Brother Joe came down just now and told me he must hear your letters read aloud. I read him most of yours, and Pa's. He was delighted with the cheerful tone of it, he said, joked awhile with me, laughed about my strait lines, and went home.

Malie Bradford comes down at night, but all day I am entirely alone. I have become quite a savage, I declare, I feel better alone than with any one, though my one plate looks very lonely, and I tear my food in silence. Sister Amanda's children are so *very* destructive, so very unruly that I do not like to let them come—they ruin my carpets, throw food from one side of the room to the other, and it gets mashed on the floor. Woman was made to live alone, if man was not. Well, I have just got room for love to the little ones, and kisses a plenty, with a howdye to the servants.

Varina Davis

5th, Brierfield

I heard from Jeff, his letter was dated the 10th of December, and I do not see how in the world he could have been at Camargo on the 10th, or even at Monterey. I enclose the letter, please take great care of it and send it back to me.

Thank you, dear Father and Mother, for your New Year's salutation—I spent my New Years at home entirely alone, putting down
and stretching carpet. I sung as loud as I could every thing I could,
not forgetting "ni-ni-na." It was a brave sight I tell you to see us
ushering in the New Year with such loud and triumphant songs, and
such undeniable hard work. I have got my parlour and dining room
fixed. My bedroom, and the one back of it, remains to be arranged.

Now as to pumpkin pies!!! I made twelve myself—and, though
I say it that should not, I do not think there is a man in Mississippi,
be he ever as tall and sturdy as Jesse Speight, who would not have
measured his length on the ground had he been even gently struck
by a fraction ever so petite of the crust. Malie and I made pastry
last night for the fun of it, and made some mince pies—they are
excellent. I cut a piece of citron and put in it—it improves it
wonderfully I also added more brandy.

As to my improvements—better had the speculative philosopher
attempt to square the circle, better had the profound astronomer
attempt to form some sentimental intimacies on the moon, or some
of the comets than to attempt to tell when William Chew, Esq. of
Brierfield, Mi. will finish nine foot square of weather-boarding—
he who cleaned out the Augean stables did not half such work as
William. But all the negroes seem to try their best at the carpenter-
ing, and I cannot find fault. In a few weeks I intend setting the
negroes to Brick making, and do hope I may be able to make brick
enough before Jeff comes home to make the house he wants me to
build.

I spend my days here pretty much as I do everywhere—projecting
immense improvements, thinking of Jeff, and wondering if I ever
shall see him again— [*The rest is lost.*]

Jefferson Davis to Varina Davis

Davis's few extant letters to Varina from Mexico are laconic. The
business of war took up his entire time. This letter, written after the
decisive battle of Buena Vista when Davis saved the day for Zachary
Taylor with his inspired V-shaped formation and won the newspaper
plaudits of Europe as well as the United States, is characteristic. He
had been painfully wounded early in the battle when a ball pierced his
ankle and embedded slivers of his brass spur in the flesh. But he refused

to leave the field until the Mexicans were routed and stayed in the saddle most of the day with blood filling his boot. The anxious General Taylor had him constantly tended to prevent blood poisoning. The day he was removed to Saltillo, after preparing a long official report of the action of battle, Davis writes reassuringly to his wife. He speaks modestly of his regiment and minimizes his incapacitating wound.

Saltillo 25th Feby 1847

My dear Wife,

I wrote to you a few days since anticipating a battle. We have had it. The Mississippians did well. I fear you may feel some anxiety about me and write to say that I was wounded in the right foot and remained on the field so long afterwards that the wound has been painful but is by no means dangerous. I hope soon to be up again. My friend Mr. Crittenden will write on this sheet to Brother Joe and give him more particulars. God bless you

affectionately
your husband

Jefferson Davis to Varina Davis

Now Jefferson Davis is on his way home as a hero.

Mouth of Rio Grande
27th May 1847

Dear Wife,

I have just arrived here and have a moment to say that we are on our way to New Orleans and will leave by first conveyance. Early in next month we will probably be in New Orleans and soon thereafter I shall be at home. I cannot walk yet but am steadily recovering. God bless you my dearest and preserve you in all things for the great end of our life, substantial, mutual happiness.

Farewell
Your Husband

Varina Davis to Her Mother

Jefferson Davis has returned on crutches from the Mexican War to New Orleans, where he was accorded a mighty hero's ovation. He still suffers considerable pain at Brierfield. But he suffers even more because of a disagreement with his brother Joseph, with whom Varina has been quarreling. In the building of the large new house at Brierfield, Joseph had wanted two kitchens, so that his widowed sister Amanda Bradford and her seven children could occupy half the house or at least while the Jefferson Davises were in Washington. Naturally Varina opposes any such arrangement. Jefferson is torn between the strong wills of his old brother and his young wife, and also feels a sense of duty to his widowed sister. But the families keep up a show of friendliness.

Brierfield
[Summer, 1847]

My dear Mother,

A few days ago I wrote to Father expecting the letter to go down by the *St Mary's* but I suppose it accompanies this to Natches. Jeff is not well, or like himself—he never complains, but he is quite feeble. This miserable business of Brother Joe's has given him more pain if possible than I expected, however I have determined to preserve perfect silence upon the subject until we can talk about it without it exciting either of us. The family and myself are upon as good terms as usual. I do not go there oftener than I can help, and they come down almost every day to see Jeff, and treat me with respect. My good Sister Amanda and the girls come when they can, and I feel always glad to see them. Brierfield has treated me better than I did it. I have lost but few of my trees, and the vines grow beautifully. The cedars you sent me all lived with one exception, and look green, and thriving. If Billy would send me two or three little pines they would beautify me wonderfully.

Jeff's heel is better a great deal, and I think will soon be well. He lets me dress it, which you know is a great pleasure to me, somehow I always imagine Dr Mitchell hurts him. Jeff bandages it himself.

Well! I believe I have given you an account of every thing of consequence except that Sister Amanda expects you to write to her, and that Jeff intends writing to Pa as soon as he feels well enough to do so.

I beg that you will feel perfectly at rest concerning me, "all will be happy yet" I hope, and I would not add even a feather, my dear Mother, to your already heavy burthen, if I could help it. I do not think circumstances can make any one happy; the heart at last, if it is well governed, makes the heaven. Love to all who love me, or whom I love—and for yourself, my dear Mother, the tenderest thoughts of

> Yours affectionately
> Varina

FIRST YEARS IN THE
SENATE

Varina Davis to Her Mother

For his signal bravery and success in Mexico Jefferson Davis was appointed a Brigadier General by President Polk, but he declined the honor. However, a few days later he accepted from the Governor of Mississippi a place in the United States Senate made vacant by the sudden death of Senator Speight. Davis arranges plantation affairs so that he can leave for Washington.

Brierfield

Thursday—October 17th 1847

My dear Mother,

Your letter arrived this morning and you may be assured rendered me very happy. I feel sorry that you should so unnecessarily have felt anxious for me. I am quite well now—only having had two chills since I came up, they were slight.

Jeff's health is better. His foot is much improved, and his appetite uncommonly good. He walks with one crutch pretty well. He speaks of starting for Washington in a week, or at most two.

I spent the day yesterday and the night before last at the Hurricane, and every one was very busy.

Lieut. Arthur paid Jeff a visit and staid here all night—they of course "fought their battles o'er again."

Please give my love to Pa and Judgy, and Billy, and all the little ones. Jeff sends his love also. God bless you my dear Mother prays

Your affectionate daughter

Varina

Varina Davis to Her Mother

Though not fully recovered from his wound, Jefferson Davis has left for Washington to take his seat as United States Senator. Senator Henry Foote was a wily politician, who became a turncoat during the Confederacy and Davis's most vicious enemy.

Brierfield
Friday—Nov. 12th 1847

My dear Mother,

Jeff has left to go on the Northern route up to Washington. At dinner time I expected he would go the Southern route, but Sen Foote, who is to travel with him, sent him a letter saying that the Alabama river was so low as to require him to go in a stage instead of a boat—he is so weak that he could not bear the stageing, and is troubled with a constant back ache from his wound. Of course, we were hurried nearly to death with our preparations—we sat up until 1 o'clock the night he went away, and went to Brother Joe's by sunrise the next morning—he left on the *Magnolia*.

I never felt so much before at leaving him, it really seemed to me that I had rather die than take leave of him. His health is better than when you saw him, but still very bad, and I felt what a comfort it was to us both to be together. He would have written to you if he had fifteen minutes to himself, but he wrote and talked to Brother Joe on business up to the last moment of his departure.

I could not go with Jeff when I might have been with him to the last because I had not one dress I could receive the visitors who would crowd to see Jeff. He went from me comfortable, and as happy as the circumstances would admit of. He sent you and Pa much love, and said he would write. Do write to him often.

Please accept the vest I send for Billy. It is but slight worn if at all, and it is too short waisted for my good man. I will send the cow with pleasure next week. I will also make George Trigler glue the piano and send it and your preserves to you—also 30 or 40 pounds of loaf sugar from my barrel, and several hams, not that

I have the impertinence to think you need them, but for the same reason that the lady went to bathe—sheer wantonness.

As ever most affectionately,
Your Daughter
Varina D.

Varina Davis to Her Mother

Jefferson Davis Howell, the youngest of Varina's brothers, is merely one of the numerous boys, in the family and out, named for Jefferson Davis before 1848. Scores of boys were named for him later.

Hurricane
Nov 26th, 1847

My dear Mother,

Your letter gave me so much pleasure that even if I had not been feeling particularly well, I should have been happy all day. I am glad you liked the hams, and will send you some butter and eggs tomorrow if they can be procured. There was ice here this morning.

I have received as yet no news from Jeff. I hope to hear on Saturday. I see him suggested in several papers as Vice President to Dallas in the election of '48.

If I had wanted the money I sent, I would not have sent it, having so fond an admiration of it when it is at all useful to me. I wish it had been more.

I suppose Gen Quitman has arrived—"and how is Massassippi and how does she stand?" Oh! Mr. Marsh has arrived, the man I told you preached to the "poor benighted sufferers" here last year, mended the steam gin, put the spinning Jinnys to work, and came all the way from Nova Scotia to see Brother Joe.

If you would cut out Jeffy D's little slips, and send them to me I could bring him a supply next time I come. *Please do it for once,* Ma. I might as well make for Jeffy D, as for Jeffy Harris. There is Jeffy Howell, Jeffy Laughlin, Jeffy van Benthuysen, Jeffy Harris, Jeffy Bradford, and Jeffy Gilbert. I do not think they would make a bad settlement to go to a new country.

I had intended to write to Brother tonight but I unfortunately got hold of a villanously long article of the Unions, and Brother Joe said I read so well he could not let me go to bed until he did, so I waded with all my strength through it. So I "very imprudently" stayed until bed time. Randall is to make the garden fence, and Christmas is certainly coming without any trouble in arranging matters so that it will be here.

Good night, my dear Mother.

Yours ever
Varina

Varina Davis to Her Mother

Jefferson Davis was now in the Senate in Washington. The portrait cameo is owned today by the eldest great-granddaughter, Mrs. John Wolcott Stewart of Santa Barbara, California.

As to the "revelations," Mrs. Howell is accusing Joseph Davis of holding out some of Jefferson's share of the money realized on the sale of Brierfield cotton.

Brierfield
January, 1848

My dear Mother,

I received safely your kind letter and the bundle. Jeff's miniature came safely to hand, and is a splendid cameo, white on a deep lead-colored ground, set in a splendid broad band of gold for my wrist. He looks beautiful in a cameo—it is exactly like him. Also he sent me a beautiful little gold chain, and gold pencil and pen altogether, with a lovely little seal on the top he had engraved. I have received no letters from him for a month, but expect some by this boat. I will have my portrait taken in a black velvet, if the artist can paint it without my getting one. Well, I am surprised at the revelations you mention, but have burnt the letter, and cannot but hope is not so.

I have letters upon letters to write—please don't be angry at this, whatever happens you shall know. Everyone is affectionate—some decision has been arrived at about the house, but as I am so little concerned it has not been thought proper to inform me. I always speak as if it were mine, and no one's else, so I suppose all will be straight. The subject is never mentioned. They are as affectionate as they can be, and in trying to do my whole duty, I am happy, and absolutely look upon Jeff's displeasure or pleasure as a minor consideration to my own duty. I have not been low spirited for two months or cross for I do not know how long.

As ever affectionately
Your Daughter
V. D.

Varina Davis to Jefferson Davis

Varina is visiting her parents in Natchez.

Briers, Natchez
Jan. 24th, 1849

My own darling Husband,

I saw by the papers today that Major Dix had died of the Cholera at Cumberland; and conclude that ere this you are in danger of taking it. Take laudanum and camphor the *first* slight pain you feel. Only come back to me safe in person and I can bear all other evils. Much as I have loved and valued you it seems to me I never knew the vastness of my treasure until now. If you have no fear for yourself, have it for your Winnie, your thoughtless, dependent wife, and guard your health as you would my life. Sweetest, best husband, don't go out at night, don't drink wine, don't eat any fruit. If you feel any temptation to be imprudent just recall the question to your mind if you have any right to blast my life for your gratification of the moment. You were never selfish, then be yourself now, and think of your wife. Jeff, my sweetest, write oftener if you can, though God knows your letters have been very, very frequent. Write to me every day, only three words "I am well" will suffice, if you have not time for more. My better life, my nobler self, farewell, as ever I am,

Your devoted Wife
W. Davis

Varina Davis to Jefferson Davis

Natchez
January 25, 1849

My darling Husband,

You could not assist me in the least in my illness unless looking into your sweet eyes would be balm for all wounds.

In the papers you sent me I saw your very forcible little speech in partial answer to Mr. Hale's vituperations against slavery. It was a little too violent, more so than I would have liked to hear you be, however well deserved the censure might be.

Thank you for Dickens' pretty little Christmas Tales. If you read it you admired the character of Milly, did you not? I have not been reading much lately, in fact nothing but Mrs. Ellis's Guide to Social Happiness, which as it treats of woman and woman's trials could not interest you, but it will help "Winnie" to be "Wife."

My own bright love, farewell. Kiss wife, and say goodnight. Winnie is Husband's baby and baby is your

devoted Wife
Winnie Davis

Varina Davis to Her Mother

The Davises and some other Southern senatorial families rented a house next to the United States Hotel and took their meals in a private dining room. Mrs. Armistead Burt is a niece of John C. Calhoun.

Zachary Taylor, Jefferson Davis's first father-in-law, is President and his daughter Betty Bliss acts as his hostess because his wife, Margaret, is in frail health. Betty at twenty-five looks so remarkably like the dead Sarah Knox that Davis was startled when he saw her. As a little girl in Prairie du Chien, Wisconsin, she had been devoted to him.

William W. Seaton, an editor of the famous *National Intelligencer*, often entertained the Davises as well as foreign celebrities. Lady Bulwer was the wife of the British Minister.

Washington
January 6, 1850

My own dear Mother

It does seem to me, my dear Mother, that I never will get time to write there are so many interruptions. Well we left Godshys and went up to the west end to board, to Mrs Wise's, but there was a mess of clerks, and that sort of people there, and wretched living. However it was a good situation, but I tell you I did really feel lonely and dull. So Mrs Burt of South Carolina, Mrs Toombs of Georgia, and Mrs McWillie of Mississippi and I concluded to live together. We have the whole house, and there is a little platform which leads to the ladies' ordinary where we have an elegant table, all sorts of nice French dishes. We have a right nice parlour and I hired an excellent piano, and we sometimes have music in abundance. It is true we live on the avenue, and next to the United States Hotel, but I like to see the bustle. Gen Taylor and his family have been very kind. Mrs Bliss is, as I expected, less lovable than the rest of them, that is, she is not a cordial woman. I have been out but little since my arrival. I went to dine at Knox Walker's, and met there Mrs R. G. Walker, Mr Cass, Mr Winthrop and wife, and Mr Cobb, the speaker, Mr Corcoran, and Judge and Mrs Douglas, and Mr Seaton and Wife. It was the most beautiful dinner I ever saw. The table had nothing but immense candelabras and flowers on it except two brown candy trees hanging with white grapes, three feet high. There was an immense number of courses, and a beautiful dessert.

I wore my light brocade with a thread lace cape and cherry colored bows, and a white rose and buds in my hair. But I hate dinners, I declare I thought my back was broke before we got away. We did not dine till seven, and came away at eleven. You may imagine how tired I was. We have been to the President's to several levées, and night before last I went and had the pleasure of seeing Lady Bulwer and her good gentleman. She is in court mourning for Queen Adelaide. She is a little common-looking woman, with low forehead, light brown hair. It was fixed in a little knot behind, and she had black tinsel grapes full-size in two bunches as large as your fist on each side of her head. She had a black lace dress ruffled with broad black lace, and a black lace Bertha. He had a silk collar to his coat, and whiskers.

On New Year's day I went to the President's also, and certainly I never saw anything like the rich uniforms and orders of the foreign ministers. The coats were nearly covered with embroidered gold leaves, some were oak leaves and acorns, and the orders fairly blazed with jewels. But I did not enjoy it at all. The President had no refreshment, but everybody else almost had. I laughed until I almost died at the Mexican Minister. He left his cards for us, and we returned the visit New Year's day, and when we went in I took him for a mulatto. First is "pass this way," second is a cup of eggnog, the third, his bow to me. He could not say one word but "pass this way," and every time he said "pass this way," I thought he felt as triumphant as Mouse Hedrigg did when she had "luppen a ditch." [*The rest is lost.*]

Varina Davis to Her Mother

This fragment of a letter from Varina to her mother speaks of John C. Calhoun's funeral.

Washington
[Late April, 1850]

I could not help crying, but they would not hear to putting off the ball. There were a hundred and two carriages in the funeral, and twelve white horses with a Negro at the head of each to lead them drew the hearse; the negroes were substituted in the place of white men by the committee for the edification of the free soilers. I will bring you a piece of his [Calhoun's] hair when I come home.

I will write Maggie a full description of the May ball as soon as it is over. It is now the fashion to give real dinner parties to children, courses and every thing like big people. I have been keeping french kisses for each of them all the winter, and have a good many. The last ball I went to a young lieutenant in the marines came rushing up to me—my dear Madam, I have been every where looking for you—here are some kisses for your little Sisters—and he was perfectly out of breath. It produced a general laugh around, and I felt pretty mean.

Now my dear Mother you must write, and tell me about all your plans, and prospects. What you expect to do. God grant you may be more comfortable and happier than now. With love to my dear father as ever

Your tenderly attached
Daughter

Varina Davis to Her Mother

Jefferson Davis went to Charleston for Calhoun's funeral as one of "the escort of honor."

The Davises frequently attended dinners at the White House, but Mrs. Zachary Taylor almost never appeared at public functions. "Malie" Bradford, Davis's niece who accompanied the Davises to Washington in November, 1845, is married to Charles Brodhead, Pennsylvania Representative.

Washington
May 18th, 1850

My dear Mother,

Jeff returned much improved from Charleston, and sooner than I expected. We have been expecting to move from day to day to the west end of town, but I have concluded there are no such rooms anywhere as here and we have a parlor all to ourselves. I am invited to the President's to dine again on Thursday, but I think I had rather take a whipping than go. The lilac silk has been to every party this winter, so I must get a new dress, and it hurts my conscience dreadfully.

May 20 1850

Well, darling sweet old Mammy doogle, I went to the President's in a sky blue silk ruffled up to the waist, and made with a train, with scarlet rosettes in my hair and bosom, and short sleeves. I had a sweet time I can tell you. It is the only dinner party I have enjoyed for some time.

The same evening after dinner I went upstairs to see Mrs. Taylor. I found the old lady sitting with her feet in the fender shivering, and she seemed so charmed to see me, said she felt so wretchedly lonesome, and chilly. I talked as long as I could, but had told Betty to call for me to take her to a party at ten, and she had been waiting some time so we started out to the party.

I am going next week to stay with Malie until after her confinement. Charles Brodhead, Malie's nephew, comes over for me to take me to Easton, and I expect to go in his carriage from Philadelphia out to Easton. Jeff will go over to Baltimore with me, and from there we will go to Philadelphia that night. Poor little Malie seems delighted to think I will be with her in her trial. She is so far from any of us that I felt as if it would be mean to be so near her, and not go.

I will keep this letter until I go there and write more to my own sweet good Mother.

Varina Davis to Her Mother

This letter of the twenty-four-year-old Varina is vivid with eye-witness details of the death of President Zachary Taylor on July 9, 1850.

"Through the torture of a state funeral" on Saturday Varina was a great comfort to Mrs. Taylor, who lay in her bed trembling violently when bands "blared the funeral music of different military units," and "cannon boomed to announce the final parting."

Washington
July 10th, 1850

My dearest Parents,

You will have before this heard of Gen Taylor's death, and I have been with the family every spare moment since. The fourth of July after a hearty dinner, or before a hearty dinner of cherries, with a slight diarrhoea, he went over to the Washington monument to hear Mr Foote's oration, and it was excessively hot. He came home feeling very unwell—that was Thursday. Friday he had fever all day. Saturday the same. Mrs Taylor implored him to send for a Physician but he would not. Sunday they sent, whether he would or not. He continued hot, and cold by turns, and Tuesday (yesterday) congestion of the brain took place, and last night he died at half past eleven.

As soon as we heard he was worse we went up and found his family round him, poor Mrs Taylor on the bed chafing his hands, and telling him she had lived with him nearly forty years and he must talk to her, begging him to tell his poor old wife if she could do nothing for him. Of course, he could neither see or speak. In the midst of it all the cabinet ministers came in with their heads bowed, and one after the other took his hand and kissed it. And after a gentle breath he died like a child going to rest.

Then the tearing Mrs. Taylor away from the body nearly killed me—she would listen to his heart, and feel his pulse, and insist he did not die without speaking to her. Poor little Mrs Bliss, and Mrs Wood, and Col Taylor's grief, the bells tolling and the servants crying altogether I liked to have gone mad. I stayed until one o'clock and then came home. I went again this morning and stayed all day, and shall go again tomorrow and every day as long as they stay here. They will, I think, leave immediately after the funeral for Baltimore, and stay there until some further plans are made. The funeral takes place on Saturday. He is in a refrigerator until then, frozen, when he will be laid in state in the east room for a few hours. The last distinct words he said were to Jeff. He suddenly spoke, and said, "Apply the constitution to the measure, Sir, regardless of consequences."

I have been thus particular because I know you admired him so much. This morning when I waked up such a weight of thankfullness came over me when I thought I have Husband, and Father, and Mother, and I am almost an old woman. But enough of this mournful subject. I am so tired I must say good bye to you both, my own precious Father and Mother. With love from Jeff to you both, I am, as ever, my best dearest friends,

Your affectionate Daughter

Varina Davis to Her Parents

To please the Democrats of Mississippi, Jefferson Davis had given up his seat in the Senate to run for Governor, because there was no other man considered strong enough to defeat the Whig candidate. Davis became ill and could do little campaigning. He lost by a narrow margin.

Brierfield
Oct 28th, 1851

My dear Parents,

No letters from Jeff since he left Jackson, and he promised so faithfully to telegraph me that I feel anxious about him. Poor fellow, he is just finding out what I predicted, and everybody but his friends knew, that the Southern Rights cause is the losing one now, whatever it may be when further aggressions have been perpetrated. Pecuniarily, defeat would be the very best thing which could happen to us, for the outlay upon servants, silver, china, cutglass, table linen, bed linen, and carriage and horses would be *immense* for our fortune, to say nothing of the dinner parties given to the members and the wives and so forth. I have at present the immense stock "in my cellars" of six bottles of port wine, and a gallon of vinegar and one of brandy.

So far as its influence upon Jeff's popularity would go, I doubt my power to bear with insolence and to conciliate fools and busy-bodies, and his to bear with tiresome friends, and I am afraid that some time when the people are flying in on "loose" nights I might get tired standing and sit down, and get to talking and forget the strangers. All those things I have balanced, and am as contented as possible to remain where I am.

Now to more agreeable things. I am very busy making a fall garden. I have a vegetable ivory nut growing, and some beautiful plants from Chili, Brazil & Turkey, some from John Perkins, some from my kind old friend, Mr. Seaton in Washington. So much verbena that I cannot get it all planted, scarlet, pink, white, lilac, royal purple, and crimson.

I feel almost babyish about seeing you all. Nothing but the necessity of remaining here prevents me from deserting, and going down. However I don't think Brother Joe would let me go now if I was ever so uproarious, for poor Shook went to New Orleans about three weeks ago, and returned sick, and died with yellow fever day before yesterday, bleeding at the mouth and gums. Brother Joe seems dreadfully cast down by it. He was very kind to the poor fellow, had him brought to the house, and taken care of. [*The rest is lost.*]

Varina Davis to Her Mother

After seven years of marriage, Varina is pregnant. Now out of the political arena, Jefferson is enjoying plantation life and working hard at it. Varina delights in her flower and vegetable gardens. While relations with the Hurricane family are still strained, the Jefferson Davises go there frequently.

Brierfield, March 4 1852

My dear Mother,

Everything here is about as usual except that I am generally much better. All at the Hurricane were well when I last saw them which was Sunday, except Sister Eliza who is quite delicate, and most always sick. They talk of going "hither and yon" this summer, but I think will wind up as we have in determining to stay at home. I feel able to ride up there now but Jeff won't listen to any proposition of the kind so I have to be satisfied with going in the garden two or three times a day. Did you ever see as forward a spring? All my roses are in bud, some just ready to bloom—which were planted this spring, but if a frost should come we would be in a forlorn condition. I have tomatoes a foot and a half high, and beets with four leaves, eggplants with six, peppers with 8, and by the hundreds.

Jeff is quite well, and so busy at his field that I scarcely ever see him except when he is too tired to talk. He seems satisfied with home, and certainly I feel much happier here than in Washington. My dear affectionate sister now and then enquires if I don't think I should like to go on, and if I don't miss the trip, and suggests that Brother Jeff will never, she thinks, be successful after a defeat so utter &c. But you know my heart never went with Jeff in politics *or* soldiering—so it does not feel sore on the subject of his defeat—and there never was a time when his presence was more opportune than it has been to me this winter.

If you don't come, as soon as I am able I will come down. I can't bear the jolting over the stones, if I were able to get up the steamboat steps which I am not, but in two or three months I hope this pain in my hips may disappear, and then I will come, if Jeff is not so dreadfully concerned as now. Do come up. It is the longest time I ever was away from you. Do come and see Jeff for the first time with no political troubles, and see how agreeable he is.

Please write soon, and tell all about everything concerning yourself, and your home, as I do of mine.

Your devoted Daughter,
Varina D.

Varina Davis to Her Mother

Why Varina, who was an expert seamstress, has neglected to make baby clothes is unexplained, as she is expecting the birth in late July. In May Payne and Harrison of New Orleans had sent a bill for $9.02 for bird's-eye diaper cloth. Now she is suddenly frantic.

Brierfield

June, 1852

My own dear Mother,

I am so generally unwell that I can do nothing. Jeff gets so much frightened that I am almost afraid to say how bad I really do feel, and did without my knowledge send for Dr. McElrath by the boat, and I am in dreadful expectancy of him this evening. I expect Mrs. Bennett had better come the 7 or 8th of July, for I have been suffering so much from shooting pains that I have got uneasy, for if any thing should happen unexpectedly the old negroes here are very ignorant, and the water is too high to go to Warrenton for a Physician, and there is no skiff to send. What I shall do, God only knows. My chemises are all torn up. I have no baby clothes, and no night gowns.

Ma, do for Heaven's sake send me a few little patterns—indeed I will not be well enough to sew by the time you get here, and I hate in case of my death to leave the poor little thing without common necessaries. Please send me the lawn, or let me know by the *Frank Lyon* if you have bought it because I can send to Mr. Payne for it. I have not more at the very farthest than three weeks to go on, and not a shirt, not a petticoat, or slip, and only twelve diapers altogether. Please don't think me importunate but the thoughts of it nearly sets me crazy. Could you get me a very large bedstead, with very high posts, and low off the ground, and if a spring mattress is not too expensive—that is, more so than two hair ones—please get me one to fit it. I care more for the extra size than any thing else. All I care for is an extra-sized mahogany bedstead, low from the ground, and high in the ceiling with a low footboard. Jeff says if you will send him the bill, he will pay it.

I sat down to write you a long letter, but am suffering so from pains in my back and side that I cannot write. Jeff sends his very best love.

Your devoted daughter
V. Davis

Margaret Howell to Her Husband

On July 30 a boy child was born to Varina and named Samuel Emory for Jefferson Davis's father.

Franklin Pierce had been nominated for the Presidency at the Democratic Convention in June and Davis feels impelled to do some campaigning for his friend.

Brierfield
August 20th 1852

My dear Husband

Our dear little grandson continues healthy and is growing finely. I cannot say I feel any older than I did—being at least 20 years older than I ought to be. Varina goes about everywhere, and Jeff is the proudest, fondest father I ever saw—and the best husband. He is more like a woman about his "li' man," as he calls him, than any one I ever saw. He wishes you to purchase for his boy a little barouche with two seats—get it handsome lined. I mean a real little barouche for a child—such as the nice little children are pulled about in the city—stout, well made and good springs and wheels. This boy is to have nothing common.

Jeff leaves us this evening for Natchez where his friends had made an appointment for him without his knowledge. He will be absent a few days. I did not know he was going in time to write you a long letter.

Varina, Jeff and the children all join me in love to you all.

Your affectionate
Wife

SECRETARY OF WAR

Jefferson Davis to Varina Davis

Jefferson Davis had reluctantly accepted a post in Franklin Pierce's Cabinet as Secretary of War, in which even his enemies later acclaimed his superior qualities and achievements. In March he took the oath, and now he is looking for a suitable residence before his wife and first-born baby, Samuel, arrive.

The Howell family was originally from New Jersey, where Varina's grandfather, Richard Howell, was eight times elected governor. The Howells mentioned below lived in Pennsylvania.

Washington
April 17th 1853

My dear Winnie,

Your letters have come at last, just now yours of the 7th reached me and brings the disagreeable intelligence that my dear "li' man" has the whooping cough. Thank God he is at New Orleans, not Washington, because there the weather must be warm; here it is cold and changeable. I am paying dearly indeed for public honors, worn out by incessant boring and separated from all which brings freshness to my heart. The eternal round of labor has given me little opportunity to plan for the future, but to your inquiry as to when you should come on I would say for your own and Sam's sake it would probably be best to postpone the trip until the weather is warm enough to escape the effect of the change of climate. Col Taylor offered his services, Mr. Brodhead proposed to go for you, but I answered to both that I hoped to go for you myself as early as it would be desirable for you to come.

In former letters I have answered your inquiries about my place

71

and mode of living, and asked for your views as to the future. It may be that events in Missi. will enter as a diverting element into our arrangements. I recently received a letter from your Uncle Jos. B. Howell, and one from your Aunt Agnew; they both make inquiries concerning your Pa and his family. You have not told me how far your visit at Bayou Sara was agreeable and I have feared it was attended by some unpleasant event or indication. I wish you always to speak freely and explicitly of every thing which concerns you because it must be equally my affair.

Kiss my dear child for his Father, who hopes not soon to be again so long separated from him.

Give my love to Pa & Ma & all the young people.

Farewell, my dear, and let us hope that happier days will come when our trials have passed, but there can be none in which you will be dearer and nearer to the heart of

Your Husband
Jeffn. Davis

Varina Davis to Her Mother

In July Jefferson Davis, Secretary of War, accompanied President Pierce on a kind of whirlwind royal progress through Delaware, Pennsylvania, New Jersey, and New York. He made many speeches and returned to Washington with increased political stature.

July 26, 1853
Washington

My own dear Mother,

Jeff's trip to New York, I think, did him some good. He talks about going again, but I hardly think he will do so. Your little Sammy is the sweetest thing you ever saw. He calls his Father "Boo," and himself baby—calls me mammam—whistles when he is told and mocks the cows. He is devoted to Jeff—let him be sucking ever so greedily, if Jeff speaks to him he lets go and goes to him. He sits up company or no company and takes his meals with us and is waked up if he is asleep to come and eat his dinner.

July 30th. We had a little dinner today on the occasion of Sam's birthday, and a little cake with Saml E. Davis on it. Maggie was spending the day out, but hurried home with little Agnes Irvin to dessert, and we all drank his health.

Does Billy want me to get him a suit of winter clothes? Ask Pa to send me his measure for a coat and pantaloons. The children send their best love to you, and canvass what they think will be done when Jinny and Ma, and Pa, and Jeffy come on—

As ever, dear Mother, I am

Your devoted daughter,
V. Davis

Jefferson Davis to Varina Davis

Varina's sister Margaret and brother Becket are living with the Davises in Washington and being educated at Davis's expense.

Alexander Dallas Bache, great-grandson of Benjamin Franklin, had stood at the top of his graduating class at West Point when Jefferson Davis was a plebe. Young Davis almost always chose his friends from those older than himself, and the two men had remained warm friends. The Baches had been most attentive when Davis first went to Washington as Congressman. Later when Davis was in the Senate he had risen from a sickbed to make a powerful address urging a substantial appropriation for Bache's important coastal surveys.

Blue Mountain, Me.
28th Aug. 1853

My dear Wife:

I arrived at this the present station of the coast survey last night, and am now under canvas enjoying the hospitality of Mrs. Prof. Bache. To both I am indebted for many attentions and much cordiality of which I will speak more fully when we meet. I am far up in the mountains and far "down east in Maine." The wind sweeps over the tent with the chilly feeling and hollow sound of wintry weather, but every thing is so well arranged that the portable stove renders the inside of canvas very comfortable.

Since I wrote to you our time has been mainly passed in the White Mountains. We slept on the summit of Mount Washington the highest peak in the range and travelled over worse roads than even in your swamp experience you ever saw. This being Sunday I can see but little of the survey. Tomorrow I hope to make the tour of the station, and, though the stay here being both pleasant and instructive might be prolonged even to the limit you indicate, other considerations prompt me to turn my steps towards Washington and I expect to leave in the course of Tuesday.

If my dear "Li' man" looks out for his Father our thoughts meet, for there is little which does not associate itself in my mind with him.

Tell Becket and Margaret and Sam to be good children and give them my sincere love.

Farewell for a little while, my dear Waafe, and be assured that in the meantime whether sleeping or waking the fondest affections are with you which can be offered by the heart of

Your Husband

Varina Davis to Her Mother

The Davises have rented the Edward Everett house of twenty rooms at the corner of F and Fourteenth Streets, where they remain while Jefferson Davis is Secretary of War.

Washington
January, 1854

My own darling Mother,

I have been literally run off my feet the month of December. I only wrote once because I was so weak with moving and hurry that I was glad to get a moment to sleep quietly. I fear my heart will not be improved by my sojourn here. Every day I have about 30 calls, and the only way to do is to get in a carriage, and ride up and down to avoid them. The fact is I never led such an unsatisfactory life in all my days. One week I give a dinner, and a party the next week, and every Tuesday morning a reception, to which about sixty people call, sometimes more, and I must stand until half past four, from 12 in the morning. And then my servants and house keeper distract me with complaints of being run to death with company, and Sam in the midst of it all is occasionally threatened with the croup and keeps me on the qui vive about him.

Nothing in the world compensates to me for your absence, and I never have felt so homesick. I am so be-flattered and courted that I long for some good old home rudeness. I had twenty dollars in gold and I send it to you to buy turkeys, and pans with, or rather "Aam," as he calls himself, sends it to his "Danaman."

Sam is the sweetest little boy you ever saw, but he has learned to fight and scratch, and he screams to have his fine dresses put on him, and whenever any one goes out he stamps his foot, and says, "back, back"—if it is me he says "back ba bam" for "please maam." When chicken is cooked and set on the table, he crows and flaps his wings for some. However, Jeff will write and tell you about him, he says. I am going out to dine this evening, and since I began this letter I have had four or five people in, and all excuse themselves for interrupting me, but still stay. God bless you my own dear Mother, as ever you are inexpressibly dear to your

devoted Child
V. Davis

P.S. Sam calls cake and what he likes "grand ma."

Varina Davis to Her Mother

President and Mrs. Pierce took a great fancy to Little Sam, and Mrs. Pierce would often call for him in her carriage to take him driving with her.

Washington, March 3rd 54

My dear Mother

Your little Aam, as he calls himself—he is getting very much better, but so bad. He has found out that "bamam" (please Maam) will get him anything, and you ought just to see him, he stamps his foot, and bullies. He is the most perfect monkey I ever saw, and he is real pretty. Today is one of the most lovely days I ever saw, and I took him out in our Phaeton to drive, and you ought to have seen his little bright face, he kept looking, and saying Mama "little 'al," (gal), "little boy," and when we passed Mr. Pierce who was riding on horse back, he stopped to talk to me, and Sam kept clicking his horse to go, and kissing his hand to him.

Billy leads me to hope you will be on in the summer. Why not just take your passage on a steamship to New York and let us meet you and Pa there. I have five spare bed rooms, and two carriages— so that we would have elegant times. I have a girl who sews in the house who would soon fix you up, and we would not see any one until you choose. Do think of it.

God bless you my dear Mother, and Father, no child can love you more than

Your devoted Daughter

Varina Davis to Her Mother

President Pierce drops in at the Davises often and unexpectedly. Nina Wood is the oldest daughter of Zachary Taylor. Little Sam is the victim of some undiagnosed malady that shortly brings his death.

Washington—March 26, 1854

My own dear Mother,

Upon the whole the news from home was pleasant, and that always seems to render me happy though I have nothing particularly so here just now. Sam's mouth is broken out, and he has been having a rising on his little middle finger which gives him a good deal of pain. Whenever I go to touch it he says "please Mamma don't," as plain as you could, and sometimes he shakes his finger at me and says "now mind, I say mind." Last night the President came down with a lady staying with them to see me, and Sam ran round the chair and looked, and called out "pretty man, pretty man." He has no more fevers, but sucks all night and fights if I attempt to do anything to him.

Jeff's health is rather better than it was this time last spring. He often talks to Sam of his grand Ma and Pa, and Sam listens very attentively, but I am getting perfectly miserable about home. I do want to see you all so very badly. I think I will go and talk to Jeff about going home—he won't hear of my going, says I could not possibly do it.

I have Nina Wood again staying with me. She came over to go to the Brazilian Minister's ball. I did not go, but Nina and Jeff described it to me as the most splendid ball they had ever seen. Lackeys in maroon velvet jackets embroidered with gold stood at the door and marshalled them in. It was said to have cost $6000. I had not intended going, but if I had would have been too tired to do so, as we had a gentleman's dinner of 22 that day, and did not rise from the table until near ten o'clock. Tell Billy, I am universally acknowledged to give the finest dinners in Washington, with the most elegant decorations—but all would I give to run round the corner with him and stuff bananas.

For gracious sake don't give up the idea of coming on this summer, I can't bear to think of it.

Jeff says I must give his love to Pa and you and the boys and kiss the children for him. He says that when he can get time he will write, but poor fellow, I cannot tell when that will be—he is as thin as a lath. God bless you both prays your

devoted child
V. D.

Varina Davis to Her Mother

Jefferson Davis was one of the most active of the fourteen regents of the recently established Smithsonian Institution and always enjoyed entertaining the distinguished American and foreign scientists who met in annual convocation.

Davis is gravely concerned about his little boy's strange illness and the coolness between him and his brother Joseph. Varina is aware that she caused the trouble.

Washington
April 29, 1854

My dear Mother,

I wrote to you this day three weeks and I suppose you thought mine a very short, and exceedingly unsatisfactory, letter but Sam has been very sick and was then and I feared to tell you how wretchedly miserable I was. Now he is better and I can tell you. His poor little mouth began swelling and then blistered, and every time he laughed he cried, for it broke open and bled, then his poor little eyes became blood red, and he fretted, and sucked incessantly. I gave up visiting and receiving people and drove him out in the country but all would not do, he drooped steadily, and I felt as if the world was coming to an end, but charged Maggie not to say a word of it in her letters to you. Then his sores extended almost over his face, but we cured them up, and now his little head is a perfect mat of scabs, and I have cut his hair close to his head— he stopped walking, and does not walk much yet, but is well except occasionally a little fever. I give him no medicine but a little elixir of vitriol occasionally—he can say aitch, for yes, and hoitch for horse—and sits up at table and hands his plate like a man for what he wants. He holds up his arms, catches our faces, and says "Kish nam" for kiss Sam. Jeff is absorbed in him to a fearful extent.

Washington is thinning now very much, and the weather is becoming very pleasant. Thursday night we received the savants here who meet at the Smithsonian this year to read their papers of discovery. Really it was a splendid sight, and I regretted extremely that I did not have time to talk long to any one. We gave them refreshments, and invited a good many of our friends to meet them. I thought so often how you would love to see them.

We hear but seldom from the Brierfield, and then it is always of some new disaster, until really I feel as if everything were going to ruin. Jeff is wretchedly thin, and at times very weak, but then he recovers, and is gay for a week or ten days. I think his Brother Joe's alienation preys upon his mind, but he never speaks of it. [*The rest is lost.*]

Varina Davis to Her Father

On June 30 Samuel died. It was the first deep sorrow Davis had known since the death of his bride Sarah Knox Taylor in 1835. Though he was stoical in self-control, Varina wrote weeks subsequently that "he walked half the night and worked fiercely all the day" and that "a child's crying in the street would cause him acute distress."

Washington
July, 1854

My dear Father and Mother
I have made several efforts to write to you since our loss, but could not. My child suffered like a hero. A cry never escaped his lips until his death, but he would say, "Mamma, I tired, I wana walk, I wan bed," showing restlessness, and suffering—and would hold up his mouth to kiss me to make me stop giving medicine, and if I was out of his sight a minute he would call out "Mamma gone." We have had great sympathy shown us, and I am tortured with letters of condolence and it gives me nothing but unmitigated pain to see people, and hear the set forms of consolations.

I thought I could write, but cannot— The children [Becket and Margaret] are well, and both at school. I think of boarding Margaret at Miss Tyson's during holidays on account of her music, as also that we anticipate taking a short journey. Jeff is weak and low, and my own health has unaccountably failed.

When I can I will send you some hair and a miniature of Sam.

Your affectionate child
Varina Davis

Margaret Howell to Her Husband

Mrs. Howell is visiting the Davises in Washington. Varina is expecting another baby in late February, 1855. Joseph Howell is in California.

Washington
October 29, 1854

Dear Husband—

No one has been more kind to me than Mr. and Mrs. Pierce. The society here is really delightful. Everybody is well read and well informed. You are well entertained if you only sit still and listen. Talent makes the aristocracy *here*—money has its admirers too—but talent outranks it. Jeff leaves tomorrow for a short trip to West Point by way of relaxation from duty. He will be absent five days. His health is about as usual. He had escaped his usual attacks of fever this fall for the first time since he has been in public life. He looks well though thin. We play backgammon every night late and sometimes too late. Varina's health and spirits are much improved, though she suffers sometimes from toothache—a natural consequence I think of her *situation*—and a cough which her physician says is altogether nervous. When she has the one, the other is entirely relieved.

We have had three letters from our Joe—but there was no money in any of them. [*The rest is lost.*]

Varina Davis to Her Parents

The second Margaret was the first Davis girl, born in February, 1855. Sometimes called Maggie, she was generally called Pollie, and she was her father's pet throughout his life. The Joseph Davises have come to see the Jefferson Davises at a summering place near Washington. They are apparently reconciled.

Adèle Cutts, beautiful, large blonde, was the niece of Rose Greenhow, the famous Confederate spy. She was marrying the widower Stephen A. Douglas, whose nomination as the Democratic candidate for President in 1860 caused the party to split into three parts and brought about the election of Abraham Lincoln and the War Between the States. Adèle's proud, aristocratic father had only a meager salary in an inferior government post. Mrs. Davis regarded Douglas as a dangerous demagogue of remarkable personal untidiness.

Redwood, Maryland, Sep 15th 1856

My dear Father and Mother,

I have reason to be grateful that both here, and with you, all my nearest and dearest are well. Our health has been uninterruptedly good, and I don't think I ever saw the two Margarets so well.

Brother Joe and Sister Eliza, with Joe Mitchell and the Culbertsons, came on some days since. He came out with Jeff immediately, and seemed charmed to see me and the baby, and delighted with Maggie [Howell]. Yesterday we gave Brother Joe a beautiful dinner. He gave the baby 60 dollars in gold to get her a present, whereupon she kissed her hand to him, and said "ta–ta," making a curtsy at the same time. He thinks she is wonderful, and looks like you. Yesterday while the gentlemen were taking coffee she danced for them "You can't come the gammon over me, young man."

Jeff and I both can't leave home in October, so I prefer staying here until March when I shall come back, and, as soon as the house is made bearable for Jeff, come down to see you. I don't know that I would not be tempted to leave the servants to their own devices and go home with him in October, but he must travel post, as altogether he can be gone but three weeks, and I suppose you would expect the baby too, and I could not take her so fast as that.

We are all expected at a family what's-a-name at the President's tomorrow. I shall give you an account of the dinner.

Ada Cutts who continues "bigger than all the men at the springs" is to be married immediately to Judge Douglas—and any amount of first love and sentiment is talked upon the occasion, and the dirty speculator and party trickster, broken in health by drink, with his first wife's money, buys an elegant, well-bred woman because she is poor and her Father is proud. However, water is going to be introduced into the city, and I trust with a view of making a little more out of the public, and sparing his wife's olfactories Douglas may wash a little oftener. If he don't his acquaintance will build larger rooms with more perfect ventilation. However, this wedding has put me out of patience.

I have been reading a good deal this summer, and rose from "John Halifax Gentleman" more charmed than I can express. Both of you must read it.

Please give my best love to the children, and, my dear parents, believe Jeff is as much attached nearly as your devoted child

V. Davis

Dr. Robert C. Wood to Mrs. William B. Howell

Dr. Wood has been unremitting in his attentions and writes by request of Varina. She had come near dying at the birth of Jefferson Davis, Jr., on January 16, 1857. Dr. Wood married Ann, eldest daughter of Zachary Taylor, and became Surgeon General of the Union forces during the Civil War. His son, John Taylor Wood, fought with the Confederates and was with Jefferson Davis when he was captured in Georgia, but Wood bribed his captor and escaped.

Washington, D.C.
Jan. 24/57

My dear Madam,

You have already been informed by telegraph that Mrs. Davis was confined eight days since and was well.

The child, a boy, is a remarkably strong, well-developed and promising infant, and Mrs. D. is at the present time doing remarkably well. Some untoward symptoms supervened which have been relieved.

The boy has not been unwell a moment.

Mrs. D. has been in the hands of considerate and kind friends who endeavoured to supply your absence.

Your daughter Miss Maggie is in fine health, and spirits, and Col D. in his usual health.

With kind regards in which Mrs. W joins, very respectfully,

R. C. Wood

Varina Davis to Her Mother

Though Mr. Howell did not care greatly for children, his long-suffering wife bore him eleven. Jefferson Davis had a special affection for children.

Washington
Jan 31st 1857

My dear Mother,

This being the first time I have been able to sit up I write to let you see I am not dead, though I have been very near it. Dr Miller stopped coming today however, and says I am in a fair way to be soon on my feet again. The baby is a very fine one. He looks exactly like his Father, and I expect to call him Jeff though his Father is very much opposed to it.

I have had every attention that humanity is heir to, and poor Jeff just gave up every thing, and never left me for nearly two weeks, but now has resumed his duties much cheered. The baby and Maggie are well, and both in high feather at my being able to have them in the room again.

My love to my dear Father, and say I took a long cry when he wrote such a short, mercantile letter about the baby, but I then reasoned that it was a long time since I had seen him, and like myself he don't care for children, and therefore that it was so much as I could expect. But if any boy or girl could pay for puerperal fever mine has paid me, and I think his grandpa will be very fond of him. I am tired and must close. Do kiss all for me, and believe me, dear Mother, your affectionate child

V. Davis

Varina Davis to Her Father

James Buchanan is the President Elect. Since Jefferson Davis is not to be in the new Cabinet, he is giving up his large house and taking a smaller one as Senator from Mississippi.

Feb. 13th 1857

My dear Father,

Your very kind letter gave me so much pleasure. I have no recurrence of chills, and if I had a few lake shrimp could eat with fine appetite.

I must try my chances travelling with the young ones, and we will take the easiest route home, via Brownsville and Pittsburg, and soon thereafter as I shall have made home comfortable, I shall come down to New Orleans, but I cannot say how long that will take, for Jeff tells me the house was thoroughly dismantled when he last saw it—even the locks being off the doors, and no knives and forks, too.

My boy is the finest baby I ever saw, large and strong, and comely, and so like Jeff that every one remarks upon it. He never cries except from hunger, and then "roar" is the word for his performances. Little Maggie is the pet, and pride of the house—she is very like Ma and exceedingly pretty and smart.

We have had a visit from Mr Buchanan, the rising sun, and the poor old man has been talked within an inch of his life and advised and courted. We, of course, could not entertain him, but everybody else did. He is to be here again the 25th of this month, so quidnuncs say, with a cabinet made out. But as I am not in it, his decision will not distress me, but I know half a dozen men who walk conscious of being secretary of state, but try not to be proud.

Jeff, since my partial recovery, looks pretty well, and seems to anxiously look for the time when he will go out of the Cabinet, but I am so oppressed with the numberless things I have to do that I don't contemplate it with pleasure. When I get out don't be anxious if you don't get a line until I get home, for I have my large house to break up, a small one to fit up—four dinners, and a reception to give, and return my visits in the space of eighteen days and am so weak I think I shall probably stagger for two months—so you see I am in a fair way to earn my part of the salary.

Please kiss my dear Mother for me. Affectionately your daughter
V. Davis

IN THE SENATE AGAIN

SECESSION LOOMS

Jefferson Davis to His Father-in-law, William B. Howell

At nine o'clock on March 4, 1857, Jefferson Davis took leave of President Pierce. "I can scarcely bear the parting from you," Pierce said. "You have been strength and solace to me for four anxious years and never failed me." Within twenty-four hours after he had ceased to be Secretary of War, Davis was sworn in as Senator from Mississippi. After two months in the Senate Davis has returned to Mississippi for the summer vacation.

Brierfield
May 12, 1857

My dear Sir,

I have the pleasure of announcing our arrival at home. Varina and the little boy Jeff are better, but not entirely well.

Maggie is quite healthy and has many speculations about the event of meeting her grandpa and grandma. She is very smart and talks plainly. We are anxious to see you and had the condition of my family justified it I would have gone down for that purpose to your house. Cannot Mrs. Howell and yourself come up to see us? I write in great haste as the hour has arrived to despatch our letters. With love to Ma and all the children I am as ever

very truly yours
Jefferson Davis

Varina Davis to Her Mother

Varina writes in detail vividly about the vicissitudes of moving and traveling with children. However, she always seems to have numerous friends to help her. The destruction she found at Brierfield was appalling.

Brierfield
May, 1857

My dear Mother,

I was grievously disappointed at the reception and Pa's refusal to come up. However, I felt as if I did not wish you to make any sacrifice to come, for I hope to get down as early in the fall as the health may decree. I have regretted a thousand times that you did not live in a healthy place that I might spend my summer with you. I see by your letter that you have had none of mine since I moved, so I will begin back.

When the baby was two months old we decided on the score of economy to straightway pack up and leave the house. On account of our weak condition, at least of mine, we could not leave immediately, so took rooms. Just as I was setting to pack up, Jeff decided in my wretched weak condition I could not go home, and he would come for me in midsummer, and take me home slowly by the lakes. Then in the Everett house I packed to go to rooms for the summer, and they not being ready by the time the auction was advertised in the Everett house, I went to Mrs Emory's, with Kate, Betsy, and the children. Mrs. E. was sick and I would not let her give up her room, so I took her bathroom, fitted up very nicely, and the children went in the garret. The house was heated to suffocation, and the weather very cold, and Jeff was the second day taken quite ill with an attack of his head, and his ear rose and broke. Betsy had a quarrel with Kate the day we reached Mrs. Emory's and went to bed where she laid one week, and would not even hold Jeffy for Kate to get her breakfast—so three, or four, sometimes five or six times a day I had to climb the stairs from the ground floor. Finally before their father got well both the children were taken sick with cold, Maggie far the worst of the two. I sent for Dr. Miller who did not feel much concern for Jeffy, but thought Maggie threatened with croup, as she had fever. At last one evening he came, and told me he thought Maggie better, but I must be careful, that Jeffy's feet must be bathed, so about two hours after he left Jeff and I went up to see them—and found Jeffy asleep in his crib, his little face purple with strangulation and shaking his whole body at every gasp. We sent immediately for the Dr who came, and pronounced it an acute case of pneumonia—he staid all night but could not vomit him. Mrs. Hetzel was ill and could not even hear anything painful, Mrs Campbell in New York, and there I was. I sent for Mrs Wayne, and we nursed him between us. Dr. Miller and Dr. Wood stayed with us alternately the whole time, and Malie hurried the landlady with the rooms—which were two which communicated with each other on the third floor and that day we put him in the carriage and took him there. Every time I asked the Drs what they thought they said while there was life there was hope—they would save him if they could—his little hands had death damp on them for four days—and for two weeks this horrible suspense continued. Eliza Bache, Mrs Campbell, Malie, Mrs Wayne all nursed him. My milk gave out, and he cried from hunger as well as pain—his little chest was blistered, his poor little back cupped. His Father got so frantic seeing the blood run down he would not have but two of the four ordered put on. Then they decided I was too low to nurse him so we scoured the town for a wetnurse. However I put down my foot that I would not have one with a child, so they were defeated, and my milk must depend on gum Arabic water for assistance.

In that state of things Jeff determined to leave, and I asked to come, too, thinking him not by any means well, so the Drs thought the change and travel would be good for Jeff, therefore I had to unpack everything root and branch to repack for here, and I was so weak I could not stand up five minutes. Mrs. Graham and Eliza Bache came down and did it with my help, and *then the cars left us*—we had to come back to Malie's to spend the night. Maggie had been taken with the chicken pox dreadfully, and cried incessantly, Jeffy kept her company. However we got started, and got down to Wheeling, when little Jeff took it, too, and cried a little harder than usual—he could not have cried more constantly—until we landed at the Hurricane, where we found two of the carriages of the place waiting for us, as they had done for a week, and went up to the house and found the parlor and tea room fitted up for us, and even a crib for the baby.

We stayed there that night, and the next day left for home—and the destruction I cannot speak of. All the locks spoilt, sheets cut up for napkins, towels and napkins swept from the land—nothing even to cook in—nothing but fruit trees which was not destroyed. I just sat down, and cried. And so would Jeff I am sure if he could. However, we concluded not to get anything new we could avoid.

The whole family have been forced to sleep without bars in the mosquitoes ever since we got here. We have had some gentlemen staying with us in this condition. I have even got to furnish the negroes with summer clothes. So much for my present condition, but for my sewing machine I don't know what I should do for someone to work—making pillow cases, sheets, towelling, and napkins—and tablecloths. Both children are pretty well now.

Jeff is in Vicksburg *receiving* his *reception*. He is quite well. He counted certainly on seeing you and Pa. I expect him in a week back again. I shall leave here the third week in June, and if I go to Mississippi City will pass through New Orleans if only to say howdy-do—but if I go to the Knobs of Tennessee I shall come as soon as the health permits in the fall. If I thought either of the children not able to have a disease I should come now, but if Jeff should be seized with whooping cough, measles or scarlet fever I am sure I should lose him, and then I think I should give up the ghost myself. His head is very large and his lungs seem to choke up directly—he sweats a great deal and often has cold feet and hands, and always a cough. Maggie is cutting her last four large jaw teeth and is anything but strong—so much for myself.

I am glad after reading your letter that I did not come down last week, my dear Mother, with all your household troubles thick upon you. I think if you consult a physician about Chaney and Venus you will find it much cheaper than tormenting yourself with their vagaries. Can't you hire them out, and get two good white women to do the work? I hate for you to be wearing out your life nursing and waiting on those two negroes, who never were worth their salt.

I wish you had a bunch of my flowers—they are splendid, what of them is left. And I shall have so much fruit I cannot use it all this summer—expect it every week. Can you send me up a bundle of fig cuttings in wet moss next week by the boat? Please kiss Pa for me. My love to the boys, and please say to Becket that I would send Maggie willingly enough if it was in the country—and that she is as old fashioned and cute as he was when he was small. Her Father asked her to sing the other night after she had her nightgown on, and she said with quite an air—"I cant thing, I ain't got on nany belt." She was standing by me kissing Jeffy the other day and I took no notice of her until he screamed out, when I said, my poor little son have you got colic? "No" said she, "me bit him, he'll sthop directly, it don't hurt him very much and I won't bite him nany more, ain't I bad nasty little child." She is as smart as she can live. God bless you, my dear Mother, and believe me as ever most affectionately

Your devoted child
V. Davis

Lucinda Stamps to Jefferson Davis

Lucinda Stamps and her second husband are living in the Davis family place at Rosemont near Woodville, Mississippi. From the age of three Jefferson lived here except when he was away at school and college. His mother died at Rosemont and is buried in the little walled family cemetery near the house, along with his sister Mary and numerous other family members.

Rosemont
May 29th 1857

My dear Brother,

I received your kind letter and it gave me a great deal of pleasure, it had been so long since I had heard from you (except through the news papers) that I began to think you had no time to think of or write to your Sister so far away.

I am sorry to hear that Varina's health is not good, but hope her visit to the South will perfectly restore her and make the dear little boy healthy and strong. I feel so anxious to see your children I hope it will not be long before you can come with Sister Varina and the little darlings to see us.

I hope we shall not be disappointed this summer in your visit. I shall be so glad to see you. It has been long indeed since we met, and many changes have taken place as years roll by, but not in the love I feel for my brother. It will remain the same while life lasts and I do not feel more proud of him now than I did when he was a little boy and searched over the orchard for the ripest and best fruit for his sister.

You must make your visit long enough for the dear little children to know and love me. I think a visit to your old home would do you and them good, and Varina would grow strong here if she would stay long enough in this healthy country.

As ever affectionately
Your Sister
Lucinda

Jefferson Davis to James Buchanan

Warren County, Mi.
June 19, 1857

To the President

My dear Sir,

It has long been the subject of remark that the graduates of the Military Academy whilst occupying the first rank as scholars in the exact sciences were below mediocrity in polite literature. Their official reports frequently exhibit extreme poverty of style. To remedy this, I increased, when in the War Dep't, the course of English studies, and in the examination of the text books found among other objectionable and defective features that Wayland was the author used for instruction in moral philosophy.

Not to weary you with details I will only say that the course of studies of Cadets and the little preliminary education exacted for admission, requires that the text books should have a special character. To train the men who are at the head of armies, to maintain the honor of our flag and in all circumstances to uphold the constitution, requires a man above sectional prejudices and intellectually superior to fanaticism.

Very truly your friend,
Jeffn. Davis

Varina Davis to Her Father

While Mrs. Davis is boarding on the Gulf Coast, Davis is attending to plantation affairs at Brierfield. Overseers are always a problem. Mrs.

Davis, who was later to say she hated the Gulf Coast, now buys lots on the water and looks to building a house there.

Mississippi City
Aug 9, 1857

My dear Father,

Your kind letter reached me this morning, and I sincerely regretted my laziness about writing when I found you had taken a trip down the coast in the railroad to meet Ma. Her health is fast improving, yet she says she must positively go over in the evening as she feels anxious about a house, and wants to settle home affairs a little so she leaves here tomorrow. I would give any thing if you were here today, the sea is so splendid, and the tide so high. My children are both tolerably well, and Maggie loves dearly to bathe.

I had a letter from Jeff since the one you sent me. He lives well, but very busy with the crop, and waiting for a new overseer whom he was expecting, so that by this time I think he is in North Mississippi. He thinks he has been able to redeem a great part of the crop. I have concluded to buy the place I spoke of when you were here, and think though it was high, that I shall not regret it, so have done so, and think of at the same time buying a hundred and twenty-five feet more, which will make the whole lot cost me $2000—$1000 cash.

God bless you my dear Father, as ever I am affectionately

V. Davis

Jefferson Davis to Varina Davis

Perhaps no man in politics ever spent less time than Davis visiting his constituents. His Representative and Senatorial positions had been handed to him with little or no canvassing.

Brierfield, Mi.
Aug 23, 1857

My dear Wife,

I am doomed to delays & at the same time more and more urged to fulfill my promises in answer to invitations to visit my constituents.

Brother Joe arrived yesterday. Eliza returned with him. They are well and report the children all well in Ky.

The measles continue at the Hurricane and must sweep the place before stopping. No case here yet. Things get on here as usual. William is no gardener, and has not mind enough even to make one. He had forgotten to plant any thing for a fall garden, and I need not tell you that when I thought of it, which was quite lately, I had little knowledge as to what ought to be planted, and found no seed for such purpose.

The packet has met with an accident below and we received nothing yesterday. I am the victim of gnats and am now suffering from one which met me with an evil eye, yesterday evening, and straight rendered my eye so evil that I write with pain. God bless and preserve you all and grant me soon again to have "my arms about my dearie O."

Your Husband

Varina Davis to Jefferson Davis

Mississippi City
August 31st '57

My dear Banny:

The family here continues to be very very kind to us, and I am about as free as I should be at home.

I shall probably fence in three acres of the lot, or lots purchased as the case may be, and of course put a board fence around it. I shall sow Bermuda Grass or rather sod Bermuda all over the part cleared. And if we purchase the new lot, leave it to amuse you when you come down. It is covered with a thick growth of young live oaks—two of the grandest pines on the coast and some rich magnolias, and live oaks full size for this place. This is the handsomest lot I have ever seen—maple, hickory, magnolia, live oak, jupon pine and sweet bay in a dense shade.

Jeffy!!! bit boy, smart bit boy, grand old boy, big as him's Fader—him was big again as when his Fader left him, and not a single tooth. He's the sweetest thing you ever saw and good as gold—not at all precocious however—and I am thankful for it. Maggie is very little less fleshy than she used to be in Washington, and the smartest thing I ever saw. She calls out to go bathing and when she gets in plays about like a fish.

Whenever I go to Handsboro the people ask for you, and want to know when you will come.

Take care of yourself my own old Ban, and write when you can. God bless and keep you is the prayer of your devoted wife

W. D.

Varina Davis to Her Father

Mississippi City
September 27th, 1857

My dear Father

Jeff arrived much to my delight about daybreak in the morning, after having been all night beating about in an oyster boat, it being the only conveyance he could get to bring him.

I had built upon your and Ma's coming over with him, and now let me implore you to come if only to "right her up"—and to fish yourself. We went this morning, and the rest caught perch a foot long just as fast as they could pull them out, and one Spanish mackerel. I felt too much indisposed to hold a pole even, so did not fish, and coming home I went to get out of the boat and felt so weak I lost my footing and fell in heels over head under the bath house. Jeff jumped in and fished me out, and I have felt pretty well worsted since, but tell Ma it was the first time I felt how ducking felt since my childhood. I believe no matter how Ma moves so she gets the things put together, and I will help her in everything, and you know I am a horse when I turn in.

Jeff speaks here Friday. Can't you and Ma come? If you can come, maybe Saturday we can go to Ship Island. Come and bring the children. Do come. Please let us know by return of mail so the carriage can meet you.

God bless you all until I see you again.

As ever your devoted child
Va. Davis

Varina Davis to Her Mother

Jefferson Davis Howell, generally called Jeffy D., was supported and reared as a son by Jefferson Davis. He became a cadet of the newly formed Confederate Naval Academy during the War Between the States.

Brierfield
October, 1857

My dear Mother,

Without solicitation, and without even a suggestion Jeff offered to take little Jeff, and educate him if you would let him go to Washington with us. I will send my butter money for you to fit him out, and need I say, my dearest old Mother, that no effort will be spared to make him a comfort to you. I will keep him with me and watch him until he is large enough to go to school, and you shall have no anxiety about him. I know it is hard to offer to take him from you, but I believe his welfare much concerned in it. If you let him go write immediately and I will send the money. I'll get him clothes and prefer it at the North because they are cheaper. I'll make him visit with me, and keep him with me, and try to give him confidence in us. Don't be afraid Jeff does not mean all this, for I told him I would rather not offer if he did not feel able. For God's sake, Ma, consider what a place New Orleans is to bring up a boy in, and don't refuse. He shall go to college, West Point, or the Army as he chooses. Pa will counsel with you.

I have been trying to get your comforts made, but am slow, having only Betsey sick for a house servant, the rest picking cotton. I will send you some eatables as soon as there is a boat stops.

I am hurried out of my boots. God bless you, my dear.

Affectionately
V. D.

Varina Davis to Her Mother

Now that Congress is in session, the Davises are settled again in Washington. Mrs. William Gwin, wife of the wealthy Senator from California, gives elaborate parties, as does Lord Napier, the British

Minister, whose wife became an intimate friend of Varina's. The other persons mentioned were prominent in Washington society in the late fifties.

Washington
Sunday Even, December 16, 1857

My dear Mother,

With Jeffy D on one side studying his lessons, and Margaret on the other, I am writing to you. My own two are in bed. Jeffy D. gets on pretty well at school, because I make him study at home at night, but I find the difficulty with him is that he can't study long without getting exceedingly tired. He is inclined to sit with the servants, but I don't wonder at that, so I forbid it, and occupy him at night so that he can't do it if he would. He is a good little boy, and I think when he improves in his retentive faculties will learn very fast. As yet he takes no interest in his studies. Jeffie and Granville Brown, the postmaster general's son, are great friends, and Mrs. Brown is very kind to him.

Margaret is so nearly a young woman that I do little more than suggest to her. She is a very fine looking and dignified girl, pleasant and quiet, but not *notable* at all. She has learned to govern her temper wonderfully, but is positive to the back bone, and never says die.

I went to Lord Napier's party, to a dinner at Mrs Gwin's, and to one at the President's. To both places I wore the old gold coloured silk with a width of black velvet let in the sides, and black lace each side, also a black bertha of lace and lemon colored bows. Lady Napier is a pretty, middle-aged woman; she seems a truly pious woman too. The lancers, a new dance, is all the rage, and all the old married women lance but me. At Mrs. Gwin's John Bull took me in to dinner, and William H. Seward sat opposite to me, Solomon Foot next, still they were pleasant. Addie Douglas ranks me—but she was sweet and affectionate, and I did not care for the place, though it was mine by rights.

At the President's I had expected to shine in a blue moire antique, with white satin spots, and point lace, but it did not come, and I rigged up my old red velvet nearly tight over my hoops, and left determined like Mark Valentine to throw myself into the breach, and be agreeable. Sir William Gore Onsely took me into dinner, and was really charming, though he is a fat old Englishman. Since this time I have dined with the Ogle Taylor's, and Lady Onsely was again of the party, Mrs Stoekel, Mrs Albuquerque, and Mrs Erastus Corning of New York, Mrs Jude Rosevelt of the same place, blazing in diamonds. It was the loveliest dinner I ever went to, such exquisite wines, and so little victuals, hardly more than just enough. Then for some reason or other I was a lion, mane and tail—so that I enjoyed it. [*The rest is lost.*]

Alexander Dallas Bache to Jefferson Davis

Senator Davis had secured a substantial appropriation for Bache's coastal survey. Bache is expecting a visit from Davis and his family at his experimental camp in Maine.

New York
July 2, 1858

Dear Mr. Davis,

Last evening I recd. a telegraph from Mrs. Davis, which has decided in part measure my plans to-day. My object in hurrying back was to meet you & as you only reach Portland on Sat., you would not be ready to go to camp on that day. So I am concluded to accept the invitation to meet the officers of the "Guyan & Inders" at Mr Fields', to report myself in Portland on Tuesday, with the little lady my spouse. I shall expect you to go to camp with me & if you do, I will wait until the next day. Mrs. B. will stop or go on to Bangor, according to Mrs. Davis' movements or stayings in Portland.

We shall have as many days before the party breaks up in camp as you will care to stay, & I only hope the weather may be propitious. Should any rail road accident or other contratemps occur to spoil my programme I will telegraph you.

Mrs. B. unites with me in kindest regards to Mrs. Davis. Yesterday was the rowdiest day I ever saw. There must have been some 500 to 600 thousand people collected in N.Y. all in Holiday dress and from morning to night was one rejoicing. More when we meet.

Ever truly yours,
A. D. B.

Varina Davis to Her Mother

The Davises had taken the two children with them to Maine. Davis, who had gone "down East" to recuperate from a serious illness in which he almost lost his eyesight, is feted and makes speeches at the State Fair and on several other occasions. He speaks twice in Portland, reviews troops at Belfast Encampment, and accepts an honorary Doctor of Laws degree from Bowdoin College.

Humpback Station, Maine
Sep 15th 1858

My dear Mother,

I received your letter on the eve of starting for Professor Bache's camp—it being the first since the first week I arrived in Portland, and that was the only one since a letter written after Jeff's sickness.

Upon the whole I have had as nice a summer as I could expect—the pleasantest part of the summer has been this under canvas. We have quite an encampment here and nice living as ever I saw, the best mutton, and the best chickens, and elegant cooking. We are three miles or twelve hundred feet above the surrounding country in quite a wild district, and we see from the top spur of the mountain over eighty miles. The mountain is only approachable to ladies by a wood sledge drawn by oxen on which we accordingly came up, Mrs Bache & I—the next day the children. We had the equinoxial gale here, but though trees were blown down all around us, we had no accident. The encampment breaks up tomorrow and we will all go down to Portland again. From there we will go through New York to Philadelphia where we will see Uncle Joe Howell, and take up the children, and go home—for their holiday, and winter outfit. I enclose a letter from Mr Chetwood, Jeffie's teacher, and his report, which I will remit to you regularly.

I have been begging Jeff so hard to let me go south with him this fall, and leave the children. He does not say yea or nay. If he goes before Jeffie & Maggie's holidays are over, I must of course give it up, Maggie is quite too womanish to be left alone. In this weary pilgrimage I am never more to do as I please.

Your devoted child
V. Davis

Varina Davis to Her Mother

Lord Napier is the British Minister. Varina saw to it that Margaret and Jeffy D. Howell associated with the best children. Jefferson Davis Bradford is the son of Davis's sister Amanda. Jeff Davis, Jr., is not yet two years old.

Washington D.C.
Nov. 21, 1858

My dear Mother,

Maggie has left for school, and Jeffy D. is deep in Monroe's school here—they are both well.

Jeff Bradford leaves me tomorrow, and I shall have no one but little Jeffy D to go round with. He brought the Napier boys home to dinner with him yesterday, and I wish you could have seen the English boys brag, and the Americans playing them off. Jeff's cheeks were purple with suppressed laughter. While Jeff Sr is away I am letting him [Jeffy D.] invite who he chooses to take dinner with him. It cultivates his gentlemanly feelings I think to feel that he has company.

Ever since the week after Jeff went away one of my horses has been lame, and I have been compelled to walk. The woman who made Jeffy's clothes lives half a mile from here, and I have walked out there times without number to get them done. You would think your little Jeff so very pretty—he is so big, and white, and fat— He has a great way of saying, "Ill boom ee in e eye, Mamma," and then doing it, and the other day I slapped his hand, he went off furious. If he is hurt instead of crying he gets puffed out like a frog, and pitches in to the first thing he sees. He goes round singing "I want Daddy home" all day long. I have had but one letter from Jeff since he reached Brierfield, however he was well. I don't much expect him before the second week in December. He has found everything in a very unsatisfactory state at home and *scant* half a crop.

Maggie is quite well, and very smart—she and Jeff play together very nicely now—though Maggie is always saying "life is not worth the struggle." Sometimes she says "Ill give you my word in honor I'm really sick for a apple."

All your friends here are well, and are preparing for the winter. Oh, how I would like to be free of care for a few days if only to know how it would feel, if I should not have to lose the objects of those cares. Cares do wear out one's youth, but I think they refine and purify at the same time. But my flights are at best lame efforts, so I'll "jist let ye off."

Your affectionate child,
Varina Davis

Malie Brodhead is going to have a baby in January—I'm glad it is not the likes of me.

Thomas J. Coe to Jefferson Davis

This letter from Coe, the latest overseer, reveals something of Davis's problems as a Delta planter who had to be in Washington most months of the year.

Brierfield Jan 31st 1859
Col Davis
Dear Sir
I can report the place in tolerible good helth, but cant make a very good report of my proggress in work we have had very bad wether rain constantly. I have just started my plowes, & the ground is not now in good order, but getting late.

I see in the Book you left to keepe som of the negroes supplied with flower molasses coffee shagor & tobacco but fine none of the above named things here to give them. Must I send for them. Please write me

The stock keeps up better than I thought for I keep them well attended to. & give them the sun of the field in dry days. & give them cotton seede & salt them well.

I am getting oute som logs to bild a crib two pens 17 ft swuar entry 12 ft. shedded all round I had a thought to fix the old hospittle but find I will have to put on a new roof & the post are all rotten. & will let all a lone untill you return home. I wish to consult with you before Building. Matilda has a fine child, *Jacks wife*. I am commenced to garden a little.

Hopeing this may find you & family well. your Brothers helth is just tolerible but he is oute most evry day

Yours truly
Thos. J. Coe

Varina Davis to Her Mother

Fanny Kemble, "the lovely English actress," who had made her debut at twenty as Juliet, was a great favorite in America.

Washington, D.C.
March 1st 1859

My dear Mother,

There is no change in us since I last wrote. Jeffy D. is quite well, and in the glorious anticipations of hearing Fanny Kemble read Shakespeare to-morrow night. We have been going for several nights to hear Fanny Kemble read. It is the most wonderful performance I ever saw. She really seems to change the scene. Do see her when she goes to New Orleans.

Jeff goes away in the morning, and stays until one o'clock at night at the Senate, and if I did not have a mountain of work to do I don't know what I should do waiting all day, but Jeffie D lost all his shirts at Burlington, has torn up his drawers, and outgrown them, also his spring clothes, so with the two children, Margaret and Jeff to get ready, that my sewing machine doesn't burn up the box is a blessing. I am in hopes Jeff will leave as soon as the adjournment of Congress. Mrs Montgomery Blair has half promised me a small house of hers about nine miles from town, only four rooms, but quite healthy and in deep woods. I shall stay here until Jeffie D's schooling is through, then move into the country for the summer, with plenty of books and work hope to get through comfortably, if not very cheerily. Jeff has stood the unusual fatigue better than I hoped so far. I don't know what the night will bring forth. The children are stirring round like mad, so I will close.

As ever affectionately
Your daughter
V. Davis

Jefferson Davis to Mrs. William B. Howell

Francis C. Blair, Sr., owner of Blair House in Washington, is a Maryland-born newspaper mogul and wily politician, who turns Republican and has considerable influence on Abraham Lincoln. It was his son, Montgomery, who as Postmaster General of Lincoln's Cabinet threatened to resign if the President did not send the so-called "relief" squadron to Fort Sumter in April, 1861, which brought on the War Between the States. Though Davis mistrusted the Blairs, Varina became intimate with them, and Montgomery virtually gave her his suburban house for the summer of 1859.

Davis is at Brierfield because of the threat of a flood from the river.

Brierfield Mi.
March 28, 1859

Dear Ma,

I left Varina and the children on the 16th Inst. They were in usual health and will remain at Washington until I rejoin them, say about the 1st of May. If it should be in my power to do so I will see you before I return. Our arrangements were imperfect, but we will probably seek a summer residence in the mountains as near to Washington as we can find a suitable place. Varina having strong "free sail" proclivities, as you know, seemed disposed to go out to the neighborhood of Mr Blair. He had a house which he offered to her at a nominal rent. What guarantee he offered for keeping the peace with me I did not learn.

Maggie wanted to come with me to keep house for me at "the Blierfeel" and if I could have hoped she would be as good all the time as she was at the start, I would have brought her with me. She is very smart and very pretty, she talks a great deal about you all, and we hear occasionally of quaint descriptions she gives of her relations when she goes out visiting. She has a much greater facility in forming acquaintance than her parents, and watches at the yard gate until she sees some body's feet on the pavement, when she calls out to them to open the gate for her, stating that she is not tall enough to reach the latch; as soon as the gate is open, away she goes to some house where she is welcome, and stays until a hue and cry detects her hiding place.

Jeff is a large strong fellow and the most manly, affectionate little fellow I ever saw. You will probably suspect me of a partial judgement, the verdict, however, is sustained by *public opinion* in which I feel full confidence.

The river here is high and rising rapidly. Our levees have been improved but the excessive rains have injured our prospect for a crop, and greatly embarrass us by destroying the pasturage on which we have been accustomed to rely.

My general health has improved. The eye of which the sight was almost lost has slowly recovered and hopes are entertained that by quiet and proper treatment during the approaching summer the sight may be restored so as to make it again useful for looking in two directions. Varina, I suppose, keeps you informed of most things concerning Maggie H. and Jeffy D.

I will write very soon to Mr. Howell, to whom and the young folks please present my affectionate remembrances. As soon as I am relieved from anxiety about the river I intend to go out to the interior of Missi. but my stay must be brief.

Accept assurances of the affection with which I am as ever, your Son.

Jeffn. Davis

Varina Davis to Jefferson Davis

Because of the raging Mississippi River flood, Varina had urged her husband to go to protect the Brierfield property, although she was expecting a baby in a few weeks. Lord Napier is the outgoing British Minister. Lord Lyons is the newly appointed one.

Washington
April 3, 1859

My dear Husband,

I see by the papers that you reached our home the 22nd for which I am thankful.

Eliza Bache came on to see me about some business the day before yesterday and is staying with me. She has cheered me more than I can express. All my friends are very kind in coming in frequently as my feet don't permit me to walk now.

The weather here is lovely, warm enough to dispense with fires.

Maggie is more changed than any child I ever saw. She continued to run away to Mrs. Phillips every few hours and Mrs. P. amused her guests making her curse, until I had to whip her three times. Since which she is perfectly biddable, good-tempered.

The Napiers left here for Annapolis a few days since, but the new arrival of Lord Lyons has induced the fear that the ship has been lost in the severe gales. They are coming back tomorrow to the Corcoran wedding, which is to be a small Rothschild's affair.

I enclose you some cotton seed, and a letter that will explain them.

Don't feel uneasy about me. I am pretty well and quite hopeful. *Pray keep out of the sun* and night air, and try to take my heart trouble lightly, so long as our little home circle is complete. That God may help you and keep you safe is the nightly prayer of your devoted Wife, W. D.

Varina Davis to Jefferson Davis

Washington
April 10, 1859

My dear Banny:

I received your letters of the 24th and 25th yesterday, it being the first news of you since you left Memphis.

All this time I have been hoping that the high water accounts were exaggerated by the papers. I am glad I persisted in urging you to go home. I have not the least doubt that your presence has averted a crevasse. I hope that you may be able still to do so. But the state of watchfulness and uncertainty must keep you in a nervous condition. I was just going to break out in a series of useless regrets that at the only home we have we cannot be together, but it is useless, and idle, and does not tend to make either of us feel happier. Your return must necessarily depend upon so many contingencies and I must reconcile myself to look upon it as the church does Easter, i.e. a moveable feast.

Little Jeff is constant to a degree. I have never seen a dearer baby before. He shouts fifty times a day—"I love my Daddy, I love Mr. Davis, I do!" He and Maggie ran away day before yesterday and were discovered across the street taking a stroll hand in hand "like the babes in the woods," as Maggie says. Dr. Lawson's garden is a perfect blessing to us, they trot around there all day long, and Eliza [the nurse] seems to enjoy having them penned up securely in so large a stamping ground. I am doubly glad because the scarlet fever is very prevalent.

Maggie and Jeff are both as well as possible, only Jeff is burnt quite red, his cheeks look so red they would do honor to a winter apple. He is singing from the minute he gets out of bed until his mouth is stopped with his own delicate mixture of fish roe and molasses.

Being rather more helpless than usual my friends are very kind. That is Mrs Hetzel, and Mrs Emory and Mrs Graham. They come very often to see me which relieves me of many weary hours, for now I am unable to go out but for a little while in the carriage and find it impossible to see strangers as I can't bring them upstairs. Strange to say the most affectionate remembrance I have had was from dear Lady Napier, who has knitted me some little socks and not only written to me from Annapolis, but written to friends for news of me. Lord Lyons (the new British minister) is very taciturn and very stupid, so the people say who have seen him.

I have sent off over two thousand speeches, etc. The Boston, Jackson, etc. speeches are now in the process of being franked. My time of trouble is so near that I cannot look a day ahead, so I am getting the envelopes ready.

I have deposited a $1000 check from Payne and Harrison in Riggs' bank and paid Mr. Ledyard $285 for the cameos. Mrs Hetzel will take charge of my money matters and household affairs and the children when I can do so no longer. So don't feel uneasy about us all.

I shall hope to see you by the first of June, should we all be spared, and trust you may induce Brother Joe to come with you. You must try to spend your birthday with us.

The thing most urgent in the garden I think cannot be done until the fall—trimming the roses, planting new ones, and dressing and replenishing the *new asparagus* bed near the backyard, and dressing and dividing the strawberry bed. The quinces want cultivation.

God bless you, my dear Husband, much more love than can be expressed, is in the heart of your

Waafe

W. D.

Varina Davis to Jefferson Davis

Jefferson Davis is kept at Brierfield because of the alarming floods. Varina is about to be delivered of her fourth child. She always dramatized her pregnancies and fancied that she might not survive the ordeal. Jeff, Jr., had his second birthday in January. President Buchanan was on more or less intimate terms with the Davises, though by no means as close as Franklin Pierce had been.

Washington April 17, 1859

My dear Banny,

Jeff is the "friend of my bosom, the balm of my life" as I felt he would be from the minute he was born. If I should not live to tell him so, you must when he can understand it, but I pray every day to rear him.

The only person I have seen in high spirits for some days is Mr. Buchanan, who paid me a very long and very pleasant visit yesterday, congratulating himself that there was no news—thank goodness.

If I am not taken sick before Wednesday I shall have franked 2780 envelopes, and about five hundred ready. It gives me pleasure to be doing something which seems to bring us nearer to each other. I do so long to see you, my dear Husband. It saddens me to realize that there is so very much in one's being the first love of early youth. Often since you have been away this time I have experienced that queer annihilation of responsibility and of time, and gone back fourteen long years to the anxious, loving girl, so little of use, yet so devoted to you—and nothing but my grey head, swollen feet, and household cares awake me from the dream. But indeed I am becoming sentimental, and if this reaches you in broad sunlight, busy with the levees, answering the negroes' questions, or with weak eyes when you don't want to read bad writing you will wish my romance had been indefinitely postponed, so I can only promise to run off no more, but assure that hourly my prayer is that "the Lord bless thee and keep thee."

Your affectionate Wife
V. Davis

Jefferson Davis to William B. Howell

In the midst of the worst flood ever recorded in the Delta, Varina had given birth to another son in Washington on April 18. Jefferson Davis, directing salvaging matters at Brierfield, was torn by anxiety about his wife.

Brierfield, Miss
April 24, 1859

Dear Pa:

I accept thankfully your congratulations, but my anxiety for Varina is so uncontrollable that the intelligence has caused me depression rather than joy.

I have sent off last evening the residue of my stock and am hastening to leave for Washington, as soon as provision is made for the negroes who I am unwilling to send away. The water runs with strong current across the main ridge which was dry in the flood of 1828, and was considered above any possible rise of the river. [*The rest is lost.*]

Varina Davis to Her Mother

Varina is in a highly emotional state because Jefferson urges that the baby be named for his brother Joseph.

Washington
April 25th 1859

My dear Mother,

I have never had so comfortable a confinement *after the baby was born,* though I cried until I had a nervous headache for five days about the proposed name and our home troubles. We have lost *every thing.* Jeff gets into a boat at our steps at Brierfield and goes up all the way to the Hurricane through Sister Eliza's garden to the Hurricane back steps. The stock have been boarded out at Grand Gulf and he thinks we will have perhaps to send away the women & children too. And this when we looked forward by severe economy to increasing our land and force—with last year's heavy losses to contend with. I never have known Jeff so distressed and broken down. He seems to feel for me the utter destruction of our garden and orchard. He has evidently cried over some of his letters. However I can give up many things better than he should be troubled.

I have had a lonely time since I was sick. The Dr. thought me in such a very unfavorable condition before the baby's birth and I had fever so constantly that he has forbid all friends even yet—no one but the nurse and Mrs Hetzel & Mrs Emory—and they don't come often or stay more than a very few minutes. Had I told you that I had partially lost the use of one hand, that I could not turn over at night without my right leg slipping a little out of joint, that I was so swelled that part of the time I could not walk because the soles of my feet were so swelled, you would have had a terror not all commensurate with the amount necessary as it has turned out. Jeff was away ignorantly supposing he could be with me, so I saved all parties something, for I expected as did Dr. Miller puerperal fever and knew nothing could be done but just to suffer. And if I had to die it was useless to make you all wretched, so I sewing-machined with my disabled hand, and got all the children, Margaret included, in such a condition that if I died they could do without attention until their friends "hove in sight." And here I am high & dry—the children clothed and the little fellow pretty well provided for with his Brother's old things, and the pretty things her grandmother sent Maggie "long ago." Jeff Jr is visiting with Mrs Emory, and behaving as well as can be in every way.

The little fellow is a pretty boy—very Davis. To tell you the truth he looks enough like his Uncle Joe to be his child, small build, grey eyes, large nose, and black hair. However, I pray he may grow out of the resemblance. If he doesn't, it will be external only, unless Howell & Kempe blood has run out.

I have a very sick household, cook, man servant, and Kate—the latter threatened with a miscarriage. Eliza and a supernumerary I hired since I have been sick do well all they can, but I must say I eat by hook & by crook, and pretty crooked at that. I am not able to sit up yet, and must close as my headache still lingers.

Your devoted child
Varina Davis

Varina Davis to Her Mother

Caroline Leonard is Joseph Davis's third daughter, now living in Norfolk, Virginia. Varina resents bitterly having to name her son for her husband's brother, Joseph Davis. However, the child was named Joseph Evan Davis, Evan for Jefferson Davis's Philadelphia-born grandfather.

Washington
May, 1859

My dear Mother,

I received today your and Pa's generous letters about my boy's name—but I *cannot* reconcile myself to it. I shall hand them to Jeff and he may do as he chooses, but the child was only welcome to me as being the means of offering Pa a compliment—I have had it nearest to my heart to pay him since my first child was born. I could not wait, so I wrote to Jeff the second day the baby was born, and told him how I hated the thought, and I don't think he got it. I cried myself sick and had to take quinine. Malie wrote me a letter of congratulations, and went out of her way to say that she wished I could name him Joseph. I thanked her for the opportunity, and wrote her in return that I had but one wish, and that was to name it after my dear Father, and that it should be like him. However, until I saw Jeff I could not tell what he wished but would think it quite natural if he wished to name it for his Brother. And of course he had a perfect right to do so, however, I could never participate in paying, in my opinion, the highest compliment in a woman's power to a man whose very name was only suggestive to me of injustice and unkindness from my youth up to middle age. I thought if she fished she should have a gudgeon.

I then wrote to Caroline Leonard, whose letter was really affectionate and said that if the boy was not named for Pa I didn't care if he was called Elihu, Moses or "Deutioneramy & them." I don't abuse Jeff's Brother, but I come so near hating him that I should hate mightily to be as near the edge of a precipice, for I am afraid I shall fall off—but enough of this.

I expect Jeff here on Thursday or Friday. He has started to come, then I will speak fully about it.

Jeff, Jr. is well, and very good, and slovenly—but he is a dear little heedless, provoking boy, with no vices. He is growing, and is healthy as a bear, never impudent, and if I can lay my hands on him, minds me. He is much like what Billy was. [*The rest is lost.*]

Varina Davis to Jefferson Davis

After settling his family in a summer resort, Davis had to return again to Brierfield because of the flood wreckage. Varina now seems reconciled to the baby being named for Joseph Davis.

Oakland, Maryland
July 2, 1859

Dearest Husband,

It was so thoughtful of you to write me from Cincinnati. You would have been gratified if you could have seen Jeff. He was in a high play in the street and I told him I had a letter from you and he should read it—he came in blowing, asking "did it tome on the tars"? He sat down, opened it, and began "dear Daddy, I love ou too moch." He kissed it at least a dozen times. He is truly a precious boy of such a noble heart. Maggie is about as usual, pestiferous, honorable, but not remunerative as yet.

How I do look forward & long for the time when we may walk about here together if God only gives you back to me safe. My little Joe seems blessed to me, and all the sweetness of our happiest hours seems to have returned with his birth, and I hate to give you up even for a day. May God keep you safe, my only love, and give you to me again in health. But please don't stay long—I feel so unwilling for you to run so great a risk. Do remember that you are a part of a powerful party and therefore can be spared, but you are all to your wife and babes. But I get so worked up and so frightened when I think of your danger I am hardly coherent.

And now my precious good Husband, farewell.

Your devoted Waafe
W. D.

Jefferson Davis to William B. Howell

Jefferson Davis was endeavoring to help his father-in-law in New Orleans in one of his various projects which always went awry. Davis is still laboring with the problems of a plantation on the Mississippi River. The new tie was for baling cotton.

Dr. Leacock, an Episcopal clergyman of New Orleans, was the father-in-law of William Howell, Jr., Mrs. Davis's second brother.

Brierfield
Nov. 24, 1859

My dear Sir,

Mr. Garrett called at my lodgings in Jackson and left your letter of introduction, but gave no clue as to his whereabouts and I was unable to find him.

I called the attention of the President of the Society to his tie and also asked the consideration due to it of one of the Judges. If you could have been there in person or have been represented by an active agent more notice would have been secured for the tie. It would have given me pleasure to have seen to an experiment such as you describe and to have written to you on the subject, if the tie had been received in time. I will instruct my overseer to give the subject special attention and to write to you when the cotton is shipped. We have made very little and have ginned none; for this there are two reasons, first the chute is so low that we have no opportunity to ship from the usual landing, and second the mules are employed in repairing levees.

I expect to hear from Washington to-morrow. It will be necessary for me to go by way of Jackson and the time is so short that I must adopt the quickest route. A note from Dr. Wood informed me that Varina and the children were well on the 7th Inst. I cannot imagine where Varina's letters have strayed as it is not supposable that she has not written to me since we parted.

My days here have been days of constant toil and there is yet so much to be done that I feel reluctant to leave. If Varina and the children were with me I should borrow some time from the public and allow the session of Congress to open without my presence.

Dr. Leacock and William made me a hurried but to me very

gratifying visit, and I felt when they had gone the want of their interesting conversation. The Doctor possesses such varied attainments and takes such striking views of things that I was constantly impressed with the blessing such an acquaintance must be to one who wearies of the common-place hum-drum people who make up everybody's world.

Present me affectionately to all the family and believe me very truly yr's,

Jeffer. Davis

Franklin Pierce to Jefferson Davis

Ex-President Pierce is about to sail for Nassau and thence to Europe for his invalid wife's health.

Clarendon Hotel
New York
Jany 6, 1860

My dear Friend—

I wrote you an unsatisfactory note a day or two since. I have just had a pleasant interview with Mr. Shepley whose courage & fidelity are equal to his learning and talent. He says he would rather fight the battle with you as the Standardbearer in 1860 than under the auspices of any other leader. The feeling and judgment of Mr. S. in this relation is I am confident rapidly gaining ground in New England. Our people are looking for "the coming man"— One who is raised by all the elements of his character above the atmosphere ordinarily breathed by politicians—A man really fitted for this emergency by his ability, courage, broad statesmanship & patriotism. Col. Thos H. Seymour arrived here this morning, and expressed his views in this relation in almost the identical language used by Mr. Shepley.

It is true, that in the present state of things at Washington and throughout the Country, no man can predict what changes two or three months may bring forth. Let me suggest that in the running debates in Congress full justice seems to me not to have been done to the Democracy, of the North. I do not believe that our friends at the South have any just idea of the state of feeling, running at this moment to the pitch of intense exasperation, between those who respect their political obligations, and those who have apparently no impelling power but that which fanatical passion on the subject of domestic slavery imparts without discussing the question of right—of abstract power to secede. I have never believed that actual disruption of the union can occur without blood, and if, thro the madness of northern abolitionism that dire calamity must come, the fighting will not be along Mason's and Dixon's line merely. If may be within our own borders in our own streets between two classes of citizens to whom I have referred. Those who defy law and scout constitutional obligations will, if we ever reach the arbitrament of arms, find occupation enough at home.

Nothing but the state of Mrs. Pierce's health would induce me to leave the Country now altho it is quite likely that my presence at home would be of little service. I have tried to impress upon our people especially in N.H. and Connecticut where the only elections are to take place during the coming spring, that while our Union meetings are all in the right direction and well enough for the present, they will not be worth the paper upon which their resolutions are written, unless we can overthrow political abolitionism at the polls and repeal the unconstitutional and obnoxious laws which in the cause of "personal liberty" have been placed upon our statute books. I shall look with deep interest and not without hope for a decided change in this situation.

Ever & truly
yr Friend
Franklin Pierce

Varina Davis to Jefferson Davis

Jefferson Davis was in Mississippi sitting up half the nights trying to persuade his State not to rush into secession.

William M. Browne, a naturalized Irishman, believed so wholeheartedly in a strict construction of the Constitution that he became known as "Constitution" Browne. Later he became an aide of President Davis.

Washington
November 15th 1860

My dear Husband,

I am very anxious to hear from you. I trust from the News Paper accounts you are quite well, and Mr Wigfall tells me you were in good spirits when he saw you, and looking well.

By the time this reaches you, unless you stay till the opening of the extra Session the Gov. has convened, I suppose you will be on your way home. Your last letter was dated the fifteenth of Oct.

There is intense interest felt here to know what you are doing or will do. I always say I don't know, and can't guess—that there is but one thing we do know, and that is that we quit here the 4th of March. Not one of your speeches has been reported, not even a digest of them. People talked so impudently of disunionism before me that I hunted up my old white satin flag: "If any man call me a disunionist I will answer him in monosyllables. Jeff. Davis," and declared to hang it up and quarrel with the first person who said a word. Mr Buchanan has taken it, however, and vows I shan't have it again. There is a settled gloom hanging over everyone here. Duf. Wallack has gone for Lincoln and is as fierce as a buck rabbit on Southern seceders—I say gone for Lincoln, he thinks he will make a strong, impartial, conservative President. *Everybody is scared,* especially Mr. Buchanan. Wigfall is talking to the bitter end. Hunter opposes secession. Jacob Thompson is prepared to go with the majority for everything. Toombs blathering about a resignation (in future). No one rings like the true metal so much as Constitution Browne who is enthusiastic and thoroughgoing, repudiates Mr. Buchanan's views openly, assuring secession responsibility. Good bye, dear Husband, I hardly think you care to hear from me since you don't write, though you have been so busy I won't stick to that. May God direct you right prays

Your Wife V. D.

THE WAR COMES

ON APRIL 23, 1860, the Democratic National Convention met at Charleston amid impending party strife. Though Jefferson Davis did not attend, the Massachusetts delegation led by Benjamin F. Butler voted for the Mississippian in fifty-seven sequent ballots. And Butler, who later became a name of infamy in the South, always maintained that if Davis had been nominated he would have won the Presidency and reconciled the opposing factions of North and South. But the Democratic party split asunder; the Lower South's delegates bolted because of the strength of Stephen A. Douglas. Finally there were three different Democratic candidates of opposing modified parties on the national ballot. This split of the Democrats made possible the election of the Republican's Abraham Lincoln on a partisan ticket. Though he had a million votes less than a majority, Lincoln became the President. Despite his reasonable protestations, the South regarded him as the embodiment of Republican ill will. With this presage of doom, all over the Southern States voices were raised urging withdrawal from the Union.

On December 17, 1860, Horace Greeley, famous abolitionist editor of the New York *Tribune,* wrote in an editorial: "If the Cotton States shall become satisfied that they can do better out of the Union than in it, we insist on letting them go in peace." Three days later South Carolina, without consulting the will of the other Southern States, made the drastic gesture of seceding from the Union.

In the early morning following Christmas Day, 1860, Federal Major Robert Anderson, in command of Fort Moultrie in Charleston Harbor, spiked his guns there and, under cover of darkness, removed to redoubtable Fort Sumter, which was out of range of most of the shore batteries. South Carolina chose to regard Anderson's move as an act of war. In fact, it would later be pinpointed as the deed which actually sparked the War Between the States.

On January 9, 1861, Mississippi seceded. But since Senator Davis had received no official notification, he made a powerful speech of some 15,000 words in the Senate on the danger of a terrible war that might come, but which might be avoided. "I have striven unsuccessfully to avert the catastrophe which now impends over the country, and I regret it," he said. "If you will but allow us to separate peacefully since we cannot live peacefully together, there are many relations which may still subsist between us, which may be beneficial to you as well as to us."

For months Jefferson Davis had been laboring to prevent a rupture of the Union. Now with the accumulation of strain he became so ill that his physician ordered him not to leave his room. But on January 21 he rose and went to the Senate to make his last appearance. In announcing that Mississippi had declared her separation from the United States, he made one of the most moving and eloquent speeches in American history.

Then, with his family, he took the train for Mississippi. At Jackson he was made a Major General, in command of the State's defenses. At his home, Brierfield, Davis had begun to put plantation affairs in order, when on the afternoon of February 10 a messenger from Vicksburg arrived in hot haste with a fateful telegram. Jefferson Davis had been unanimously elected President of the newly formed Confederate Government in Montgomery, Alabama. The news was hard to take; he had prayed to be spared that executive position. But he accepted the cup as his duty, and, on February 12, he formally resigned his generalship. On the night of February 16, after a roundabout railway journey, because there was no railroad line between Jackson and Montgomery, he reached the first capital of the Confederacy. In his introduction to the welcoming crowd, William Yancey proclaimed, "The man and the hour have met." On Monday, the eighteenth, Davis took the oath of office as provisional President.

When President Lincoln sent the heavily armed so-called "relief" ships to Fort Sumter, Confederate batteries reduced the fort to surrender on April 13. Two days later Lincoln, without the authority of Congress, called for troops and the war between brothers was launched.

President Davis's task was stupendous. He was called upon to administer a brand-new nation, which was virtually defenseless, with no army, navy, arsenal, or shipyard, with few manufactories of any kind, and a woefully scant railway system. Cotton was the only plentiful commodity. Davis had to establish a foreign policy, and at the same time to appease the hundreds of office seekers who did not get the positions they clamored for. An army had to be organized with a formidable want of manpower, for the Southern States had only one-fourth the white population of the North. In the face of obstacles to stagger the imagination of any statesman, Jefferson Davis began to labor to the utmost of his strength, while praying to Deity for guidance and support.

After six weeks the capital of the Confederacy was moved from Montgomery to Richmond. President Davis went on ahead while his wife and the children followed shortly.

Davis arrived on May 29 to an overwhelmingly enthusiastic reception. The Richmond *Daily Enquirer* declared, "The mantle of Washington falls gracefully upon his shoulders. Never were a people more enraptured with their Chief Magistrate than ours are with President Davis."

The bulk of Jefferson Davis letters of the January, 1861–April, 1865, period have been reproduced in the *Official Records* or in Volumes V and VI of Dunbar Rowland's huge compendium, *Jefferson Davis: Constitutionalist*. Many specimens have been used in excerpt throughout my own *Jefferson Davis: Confederate President* and in the first two hundred pages of *Jefferson Davis: Tragic Hero*. In the Jefferson Hayes-Davis Collection there are comparatively few intimate family letters during the war, for most of the four years the family was together. Many years ago some of these were given to the Confederate Museum in Richmond, and others to Confederate Memorial Hall in New Orleans. The twenty letters of this period included herein have been arbitrarily selected for economy's sake, for their varied flavor, and to carry on the story from Mississippi's secession to the evacuation of Richmond in April, 1865.

Jefferson Davis to Franklin Pierce

From his sickroom, on January 20, Davis wrote a sad letter to Franklin Pierce, whom he loved above all other men except his brother Joseph and perhaps Albert Sidney Johnston.

Caleb Cushing of Massachusetts had been the Attorney General in Pierce's Cabinet, when Davis was Secretary of War. These two men were devoted friends.

Washington
Jan. 20, 1861

Dear Friend,

I have often and sadly turned my thoughts to you during the troublous times through which we have been passing and now I come to the hard task of announcing to you that the hour is at hand which closes my connection with the United States, for the independence and Union for which my Father bled and in the service of which I have sought to emulate the example he set for my guidance. Mississippi, not as a matter of choice but of necessity, has resolved to enter on the trial of secession. Those who have driven her to this alternative threaten to deprive her of the right to require that her government shall rest on the consent of the governed, to substitute foreign force for domestic support, to reduce a state to the condition from which the colony rose.

When Lincoln comes in he will have but to continue in the path of his predecessor to inaugurate a civil war, and, leave a *soi-disant* democratic administration responsible for the rest.

Genl. Cushing was here last week and when we parted it seemed like taking leave of a Brother.

I leave immediately for Missi. and know not what may devolve upon me after my return. Civil war has only horror for me, but whatever circumstances demand shall be met as a duty and I trust be so discharged that you will not be ashamed of our former connection or cease to be my friend.

Do me the favor to write to me often, address Hurricane P.O. Warren County, Missi.

May God bless you is ever the prayer of your friend

Jefferson Davis

Jefferson Davis to Varina Davis

Davis's first letter to his wife after becoming President of the Confederacy "bears the imprint of a patriot's weight of care and sorrow," and reveals no elation of the ambitious.

Montgomery, Ala., February 20, 1861

My dear Wife,

I have been so crowded and pressed that the first wish to write to you has been thus long deferred.

I was inaugurated on Monday, having reached here on Saturday night. The audience was large and brilliant. Upon my weary heart was showered smiles, plaudits, and flowers; but, beyond them, I saw troubles and thorns innumerable.

We are without machinery, without means, and threatened by a powerful opposition; but I do not despond, and will not shrink from the task imposed upon me.

All along the route, except when in Tennessee, the people at every station manifested good-will and approbation by bonfires at night, firing by day; shouts and salutations in both.

I thought it would have gratified you to have witnessed it, and have been a memory to our children.

Thus I constantly wish to have you all with me.—Here I was interrupted by the Secretary of the Congress, who brought me two bills to be approved. This is a gay and handsome town of some eight thousand inhabitants, and will not be an unpleasant residence. As soon as an hour is my own, I will look for a house and write to you more fully.

Devoted love to you and the children,

Your Husband

Varina Davis to Her Mother

Varina has just arrived in Richmond. Though a house has been selected for her it is not ready, so she is staying in a suite at the Spotswood Hotel. At this time President Davis is enormously popular—"man worship," as his wife expresses it.

Richmond
June, 1861

My dear old Mother,

I arrived here safely after such a trip as few would like to take (four nights & three days *constant* travel without sleeping cars). The troops on the road delay everything. I really felt as if we would never get here. We are now in a hotel & I have not a moment to myself. Everything seems to me turned topsy-turvy. Jeff has had no return of chills.

In this hotel we have a private table and parlor, but, alas, that is all a name. It is crowded—fifteen or twenty ladies, each with one or two gentlemen every evening. I do get so tired, & so weak sometimes, however I am very much better since we came to Richmond in every way. The place is a most beautiful one, but it is hilly.

When we reached here tired & travel stained, Jeff, Jr. having gotten in a fury & thrown away his hat, being therefore hatless, who should appear but Jeff at the cars in the midst of hundreds of people, and a carriage furnished us by the city with four horses, and open, with yellow satin lining. As we proceeded up the street bouquets were showered into the carriage, and hurrahs for the children. It is perfect man worship. The place is one vast camp— all day long the troops are swarming in. If we meet them they all salute. When Jeff goes to the encampments they go on like wild Indians, scream, catch hold of him, call out "I am from Tennessee, I'm from Kentucky, I'm from Mississippi, God bless your soul." The other day a volunteer stepped up to the carriage & said "God bless you, Madam, & keep you well," with a deep bow. They seize little Jeff & kiss him. It seems as if Jeff's stock had suddenly risen. Amidst all this enthusiasm however comes over me the deep horror of our not being ready & armed. *Their* hordes are very near & their bitterness is very great. *They* have manufactures of arms—we have none. I made up my mind to come here & to be happy no matter what danger there was & to be with the rest if needs must be. They have taken a very fine house for me. I send you a poor plan, only to show you the style. It is a very nice place, but the woman seems never to be going to move out of it. As usual, I am interrupted. I will write again in a day or two, & telegraph today.

Give my best love to all.

Your devoted daughter,
V. Davis

Varina Davis to Jefferson Davis

Mrs. Davis and the children have been sent to North Carolina for safety. Colonel Custis Lee, the eldest son of R. E. Lee, is an aide-de-camp of the President.

Raleigh, N.C., May, 1862

My darling Husband,

The telegrams bring fearful news from Richmond of gunboats approaching within ten miles, etc. No one seems troubled about anyone there except me and I am so wretched I feel happier writing you in whose existence is bound up my future & that of our poor little helpless children. Our good it must be right to consider, else why did God give us you. Don't risk your precious life, my own noble Husband, in any unnecessary manner.

Col Lee has called for the letter & I can say no more—

God bless you precious Husband, and may he protect his own is the prayer of

Your devoted Wife

Varina Davis to Her Brother, William F. Howell

Margaret Howell, who had been given a sum of money by Jefferson Davis for the comfort of Varina's family, has joined them in New Orleans.

Raleigh, N.C.
May 28, 1862

My darling Boy,

I am so happy to hear you are getting better, and do so trust you may be able soon to come on with Pa. You ask me what I think for Minnie of a retreat to the North Carolina Mountains. I have been trying to find out for weeks some place here, but food is very scarce & all the places crowded and inaccessible, and prices fabulous. I don't expect to stay here any longer than the impending battle is in abeyance. If defeat comes, I shall probably come further south, if not, shall go back to Richmond, as expense is to me now a great item.

When we meet we will talk over these things more at length. I think Macon or Marietta the best place for Minnie. I have friends in both places. The frontier is no place for people who can't afford to run. Jeff begged me to go to Marietta and I will do so if necessary, but linger near him. One of Jeff's aides has his wife and children there—it is high, healthy, & cheap comparatively. I board my servants out here for $13 a month with free negroes, and they wait on me just as well.

Pa says Ma is not very well. Whatever can be done for her comfort Margaret has money to do—pray look after it.

Kiss your dear wife & babies for me—love to all

Your devoted Sister

Jefferson Davis to Varina Davis

Dr. Garnett was the Davises' family physician in Richmond. He took the arduous trip to Raleigh to minister to the youngest Davis child, William Howell Davis, who was born on December 16, 1861, and always called "Billie" or "Billy."

Richmond, June 12 '62

Dearest Wife,

Your telegram was received and I sent forthwith for Dr. Garnett. He said he would go by first train, that the afternoon train would not take him beyond Petersburg and he would get to Raleigh as soon by starting in the morning. God grant that my dear Baby may be relieved before the Doctor gets there. It is hard that I cannot go. Kiss my dear children.

Ever devotedly,
Your Husband

Joseph E. Davis to Jefferson Davis

Joseph Davis has had to leave his plantation as the Federals approach. He has a large number of slaves to move and care for. He takes his people to Bolton, Miss. President Davis sends him $3,000 to provide for his own smaller number of Negroes. Jefferson Davis's books and boxes of personal papers, including letters from his parents when he was away at school, were stored in O. B. Cox's attic and taken in 1863 by Union soldiers.

Aug. 23, 1862 (O. B. Cox's)

My Brother,

I have been looking for some time for a letter on the subject of sending your people to H. P. Davis. He offers to take them and think provisions cheaper there; it seems difficult to find shelter for them here. I am still in search of a plan; property is higher than before the war and provisions three times, every thing is high except labor. I find it difficult to find plans to bring them. Our stock have fared badly, many have died, & think of taking such as would not likely be stolen by the enemy back to the river, the want of salt is in part the cause, we are now trying to procure salt from lake near Shreveport, La. It is now $45 a sack. Mr. Barnes has just left here. I told him to get ready for a move, of all except a few of the old people, and I am to let him know as soon as I hear from you. The sickness among the negroes is painful and some still are convalescent, some look like they could never get well, your boy Ed seems to be of this assumption.

You will see from the papers the depredations of the enemy on the river, Madison Parish, La.

I went to the Post office to mail this letter and received yours of the 13 & 14, the latter with the $3,000.

I have several places offered and hear of many more. You will be surprised when I tell you the most favorable offered was Young Shotwell's at $40,000. This might be sold again for the purchase money, but such a debt I am unwilling to incur & therefore must take over when the liability is less. In Rankin County some pretty good places may be had, it is said, at $10 per acre, but none with shelter for half the number of our people. A little place near here if building material can be had might answer for most of them, the price is $25 per acre.

I saw General Van Dorn this morning. He seemed heated & agitated. I did not learn the cause.

Affectionately
Yr Brother

Maggie Davis to Her Father

Mrs. Davis with their son Joe has apparently returned to Richmond to see about bringing the other children back. Catherine is the children's Irish nurse. Helen Keary is Davis's niece, married to a Confederate colonel.

Raleigh, Aug. 28th, 1862

My dear Father,

We are all well. Jeffie and I have been sick, but we are well now. Billy is so sweet—he is growing so fast and laughs so loud. Jeffie and I say our lessons ever day and nearly always get A. This ink that I am writing with I made myself with red paint!

Please Father let us come home. We love to be with you. Kiss my dear Mother and sweet little Joe for me. Catherine sends a kiss to Joe. Cousin Helen and Jeff join me in love to all.

Your daughter—Polly

Jefferson Davis to Varina Davis

President Davis is making a trip to the army in Tennessee to stimulate morale. Joe Mitchell and Willie Farish are great-nephews of Jefferson Davis. A son of this William Farish, William Stamps Farish, eventually became the president of Standard Oil (New Jersey).

Clement C. Clay, Jr., a former United States Senator from Alabama and now in the Confederate Senate, was to be imprisoned with Jefferson Davis at Fort Monroe in May, 1865.

Chattanooga, Tenn.
Dec. 15, 1862

My dear Wife,

We had a pleasant trip & without an incident to relate reached this place on the 11th.

The troops in Murfreesboro were in fine spirits and well supplied. The enemy keep close within their lines about Nashville, which place is too strongly fortified and garrisoned for attack by troops unprepared for regular approaches on fortifications.

Many of your acquaintances made kind inquiry of you. Especially Genl. Hardee. I saw Joe Mitchell and Willie Farrish, both were well. Last night on my arrival here a telegram announced the attack made at Fredericksburg. You can imagine my anxiety.

There are indications of a strong desire for me to visit the farther West expressed in terms which render me unwilling to disappoint the expectation. Mrs. Joe Johnston is well, not quite pleased with her location. Genl. Johnston will go directly to Miss. and reinforce Genl. Pemberton. I saw Mr. Clay, who gives a discouraging account of the feeling of the people about Huntsville. He says the fear of the traitors is so great lest they should in the event of a return of the Yankees bring down vengeance on the true men that our friends look around to see who is in earshot before speaking of public affairs.

It is raining this morning and unreasonably warm. I have traveled constantly since starting and feel somewhat the want to rest, but otherwise am better than before the journey. Joe was a little unwell yesterday, but seems bright today. Many of the officers inquired for Col. Preston Johnston and felt, as I did, regret at his absence.

Kiss the children for their loving Father. They can little realize how much I miss them. Every sound is the voice of my child and every child renews the memory of a loved one's appearance, but none can equal their charms, nor can any compare with my own long-worshipped Winnie.

> She is na my ain Lassie
> Though fair the lassie be
> For well ken I my ain lassie
> By the kind love in her eye.

Ever affectionately,
Your Husband

Robert E. Lee to Jefferson Davis

After the unhappy third day of battle at Gettysburg, July 3, and the capitulation of Vicksburg on July 4, the South was plunged in deepest gloom. There was sharp criticism of Lee's direction at Gettysburg, though never one hint of disapproval ever came from his Commander-in-Chief. Both men were excessively fatigued, not only by the depressing burdens and enormous responsibilities heaped upon them, but by the direct attacks and snipings of censuring newspapers.

Lee chafed for a month, and then on August 8 he came to a momentous decision. He wrote a letter to the President asking to be relieved of his command. Davis was appalled. To lose Lee would be worse than losing his right arm. The two men exchanged letters which have been quoted in extracts in various works. They are reproduced in this volume to reveal the close sympathy and mutual respect of the two foremost

Confederates. As one historian has pointed out, these two letters are true "mirrors of the souls of Davis and Lee."

The original of Lee's letter is owned by the Confederate Museum at Richmond. Davis's letter is taken from the President's letter book now in the Howard Tilton Library, Tulane University.

Camp Orange, Aug. 8, 1863.

Mr. President—Your letters of July 28 and August 2 have been received, and I have waited for a leisure hour to reply; but I fear that will never come. I am extremely obliged to you for the attention given to the wants of this army, and the efforts made to supply them. Our absentees are returning, and I hope the earnest and beautiful appeal made to the country in your proclamation may stir up the whole people, and that they may see their duty and perform it. Nothing is wanted but that their fortitude should equal their bravery, to insure the success of our cause. We must expect reverses, even defeats. They are sent to teach us wisdom and prudence; to call forth greater energies, and to prevent our falling into greater disasters. Our people have only to be true and united, to bear manfully the misfortunes incident to war, and all will come right in the end.

I know how prone we are to censure, and how ready to blame others for the non-fulfillment of our expectations. This is unbecoming in a generous people, and I grieve to see its expression. The general remedy for the want of success in a military commander is his removal. This is natural, and in many instances proper. For, no matter what may be the ability of the officer, if he loses the confidence of his troops, disaster must sooner or later come.

I have been prompted by these reflections more than once since my return from Pennsylvania to propose to Your Excellency the propriety of selecting another commander for this army. I have seen and heard of expressions of discontent in the public journals at the result of the expedition. I do not know how far this feeling extends in the army. My brother officers have been too kind to report it, and so far the troops have been too generous to exhibit it. It is fair, however, to suppose that it does exist, and success is so necessary to us that nothing should be risked to secure it. I, therefore, in all sincerity, request Your Excellency to take measures to supply my place. I do this with the more earnestness because no one is more aware than myself of my inability for the duties of my position. I can not even accomplish what I myself desire. How can I fulfil the expectations of others? In addition, I sensibly feel the growing failure of my bodily strength. I have not yet recovered from the attack I experienced the past spring. I am becoming more and more incapable of exertion, and am thus prevented from making the personal examinations and giving the personal supervisions to the operations in the field, which I feel to be necessary. I am so dull that in making use of the eyes of others I am frequently misled. Everything, therefore, points to the advantages to be derived from a new commander, and I the more anxiously urge the matter upon Your Excellency from my belief that a younger and abler man than myself can readily be obtained. I know that he will have as gallant and brave an army as ever existed to second his efforts, and it would be the happiest day of my life to see at its head a worthy leader; one that would accomplish more than I could perform, and all that I have wished. I hope that Your Excellency will attribute my request to the true reason, the desire to serve my country and to do all in my power to insure the success of her righteous cause.

I have no complaints to make of any one but myself. I have received nothing but kindness from those above me, and the most considerate attention from my comrades and companions in arms. To Your Excellency, I am specially indebted for uniform kindness and consideration. You have done everything in your power to aid me in the work committed to my charge, without omitting anything to promote the general welfare. I pray that your efforts may at length be crowned with success, and that you may long live to enjoy the thanks of a grateful people.

With sentiments of great esteem, I am very respectfully and truly yours,

R. E. Lee, General

Jefferson Davis to Robert E. Lee

Richmond, August 11, 1863

General:

Yours of the 8th inst. has been received. I am glad to find that you concur so entirely with me as to the want of our country in this trying hour, and am happy to add that after the first depression consequent upon our disasters in the West, indications have appeared that our people will exhibit that fortitude which we agree in believing is alone needful to secure ultimate success.

It well became Sydney Johnston when overwhelmed by a senseless clamor to admit the rule that success is the test of merit, and yet there has been nothing which I have found to require a greater effort of patience than to bear the criticisms of the ignorant, who pronounce everything a failure which does not equal their expectations or desires, and can see no good result which is not in the line of their own imaginings. I admit the propriety of your conclusions, that an officer who loses the confidence of his troops should have his position changed, whatever may be his ability; but when I read the sentence, I was not at all prepared for the application you were about to make. Expressions of discontent in the public journals furnish but little evidence of the sentiment of an army. I wish I could feel that the public journals were not generally partisan or venal.

Were you capable of stooping to it, you could easily surround yourself with those who would fill the press with your laudations, and seek to exalt you for what you had not done rather than detract from the achievements which will make you and your army the subject of history and object of the world's admiration for generations to come.

I am truly sorry to know that you still feel the effects of the illness you suffered last Spring, and can readily understand the embarrassments you experience in using the eyes of others, having been so much accustomed to make your own reconnaissances. Practice will however do much to relieve that embarrassment, and the minute knowledge of the country which you have acquired will render you less dependent for topographical information.

But suppose, my dear friend, that I were to admit, with all their implications, the points which you present, where am I to find that new commander who is to possess the greater ability which you believe to be required. I do not doubt the readiness with which you would give way to one who could accomplish all that you have wished, and you will do me the justice to believe that if Providence would kindly offer such a person for our use, I would not hesitate to avail of his services.

My sight is not sufficiently penetrating to discover such hidden merit if it exists, and I have but used to you the language of sober earnestness, when I have impressed upon you the propriety of avoiding all unnecessary exposure to danger because I felt our country could not bear to lose you. To ask me to substitute you by some one in my judgment more fit to command, or who would possess more of the confidence of the army or of the reflecting men in the country is to demand for me an impossibility.

It only remains for me to hope that you will take all possible care of yourself, that your health and strength may be entirely restored, and that the Lord will preserve you for the important duties devolved upon you in the struggle of our suffering country, for the independence which we have engaged in war to maintain.

As ever very respectfully and truly yours,
Jeffn. Davis

Mary Stamps to Jefferson Davis

Mary Elizabeth Humphreys Stamps, daughter of Governor Benjamin Grubb Humphreys of Mississippi who had been a classmate of Davis at West Point, was the twenty-six-year-old wife of Davis's nephew, Isaac Davis Stamps. She had been staying with the Davises in Richmond when her captain husband was mortally wounded at Gettysburg. General Humphreys, who was in the battle, was with his son-in-law shortly before the end came. A beautiful young woman with superb carriage, Mary Stamps had both brains and character. She was greatly admired by the fifty-five-year-old President. At the time of her tearing grief over her husband's death, he was of immeasurable consolation to her. But neither she nor her uncle dreamed that their mutual sympathies and extraordinary compatibility would flower into such an attraction of mind and spirit as would evolve in the next decade. The following letter written after she had left Richmond is the only one extant to Davis. Many of his later letters to her have been preserved and are now owned by the University of North Carolina, but those from her to him were lost or perhaps destroyed by Varina.

Fincastle, Virginia
Aug. 16th, 1863

My beloved Uncle,

On reaching this place I found a letter from you which Genl Preston had forwarded from Abingdon, and I regretted very much that it had not come before I went to Richmond that I might have replied to your kind and comforting words.

I have been confined to my bed almost every day since my return and am still unable to get up. Dr. May, a physician from Petersburg, has been attending and tells me today that he hopes the disease is not as he feared, dropsy. My whole body has been so swollen that it was with the greatest difficulty I could draw each breath. Today however the swelling is subsiding, my breathing almost free again and much less pain in every respect.

I rec'd letters several days ago from my dear Soldier's comrades and wished to write to you at once but was prevented by my sufferings. I wish very much, dear, gentle, sympathizing Uncle that you could read them, but as almost every memento I had of him, his presents to me, his likeness and your letters so prized were all lost in my trunk, I am almost afraid to hazard them. Dr. Peets, the surgeon, writes to me confirming all that I heard from those hospital soldiers in Richmond. He was carried on litter very soon after his fall to the surgeon who chose he says "a soft spot in a wheatfield under a medium sized oak." From his own lips and from his paled features he at once learned that the wound was mortal and confirmed my darling's inquiring look by a burst of tears. His first words were, "Dr. I am mortally wounded, Oh do you think Mary can bear it? My poor wife, my poor Mary, and my blessed children." He suffered lacerating pains and pled for something to make him insensible. Morphine was administered and gave partial relief, with recurrences of great pain til an hour before he died.

During the early part of the night the lieut. of his company got leave to go and see him. I rec'd a letter from him telling me as nearly as his memory could suggest every word that he uttered to him. "Press, is that you? I am glad you have come to see me— Oh! Press, my dear wife. Tell her I am ready to die and not afraid. I wouldn't mind it if it were not for her and my children. I had rather die on the battlefield in defense of her and them and my country than to live and see it subjugated." He then asked how the battle went and they told him that he was dying in the greatest victory of the war, for *then* they believed so, and he exclaimed "Thank God! Thank God! I die contented—"

After this he manifested a desire to be quiet until my Father came. My Father remained with him the rest of the night.

He told Dr. Peets to write to me and tell me everything—and

that he died like a brave soldier and to take good care of his sword that his Uncle [Jefferson Davis] gave him and send it to me and tell me to keep it for his children. He gave him his pen knife and told him to send it to me, as I had given it to him.

He staid all night on the field in the open air from preference— and was attended there in the moonlight by several friends who never left him. Next morning he was carried in an ambulance to the rear to a hospital. At 2 o'clock he passed from us quietly and peacefully, blessing all around him.

Let me know all you hear of my dear Mother and Father Stamps. I have not found the heart to write to them yet. Oh how gladly I would drink of this cup alone, if it could pass from their blessed lips.

Were it not, my dear Uncle, that I knew you wanted to hear all about "the dear boy," it would be sufficient apology to say that it comforts me to write you about it. I often wish during the day that night would come, when the company all gone, I might see my dear Uncle's face and live over part of Isaac's life in tender recollection. As day after day passes with no more to do for him and no more to hear, I find myself bowing before the reality of my lonely lot.

Dear Uncle, you will forgive me for leaning, along with my country and as a part of it, upon your great heart. It is not that I would oppress it, but that it comforts me. You can lean only upon its God, and through Him, our common Father, I hope to repay a part of your tenderness to me.

Give much love to Aunt Varina and kiss the dear children for me and tell Jeffy I miss the paper he used to bring to me very much.

Let me hear from you sometimes, my dear Uncle, and believe me always Your loving niece

Mary Stamps

The beginning of this letter was written yesterday. I have been up all today and walked out this evening.

Varina Davis to Jefferson Davis Howell

Varina writes her young midshipman brother about the notorious Dahlgren Raid led by the twenty-two-year-old son of Federal Admiral

John Dahlgren. Becket, Varina's third brother, is an officer on Admiral Raphael Semmes's famous *Alabama*, destroying enemy ships in various seas.

Richmond
March 4th 1864

My dear Son

Well, my dear boy you will see by the papers that we have had quite a raid upon Richmond. We have driven off the enemy and captured some of them, but they have burned and destroyed everything in their way—robbed and laid waste. Their colonel, Ulric Dahlgren was killed and in his pocket was found a copy of his orders to his men. They were to kill everybody of any importance here, burn and destroy the City, and carry off all that was valuable. The vile wretch was shot as he deserved and killed instantly, he had no time to ask for forgiveness—may God judge him more mildly than I can.

I could not help laughing at Maggie and myself—neither of us were at all frightened but determined if we had to run (which I did not think at all probable for you know how much faith I have in a protecting providence) we wanted to have clothes enough. We had no horses or carriage or any way to ride out or carry baggage—so we put on all the clothes we could. I had on seven petticoats, 3 chemises, 2 pair of stockings on my legs and six pair buckled round my legs by my garter. Maggie had on quite as much with the addition of two dresses and her cloth cloak. The Yankees would have caught us certainly, for we were so heavy we could hardly walk, running would have been impossible. The vile villains are now forty or fifty miles off but say they will pay another visit very soon when they hope to do better.

I was astonished to find I had only sent you 5 dollars when I was certain I had put in ten, but you will certainly find ten in this letter, and also a few stamps. I felt like crying when I saw my mistake.

I heard you were still suffering from those boils. Do let me know about it, and take care of yourself. I am very anxious about you my darling son. Now you must answer all my questions and write often to me, direct to this place until I tell you not.

I saw today the wife of Becket's Capt Semmes. She told me she had letters from her husband last Christmas that Becket was well and in good spirits, which I was gratified to hear as you may suppose. I will try to send a letter to him in same way she sends hers if I can.

Oh how anxious I am to have this dreadful war over, that I might once more see my dear boy back home. I sometimes feel nearly wild but pray continually to God to keep all of mine and me in the right way or I would be a maniac. May God bless and keep you, my dear child, from all harm and guide your steps aright—

Your devoted
Mother

Varina Davis to Mrs. Richard Griffith

Mrs. Griffith was the widow of Brigadier General Griffith, Philadelphia-born Confederate officer who had been killed at Savage Station in June, 1862. Mrs. Griffith is now living in Jackson, Mississippi. Mrs. Davis's letter is in response to one of the hundreds of letters of condolence that poured in after the death of five-year-old Joseph Davis when he fell from a side balcony of the Executive Mansion on April 30, 1864.

Richmond
May 8, 1864

My very dear Friend,

Your letter reached me only a few days since, and found me in the deepest affliction, yet grateful as I must ever be for the remembrance of friends. One week ago I should have been able to tell of my most beautiful and promising child. Now I can only tell you that I have three left—none so bright, none so beautiful, but all infinitely precious. Maggie and Jeff are the children you remember. They are well & quite bright and tolerable biddable, as children go. My youngest, William, is an unusually fine boy. He is as large at two years as other children at three. Very active and very good. I think his mind is like his dear father's.

While I write the alarm bells are ringing, and the poor fellow is in a state of anxiety, which he does not express but that which I cannot fail to participate in. The enemy are pressing us everywhere and Genl Lee is fighting desperately alone, hopeful of pre-

venting the siege of Richmond. However God in his Mercy over-
rules the destinies of men, and can save by few as by many. In Him
does he put his trust.

Devotedly,
Varina Davis

A. Dudley Mann to Jefferson Davis

Dudley Mann was a Confederate Commissioner stationed in Brussels.
Mann had been sympathetically received in audience by His Holiness,
Pope Pius IX, in December, 1863.

Brussels, May 9, 1864

Mr. President:

Herewith I have the honor to transmit the Letter which His
Holiness, Pope Pius IX, addressed to your Excellency on the 3rd
of December last. Mr. W. Jefferson Buchanan has obligingly undertaken its conveyance and will deliver it in person.

This Letter will grace the archives of the Executive Office in all
coming time. It will live too, forever, in Story, as the production
of the first Potentate who formally recognized your official position
and accorded to one of the diplomatic representatives of the Confederate States an audience in an established Court Palace, like
that of St. James or the Tuileries.

I have the honor to be, with the most distinguished consideration,

Your Excellency's obedient servant,
A. Dudley Mann

Jefferson Davis to Hugh Davis

Hugh was a planter son of Jefferson Davis's sister Lucinda Stamps
by her first marriage to Hugh Davis, a South Carolinian and no relation.
In this personal letter the President of the Confederacy unburdens his
full heart concerning the troubles he had been having with some of the
Southern people and many State administrators. Chief among those in
high position who had exhibited conduct near to treason were Vice-

President Alexander H. Stephens and Governor Joseph E. Brown of Georgia.

Richmond, Va.
8th Jany. 65

My dear Hugh,

The departure of Major Keary furnishes a safer opportunity to write to you. I have felt very anxious about your son not having heard whether he was exchanged. It has sometimes happened that military commanders have been able to exchange equivalents before the prisoners have been turned over to the officers having special charge of them, when after being so turned over the orders of the Yankee Govt. rendered it impossible to obtain the release of our men. As soon as the case was made known to me I directed the authority to be given to General Hodge to make the exchange if he could and only regretted that he had not known our practise not always to approve such action on the part of any commander similarly situated. We want all of our own soldiers.

The movement of the contending armies in Ga. has resulted very disadvantageously to us. I had hoped Genl. Hood would have compelled Sherman to go North from Atlanta and perhaps to beat him by selecting a strong position in the mountains between Atlanta and Chattanooga, and such was the expectations of Genl Hood when I parted from him on the Chattahoochee. It is not possible for one who was not present, and too little acquainted with the troops to judge of their spirit and condition, to decide whether it was practicable to carry out the original design or not. That army had suffered much in its morale by the long succession of retreats from Dalton and it may have been a necessity to avoid battle until it could be reanimated and to some extent recruited. After Sherman started to the South East Genl. Beauregard thought it impossible to overtake him but that his plans might be frustrated by a rapid advance into Tenn. The latter part of the opinion proved erroneous, the first part may have been right. Left with only cavalry, reserves, and militia to oppose Sherman's march, I directed the roads to be obstructed, bridges destroyed and all supplies near to his line of march to be removed or burned. His horses were poor and not sufficiently numerous to draw provisions and ammunition for his march. The faithful execution of those orders would have defeated his project.

When will our people learn to expect nothing from Yankee forbearance? An officer of our Cavalry, who served under Genl. Wheeler in that campaign, writes that the Yankees while on the march took from one man a thousand hogs and from one county two thousand horses & mules. Of corn they got an adequate amount, sometimes it being in excess, the superabundance was burned to starve the people who had left their cribs for the enemy's use.

Now Sherman is on the Atlantic coast, can be readily supplied and reinforced for future operations. The malcontents, seizing on the restlessness consequent upon long and severe pressure, have created a feeling hostile to the execution of the rigorous laws which were necessary to raise and feed our armies, then magnifying every reverse and prophesying ruin, they have produced public depression and sown the seeds of disintegration. Men of the old federal school are they who now invoke the laws of state rights to sustain a policy which, in proportion to the extent of its adoption, must tend to destroy the existence of the States of our Confederacy, and have them conquered provinces. "O liberty, what crimes have not been committed in thy name" was the sad exclamation of one who mourned such perversion of truth to the maintenance of error as now appears in the conduct of those who assume the guise of state rights men to sink the States by the process of disintegration into imbecility and ultimate submission to Yankee despotism.

Maj. Keary will be able to tell of my family and of affairs in Richmond. Of the proceedings of Congress you are sufficiently advised by the newspapers.

Now when we require the brains and the heart of the country in the legislative halls of the Confederacy and of the States, all must have realized how much it is otherwise. Our people have fought so as to command the admiration of mankind, they have nobly met the sacrifices of their position, never before was there so little despotism under such severe pressure and if there be a growing spirit of opposition to continued effort it is, I think, to be attributed to the bad conduct of those whose official position made it their duty to cultivate confidence, and animate patriotism.

Give my love to Cousin Anne and your children, also when you see them to others of our family. May God bless and preserve you and yours, and grant that before another year comes to us that our country may be in peace and independence, and that we may all meet again to cheer and sustain each other in the future trials of life.

Your Uncle,

J. D.

Maggie Davis to Jefferson Davis, Jr.

After considerable pleading, eight-year-old Jeff, Jr., has been permitted to go for a few days' visit to the edge of the battleground with his first cousin Brigadier General Joseph R. Davis. Tippy is the dog. Jim Limber is a little Negro boy Mrs. Davis had rescued from a brutal father and more or less adopted. Mrs. Omelia is the housekeeper.

Richmond March 11, 1865

My Dear little Brother—

I miss you very much and wish you would come home. I am so very lonesome. I am very sorry that I told you that I would be glad if you would go. And what do you think Tippy did? Why he killed the biggest rat I ever saw and we made such a great fuss about him that you would have thought he never killed one before. Jim Limber sends his love to you and so does Mrs. Omelia send her love to you and sends two kisses to you, My Dear little Brother. I wish I could see your sweet little face. Darling, I am now tired, but I am your most affectionate Sister

Maggie Howell Davis

James Chesnut, Jr., to Jefferson Davis

General Chesnut, former aide to the President, had taken Davis's beautiful Arabian, a gift from a friend in Egypt, to keep safe on his South Carolina plantation. Chesnut is now an active general in South Carolina.

Chesterville, S.C.
March 15, 1865

To His Excellency
    President Davis

Dear Sir,

I am very sorry to have to say that through the imbecility and cowardice of my Overseer, who was a foreigner, I have lost your

Arabian horse. Some weeks before the evacuation of Columbia, I instructed fully as to the course he should pursue in case of a Yankee raid, which if it had been done the horse would have been safe. From the same cause I have lost my entire stock of horses, mules, etc. But this gives me no concern, I would infinitely have preferred to lose them all than one you entrusted to my care. I was with the troops in Columbia at that time of evacuation, which was sudden & to most people unexpected. In truth I think the State was shamefully and unnecessarily lost. It is the common opinion, as well as my own that the enemy, having fully developed his purpose after crossing the Salkehatchie, we had time, opportunity and means to destroy him. But there was wholly wanting the energy and ability required by the occasion—and all was lost.

The devastation of the enemy in this State was great and cruel. How bread is to be made for the coming years is a serious question —the larger portion of the Country being utterly stript of its Stock— & to a great extent the agricultural implements & Mills destroyed. But still bad as it is, it is not as bad as in Virginia, & she still holds an elevated & defiant crest. She presents a worthy example for us all.

Under all the circumstances I think you did wisely to restore Genl. Johnston to command. He seems to possess the confidence of the army, and is certainly better than Genl. Beauregard, whose Star is set—& who it is believed could not have done worse than he did in this recent Carolina campaign.

Ever sincerely,
James Chesnut, Jr.

Jefferson Davis to Jefferson Davis, Jr.

Richmond, Va.
16 March 65

My dear Son,

Your very gratifying letter came duly to hand, and I was very happy that my dear boy was able to write to me about himself and to give me news from the trenches.

We all miss you very much and are only willing to spare you so long because you seem to be so happy with your Cousin Joe.

Your Mother and the children are well and are anxious to have you back.

It made me very glad to hear from your Cousin Joe that you were a good boy. With much love

Your father
Jeff'n Davis

Jefferson Davis to Josiah Gorgas

In late March, 1865, when it appeared that General Lee must give up Petersburg before the pounding might of General Grant, Davis decided to send his wife and children to a place of safety in North Carolina. He gave Varina a pistol and showed her how to load, aim, and fire it. "You can at least, if reduced to the last extremity," he said, "force your assailants to kill you."

On March 29 Davis wrote the following hasty note to General Josiah Gorgas, his Chief of Ordnance and good friend, who had been confirmed with him at St. Paul's Church in May, 1862.

Armed with her pistol, Mrs. Davis and the children, her sister Margaret, the Negro maid Ellen, the colored coachman James Jones, and Jim Limber, the little adopted black boy, left Richmond by train, escorted by Burton Harrison, the President's private secretary, and a twenty-year-old midshipman named James Morgan.

Gen'l Gorgas

My dear Sir

Will you do me the favor to have some cartridges prepared for a small Colt pistol, of which I send the moulds, and the form which contained a set of the cartridges furnished with the piece. The ammunition is desired as promptly as it can be supplied.

Very truly yours,
Jefferson Davis

29 March '65

EVACUATION OF RICHMOND

SURRENDER AT APPOMATTOX

FLIGHT AND CAPTURE

THE LETTERS THAT follow were written after the evacuation of Richmond, when the Confederate Government removed to Danville in southwest Virginia and then continued south until President Davis, his family, and some of his staff were finally captured at Irwinville, in southeast Georgia, on May 10, 1865. The letters reveal the haste, tension, and anxieties of the Davises. Although for the most part these letters are to be found in the Manuscript Division of the Library of Congress and have been published in part, they are included in this volume for their vivid sense of immediacy, and to carry on the story of the dissolution of the Confederacy in the weeks just preceding Jefferson Davis's imprisonment at Fort Monroe.

After General Lee's telegram to President Davis on Sunday, April 2, urging him to evacuate Richmond immediately, the Government staff packed documents and state papers with celerity. While Davis made hasty arrangements about disposing of some of the household possessions, Robert Brown packed the President's clothes. As a farewell present to the invalided Mrs. Robert E. Lee, Davis sent her his own favorite easy chair. Shortly before midnight the train bearing the President and his Cabinet pulled creakily out of the Richmond station bound for Danville.

At Danville the President and the Confederate officials received an "old Virginia welcome." Davis himself was an honored house guest in the mansion of Major and Mrs. W. T. Sutherlin. Temporary governmental offices were set up in the large Benedict House. The President was expecting General Lee with his army at Danville, as had been agreed between them in case of critical emergency. From Danville Lee was to proceed to join forces with General Joseph E. Johnston in North Carolina.

Jefferson Davis to Varina Davis

Mr. Grant was a kind neighbor who lived across the street from the Davises. David Bradford was Davis's nephew. General John Cabell Breckinridge was the Secretary of War.

Danville, Virginia
5th April 1865

My dear Wife,

I have in vain sought to get into communication with Genl Lee and have postponed writing in the hope that I would soon be able to speak to you with some confidence of the future. On last Sunday I was called out of church to receive a telegram announcing that Gen'l Lee could not hold his position longer than till night and warning me that we must leave Richmond, as the army would commence retiring that evening. I made the necessary arrangements at my office and went to our house to have the proper dispositions made there. Nothing had been done after you left and but little could be done in the few hours which remained before the train was to leave.

I packed the bust and gave it to John Davis who offered to take it and put it where it should never be found by a Yankee—I also gave him charge of the painting of the Heroes of the Valley—both were removed after dark. The furniture of the house was left and very little of the things I directed to be put up, bedding & groceries, were saved.

Mr. Grant was afraid to take the carriage to his house &c. &c. I sent it to the depot to be put on a flat. At the moment of starting it was said they could not take it in that train but would bring it on the next train. It has not been heard from since—I sent a message to Mr. Grant that I had neglected to return the cow and wished him to send for her immediately. Called off on horseback to the depot, I left the servants to go down with the boxes and they left Tippy—Watson came willingly, Spencer against my will, Robert, Alf, V. B. & Ives got drunk. David Bradford went back from the depot to bring out the spoons and forks which I was told had been left—and to come out with Genl Breckenridge; since then I have not heard from either of them.

The people here have been very kind, and the Mayor & Council have offered assistance in the matter of quarters, and have very handsomely declared their unabated confidence. I do not wish to leave Va., but cannot decide on my movements until those of the army are better developed.

I hope you are comfortable and trust soon to hear from you. Kiss my dear children.

I weary of this sad recital and have nothing pleasant to tell. May God have you in His Holy Keeping is the fervent prayer of

Your ever affectionate
Husband

Jefferson Davis to Varina Davis

The baby girl, born on June 27, 1864, and christened Varina Anne, is here called "little Winnie," but the children called her "Pie Cake."

Danville, Va.
April 6, 1865

Dear Winnie

Many thanks for your letter giving me an account of your situation at Charlotte. In my letter of yesterday I gave you all of my prospects which can now be told, not having heard from Genl. Lee and having to conform my movements to the military necessities of the case. We are now fixing an executive office where the current business may be transacted here and do not propose at this time definitely to fix upon a point for a seat of Govt. in the future.

Love to Maggie, little Maggie, Jeff, Billy and little Winnie. Farewell my love. May God bless, preserve and guide you.

Husband

Varina Davis to Jefferson Davis

W. L. Trenholm, Confederate Secretary of the Treasury, was quite ill and had gone to his home in Chester, South Carolina. Col. Preston Johnston, the President's aide and the son of Albert Sidney Johnston, accompanied Davis until his capture. The Reverend Dr. Charles Minnegerode, Rector of St. Paul's, remained in Richmond.

Charlotte, N.C.
April 7, 1865

My own dear old Banny

Since my arrival here I have been so busy as to have only the evening to write in, and then but one room where the children most did congregate, so I have written but one disjointed letter.

The news of Richmond came upon me like the "abomination of desolation," and the loss of Selma like the "blackness thereof."

Since your telegram upon your arrival at Danville we have nothing except the wildest rumors, all however discouraging.

I, who know that your strength when stirred up is great, and that you can do with a few what others have failed to do with many, am awaiting prayerfully the advent of the time when it is God's will to deliver us through His own appointed agent, I trust it may be you, as I believe it is. It would comfort me greatly if you could only find an opportunity to write me a full long letter. As soon as we are established here I am anxious to leave Mrs. Chesnut with the children and bring Li' Pie to see you. I do not know how soon that may be. God grant it may be soon. The gentlemen I have seen here (the officers of the Post) are exceedingly kind, and have offered me every civility in their power.

Upon the whole I do not think the shock as great as I expected. We had a digest of your address to the people today and I could not make much of it except as encouraging exhortation, am anxious to see the whole thing. Numberless surmises are hazarded here, as to your future destination and occupation, but I know that wherever you are, and in whatever engaged, it is in an efficient manner for the country. The way things look now the trans-Mississippi seems our ultimate destination—

Mrs. Chesnut wrote me a most affectionate letter from Chester today. She is staying in two rooms very badly furnished, and furnished with food by her friends there. As I shall have a spare room she will come over and stay a few days with me. I have carpets, some curtains, some window shades and three pictures and some lovely volumes of books belonging to a man in Augusta—A marble table, brocatelle chairs, nice china and nice tin basins and buckets—I am very well off—and very kindly treated by the Jewish man Wiele who owns the house—with the delicacy and hospitality of a gentleman. Harrison has been most affectionate and kind. I really regret to see him go tomorrow which is the day he proposes to leave to rejoin you.

The Trenholms left yesterday for Chester with Col. Trenholm. Our little ones are all well but very unruly—or else the small house "makes me sensible" of it.

Write to me my own precious only love, and believe me as ever your devoted wife—

Has Ives turned up? Did Preston Johnston leave his family? Did Minnegerode come out? Did we bring off anything when you came?

Jefferson Davis to Robert E. Lee

President Davis was hopefully and hourly expecting General Lee and his army at Danville when he sent this telegram before attending church on Palm Sunday. But just after noon Lee surrendered to Grant at Appomattox.

Danville, Va. April 9, 1865

Your dispatch of 6th inst. received. Hope the line of couriers established will enable you to communicate safely and frequently. Genl. Johnston on the 8th telegraphs from Smithfield, asking you to inform him how he can co-operate with you, says it is important he should know before Sherman moves. We have here about three thousand infantry and artillery. Are constructing defences and should have an experienced engineer, the ground being unfavorable.

I had hoped to have seen you at an earlier period, and trust soon to meet you. We have here provisions and clothing for your Army and they are held for its use. You will realize the reluctance I feel to leave the soil of Virginia, and appreciate my anxiety to win success North of the Roanoke. The few stragglers who came from your Army are stopped here and at Staunton bridge, they are generally without arms. I hope soon to hear from you at this point, where offices have been opened to keep up the current business, until more definite knowledge would enable us to form more permanent plans. May God preserve, sustain and guide you.

Jeffn. Davis

Varina Davis to Jefferson Davis

Chester

April 13th 1865

My own dear Banny,

The rumors of a raid on Charlotte induced me to decide to come to this place, Chester. A threatened raid here induces me to leave here without making an hour's stay which is unnecessary—I go with the specie train because they have a strong guard and are attended by two responsible men—I am going somewhere, perhaps to Washington, Ga.—perhaps only to Abbeville. I don't know, just as the children seem to bear the journey, will I decide. Gen. Chesnut seems very anxious, exceedingly kind, but is so moody that I am wordless, helpless. The children are well as are Maggie & I. Would to God I could know the truth of the horrible rumors I hear of you. One is that you have started for Genl. Lee but have not been heard of—

May God have mercy upon me and preserve your life for your dear

Wife

Jefferson Davis to Varina Davis

After the official confirmation of Lee's surrender to Grant, President Davis with his Cabinet and a military escort moved on south.

Greensboro, N.C.

14th April 1865

Dear Winnie

I will come to you if I can. Everything is dark. You should prepare for the worst by dividing your baggage so as to move in wagons. If you can go to Abbeville it seems best as I am now advised—If you can send everything there do so. I have lingered on the road and labored to little purpose. My love to the children and Maggie. God bless, guide and preserve you, ever prays

Your most affectionate

Banny

Varina Davis to Jefferson Davis

Mrs. Davis and her family are the guests of former United States Senator Armistead Burt, whose wife is a niece of John C. Calhoun. Jeffy D. Howell was one of the Confederate midshipmen guarding the treasure train. General Johnston is meeting with General Sherman to make terms for surrendering his army.

Abbeville
April 19, 1865

My dear Old Banny

The fearful news I hear fills me with horror—"That Genl Lee's army are in effect disbanded, Longstreet's Corps having surrendered, Mahone's also, saving one brigade." I do not believe all, yet enough is thrust upon my unwilling credence to weigh me to the earth. Where are you, how are you—what ought I to do with these helpless little unconscious charges of mine are questions which I am asking myself always. Write to me freely of your troubles for mercy's sake. Do not attempt to put a good face upon them to the friend of your heart, I am so at sea—

Since I left Richmond *no such heartfelt* welcome has been extended to me as the one I received here—they will hear of no change of place for the present, and urge me with tears in their eyes to share with them what little they can offer. People call promptly and seem to feel warmly—Mr. Burt really seems to feel tenderly to us, pets the children and does every kind thing in his power to me. Mrs. Burt is more than affectionate—Jeffy D was taken quite ill on the cars, and is here sick at Mr. Trenholm's who lives just across the street. He is better but not well. I shall wait further directions here. Do write every day and make the staff send the notes (I do not expect more) by officers coming this way—I am so unhappy and anxious.

Do remember me affectionately to the staff and Mr. Harrison and tell them if you cannot always write they can, but don't.

May God in His Mercy keep you safe and raise up defenders for our bleeding country prays your devoted wife—

24th

My own dear old Banny. The dreadful news, with its dreadful confirmation has rendered us very wretched. I long for one word from you. I will come to you for a day or two if this truce is really so—i.e.—if you cannot come to me. The children are all well. Jeffy D. has gotten well.

Wade Hampton to Jefferson Davis

General Wade Hampton is one of the few ardent patriots who hopes to continue the fighting. He foresees the humiliations and horrors that will follow a return to the Union with its tyrannous "reconstruction."

Hillsboro
April 19th, 1865

My dear Sir:

Having seen the terms upon which it is proposed to negotiate, I trust that I may be pardoned for writing to you in relation to them.

Most of our officers look only to the military side of the picture at present but you will regard it in other aspects also. The military situation is very gloomy, I admit, but it is by no means desperate, & endurance & determination will produce a change— Many of the Cavalry who escaped will also join us, they find that we are still making head against the enemy. There are now not less than 40 to 50 thousand men in arms on *this side* of the Mississippi. On the other are as many more. Now the question presents itself; shall we disband these men at once, or shall we endeavor to concentrate them? If we disband, we give up at once and forever all hope of foreign intervention. Europe will say, & say justly "why should we interfere if you choose to re-enter the Union?" But if we keep any organization, however small, in the field we give Europe the opportunity of aiding us. The main reason urged for negotiation is to spare the infliction of any further suffering on the people. Nothing can be more fallacious than this reasoning. *No* suffering which can be inflicted by the passage over our country of the Yankee armies can equal what would fall on us if we return to the Union. We shall have to pay the debt incurred by the U.S. in this war, and we shall live under a base and vulgar tyranny. *No* sacrifice would be too great to escape this train of horrors, and I think it far better for us to fight to the extreme limit of our country, rather than to reconstruct the Union upon *any terms*. If we cannot use our Infantry here let it disband, calling upon them for volunteers for the Cavalry—collect all our mounted force and move towards the Miss. When we cross that river we can get large accessions to the cavalry and we can hold Texas. As soon as forces can be organized & equipped, send this heavy cavalry force into the country of the enemy and they will soon show that we are not conquered. If I had 20,000 mounted men here I could force Sherman to retreat in twenty days. Give me a good force of cavalry and I will take them safely across the Mississippi—and if you desire to go in that direction it will give me great pleasure to escort you. My own mind is made up. As to my course I shall fight as long as my government remains in existence, when that ceases to live I shall seek some other country, for I shall never take the "oath of allegiance." I am sorry that we paused to negotiate, for to my apprehension, no evil can equal that of a return to the Union.

I write to you, my dear Sir, that you may know the feelings which actuated many of the officers of my command. They are not subdued, nor do they despair. For myself I beg to express my heartfelt sympathy with you, & to give you the assurance that my confidence in your patriotism has never been shaken. If you will allow me to do so, I can bring to your support many strong arms and brave hearts—Men who will fight to Texas, & will seek refuge in Mexico, rather than in the Union.

> With best wishes I am,
> Very Respectfully Yours,
> Wade Hampton

Jefferson Davis to Varina Davis

While his Cabinet members were busy composing individual opinions on the Sherman-Johnston peace pact proposals, President Davis wrote his wife the first real letter since he had left Richmond.

> Charlotte, N.C.
> 23 April, 1865

My dear Winnie.

I have been detained here longer than was expected when the last telegram was sent to you. I am uncertain where you are and deeply feel the necessity of being with you, if even for a brief time, under our altered circumstances.

Govr. Vance and Genl. Hampton propose to meet me here, and Genl. Johnston sent me a request to remain at some point where he could readily communicate with me. Under these circumstances I have asked Mr. Harrison to go in search of you and to render you such assistance as he may.

Your own feelings will convey to you an idea of my solicitude for you and our family, and I will not distress by describing it.

The dispersion of Lee's army and the surrender of the remnant which remained with him, destroyed the hopes I entertained when we parted. Had that army held together, I am now confident we could have successfully executed the plan which I sketched to you and would have been today on the high road to independence. Even after that disaster, if the men who "straggled," say thirty or forty thousand in a number, had come back with their arms and with a disposition to fight we might have repaired the damage; but all was sadly the reverse of that. They threw away theirs, and were uncontrollably resolved to go home. Panic has seized the country. J. E. Johnston and Beauregard were hopeless as to recruiting their forces from the dispersed men of Lee's army, and equally so as to their ability to check Sherman with the forces they had. Their only idea was to retreat. Of the power to do so they were doubtful, and subsequent desertions from their troops have materially diminished their strength, and, I learn, still more weakened their confidence. The loss of arms has been so great, that, should the spirit of the people rise to the occasion, it would not be at this time possible adequately to supply them with the weapons of war.

Genl. Johnston had several interviews with Sherman and agreed on a suspension of hostilities, and the reference of terms of pacification. They are secret and may be rejected by the Yankee Government. To us, they are hard enough, though freed from wanton humiliation, and expressly recognizing the State Governments, and the rights of person and property as secured by the Constitutions of the United States and the several States.

The issue is one which it is very painful for me to meet. On one hand is the long night of oppression which will follow the return of our people to the "Union"; on the other, the suffering of the women and children, and carnage among the few brave patriots who would still oppose the invader, and who, unless the people would rise en-masse to sustain them, would struggle but to die in vain. I think my judgment is undisturbed by any pride of opinion, I have prayed to our Heavenly Father to give me wisdom and fortitude equal to the demands of the position in which Providence has placed me. I have sacrificed so much for the cause of the Confederacy that I can measure my ability to make any further sacrifice required, and am assured there is but one to which I am not equal—my wife and my children. How are they to be saved from degradation of want is now my care.

During the suspension of hostilities you may have the best opportunity to go to Mississippi, and there either to sail from Mobile for a foreign port or to cross the river and proceed to Texas, as the one or the other may be more practicable. The little sterling you have will be a very scanty store and under other circumstances would not be coveted; but if our land can be sold, that will secure you from absolute want. For myself, it may be that, a devoted band of Cavalry will cling to me, and that I can force my way across the Mississippi, and if nothing can be done there which it will be proper to do, then I can go to Mexico, and have the world from which to choose a location.

Dear Wife, this is not the fate to which I invited you when the future was rose colored to us both; but I know you will bear it even better than myself, and that, of us two, I alone, will ever look back reproachfully on my past career. I have thus entered on the questions involved in the future to guard against contingencies.

Dear children, I can say nothing to them, but for you and them my heart is full, my prayers constant, and my hopes are the trust I feel in the mercy of God.

Farewell, my dear, there may be better things in store for us than are now in view, but my love is all I have to offer, and that has the value of a thing long possessed, and sure not to be lost.

Once more, and with God's favor, for a short time only, farewell.

Your Husband

The Cabinet members, including that almost incorrigible optimist, Judah Benjamin, now urged the President to sign the agreement to the peace proposal, which meant the end of the Confederate Government. It seemed the only thing to do. And in the general opinion it merely meant that "the States of the Confederacy should re-enter the Union upon the same footing on which they stood before seceding from it." Davis affixed his signature. But barely an hour after the document had reached Johnston's headquarters, the General learned from a disappointed Sherman that the Federal Government had categorically and vehemently rejected this peace proposal. Sherman then declared that he must resume the war at eleven o'clock on the morning of April 26, unless Johnston surrendered on the same terms as Grant gave to Lee. General Johnston wired Davis for instructions. Davis ordered him to retire at once with his cavalry, some light artillery and as many infantry as could be mounted on draft horses. The rest of the infantry were to be disbanded, to meet at an appointed rendezvous and proceed to the southwest. A possible line of retreat had already been agreed upon and supplies placed along it.

But against Presidential orders Johnston surrendered on April 26, and by paroles he had rendered impotent some 36,000 Confederates under arms in North Carolina. Even so Davis did not abandon all hope. He expected "to maintain his ground with small forces after the manner of Washington in the Revolution, and wring eventual recognition from the North." He purposed to reach Texas and keep up the struggle in the Trans-Mississippi until he could secure better terms for the States.

Varina Davis to Jefferson Davis

Abbeville, S.C.
April 28, 1865

My Own dear old husband,

Your very sweet letter reached me safely by Mr. Harrison and was a great relief. I leave here in the morning at 6 o'clock for the wagon train going to Georgia. Washington will be the first point I shall "unload" at—from there we shall probably go on to Atlanta, or thereabouts. Let me now beseech you not to calculate upon seeing me unless I happen to cross your shortest path toward your bourne, be that what it may.

It is surely not the fate to which you invited me in brighter days, but you must remember that you did not invite me to a great Hero's home, but to that of a plain farmer. I have shared all your triumphs, been the *only* beneficiary of them, now I am but claiming the privilege for the first time of being all to you now these pleasures have passed for me.

My plans are these, subject to your approval. I think I shall be able to procure funds enough to enable me to put the two eldest to school. I shall go to Florida if possible, and from thence go over to Bermuda, or Nassau, from thence to England, unless a good school offers elsewhere, and put them to the best school I can find, and then with the two youngest join you in Texas—and that is the prospect which bears me up, to be once more with you—once more to suffer with you if need be.

Here they *are all your friends,* have the most unbounded confidence in you. Mr. Burt and his wife have urged me to live with them—offered to take the chances of the Yankees with us—begged to have little Maggie—done everything in fact that relatives could do. I shall never forget all their generous devotion to you.

I have seen a great many men who have gone through—not one has talked fight. A stand cannot be made in this country, but do not be induced to try it.

As to the trans-Mississippi, I doubt if at first things will be straight, but the spirit is there, and the daily accretions will be great when the deluded of this side are crushed out between the upper and nether millstone. Young Haskell insists upon my going to his father's in the morning to take lunch, and his carriage to Washington. He has been more than polite to me—so have all the people here—it is like old times.

God bless you, keep you. I have wrestled with God for you. I believe He will restore us to happiness.

Devotedly—
Your wife

Kindest regards to Robert & thanks for faithful conduct— Love to Preston Johnston & John Wood.

Burton N. Harrison to Jefferson Davis

Again Davis has sent his private secretary to assist Mrs. Davis and the children.

Abbeville, S.C.
April 29, 1865

Mr. President

We had intended starting yesterday afternoon but were detained by the rain, are just about getting off now. The ladies and children are very well and in good spirits.

They move in a good ambulance and carriage and will reach Washington, Georgia, in a two days drive from this place.

From Washington we shall go towards Atlanta—there to halt until we see or hear from you. This movement was determined by your telegrams and by the belief that you would move westward along a line running north of this place.

Col Leovy has been kind enough to set out from here to meet you to explain our plans &c. He will tell you everything.

With sincere prayers and hopes for your health and safety.

Very respectfully
Yr Obt Servt
Burton N Harrison

Wade Hampton to Jefferson Davis

Yorkville, May 1st 1865

My Dear Sir

I left Hillsboro as soon as I learned of the agreement made between Genls Sherman and Johnston & pushed on rapidly to this point where I arrived at 1 this morning. A question arises as to whether I was included in this convention & I have agreed to leave it to the Sec of War for his decision. The convention and the subsequent order of Gen Johnston disbanded all the troops at once. I think you will have to rely on a small body of picked men to get you across the Mississippi River. I have some such who will go on as soon as they arrive here which they will do today. My own movements will depend on your order & wishes. It will give me great pleasure to assist you if I can do so & you may rest assured that I shall stick to our flag as long as any one can be found to uphold it. I have given Genl. Wheeler my views of this movement out west & he will explain everything to you. Should I not overtake you I beg you to believe that you have my earnest good wishes & my prayers for your success. If I remain here I shall be most happy to render any service to Mrs. Davis. That God may protect you & bring you back in safety & with success is the prayer of

Your sincere friend
Wade Hampton

Varina Davis to Jefferson Davis

Washington 9 o'clock
Morning morning
May 2

My dear Banny—

The young gentleman who will hand you this is just going by Abbeville and I cannot refrain from expressing my intense grief at the treacherous surrender of this Department. May God grant you a safe conduct out of this maze of enemies—I do believe you are safer without the cavalry than with it, and I so dread their stealing a march and surprising you. I left Abbeville against my convictions, but agreeable to Mr Burt's & Mr. Harrison's opinions. Now the danger of being caught here by the enemy and of being deprived of our transportation if we stay is hurrying me out of Washington. I shall wait here this evening until I hear from the courier we have sent to Abbeville. I have given up the hope of seeing you, but it is not for long. Mr. Harrison now proposes to go on a line between Macon and Augusta and to make towards Pensacola—and take a ship or what else I can. We have a very gentlemanly escort, among whom is Capt. Moody, who says he will see us through—there are also some Mississippi teamsters. We are short of funds, & I do not see why these trains of specie should be given up to the Yankees, but still I think we will make out somehow.

May the Lord have you in His holy keeping I constantly & earnestly pray—I look at the precious little charges I have, and wonder if I shall be with you soon again. The children are all well. Pie was vaccinated on the roadside, as I heard there was small pox on the road—she is well so far. The children have been more than good and talk much of you as does Sis Maggie. Harrison is attentive.

Oh my dearest precious husband, the one absorbing love of my whole life may God keep you free from harm.

Your devoted—
Wife

Varina Davis to Jefferson Davis

May [1865]

My own precious Banny,

How disappointed you are I know—may God give us both patience against this heavy trial. The soldiers were very unruly and had taken almost all the mules and horses from Camp. More of Wheeler's Cavalry are expected, as were the Yankees, so we thought we had better move for fear our transportation would be stolen, and moving felt it best to cross the railroad before nightfall. We will make a march tomorrow of 25 miles to pass beyond the point of positive danger between Mayfield & Macon by day after tomorrow. Mr. Harrison is quite sick tonight or I would get a note from him. Do not try to meet me, I dread the Yankees getting news of you so much. You are the country's only hope, and the very best intentioned do not calculate upon a stand this side of the river. Why not cut loose from your escort? Go swiftly and alone with the exception of two or three—

Oh! May God in His goodness keep you safe, my own. The children send kisses. May God keep you, my old and only love, as ever

Devotedly, your own
Winnie

THE PRISON LETTERS,
1865

IN WASHINGTON, GEORGIA, only a couple of days after the departure of Mrs. Davis's party for the Florida coast, Davis arrived and held a last official meeting. As President, he had no constitutional authority to dissolve the Confederacy, and he still maintained his hope of reuniting the disorganized Southern forces across the Mississippi. Though terribly concerned about the welfare of his family, Davis knew that his wife's urging him "to cut loose from escort and go swiftly with two or three" was sound. So in the town square Davis bade farewell to the saddened soldiers accompanying him, and Frank Vizetelly of the London *Illustrated News* made a pen-and-ink drawing of the occasion on the spot.

After three days and nights of riding and camping out, Davis's escape from capture by Federal pursuers seemed assured. But while evening encampment was being made on the east bank of the Oconee River, a rumor came that some disbanded soldiers planned that night to rob Mrs. Davis's wagon train, which had recently passed. The agitated President, with his exhausted attendants, rode all through the night and finally caught up with the amazed Mrs. Davis. After two days of traveling together, they separated, only to meet again because of more rumors which made Davis anxious for his family's safety.

Finally at five o'clock on the afternoon of May 9, Burton Harrison ordered camp made south of a creek just north of Irwinville, Georgia, only fifty miles from the Florida state line. Davis positively promised Harrison that as soon as he had eaten supper he would ride on another ten miles that night with his companions: Postmaster General John Reagan and the Presidential aides, William Preston Johnston, ex-Governor Frank Lubbock, and John Taylor

Wood. But a fresh rumor came from Irwinville that a party of marauders purposed to attack the camp that very night. Instead of pushing on directly after supper, Davis decided to wait a couple of hours to see if the attack materialized. With his horse saddled and hitched close to the road, he lay down to rest in his wife's tent fully dressed and went sound asleep. Reagan and the others sat up late expecting to leave at any moment; then they too dropped off to sleep.

At dawn on the morning of May 10, 1865, the camp was surrounded, not by mere marauders, but by the Fourth Michigan Cavalry commanded by Colonel B. D. Pritchard. Harrison, who was suffering from fever and dysentery, was astounded on awakening to find Davis still in camp. Pritchard, who had been hoping to capture the "Confederate treasure train," was dumfounded to discover that President Davis himself was his prisoner. John Taylor Wood escaped by bribing his captor with gold. But Davis and the others of the two parties were taken on a four days' overland march to Macon and the headquarters of Federal General J. H. Wilson. On the third day Pritchard learned of a Proclamation from President Andrew Johnson offering a reward of $100,000 for the capture of Jefferson Davis, now charged with participation in the Lincoln assassination plot.

After a day and night at the Lanier Hotel the prisoners, including Clement C. Clay, Jr., who had given himself up, were taken to the railway station bound for Savannah. A Virginia-born boy of nine named Woodrow Wilson, son of the Presbyterian minister, watched awestruck as the strange procession passed and was jeered at by aliens in the crowd.

From Savannah, the prisoners sailed on an ancient side-wheeler, the *William C. Clyde,* to Fort Monroe, Virginia. On the sultry afternoon of May 22 Jefferson Davis descended the gangplank to a boat sent out from the fort. The agonized Mrs. Davis later wrote: "As the tug bore him away from the ship he stood with bared head between the file of undersized German and other foreign soldiers, and as we looked, as we thought, our last upon his stately form and knightly bearing, he seemed a man of another and higher race."

The ex-President was put into an inner casemate cell with one low barred window giving on the wide moat. Seventy-odd soldiers were detailed to guard the state prisoner. Within the cell itself two armed guards were commanded to pace back and forth incessantly. A lamp was ordered to be kept burning night and day at the prison cot's head. By the authority of Secretary of War Stanton, the jailer, Brevet Major General Nelson A. Miles, was directed when advisable "to place manacles and fetters on the hands and feet of Jefferson Davis."

The next day's New York *Herald* commented on the imprisonment editorially: "At about three o'clock yesterday, all that is mortal of Jeff'n Davis, late so-called 'President of the alleged Confederate States' was duly, but quietly and effectively committed to that living tomb prepared within the impregnable walls of Fortress Monroe. . . . No more will Jeff'n Davis be known among the masses of men. . . . He is buried alive." Another vengeful Northern editor expressed the hope of soon seeing the body of Davis "dangling and blackening in the wind and the rain."

Jefferson Davis was held incommunicado; his guards could not speak to him; and no one would tell him the fate or destination of his family. The second afternoon of his imprisonment, on Miles's order, a captain with two blacksmiths entered his cell bearing an anvil and chained leg irons. Four guards held the outraged prisoner down while heavy iron bands were riveted on his thin ankles.

Mrs. Davis, who was returned as a virtual prisoner to Savannah, read the account in the newspapers with sickening horror. Her miserable experiences on the voyage and her first weeks under police surveillance are related in a following letter of October 10 to Dr. John A. Craven, the army surgeon at Fort Monroe. This New Jersey-born physician had been put in charge of the prisoner's health. On June 7, Mrs. Davis wrote her first piteous letter to Craven begging news of her husband's condition, which the newspaper accounts reported to be "serious near to death." But Craven was forbidden to answer.

Davis was not allowed to write to his wife or to hear from her. He was denied access to Northern attorneys eager to defend him at a trial. The good doctor did all within his power to alleviate the prisoner's discomfort and humiliations, where hostile eyes were constantly upon him, even when he washed or when a portable commode was rolled into the room.

Aroused by newspaper accounts indicating that his prison treatment might render Davis frantic, on June 23 Mrs. Davis again wrote Craven: "Will you not, my dear sir, tell me the worst. Is he dying?

With a blaze of light pouring upon the dilated pupils of eyes always sensitive to it, chains fettering his emaciated limbs, coarse food served, as the newspapers describe it, 'in the most repulsive manner'—hope seems denied me." Dr. Craven could not tell her that though the lamp flamed all night, the fetters had been removed after five days, and that his own wife prepared more palatable "hospital food" for the prisoner. Being able to converse with one kindly man like his sympathetic doctor undoubtedly saved Davis's life. And Craven was so fascinated by Davis's conversation and learning that on leaving the cell after each visit he would write down everything the prisoner said. (In the summer of 1866 he was to publish *The Prison Life of Jefferson Davis,* which shocked the nation and helped enormously to bring about the prisoner's release on bail in May, 1867.)

However, the dank, moldy cell, the tormenting sleeplessness caused by the lamp and the tramping boots, kept the prisoner in a state of prostration and brought on a near-fatal attack of erysipelas. Reporters swarming about Fort Monroe gave out lurid accounts of Davis's illness. This third time, when the distracted wife implored Dr. Craven to give her absolutely correct news, he finally persuaded General Miles to permit the prisoner to write to Mrs. Davis himself. So on August 21, after three months of enforced silence, Davis was granted pen and paper to compose a letter to his wife, which would be scrutinized by censors. And four days later he was allowed a knife and fork to cut his own food, and to peel a peach when he had one.

Jefferson Davis to Varina Davis

Fortress Monroe, Va.
21 Aug '65

My dear Wife,

I am now permitted to write to you under two conditions, viz., that I confine myself to family matters, and that my letter shall be examined by the United States Attorney-General before it is sent to you.

Tomorrow it will be three months since we were suddenly and

unexpectedly separated, and many causes, prominent among which has been my anxiety for you and our children, have made that quarter in seeming duration long, very long. I sought permission to write to you that I might make some suggestions as to your movements and as to domestic arrangements.

This will sufficiently explain to you the omission of subjects on which you would desire me to write. I presume it is, however, permissible for me to relieve your disappointment in regard to my silence on the subject of future action toward me, by stating that of the purpose of the authorities I know nothing.

I often think of "old Uncle Bob," and always with painful anxiety. If Sam has rejoined him he will do all in his power for the old man's comfort and safety.

I have the prayer-book you sent, but the memorandum placed in it was withheld.

The confidence in the shield of innocence with which I tried to quiet your apprehensions and to dry your tears at our parting, sustains me still. If your fears have proved more prophetic than my hopes, yet do not despond. "Tarry thou the Lord's leisure, be strong, and He will comfort thy heart." Every day, twice or oftener, I repeat the prayer of St. Chrysostom.

To the surgeon and regimental chaplain I am under many obligations; the officers of the guard and of the day have shown me increased consideration, such as their orders would permit. The unjust accusations which have been made against me in the newspapers of the day might well have created prejudices against me. I have had no opportunity to refute them by proof, and can, therefore, only attribute the perceptible change to those good influences which are always at work to confound evil designs.

Be not alarmed by speculative reports concerning my condition. You can rely on my fortitude, and God has given me much of resignation to his blessed will.

Men are apt to be verbose when they speak of themselves, and suffering has a rare power to develop selfishness, so I have wandered from the subject on which I proposed to write, and have dwelt upon a person whose company I have for some time past kept so exclusively that it must be strange if he has not become tiresome.

It has been reported in the newspapers that you had applied for permission to visit me in my confinement; if you had been allowed to do so the visit would have caused you disappointment at the time, and bitter memories afterward. You would not have been allowed to hold private conversation with me.

Remember how good the Lord has always been to me, how often He has wonderfully preserved me, and put your trust in Him.

Farewell. May He, whose most glorious attribute is mercy, guide and protect and provide for my distressed family.

Once more, farewell. Ever affectionately,

Your Husband
Jeffn. Davis

Judah P. Benjamin to Varina Davis

This letter was written by the recent Confederate Secretary of State just after Benjamin's arrival in London following a harrowing escape. On August 30, in an interview published in the London *Times,* he extolled the President of the Confederacy and absolved him from all blame. At a pause at Vienna, Georgia, during "the flight from Richmond," Davis had a last conference with the loyal Benjamin and sent him to attend to some Confederate business in Havana and Nassau, after which he fully expected to join the President in Texas. C. J. McRae was the Confederate business agent in Europe.

London 1st Sept 1865

My dear Mrs. Davis

I only arrived here night before last, and my first care yesterday was to relieve as far as possible the anxiety which had been increasing during my whole trip relative to the practicability of aiding yourself or your husband in any possible manner. I learned with satisfaction that ample means have already been provided for defraying all expenses that could be incurred in behalf of Mr Davis, as well as for the defense of those unfortunate gentlemen who were associated with us in the administration of the government and who are now in the hands of the Federal authorities. I found, however, that no provisions had been made for paying to you the amount of the President's salary, which I thought should be sent to you, if any means remained within my reach. Mr. Mason had sent to you through a friend a check for two hundred pounds and an intimation that he would send further supplies as soon as he could hear of your receipt of the first remittance, and could learn in what way you wished the remittance made.

Knowing as I did how completely your resources had been exhausted before my departure from Georgia, I consulted with Mr. Mason and Mr. McRae, stating that I considered yours was the first and most sacred claim and that one year's salary of Mr. Davis ought to be placed at your disposal by sending to you a letter of credit on a London banker. It is but bare justice to both these gentlemen to say that not only did they heartily concur in the justice and propriety of this, but showed me by their correspondence how deeply the whole subject had engaged their warm and earnest sympathy long before my arrival. The only question was whether we could command the means. As I knew however of the need of immediate action, we provided at once for six months' salary and have now at your disposal twelve thousand five hundred dollars, being the President's salary up to 30th June last, which would be sent by this mail if we were confident it would reach you. It will be placed at once to your credit, and we will send you a banker's credit for the amount as soon as we get your instructions about the proper mode of securing your safe receipt of it. I have every hope that we will be able to send you a second remittance of like amount as soon as we can get together the wreck of such means as can still be commanded here, but my time for examination into the condition of affairs here has been as yet so limited that I cannot speak with entire certainty.

The money now placed at your disposal, my dear Mrs Davis, is your husband's: it is the money of the government paid to you in his behalf: you are indebted for it to no individual and are under no obligations to any one for it. You can therefore use without any scruple of delicacy. I beg however that you will not apply any of it toward the personal use of Mr. Davis or any expenses of his trial or defence; for I *know, I am absolutely certain,* that a very large sum, five times as much as will probably be wanted, is already placed in perfectly safe hands, to be used solely for his service, and for the expenses of his defence and that of the other prisoners, until his release from captivity.

Having thus disposed of pressing business matters, I refer to others which it is impossible to touch upon without the deepest emotion. God knows what I have suffered since my first reception of the horrible news that my beloved and honored friend was in the hands of the enemy. It was in May that I first learned the fact from John Taylor Wood, whom I met in Florida and who had just escaped from the scene of the calamity. I toiled on, night and day, with the vague hope that I could do something to aid him, if I were once beyond the limits of the U.S. I was very unlucky in my efforts.

I will not recount to you the details of my journey nor the scenes through which I have passed. After weeks spent in solitary travel on horseback through the forests and marshes of Florida in constant peril of capture: after passing twenty-three days in an open boat at sea, and crossing the Gulf Stream in a yawl: after being forced to put back to St Thomas in the Steamer on which I had taken passage for England in consequence of the ship's taking fire at night at sea; after every imaginable contretemps and danger, I reached London on the night of the 30th instant *nearly four months* after I parted from the President, *charged by him to perform certain public duties in Nassau and Havana, and then to rejoin him in Texas.* During this whole time, I have been incessantly harassed by the most poignant anxiety both on your account and his. Knowing your devoted love for your husband, I cannot imagine how you have survived the terrible distress which must have overwhelmed you when the extent of the calamity became apparent as revealed by his barbarous treatment, and aggravated by the inhuman refusal to allow you access to him.

However, I am here at last, without means, but with unimpaired health and undiminished energies. Can I, my dear friend, do any thing, in any way, by any sacrifice, to aid you or Mr Davis in this dreadful crisis? If so, command me without scruple. Suggest any idea that occurs to you as opening any chance of benefit to him or yourself and I will leave no effort unemployed to accomplish something. You know me too well to harbor a moment's suspicion that I am making mere profession: you know that I mean all that I say.

Good bye, my dear Mrs Davis. God bless you and your little ones. I dare not trust myself with the expression of my feelings for your noble husband, for my unhappy friend.

Ever yours devotedly
J. P. Benjamin

P.S. I have not yet seen my family, but shall go to Paris in a day or two, and return the following week. I will probably be a month or two settling up the public business here, and have a project as yet not matured, to commence the practice of the law here in London. Write me under envelope addressed to "John K. Gilliat &

Co., Bankers, 4 Crosby Sq. E. C. London" Be sure to give plain and clear directions for communicating with you safely. Yours again truly—J.P.B.

Varina Davis to Jefferson Davis

Mrs. Davis, who for the first months had been restricted in Savannah by the Federal authorities, has been allowed to accept an invitation from Mr. Schley to stay on his plantation near Augusta, Georgia. The Davis children, all except the baby, Winnie, have been sent to Canada for safety with their grandmother, Mrs. Howell, and Robert Brown, the colored servant, to look after them. The loyalty and devotion of Brown to the Davises is an example of the frequent affection Negroes retained for their white families. Ellen, a onetime Davis servant, was forced by her husband Charles to leave the ship at Old Point Comfort in May, but they remain friendly. Mary Ahern is the white nurse who was to be in the Davises' employ for a dozen years. In a subsequent letter of October 23, Mary's background and credentials are explained in detail.

Mill View, Ga.
Sept. 14th, 1865

My darling Husband,

"And art thou sick and I not with thee," can it be that your nights of pain are passed without one loving hand to touch you? I wake and weep, watch and pray to be granted strength to wait, to possess my soul in patience so that I may tarry the Lord's leisure and be strong. It was mistaken kindness in you to refrain from telling me how unwell you were. Do you not know I could take my death warrant from your lips better than joyful tidings from another.

My dear, dear Husband, tell me precisely how you are. Do not let my inevitable sorrow be swelled by uncertainties. You do not save me anything. I see in the papers accounts of every pang. Why not tell your poor helpless wife in your own sweet kind way the worst, and thus enable me to defy the penny-a-liners who for an item would wring the last drop of blood out of a broken heart. If your health has failed to the extent represented, am I not the one most deeply interested?

Genl Stedman has kindly given me permission to telegraph Genl Miles, but I do not know if he will answer me. I have written to the President, and to Mr Atty Genl Speed "making request if by any means now at length I might have a prospect by the will of God to come unto you."

Do not discourage me from coming if I get permission. It is my only hope of peace, to be near you. As to "bitter memories" these will be my bitterest, that I have not been able to help you in your time of need.

I have no recent news of our dear children. Ma has failed to write. I occasionally see a notice in the newspapers of them. Our little Pie Cake is as well as could be expected as she is cutting several jaw teeth at once. Her eyes look so like yours at times that I thank God for it.

I do not propose leaving Mr Schley's house until I hear something of you. I am as my sorrows permit.

My Ellen is at Old Point, as I hear from a letter of Charles to me expressive of sympathy, and anxiety on the part of Ellen. Our servants have not maligned us I am glad to see—it is a comfort to find that some one is not waiting for an opportunity.

Winnie's nurse is a sweet-tempered, kind creature, simple-hearted, and never having nursed before is devoted. She thinks everything Winnie does is so very smart. She is Irish born, but came to Georgia when three years old, and her father cultivates a little place near Savannah. The baby loves her very dearly—calls her Mamy, and has not much use for her Mammam except to nurse. Mary seems to be destitute of a "skeleton in her closet"—talks freely of her affairs like an honest child—I feel peculiarly fortunate.

As to Robert Brown I could not tell you what he has been to me. I gave him seventy-five dollars, which was the sum he specified as necessary to replace a part of the clothes taken from him by the Federals at our capture, but very soon found that he paid bills for which he had received no money, and called him up to give an account of money expended. He seemed much hurt when I told him that I did not desire to take his money, and said "Mistress, then you do not consider me as one of the family; I am nothing but a hired nigger." He then went on to tell me that he could idle as well as any other man if there was nothing to do, but that so long as the children wanted an education and his hands could make it for them, they could not want.

When I read the newspapers to him in which he was represented as happy to get rid of you and indifferent at parting, he remarked,

"Yet, he gave me charge of his family, and was too manly to make a scene, and I would not expose him and myself by showing what I suffered." He, however, was entirely willing to be imprisoned with you. You know how irritable and fastidious he has always been about work of a particular kind. He even nursed the baby and washed her clothes. Billy is his pet; but he watches over all. The only use he has made of his newly acquired freedom was to knock a white man down who made use of some abusive remarks before the children, when he was going to New York on the ship, and he was borne out in his course by the Captain, who examined into the case and pronounced the assault justifiable.

I have written to Brother Joe and urged him to take one hundred dollars from my little store. I hope he may consent, for I hear he is quite poor. Being at no expense now I could spare it. Did I tell you that the negroes at the two places think they can get about 1500 bales of cotton this year off them. Every tree has been cut down at both places, and cotton planted up to the steps of the houses.

My dear Lizzie Blair has followed me with constant solicitude and affectionate letters. Mrs Lee, Mary Lee, Mary Pegram, Gussie Daniel, Mrs Berin, Mrs Caskie, Mrs Grant, the Ritchies, and the Harrisons, dear Mr Burt—everybody is kind.

May God bless you and keep you, dearest honored husband. The all absorbing love of my whole life seems so poor a tribute to your worth. I can never hope to be worthy of you, only count all my love to one for rightness and pray that I may soon see you—the prayers of the righteous avail much.

Devotedly
Your Wife

Jefferson Davis to Varina Davis

Fortress Monroe Va. 15 Sept. 65

My dear Wife,

I wrote to you on the 21st Ulto. and have anxiously expected an answer until so much time has elapsed that I have come to the conclusion that you did not receive my letter. It was sent as required via Washington D.C., to be inspected by the Atty-Genl., who was requested to ascertain your address and forward it. Genl. Miles had previously at my request inquired, by telegraph, whether you were still in Savannah, but received no reply. You can readily imagine the painful solicitude I have felt and feel concerning you and our children. From newspapers it appears that the three older children have been with your Ma in Montreal and that they have left there, whither not stated. In my former letter you were reminded of the importance of your presence with the children and urged not to allow your care for me to prevent you from going with them to some suitable place for them and for you.

I hope soon to hear from you and to know of all which concerns you and which has been by day and by night the subject of my thoughts. How is Pie Cake? Her bright little face is ever before me and I thank God that she is unconscious of all which distresses those nearest to her.

Endeavor to be cheerful and hopeful. Have confidence in my ability to resist both physical and mental burthens, under the supporting grace of our Heavenly Father, who sends His comfort to alleviate my afflictions.

I cannot write you as often as I would, for special permission is each time required and the requisite materials are furnished for that occasion only.

Farewell, my loved Wife, remember that you cannot diminish my griefs by sharing them, and strive to preserve the tone of both your mind and your body by cultivating cheerful views of all things and charitable feelings towards all men. Kiss my baby. God guide you, and believe He will restore us to each other in this world, ever prays your Husband

Jeffn. Davis

Varina Davis to Jefferson Davis

Margaret Howell has left Savannah to join her mother and the Davis children in Montreal. In a false bottom of her trunk are secreted valuable Confederate papers and President Davis's letter book, which are to be stored in the vaults of a Montreal bank.

Clement C. Clay, Jr., onetime United States Senator and a Confederate Senator, was sent to Canada by President Davis as a peace commissioner in April, 1864, to meet with Horace Greeley and other Northerners in an attempt to stop the war. In May, 1865, along with President Davis and several prominent Confederates, Clay was accused by the Federal Government of conspiring in the Lincoln assassination and a reward of $25,000 was offered for his arrest.

Mill View—five miles from Augusta
Sept. 22nd 1865

My dear Husband,

I have looked in vain for another letter from you. How did you bear the long hours of suffering from erysipelas and I not with you? I see that you have been removed from the damp cell to a dryer "hall." If it is so, I thank God, for I dread worse still than erysipelas if you remain there.

There has been more delay about getting the baby's photograph taken than I anticipated, but at last I send it. Is not Pie a cunning looking little thing? I am without late information of our children but am sure they are well. Ma will surely write often, but I have received but one letter since they left me. Am anxious for Maggie to reach them—on many accounts. This is written by snatches as I am nursing mercurial little Pie.

If you can, dear, do tell me how Mr Clay is—so that I can send word to his wife. Perhaps, however, he is allowed to write to her. I have not seen her since she left Savannah, where she was not restricted, but permitted to go at will. I was at the time forbidden to receive letters, except through the Provost Marshal and after inspection, so she did not write. Well, I will not complain, for friends have raised up everywhere for me and mine. God bless you and keep you is the never ending prayer of

Your devoted
Wife

Jefferson Davis to Varina Davis

Fortress Monroe, Va.
26 Sept. 1865

My dear Wife

Your much wished for letter of the 14th Inst. reached me yesterday and today I have been furnished with writing materials to enable me to reply. Your well known and beloved hand brought comfort to me before the envelope was broken. The spirit which attends me waking and sleeping seemed to be brought more into a real presence. Your letter informs me of much which you did not intend to communicate. I hope you are better now than when you wrote, as the weather must be less oppressive. One of the causes of my anxiety that you should go with the children was the expectation that your health would suffer if you remained in that hot, crowded, and to you strange place.

It is true that my strength has greatly failed me, and the loss of sleep has created a morbid excitability, but an unseen hand has sustained me, and a peace the world could not give and has not been able to destroy, will, I trust, uphold me to meet with resignation whatever may befall me.

If one is to answer for all, upon him it most naturally and properly falls. If I alone could bear all the suffering of the country, and relieve it from further calamity, I trust our Heavenly father would give me strength to be a willing sacrifice.

The great mass, accepting the present condition of affairs as the result of the war, and directing their attention to the future issues which are involved in the changes produced, would bury the inevitable past with the sorrow which is unmingled with shame.

My dear Winnie, I felt how anxious you would be to be with me if you knew that I was sick and in pain. Need I say that every pang reminded me how often your soft touch and loving words had soothed me in like times of suffering. How sadly I felt that public cares and frequent absence and preoccupation with disagreeable subjects had prevented me from making even the poor return which it was in my power to give.

My good Wife, the Lord will care for you, there always seems to me to be an assuring answer when I pray especially for you. My heart is sustained by the conviction that we shall meet again in this world, that even before human judgement my innocence of wrong to my fellow man will prevail though many seek my destruction.

May the Lord guide and comfort you ever prays with all the fervor of devoted affection your Husband

Jeffn. Davis

P.S. I met Mr. Clay in our walk, he asked me to give his love to you and the children. He is now in better health, but is much changed. Hair and beard quite gray. We are not allowed to visit each other or to converse when we meet in the open air.

Varina Davis to Jefferson Davis

The loyal and devoted William Preston Johnston is a refugee in Montreal.

> Mill View, five miles from
> Augusta, Ga.
> Oct. 1st 1865

My darling Husband,

Where my many letters have been taken to I do not know. They too were sent through the proper channel. I hoped they had cheered your sick bed. Lest you should not have received them, I repeat that the Soldiers petted the children a good deal, and I suppose without any intention of doing harm, taught Bill derisive songs— horrible for me to hear come out of his rosy little lips about his Father. And Jeff happening accidentally to come into the parlor of the Hotel where was the wife of a lieutenant on duty in Savannah, she took occasion *without provocation* to say such things of you to him, as sent him pale and tearful to me. Then I would hear from the window such speeches as these, not intended insultingly, only jocularly—"Jeff what will you do with all your money?" "I have none, sir, my Father is poor." "Why, child, he stole enough for you to live like a lord."

Robert pled with me to send them away—and I felt as I was a prisoner within the city limits, and not likely to be set free, that I had better put them out of the way of seeing the jewel and pride of their life, their blameless Father's fame, tarnished by idle and unfeeling talkers. I then too hoped soon to join them and to say to you in person the reasons why I had sent them. But leave to go into "Georgia" was all I could obtain.

You may say why not then have gone into the country in Georgia. The country is not safe—it is infested by bands of robbers, negro and white, and if it had not been, my means were too limited to permit my paying board longer, and my family way too large to visit any one. Jeff and Maggie could spare no more time—and I thought for the little time I should be separated they had better go to boarding school. I chose the Convent of the Sacred Heart near Montreal because in convents purity is enjoined as a duty even in the idlest conversations between children, and the necessity of confession keeps them true, and then means were not needed to put her there. The Catholics, God bless them, have been everything to me. W. Preston Johnston writes a friend on the 15th of Sep. dated from Montreal, "Rely upon it, just now the children are where they ought to be."

Do not say if leave were granted, we could not accept it to be together. Of course we could not be all the time, but I can eat my meals with you, read to you, walk with you, nurse you if you are sick, put your baby upon your knee to murmur a little in your ear, and then kiss you as she does me, uninvited sometimes twenty times.

Somebody asked Robert if you were a gentleman. He held up Billy, and said, "Don't you see his *blood*—did you ever see a child like that belong to common tackies?" Robert says he will plough but Billy shall be educated. [*The rest is lost.*]

Varina Davis to Jefferson Davis

Varina quotes from Mrs. Howell's letter about the schooling of the children in Canada.

Mill View near Augusta
Oct 2nd 1865

My dear Husband

Good morning and God bless you. I wrote to you yesterday at great length, so only add these quotations from my mother in Montreal: "I have taken advantage of the best advice to be had here—John Taylor Wood, his mother and wife; Preston Johnson, his wife, and Julia Davidson, his cousin, a lady of most excellent judgement, who has done everything in her power to aid me. Maggie is at the Sacred Heart Convent six miles from Montreal on the Ottawa River, the most beautiful place you ever saw and bears the highest reputation for the education of young ladies. We went all through it. Genl Wm Preston's two little girls are there, and devoted to Maggie. The big girls are kept entirely separate from the little ones, and a nun is always with them. Although the children told me they had to study hard they all said they were very happy, and they looked happy. Maggie is *really in splendid health*. I will see her every two weeks and requested the Sisters to see that she writes once every two weeks, and I will forward the letters.

"Jeff is in Lennoxville at the Queens endowed college—three hours ride from the city, telegraph and railroad all the way. I have boarded him with Mrs Morris, who is employed by the college to take charge of the small boys and whose business it is to make them perfect their lessons, and to mend and attend to their clothes. She has ten of the first boys from Montreal, Jeff and two other Southern boys of the best families. I went up and spent some hours with her. Her boys seem fond of her. Preston Johnson is living in town housekeeping and will run up every two or three weeks to see him. I will see him once a month. I have done all I can conscientiously for your dear children, and made them as happy as little children can be. They all love me dearly. Our little Billy comes up to be nursed and petted every evening, and is in my bed every morning for a play. He is seldom out of temper, and the fattest fellow you ever saw. Now I have never seen him look so well—he is pink and white as a young girl—says he is getting strong as a man, means to study hard."

Farewell, dear. I have had a great deal of good news this week. I thank God for all. But always in feeling grateful for the welfare of all my newer ties find my great bulk of thankfulness to be that I am

Your devoted Wife

Varina Davis to Jefferson Davis

Her many friends continue to write solicitously. The Lee ladies are especially attentive.

October [?] 1865

My darling Husband,

My head has been so tried, that I cannot remember even the age of Pie—without prompting. My dear, have we not been sorely afflicted? But with you I could bear anything—when I could "see the fond and fearless smile hope revived again." Have I been the half to you that you have proved to me, I wonder. It would comfort me to think so. The only comfort I feel is that few people of our years have so kept up the romance of married life that the treasure of our love be not as Tennyson says "soiled by ignoble use." Now I have ample time to remember and appreciate how dearer is the old Husband, than my young one once was, and I thought in our youth the measure of my love running over, that I had given you "all—I could no more." Of course, I do not dread poverty with you. You know I never loved a large house as you did. I fancied a small one with a large fireplace & hearth around which we might all sit. Don't take thought for the morrow. We somehow or other do well enough.

Look upon the waters for your bread. Your Mother's bread, mine, my Mother's—we cannot want. We have shared with many a Lazarus, freely and tenderly. I cannot want money, of course I am economical, but loans, ergo gifts of large amounts, could be procured if I asked for them of the people who have offered to me. But my dear Old Husband's dignity is a better mantle for me than ever so large a wrapping of green backs.

Mr Schley's Mother is living here, and his wife is living—a very large family—they are quite a pretty sight, they remind me of the "Hurricane" at table. I have a very affectionate letter from Constitution Browne. It took a gentleman born to write it—says his wife is doing her own work—and is in better health than she has been. Never woman had such friends. My very dear Richmond friends—poor, grateful little Mrs Grant—little Gussie—Mrs Anne G— all write love by every mail. Dear Mrs. R. E. Lee seems to have opened her whole heart to me—all of her girls too.

I have nothing to complain of. I suffered severely from uncertainty about your sickness. I comprehended its character and expected the termination, knew your danger. I thank our merciful Father that he has raised up friends for you in the officers, and I will teach my children to pray for dear Dr Craven all his life. Genl Stedman is very kind to me, and lets me telegraph when I please. Make yourself easy, if I or the baby either should be taken ill I will telegraph Genl Miles. So know that we are well if silent.

I hope I may be allowed to come to you. Do pray for me to come. God will answer you. And now my first and only love, farewell— May God bless you and keep you, and make His face to shine upon you is the prayer of your devoted wife—

Have you been removed to Carroll Hall as the papers say? Describe it to me, tell me how you live all day. [*The rest is lost.*]

Varina Davis to Dr. John J. Craven

In this third letter to Jefferson Davis's physician Mrs. Davis relates in detail much that had happened to her since she was parted from her husband in May in the hope that he would pass the information on to the prisoner. She did not dare risk writing him directly because of fear of censors.

Mill View (Near Augusta, Ga)
October 10, 1865

Colonel John J. Craven:

I dread paralysis for my husband, his nerves have been so highly strung for years without relief. If you can, and perhaps you may, prevail upon the authorities to let him sleep without a light. He is too feeble to escape, and could not bear a light in his room when in strong health. The sequel of these attacks has always been an attack of amaurosis, and in one of them he lost his eye. It first came on with an attack of acute neuralgia.

When he was taken from me on the ship, and after the women searched our persons, the men searched our baggage.

They then told my servants that they could go ashore if they did not desire to go to Savannah. The husband of my faithful colored nurse forced her to go. I entreated to be permitted to debark at Charleston, as my sister, Miss Howell, still continued to be ill, and I feared to return on the ship with a drunken purser, who had previously required Colonel Pritchard's authority to keep him in order; and going back Mrs. Clay, my sister, and myself would be the only women on the ship—but this was refused. Acting as my own chambermaid and nurse, and the nurse also of my sister, we started for Savannah. We had a fearful gale, in which the upper decks once or twice dipped water, and no one could walk.

God protected us from the fury of the elements; but the soldiers now began to open and rob our trunks again. The crew, however, gave us some protection, and one of the officers in the engine-room gave up his cabin and locked everything we had left up in it. The Lieutenant of the Fourteenth Maine, Mr. Grant, though a plain man, had the heart of a gentleman, and took care of us with the greatest assiduity. Some of the soldiers and crew helped me to nurse, and saved me many an hour of wakefulness and fatigue.

My little daughter Maggie was quite like an old woman; she took her sister early every morning—for the nights were so rough I could not sleep, because it was necessary to hold the infant to avoid bruising it—and with the assistance of our faithful servant Robert, who held her still while she held her sister, she nursed her long enough for me to rest. Little Jeff and I did the housekeeping; it was a fair division of labor, and not unpleasant, as it displayed the good hearts of my children.

Arrived at Savannah, we trudged up to the hotel quite in emigrant fashion. My sister with the baby, and Robert with the baggage; I, with my two little sons, little Maggie, in quite an old-fashioned manner, keeping all straight and acting as parcel-carrier; for we could not procure any carriage and must walk until we reached the Pulaski House, where, after a day and night, we procured comfortable rooms.

A black waiter, upon answering my bell, and being told to call my man-servant Robert, replied very impertinently that, "if he should see Robert he would give the order, but did not expect to see him." When Robert heard it, he waited till all the black servants had assembled at dinner, and then remarked that he should hate to believe there was a colored man so low as to insult a distressed woman; but if so, though a peaceable man, he should whip the first who did so. From that time all the greatest assiduity could do was done for me, first from *esprit de corps,* and then from kind feeling.

The people of Savannah treated me with the greatest tenderness. Had I been a sister long absent and just returned to their home, I could not have received more tender welcome. Houses were thrown open to me, anything and everything was mine. My children had not much more than a change of clothing after all the parties who had us in charge had done lightening our baggage, so they gave the baby dresses and the other little ones enough to change until I could buy or make more.

Unfortunately for me, General ——, who, I hear, was "not to the manner born," was in command of the district at the time. I asked permission to see him, and as I was so unwell that I could not speak above my breath with a cold, and suffered from fever constantly—the result of exposure on the ship—I wrote to beg that he would come to see me, for his aide had told me the night before that I could not be permitted to leave Savannah, and having been robbed of nearly all my means, I could not afford to stay at the hotel. Besides, as soon as I reached the hotel, detectives were placed to watch both me and my visitors, so I did not feel at liberty, thus accompanied, to go to private houses.

General ——'s aide, whose animus was probably irreproachable, but whose orthography was very bad, was directed to tell me that he did not go out of his office, and "all such" (which I afterward found to mean myself) "as desired to see him would call at his office." On the following day I went, accompanied by General Mercer. Need I say that General —— did himself justice, and verified my preconceived opinion of him in our interview, in which he told me he "guessed I could not telegraph to Washington, write to the heads of departments there, or to anybody, except through the regular channel approved"; and I could not write to my friends, "except through the Provost-Marshal's office"; and that I was permitted to pay my expenses, but must remain within the limits of Savannah.

In this condition I remained for many weeks, until, fortunately for me, General Birge relieved him, but had it not in his power, however, to remove the restrictions any further than to take the detectives away. General Birge permitted me to write unrestrictedly to whom I pleased, and appeared anxious, in the true spirit of a gentleman, to offer all the courtesies he consistently could.

My baby caught the whooping-cough, and was ill almost unto death for some days with the fever which precedes the cough and then she slowly declined. I did what I could to give her fresh air; but the heat was so intense, the insects so annoying, and the two rooms such close quarters that she and I suffered much more than I hope you or yours will ever know by experience.

My most acute agony arose from the publication and republication in the Savannah *Republican* of the shackling scene in Mr Davis's casemate, which to think of stops my heart's vibration. It was piteous to hear the little children pray at their grace, "That the Lord would give father something which he could eat, and keep him strong, and bring him back to us with his good senses, to his little children, for Christ's sake"; and nearly every day, during the hardest and bitterest of his imprisonment, our little child Maggie had to quit the table to dry her tears after this grace, which was of her own composition.

I believe I should have lost my senses if these severities had been persevered in, for I could neither eat nor sleep for a week; but the information of the change effected by your advice, relieved me; and I have thanked God nightly for your brave humanity.

Though I ate, slept, and lived in my room, rarely or never going out in the day, and only walking out late at night, with Robert for protection, I could not keep my little ones so closely confined. Little Jeff was constantly told that he was rich; that his father had "stolen eight millions," etc. Little two-year-old Billy was taught to sing, "We'll hang Jeff Davis on a sour apple-tree," by giving him a reward when he did so. The little thing finally told me one day, "You thinks I's somebody; so is you; so is father; but you is not; so is not any of us but me. I am Yankee every time." The rough soldiers doubtless meant to be kind, but such things wounded me to the quick. They took him and made him snatch apples off the stalls, if Robert lost sight of him for a moment.

Finally, two women from Maine contemplated whipping Jeff, because they found out that he was his father's son; but a man took them off just in time to avoid a very painful scene to them as well as to me.

Hourly scenes of violence were going on in the streets, and not reported, between the blacks and whites, and I felt that the children's lives were not safe. During General ——'s régime, a negro sentinel levelled his gun at my little son Jeff to shoot him, for calling him "uncle." I could mourn with hope if my children lived, but what was to become of me if I was deprived of them? So I sent them off with many prayers and tears, but confident of the wisdom of the decision. On the ship I understood a white man was very abusive in their hearing of Mr. Davis, when my faithful servant Robert inquired with great interest, "Then you tell me I am your equal? You put me alongside of you in everything?" The man said, "Certainly." "Then," said Robert, "take this from your equal," and knocked him down. The captain was appealed to, and upon a hearing of the case, justified Robert, and required an apology of the leveled leveller.

As soon as the dear children were gone, I hoped with my little weak baby (you see I am very honest with you) to make my escape out of the country to them; but when, upon coming to Augusta—

which General Stedman gave me leave to do immediately upon
his accession to command—I was informed by a gentleman, who
said he had been told so authoritatively, that if I ever quitted the
country for any possible object, I would—no matter what befell
Mr. Davis—never be allowed to return; and then abandoned the
intention.

Under the kind treatment I have received, the fine country air
(five miles from Augusta), and the privacy, I have grown much
better; can sleep and eat, and begin to feel alive again with the
frosty air, and loving words, and letters which meet me here as in
Savannah.

The whole Southern country teems with homes the doors of which
open wide to receive me; and the people are so loving, talk with
such streaming eyes and broken voices of him who is so precious
to them and to me, that I cannot realize I do not know them intimately. Mr. Davis should dismiss all fears for me. I only suffer for
him. I do not meet a young man who fails to put himself at my
disposal to go anywhere for me. I cannot pay a doctor's bill, or
buy of an apothecary. "All things are added unto me."

Varina Davis

Jefferson Davis to Varina Davis

Fortress Monroe, Va.
11th Oct. 1865

My dear Wife,

I have tried and not without success to possess my soul in patience. A varied life has given me experience in most forms of trial.
When a Cadet I lay for more than four months in Hospital and
rarely saw any one even when it was thought I was about to die,
then some of my friends were allowed to stay with me at night.
I should have more resources to sustain me now than then, and
as much fortitude as when you have seen me suffer.

On the second of this month I was removed to a room on the
second floor of a house built for officers' quarters. The dry air, good
water, and a fire when requisite, have already improved my physical
condition, and with increasing health all the disturbances due to a
low vitality, it is to be expected, will disappear as rapidly as has

been usual with me after becoming convalescent. I am deeply in-debted to my attending physician, who has been to me much more than that term usually conveys. In all my times of trouble, new evidences have been given me out of God's merciful love.

Misfortune should not depress us, as it is only crime which can degrade. Beyond this world there is a sure retreat for the oppressed; and posterity justifies the memory of those who fall unjustly. To our own purblind view there is much which is wrong, but to deny what is right is to question the wisdom of Providence or the existence of the mediatorial government.

Every intelligent man knows that my office did not make me the custodian of public money, but such slanders impose on and serve to inflame the ignorant—the very ignorant—who don't know how public money was kept, and how drawn out of the hands of those who were responsible for it. My children, as they grow up and prove the pressure of poverty, must be taught the cause of it; and I trust they will feel as I have, when remembering the fact that my father was impoverished by his losses in the war of the Revolution.

Our injuries cease to be grievous in proportion as Christian charity enables us to forgive those who trespass against us, and to pray for our enemies. I rejoice in the sweet sensitive nature of our little Maggie, but I would she could have been spared the knowl-edge which inspired her "grace," and the tears which followed its utterance. As none could share my suffering, and as those who loved me were powerless to diminish it, I greatly preferred that they should not know of it.

I hope the negroes' fidelity will be duly rewarded, and regret that we are not in a situation to aid and protect them. There is, I observe, a controversy which I regret as to allowing negroes to testify in court. From brother Joe, many years ago, I derived the opinion that they should then be made competent witnesses, the jury judging of their credibility. The change of relation diminishing protection, must increase the necessity. Truth only is consistent, and they must be acute and well trained, who can so combine as to make falsehood appear like truth when closely examined.

For, say, three months after I was imprisoned here, two hours consecutive sleep were never allowed me; more recently it has not been so bad, but it is still only broken sleep which I get at night, and by day my attention is distracted by the passing of the sentinels who are kept around me as well by day as by night. I have not sunk under my trials, am better than a fortnight ago, and trust I shall be sustained under any affliction which it may be required me to bear. My sight is affected, but less than I would have supposed if it had been foretold that a light was to be kept where I was to sleep, and that I was at short intervals to be aroused, and the expanded pupil thus frequently subjected to the glare of a lamp. There is soon to be a change of the garrison here. I will be sorry to part from many of the officers, but as they are to go home I should rejoice for such as are entitled to my gratitude. *Au reste,* as I cannot control, so I may hope for the best.

I have not seen Jordan's critique, and am at a loss to know where that game was played and was lost by my interference. If the records are preserved they dispose summarily of his romances past, passing, and to come. The events were of a public character, and it is not possible for men to shift their responsibility to another. The unfortunate have always been deserted and betrayed; but did ever man have less to complain of when he had lost power to serve? The critics are noisy—perhaps they hope to enhance their wares by loud crying. The multitudes are silent, why should they speak to save him who hears best the words most secretly uttered? My own heart tells me the sympathy exists, that the prayers from the family hearth have not been hushed.

I have been reading Bancroft's history of the United States. It is a work of great research and considering it is called "history" is very fair. It was to me most interesting by its reference to all the books connected with his subject I have seen; thus as it were peopling my prison with old acquaintance; and further illustrating by authority things which I had only known through tradition. In many passages his style rises to the highest level and through the whole runs undefiled the love of Justice and liberty.

John Mitchel has been released. He was permitted to take leave of me through the grates, and he offered to write to you. I have not seen our friend Clay for some time, not having been out to walk lately on account of a series of boils, or a carbuncle with a succession of points, which rose in my right armpit, and has prevented me from putting on my coat since the day I last wrote to you. I believe the disease is now at an end, and but for the rain I would have gone out to-day.

I will comply with your repeated request for a description of my room, and hope the reality may be better than you have imagined the case to be. The room is about 18 x 20 feet; is situated at the corner in the second story of a long two-story house which stands under cover of the main parapet, and was built for officers' quarters. In the centre of the end wall, is a fireplace; in the centre of each of the other walls is a door. The one opposite to the fireplace opens into the room occupied by the officer of the guard for the day, the one on the south side looks out on a gallery which runs along the building, and, beyond, is a limited view of the interior of the fort; the one on the north side connects with a passage dividing the building. The doorway into the officer's room is closed by an iron grating, with locks on *his* side of it, and, turning on hinge, affords the means of exit. The gallery door is closed by a fixed iron grating with glazed sash shutters outside. The passage doorway is closed by iron grating, and a panel shutter into which are inserted two panes of glass.

Sentinels are no longer kept *in* the room I occupy. One sentinel only now walks back and forth along the gallery, one along the passage, and one in the officer's room, so as to give each of the three a view through his door of the interior of the room. They cause the broken sleep concerning which you ask. I have endeavored to overcome the distraction and annoyance this constant passing causes in the day, and to resist its disturbing effect at night; the success has not, however, been commensurate with the effort. Formerly the circumstances were much worse; and before changes were made, a morbid condition had been produced so that wakefulness is continued by less than would have produced it.

My bed stands in the corner of the walls of the gallery and officers' room; on the opposite corner is the water-bucket, basin and pitcher, and folding screen which *enables me to wash unobserved*. On the gallery side of the chimney is a recess with a shelf for books, and pegs to hang up clothes. On the opposite side of the chimney, a closet. The bed is the common form of iron frame, two mattresses, sheets, blankets, and a cover with pillows and mosquito bar. Breakfast is sent to me about nine; dinner about four; and tea would be sent if I desired it. The food is suited to my condition and I have had no occasion to ask for change or addition. The chair, though coarse, is so much better than the one I had before it, as to be comparatively satisfactory; a stand, such as is commonly used in hospital wards, serves me as a table, and for the present there is a stool which answers for a washstand. My clothes are not with me, except those in immediate use. My valise was taken charge of by General Miles. I have not seen it since. I much regret that you did not keep the things which had a value from association, instead of leaving them in the valise.

We have had a few cold days here, but the weather is now pleasant. The trees are still covered with leaves, but they are assuming the hue of autumn. The feeling of cold carried my thoughts to the children in Canada and then to "Old Uncle Bob" in Missi. Who will take our place in regard to him and the "old people" who were with him?

Farewell my dear Wife, I humbly strive with becoming resignation to say, Father, thy will be done. Every development of truth must diminish the desire to punish me, and therefore there is reasonable ground for hopefulness.

More now depends on you than at any former time. To be equal to the trial requires sana mens in sana corpore, therefore cherish hope and cultivate cheerfulness as condusive thereto.

Once more, my love, farewell. Through my bars my free spirit flies to and hovers around you. Daily and nightly my prayers are offered for you, and there is a peace which tells me they are heard. Again dearest and yet again farewell.

Ever affectionately yr. Husband
Jeffn. Davis

Varina Davis to Jefferson Davis

Joe Smith is the son of Davis's eldest sister, Anna. General Joseph R. Davis is the son of Davis's brother Isaac.

Mill View—Oct 23rd 1865

My own dear Husband,

I can only grieve over my letters not having been delivered to you. I do not know why—God knows I repress all which might be offensive to any one. The fact is I am so full of thoughts of you, and love unspeakable for you that bitterness does not suggest itself. I wrote to you a very long and satisfactory letter about the precious children.

Joe Smith writes often, and as I told you in one of the missing letters came to me after a long search, and reached here the day after Joe R. with whom Maggie went to New York. They both came to take me home with them—full of love and generosity. Joe Smith, money if I chose to draw, but I have been careful of my money, and did not require it. Armistead Burt sent me a check for a hundred dollars in gold, which I returned with thanks for kindness and an entreaty to come to him, which I concluded on account of the deficient mail facilities there, I had better not do, though Genl Stedman gave me permission to go upon parole. Mr. Schley seems to make more, and more every day, objections to my leaving him. I am better here. The girls are sweet, amiable, common-sense girls. We all occupy a room in the yard, the old gentleman built two rooms together distant about ten feet from the main building. Mary, my nurse, and I occupy one with Pie, and the girls the other. Sometimes they come in and sit with me, but Pie is too excitable for the noise of five talkative women so I oftener go to them—they rise early, retire as early. I cannot sleep much, so I do not get up to seven o'clock breakfast, but meet them at a three o'clock dinner. The cool weather here is bracing me up— I am much better already. Pie is rosy down to the soles of her feet. She eats like a little sloth. Everybody who sees her says what a fine little boy, Madam—she is so strong featured. She is a very interesting child because very peculiar.

Mary Ahern is a warm hearted woman about thirty. Her Uncle is a grocer in Savannah; her Father has a little farm twenty-five miles from Savannah. She was educated by the Sisters in Savannah, who told me there never was such a woman and they sent in the country for her for me. Sherman desolated her old Father's place, the result of all the savings of his youth—consequently she has to go out to service again. We get on delightfully—she is so soft tempered, with an acute sense of the ludicrous which renders her quite agreeable, and a remarkable degree of *proper reticence—* dresses in her own homespuns, and "would face the devil."

Do not be anxious for me, all that kindness can do is done for me. I am much better in health, and do keep cheerful—I have always a sad expression, always when my face is still—I have gained flesh since I left Savannah I am sorry to say. I nearly lost my mind for some weeks there, but, when you were better, so was I. Do not believe anything you hear of me in the newspapers. I am doing very well and acting as I think you would approve. True I see no one, or very few, but I do not act "defiantly" or write so either.

I have appealed again and again to go to you, but never an answer. President Johnson stated to one of a committee who called upon him that my applications were not in a proper spirit. Perhaps he may change his mind. I do not know. If so, how gladly will I come to you. I am very grateful to dear Dr Craven, even if he will not consent to communicate a word *with me upon any subject.* I suppose that is a rigid adherence to his duty. God bless him "in his basket and his store," as the homely old blessing goes.

What do you think I have been reading? A literal translation of Homer's Iliad. It has a new beauty to me divested of Pope's swelling rhyming translation. I really have forgotten myself to a pitch of high enthusiasm over it a great many times. My heart actually beats when I come to such battles as the one in which "Jove withdrew Hector from the weapons." And when Achilles slept and the ghost of Patroclus came to him like to himself and then "Art forgetful of me, Achilles?" "Thou didst not neglect me when alive."—But all these things you *know* and you love to think of them.

Your letters are the sweetest books to me. I live upon one until another comes, and then I am not so ungrateful as to throw the old one by. Would to God you could write daily. Can you not describe your room? Are the sentinels with you at night? Why is your sleep broken? Tell me even what is in your room—what clothes have you. Do tell me every little thing. How infinite are the questions I might ask—how deep and tender is the love with which every thing of yours is surrounded. When I read of the heroic and good, you are my exemplar better than man can depict. Seven times tried in the fiery furnace—brighter than refined gold.

I bless God for every hour that I have borne your spotless name, and fervently trust and expect that He will *reunite* us rich in your good repute *and* our twenty-one years cumulative love together, proof against the world. My Jeff, my first and only love, farewell. Infinitely dearer in your sorrow and waning strength than you were in your power and youth, I am in life and death,

Your devoted Wife

I have written you seven times. Your letters have all been received.

William Preston to Varina Davis

General Preston, brother-in-law of Albert Sidney Johnston, has arrived as a refugee in Canada after a hazardous "escape" through Mexico which took him to England. He has daughters in the convent school with Maggie Davis and a son at school in Lennoxville. His various glad tidings gave great comfort to Mrs. Davis.

Toronto
1 Nov. 1865

My dear Madam.

I have requested a friend to forward to you the accompanying letter from General C. J. McRae, which I brought over recently from England. From it you will see that arrangements have been made to place at your disposition £2500, say $12,500, for the personal use of yourself and your family. Though now more than two weeks in Canada, I have had no earlier opportunity to make a safe and certain arrangement to get this letter forwarded to you.

I would advise you to designate at once some proper person to receive the amount for you and hold it subject to your orders.

I saw your sister Miss Maggie in Montreal. Mrs. Howell was absent and in coming through that city with my family the other day I did not have time to call. They had gone to private lodgings. I saw your little daughter at the school near Montreal. She is very bright and was very well, though she complained to me amusingly of how much she was shocked at the religious observances of the nuns. I learn through my boy that your son at Lennoxville is well and very popular with his schoolmates from his intelligence and frank character.

I fear that Mrs. and Miss H. may need means, but you need feel no uneasiness about it, as I have requested my nephew Colonel William Preston Johnston to see that they shall not experience any inconvenience.

After the investment of Richmond the business with which I was entrusted became impossible. I made three fruitless attempts to run into Wilmington or Charleston, but failed after narrowly escaping capture. I then went to Havana and though fearing all was lost, pressed forward to Matamoros and got to Shreveport. The news of our terrible disaster reached me in Texas. I reported to Kirby Smith for military service and did all in my power to make head for a campaign in the Trans Mississippi Department. For a while I had hopes, but the subsequent surrender of Johnston and capture of the President rendered further resistance impossible and the army deserted their officers, plundered the public property and disbanded. Disgusted and disheartened I refused to surrender and crossed from San Antonio to Monterey on horseback through the cut-throats of Cortinas and the marauders that infest the Rio Grande. With a few friends I arrived safely and then went down through San Luis Potosi and the City of Mexico to Vera Cruz. From Vera Cruz I went to Havana and to St. Thomas. At St. Thomas I met Mr. Benjamin, who had made a wonderful escape, & had been wrecked, but had finally got to Nassau. I sailed with him on the *Seine* for England, but the vessel took fire at sea and was compelled to put back after being very nearly destroyed. It was alone saved by the coolness and courage of the crew. I learned from Mr. Benjamin what occurred after you left Richmond, and feeling the deepest solicitude for the President and yourself, I ventured to inquire into your means, and the resources of your family and what provisions had been made for his defense.

Mr. Benjamin told me he feared you were destitute, and could not give me any satisfactory answer till we reached Europe, but manifested the most friendly interest and purpose in your behalf. I left Mr. Benjamin in Europe. He does not intend to return to America.

After remaining a short time in England, I came to Quebec to rejoin my family, and arrived on the 11th of October. We had been long separated, but God vouchsafed to me to find them once more, all well. Friends were at Montreal to meet me, and all urged me to return home. My feelings, perhaps my pride prevented me. Agents from home wrote that there was great danger of confiscation of Mrs. Preston's property from her long absence as abandoned property and urged the speedy return of my family who have been banished for more than a year. Mrs. Preston has returned home, but I remain here, until future events may determine my course.

I sincerely sympathize with you in the trials to which you are subjected, and trust that before long the perils that beset President Davis will have passed away. His own character and the public opinion of the world will in the end shield him from the wrath of his enemies.

Very truly yours
Wm. Preston

Jefferson Davis to Varina Davis

Fortress Monroe, Nov. 3, 1865

My dear Wife,

Yours of the 23 Ulto. received this day and brought the only cheering ray which can light up the gloom of my imprisonment. When I grow restless from desire to receive another letter from you I draw comfort from reperusal of those preserved.

I am sustained by a Power I know not of. When Franklin was brought before the privy council of George III, and a time-serving courtier heaped the grossest indignities upon him, he bore them with composure, and afterward attributed his ability to do so to the consciousness of innocence in the acts which he was reviled.

What, under Providence, may be in store for us I have no ability to foresee. I have tried to do my duty to my fellowmen, and I have the sustaining belief that He who is full of mercy, and knowing my inmost heart, will acquit me, where man, blind man seeks to condemn.

4th Nov. The day is dark and wet, not cold but chilly. The trees in the fort are sheltered by the defensive wall, but their leaves tell that summer has gone. I have nothing learned in regard to the purpose concerning myself. Counsel has not visited me, and the newspaper stories are so repugnant to the Constitution and the decisions under it that they must have been made by the ignorant for the ignorant.

Kiss dear little Winnie for me, and, as she grows, teach her how her father loved her when she was too young to remember. Try to make my thanks to Mr. Schley and the ladies equal to my gratitude.

Be not despondent but let us rather seek only to live that we may not fear to die. Farewell, dear Wife, my prayers go up constantly for you. Your image is ever before me, my spirit is about you. You know what I would say, at least what I always feel and, suppressing utterance, I say again Farewell, dearest, farewell.

Your Husband

Sister Anastasia to Varina Davis

Sacred Heart
Sault au Récollet
Nov. 7/65

My dear Mrs. Davis

Our Revd Mother reached home a few days ago after an absence of two months.

She desires me assure you of the deep interest she feels in your dear little Maggie, which is increased by your child's separation from you, my dear Madam.

Every attention is paid to her health and I am happy to say she has been very well ever since she has been with us. Her back does not trouble her at all and she is well provided with all that is necessary to meet the severity of our climate. She is very good, indeed remarkably so for a child of her age who has been, and is even still, very much petted by everyone who sees her.

I wish that when you have the happiness of meeting your children, my dear Mrs. Davis, that you will find that she has made satisfactory improvement in French and other studies about which you are anxious. That our Lord may soon record that favor for you and Mr. Davis is the sincere prayer of our Mother and all her community.

Col. & Mrs. Johnston have been most kind and attentive to Maggie, aiding Mrs. Howell in her care of her.

Miss Howell was here on Sunday. She and Mrs. Howell are well. I mention this knowing the uncertainty of letters.

Believe me, my dear Mrs. Davis,

Yours very sincerely
Anastasia White

Varina Davis to Jefferson Davis

Belleville Factory, Ga.
Nov. 7, 1865

My very dear Husband,

Your letter of the 20th of Oct. reached me. I thank God that you are some what better, but how wearing must such suffering be. With the bounds of Georgia only to restrain me, I find myself very much changed. Perhaps the sentinels are day and night upon my spirit and the bounds will not permit my body to follow it to the preferable place.

If I deserved like you God's immediate presence in my heart, perhaps I might like you possess my soul in patience, "shorn indeed" as I am. But I am not full of love and forgiveness. I may become so when you cease to suffer. While in Savannah, I prayed God to take you to himself. I repined that you had not died at your capture. Now I thank God that you were spared, even though we may never meet, for your heart has become the "temple of the Holy Ghost, the Comforter." Should your sufferings destroy you, it cannot be long before I come to you. But I must not talk of this until God sends also to *me* "the Comforter." He has already raised up for me, among strangers, friends and protectors—"I cannot want."

I am spending a week with Mrs. Henry McAlpin, a sister of Mr Schley's, who is in her family pretty much what Sister Lucinda is in ours. She has a family of little children in whom she is absorbed. Pie is delighted. There was once a magnificent factory here, but it was burned down by a Federal emissary from Genl Grant's army when he commanded in the West—and the loss has reduced the owners, the Schley brothers, to poverty, at least all who had embarked their whole capital in it. The boarding house for the factory operatives and the dwellings which they occupied still remain. Mrs McAlpin occupies the boarding house and I have the boarding house parlor, and she and I sit and sew all day and talk of sorrows, and past joys, and watch her baby and mine play.

Margaret arrived at Canada safely, and was in Montreal the

17th of October. The children were in every sense well. I await particulars by mail. Joe Davis took her to New York.

I have kept myself from the scores of obligations which people longed to confer as a relief to their feelings for you. I have tried to meet your wishes which I generally find are my own when I desire to do what is right, or rather when I succeed in doing what is right.

I might say much, if not forbidden, about the transition through which the country is passing. I think for many years, perhaps forever, at the South it will be unsafe for men with families to cultivate in isolated spots like ours. I look forward with horror to the coming winter. The negroes have, like La Fontaine's grasshopper, sung all the summer, and they are becoming hungry and cold, as winter draws on. When the military government is removed from Georgia and other states—"the deluge." The women are very dressy and very insolent, in some cases edging the ladies off the sidewalks. The men are less demonstrative, but more threatening in their manners.

Mr Schley had an old man who was born in his wife's family, who was probably as old as Uncle Charlie—when "freedom came." Mr Schley told them that all who desired to go were not necessitated to go surreptitiously, and "Daddy Hampshire" who had two fine-sized rooms, with furniture enough to fill three large wagons, made his preparations to go saying, "I gwine if I don't lib the week." He did not say good bye, but his old wife before mounting the last wagon load, came weeping piteously, and embracing her young Mistresses said "I lub you all, good young Mistresses but I bludged be follow my old foolish man. When he done kill, I come back soon." All were in tears. The sequel is that he worked himself down, being consumptive, and is now kept from starving, in a miserable little shanty in town in which (the room being fifteen feet large) there are three other families—by Mr Schley's money, which is given to him as he needs it to smooth his path to the grave to which freedom is leading him with no gentle hand.

What you say is true I suppose. If things were different, you might direct the labor of the negroes to their and your advantage. But emissaries of insubordination and inciters to murder cannot be kept from them. When you think you have the negroes bound by a contract for the year and that from its crop plenty may abound for you and them, they get affronted, go en masse—perhaps a circus comes, or some other phenomenon, and gathering fodder to escape the rain from a sky overcast, they throw down their sheafs and go. A contract is a rope of sand. They are like the French people—liberty with them, means "equality, and fraternity" —but unlike the French liberty, equality and fraternity means utter idleness, and fine clothes, besides.

Who goes in the change of garrison? God forever bless those who have been kind to my precious Prisoner—and forgive those who have insulted his helplessness, for I cannot. I had rather know certainly about you from yourself. You did not spare me, for I heard all and more in the public prints. I shudder when I think how much, and in what spirit promulgated. Unless I had fled to the centre of the Mammoth Cave, or some other impenetrable recess, I could not keep the children ignorant. So I made them feel it was a crown of thorns, and glory. May my sons and daughters love us like their Mother loves their Father, may their *characters* be like yours. *If they love like me and act like you,* surely the world need be grateful that we have given them birth to take their places in it.

Husband, dear Saintly Husband, if I were to give the reins to my pen, surged on by my quivering, longing heart, what might not the indifferent eyes which first peruse these whilom sacred confidences, see to. Well, well, I do not use the terms of bygone times; but the heart which dictated them is the same which has throbbed for you alone since it could feel a woman's love.

Will not you be permitted to receive books and delicacies? I have procured some very old brandy for you in Charleston, and some good cigars.

I am stopped by our little Pie coming in with a little spotless white dress, and deep pink sacque trimmed with white, and a cap of the same colors which I have just knitted for her. I do not know which is the prouder, Mary or Pie. Mary says, "Now Mrs Davis, do look at the young one—is not she as orderly and pretty as a pink?"

In this long letter have I told you one thing which has made you happy? May the Lord bless and keep you safe from harm is the constant, never ceasing prayer of your devoted wife. Dearly beloved, suffering, immeasurably precious love, with many kisses from my spirit, farewell again. May God protect his own as he did Daniel.

                                                            V. Davis

Varina Davis to Jefferson Davis

Jewett's first name was really Cornell. The *Clyde* was the dilapidated old steamer that bore the captured President and his family from Savannah to Fort Monroe in May.

Nov. 13th 1865

My dear Husband,

Robert has been persuaded by a person yclept Colorado Jewett to go abroad with him, but offers to come at any time that I desire to have him return. Ma had a letter from him a few weeks ago in Paris. I shall consider what to do before he returns there, from which they had departed before I received the letter. He has been for many months inordinately desiring of travel and excitement. Ma says he was very dutiful and they had an entirely friendly time of it, but that idleness was doing him more harm than his presence was doing good. He had a theory about travel, and it was as well to exhaust it before we might need him. Just now he could not assist me materially, and Mr Colorado Jewett seems to expect to return about the middle of January.

The dreary, dreary days, and weeks, and months—I grow hard & sullen with sorrow.

I am very sad tonight and very tired. Hearing that Mr Schley's family were all ill I came back here to help nurse them, and have been on my feet all day, three of the four ladies in the family are ill. I took the precaution not to sleep in the night air, shut our windows habitually, therefore am better than anyone else. But the southern climate is a fearful one to me. This summer it hurt me often to breathe. I became sleepless—for weeks at a time I sewed until nearly daylight and then could not sleep. But with the cool weather this nervous excitability has decreased.

Since I wrote, Maggie's letter came telling me of the change from Chambly to Montreal two or three houses off from W. Preston Johnston, who looks after them. They are boarding with a Mrs Wadsworth, have a private table & parlor, the whole four for $80 a month—very cheap is it not, for good board such as they get?

If you only could know what an awful responsibility I feel, without your counsel, your decision. I always knew where the glory and pride of my house lay, but never until now how entirely the strength was in the possession of the cause of the other two. Twenty-one years of happy dependence upon the wisdom and love of another so much better and wiser does not fit one to stand alone.

My darling Husband, my dear suffering love, I do try so hard, and succeed so poorly to be patient. But the effort becomes more and more difficult. If we are not to be reunited, may God take me to himself. Keep up your strength by every means—try to imagine I am with you at mealtimes. Eat and sleep if you can for your wife and children, who so love you, so reverence and admire you. I oftenest now see you as you looked in the music room twenty-two years gone—and as you came to me from Mexico first, but then the dearer old face looks on me with the eyes of quiet fortitude which shone on the *Clyde*. [*The rest is lost.*]

Judah P. Benjamin to Varina Davis

Paris, 16th November 1865

My dear Mrs Davis

Your most welcome letter of 9th ulto. was forwarded to me here from London, and while I am greatly relieved to hear of your being in the enjoyment of a hospitable home, and of the diminished rigors of Mr Davis' Confinement, I could not repress the swelling indignation caused by the narrative of the shameful and barbarous treatment to which you as well as your husband have been subjected. The theme however is too hateful and repulsive to be dwelt upon, and I pass to other matters more interesting to you at the present time.

I wrote to Mr. McRae, who is in London, upon the subject of the investment of the money, and we are both decidedly of opinion, that it will not do to send it across the water for the present. Mr. McRae will therefore proceed to invest it at once to the best advantage, and will write to you directly on the subject, for which purpose I have given him your address. His former letter to you with enclosure of £200, was sent by Mr D. F. Kenner, and as he has arrived safely and is pardoned, we cannot guess what obstacle has prevented his sending you the money. If you get a

chance of sending a message to him by a confidential person, there
is no doubt he would send you the remittance, which is worth in
greenbacks about $1400.

A few weeks ago I was astounded by a visit from, guess whom!
Robert. He told me he had gone with your children to Canada,
and then finding that he could no longer be useful, and that yr
mother was unable to support him, he looked about for temporary
service, and accepted the offer of Cornell Jewett to bring him over
to Europe with him, but on the express understanding that he was
to go back to his master, the moment he was permitted to do so,
or as soon as his master recovered his liberty. He seemed very
faithfully attached to Mr Davis and gave me details about yourself,
and the children. He came in Company with Mr Jewett, and when
I asked him where you were, he said he did not know, but after
he and Jewett had left the room, Robert returned and told me
where you were, saying that he did not like to tell me before
Jewett not knowing whether it was prudent to do so. This little
circumstance made on me an impression strongly in Robert's favor.
He was dressed up like a gentleman, wore kid gloves, etc. etc., but
did not seem in the least degree altered in his respectful and quiet
demeanor.

In relation to your suggestion about my writing something in
refutation of the slanders and calumnies relative to the disposal
of the public moneys that were on the wagon train, and to the
alleged cause of the failure of negotiations at Hampton Roads, I
have consulted with one or two valued and tried friends, and they
all concur with me in opinion that *this is not the time* to discuss
such issues; that it would do more harm than good. You have however seen perhaps the letter I published in the "Times" on the subject of the infamous accusation that Mr. Davis was using cruel
treatment towards prisoners of war as matter of public policy. This
letter was intended to vindicate him before the public opinion of
Europe, and I think had a very good effect that way, but nothing
can *at present* be written by *me*, that would do him any good in
the U.S. You will comprehend why I have underscored some words.
The time will come when even in the U.S. my written Statements
will be read and *believed* in spite of all the Stephens in the Country.

My wife and daughter are both well, the latter having entirely
recovered from her malady of ten years' standing, and I am enjoying a few weeks of sweet repose with my family after such a long

and terrible trial and separation as we have undergone. When I first came over I was almost penniless, but very fortunately a merchant friend, a neutral, in whose possession I had placed some cotton, succeeded in sending out to me a hundred bales, which, arriving at the highest Liverpool prices, gave me about $20,000. I am therefore above want for some years and in the mean time am making up my mind what to do. I had intended entering the English bar, but if, as seems probable, I cannot do so without a novitiate of two or three years at the Inns of Court, I shall have to try something else. I am offered a position in a financial Company now about to be formed, for the purpose of advancing money to the Southern planters and Companies, and so I may in this way be of some service to my poor unhappy Country. It is not improbable I may turn my business habits to account in that way—

I am delighted to hear of the good health of the children, and doubt not that they have been under Providence the instrument by which you have been saved from utter prostration under your trials. Take good care of your own health, my dear Mrs. Davis, and be assured that isolated as you now feel yourself, there are thousands of affectionate hearts that are yearning in sympathy for you, and that would shrink from no sacrifice to be of use to you or to my beloved friend, your husband.

Ever yours most truly
J. P. Benjamin

P.S. Among friends deeply solicitous about you, I should mention Gen John Preston and his wife and daughter, whom I saw in London a few weeks ago & with whom I had a long talk about you. Also Gen William Preston, who made the voyage with me from St Thomas to Southampton.

Varina Davis to Jefferson Davis

[*Fragment of a letter presumably of November, 1865. The beginning and end are missing.*]

I do not know how much of public matters I may tell you—if I only tell what I know it will be a very small bit of information. But Mr Speed can cut these sheets off if they are not permitted.

The people accepted their situation in the beginning of their defeat with a unanimity which I confess surprised me. They attested their faith by the purchase of everything in which our country is lacking, they looked forward so hopefully to the restoration of Civil law, that they were cheerful. But since that hope has been deferred indefinitely, they look wretched, unhappy and talk as if death were at every man's door to greet his exit. The discharged new soldiers and indeed those in commission are everyday in different parts of this state, I hear also in others, perpetrating deeds without names. Murders and arson are added to them frequently.

For my part, I have found the negroes uniformly civil to me, but then I am very careful and solicitous not to give offence and I have a white servant. I employed a colored mantua maker to sew for me by the day, and she told me she would not mind marrying a Reb, but that the field cracker who rented a house in her Mother's yard said she would not have one if he offered himself a thousand times. This is a sample of their train of thought. They have such a contempt for the free school system they say their children shall not go to school with the poor whites and those colored children who "are raised up every which way." So much for the animus. I feel so sorry for the poor things. Their children die in the most dreadful manner—women from Mr Schley's place have lost as many as six children since "freedom came." And the country swarms with those who are too poor to wear clothing, only fluttering rags cover them. They grin, chatter, flirt, fight, camp out & drink to keep themselves warm. This is no Utopia, but perhaps it is the chaos out of which (after as long a period shall elapse as the Geologists say God's six days were) will be developed the most perfect and freest type of man. May the Lord have mercy upon these whose flesh and blood and bones are to form the strata for the rising generation's glorious foundations.

Varina Davis to Jefferson Davis

In late October John Mitchel, the third political prisoner incarcerated with Davis and Clement Clay at Fort Monroe, had been allowed to take leave of the ex-President when he himself was released. He had written Mrs. Davis that he found her husband behind bars in a dressing gown and "looking haggard." "But when he dresses to go out he looks well, steps as firmly and holds his head as high as he ever did on Capitol Square."

[*The beginning and end of this letter are missing.*]

[Georgia, November, 1865]

In Memoriam seems written for me in the depth and fullness of its love and veneration for the blessed object. But it does not do for me to begin to write of the love which has been yours from my immature girlhood steadily increasing to my gnarled and well-nigh leafless middle age.

I knew that you were suffering again from boils, the papers tell me everything. Tell me if you have enough warm clothes. I know you have a new overcoat. Mr. Mitchell wrote to me the particulars of your appearance and so very handsome and kind a letter that I must write and tell how I value it. I have heard nothing from Mrs. Clay which has astonished me not a little—I do not even know where she is. Dear Mr. Clay I hope will soon be better. I am so glad you received your cigars and liked them.

I must believe that the good God has much in store for us, and oh, if He only decrees that I should have once the real home life which has been the ignis fatuus which has lured me in cheerful submission through one political bog and then another, always looking for the sunny green bank upon which we might rest and pray, work and see its fruition. If I have loved and followed faithfully the soldier and statesman, it was because I first loved the man.

Jefferson Davis to Varina Davis

F. Monroe 21 Nov. 65

My dear Wife

I have the happiness to acknowledge yours of the 7th Inst. God be praised for your welfare and for the kind friends He has drawn around you in the day of your affliction.

To make the best of the existing condition is alike required by patriotism and practical sense. The negro is unquestionably to be at last the victim; but it is possible to defer the conflict and to preserve a part of the kind relations heretofore existing between the races, when a life-long common interest united them. The object is worthy all the effort. To be successful, the policy must be as far removed from the conservatism that rejects everything new, as from the idealism which would retain nothing which is old. If catch-words determine who shall mould the institutions and administer the affairs of the Southern States—the deluge. Though neither a spectator nor an actor, a life spent more in the service of my country than in that of my family, leaves me now unable to disengage myself from the consideration of public interests.

Let me renew the caution against believing the statements of correspondents in regard to me. To calumniate a state prisoner and thus either gratify or excite hatred against him, is an old device, and never was a fairer opportunity presented to do so without the fear of contradiction than is offered in my case.

November 22d. It is six months since we parted, and I know no more of the purpose in regard to me than I did then. Measured by painful anxiety for you and your helpless charge, these months are to me, many, many years. From the anguish and doubly painful trial, because I could learn nothing of you, I have extracted the consolation of increased pride and fully sustained confidence.

I do take care of my health; the motives you enumerate are ever before me; and others, of which you are less apt to think furnish me the strongest inducements to desire life and strength to vindicate my conduct, at least to posterity, and for my family.

My dear Wife, how I long once more to speak or even write to you without restraint. But let us not repine for what we have not. Shut out from the ever changing world I live in the past with a vividness only thus to be accounted for. All the events of all the years of our love rise before me and bear witness how very dear you are to your Husband

Jeffn. Davis

Jefferson Davis to Varina Davis

Sunday 26 Nov. 1865

My dear Wife,

Many thanks to you for your letter of the 16th Inst. and its enclosure, the letter of my beloved daughter. Sweet is it to witness her filial tenderness, but very sad to see such evidence of her anxiety for me. I hope you have written to her encouragingly, and that she will look forward to my coming as an event which will bring her relief. Today as I read the service it was ever in my mind that the same words were prompting the same thoughts to you as to me. You I hope had the benefit of association with church members, and that union of prayer the value of which can only be realized by those who have been deprived of it. Though God is omnipresent and his love enables us to look up to him with trust; though we are taught that the lonely sinner is sought after by the good shepherd, and that he will rejoice in bringing him back to the fold; the heart even in its least expressible feeling profits by communion with those who sympathize.

Little Polly seems to think she has charge of her Brothers and to feel the solicitude of mature years. She will I am sure be all you expect if allowed to mature as designed by her nature.

The dressing gown you sent, the night shirts and other things are a great comfort to me. The mark on the handkerchiefs no fingers save yours could make.

I have nothing yet in regard to the course to be taken in my case. The newspapers have recently represented that I am to be tried to test the doctrine on which I acted & against it establish the authority of the general government. The question involved has been the basis of political division in the United States since the second year of the Administration of the eldest Adams, it was earnestly and fully discussed in the Colonial times, and reached back through European history to the reign of King Solomon's son. Many men have died for it, but this condemnation was not accepted as a decision concluding the question.

Since my last letter, a friend has sent to me "Schönberg Cotta Family," my eyes cause me to read at intervals, otherwise I found it so interesting that it would have tempted me to read through it without intermission. For relief to the eyes I frequently change the type. Have now Humboldt's *Cosmos,* Irving's *Washington* and Allison's *Marlborough* from the post library. My Bible, Prayer Book and a Dictionary of the Bible are my endless resource.

I am better than when I lately wrote to you. The drier & purer air of my room has caused much improvement in my health since leaving the casemate, and since Dr. Craven has furnished me with food nothing which is necessary has been wanting. You cannot be content, yet you may be assured that I am as well as circumstances permit. Let not imaginary evils distress you. Farewell my dearest. Soon I hope the truth will suppress error and calumny and restore me to you. Your Husband

Jeffn. Davis

Varina Davis to Jefferson Davis

John Reagan, Stephen R. Mallory, George Davis, and James Seddon were all members of President Davis's Cabinet. George Davis, last Attorney General, is still in prison.

Mill View
Nov. 27th 1865

My very dear Husband

Though I wrote to you very recently I write to enclose you Jeff's letter. His school-mistress tells me that he is very truthful and loveable. I enclose her letter. The Archbishop of Halifax urges that I shall send Jeff to him to educate, and he will put him to school at any college in Canada or England to which I prefer to send him— and this offer is made with a warmth which is delightful. Maggie also is to be schooled if I wish it in the same manner. God has been very good to us. The Catholic clergy have been so good to me I love the sight of one.

Mr. Reagan passed through here yesterday. I saw him, and he spoke very affectionately of you. He left Mr. Mallory in very bad health. George Davis is in Fort Lafayette; Mr. Seddon in Pulaski. Mrs Seddon is as old fashioned a wife as I am and thinks her husband improves with time.

May the Lord bless & keep you, darling, may the virtuous, self-sacrificing life which you have led be your shield as Christianity has been the banner under which you have fought & suffered is the prayer of

devotedly,
Your Wife

Maggie Davis to Her Father

The presents from the Archbishop of Halifax are owned today by Maggie's grandson, Joel Webb, a banker of Colorado Springs.

> Nov. 30th 1865
> Sacred Heart
> Sault au Récollet

My precious Father

It gave me great pleasure when I found out that I could write to you for I have written to you before but my letters have been intercepted but that does not prevent me from writing to you now.

Darling Father, I will now tell you about the children—dear little Billie is so changed that you would not know him for he is so good and looking so well and Jeff is the same way and so is dear Grandma and Aunty, and Jeff and Billie send much love to you and many kisses dear Father. All I want in this convent is you and sweet Mother and sweet little Pie Cake, for I am treated so kind precious Father.

The Arch Bishop of Halifax came to the convent and was very kind to me and in remembrance of you gave me some beautiful presents which consisted of a prayer book which was butifully bound with Ivory and the clasp is pure Silver, and he also gave me a pretty little gold Cross, it is set with rubies and in the centre is a emerald. Precious Father I send you these little pictures with more affection than I can express. Precious Father please write to me soon. I went home the other day for a congé and while I was there it snowed and Grandma let Billie go out to play in it and when he came in he wanted to know why God made the snow and Grandma told him to make the earth moist so that when Fruit came it would be good and also the people could skate. Precious Father if you are allowed please send us your picture and some of your hair. I have the ribbon for good behaveiour, and my Mistress said that she was very much pleased with me for she said that I was very good and that I was trying very hard to speak French. My Precious Father I must now stop but I will continure to write to you. All send both love and kisses. Good bye, I remain your most affectionate little Pollie

Maggie H. Davis

Jefferson Davis to Varina Davis

Fortress Monroe, Va. 2nd Dec. 65

My dear Wife,

My days drag heavily on, to what I have no means to direct or to foresee. Having no communication with the outer world, except with you, and in that restricted by the judgement of the Comdg. Officer as to what should be sent, those who choose to falsify my conduct have as safe a task as a slanderer could desire. So freely has advantage been taken of the opportunity even in regard to matters of public record and public notoriety, that you should have known how little you could trust the statements in regard to occurrences in my prison. It is true that nothing happens which does not somehow pass to newspaper correspondents, but as is normally the case with monopolies they abuse their privilege by perverting their knowledge and building a superstructure with but little regard to the foundation. You say the papers tell you every thing, but I warn you that the things they tell are not realities. This example you give will illustrate. The "new overcoat" I have *not* received; though probably when the statement was published on which you relied, at telling at least one fact, it had reached this post. The matter being of such public importance as to have been followed in its progress through the tailor's shop, and down the Bay, the journals may give you the future history before it is known to me. In a late letter I notified you of the arrival of the trunk you sent to me, and I have enough of warm clothes.

My daily walks continue, the hour dependent upon Genl. Miles' engagements, as I only go out when he can be present. Dr. Craven visits me when needful, and his good Wife sees that meals and clean clothes are duly sent to me. Do not make to yourself causeless anxiety, but the rather patiently wait for the fulfilment, believing that an unseen hand is directing our fortune according to the omniscience and infinite mercy which guides and governs all things. He gives us a hope that man cannot destroy, a refuge that man cannot invade; the foretaste of which is the trusting communion of loving hearts, where correspondence superior to the electric is neither limited by the wasting power of space, nor stopped by interposing oceans. Thus can I say to you, "Far off thou art, but ever nigh."

Sunday morning, 3 Dec. 65—The bright sun and mild temperature welcomes the blessed day of rest, which calls the redeemed to meet together, and rejoice. Though formally taking leave of you you will not be left. In the stillness of your quiet hour a Husband's love is around you.

Ever affectionately
Your Husband
Jeffn. Davis

Varina Davis to Jefferson Davis

James Speed is the current Attorney General and one of the censors of the letters that passed between husband and wife.

December, 1865

My dear Old Husband

Through Mr Speed's kindness I am enabled to send you Maggie's last letter.

Wade Hampton came to see me yesterday looking very well, and much younger than when I last saw him. Spoke of you with tearful eyes and distressed voice, but while my eyes brimmed over with tears, so did my heart with thankfulness that you were so well appreciated. All the South Carolina Prestons are gone to Europe. Hampton brought me offers of money & home—the former I am not in need of, the latter my dear old friend Mrs Cobb insists that she has a right to give me. Everyone is so kind that I sometimes wonder if I am sufficiently grateful.

Dear, dear Husband, I pray for you, love you, live for you. Would to God I had died for you if by so doing I could have saved you what you now suffer. Farewell, darling—farewell.

Jefferson Davis to Varina Davis

Fortress Monroe Va. 7th Dec. 65

My beloved Wife,

I am deeply impressed by the kindness of the Bishop, and that of the priests who have so nobly shown their readiness to do their

Master's work in relieving the afflicted and protecting the father-less. They have sent thus the sweetest solace to one in the condition of Him who went down from Jerusalem to Jericho. I feel with you, that God has been very good to us.

Reagan I knew to be a true-hearted, consistent man, and I never gave the least heed to the newspaper reports which attributed to him participation in censorious remarks against me during his confinement at Fort Warren. Some men I had to trust because of the confidence others had in them. When disaster fell upon me their desertion did not surprise me.

I have been reading "Thoughts on Personal Religion," by Dr. Goulburn. His instructions as to prayer have impressed me particularly. When we shall pass into the future state of pure intelligence, so as to judge not by external signs but by the inner motives, how different men will appear to each other from the estimates of their carnal life!

Though my prison life does not give me the quiet of solitude, its isolation as to intercourse affords abundant opportunity for turning the thoughts inward; and if my self-love, not to say sense of justice, would have resisted the reckless abuse of my enemies, I am humbled by your unmerited praise. It teaches me what I ought to be.

My incarceration followed four years of terrible war. The North put forth its whole capacity on land and sea, by ball and bayonet, striving to retain the South in one Government with it; the South strained every nerve to maintain a separate existence. By the newspaper, to-day, I see that the North, as represented in Congress, stands quite united to keep the South *out* of the legislative halls of the Union, and the South, wistfully looking at the closed entrance, stands outside—and then she is told she has all the time been inside.

The bitterness which caused me to be so persistently slandered, has created a sentiment which will probably find vent in Congressional speeches, and test all your Christian fortitude. Remember that the end is not yet. A fair inquiry will show how "false witnesses have risen up against me and laid to my charge things that I knew not of." If you will recall the very early period when I was warned by letter that an emissary had been sent to Montgomery to assassinate me, you will see misconception of my position and a cruel desire for my destruction are not new-born. When the truth is revealed, the more honorable and manly of my enemies will recoil from further association with the others. Truth and the common sense of justice will generally protect the innocent, where the trial is according to the due course of law, and is sure to vindicate the memory of a victim.

December 8th. Another day has succeeded the night. The sun has risen bright, and the cold bracing air invites animal life to activity. To me there is the same monotonous round of prisoner's life in military confinement, such as is not known to the usages of war in cases like mine. I am, however, thankful for the power to bear, and trustful that the power will be given to me to bear in patience.

The sentinel has stamped with such noise, back and forth, in front of me, that until another and more quiet walker comes on, and I recover from the effect produced by the attempt to write under such difficulty, I will desist—.

Somebody writing from Augusta to the *Boston Advertiser* makes an extraordinary statement about a letter said to have been written to someone in Columbus, by Mr. A. H. Stephens, immediately after the Hampton Roads conference—containing the assertion that terms not humiliating to the South could be obtained, but that I and my principal advisers did not want peace. Of course Mr. S. could not have said anything of the sort, as he had been twice employed to seek peace, and on the last occasion, made a report, written and oral, showing that no negotiation would be entertained.

There has been certainly much zeal displayed in the planting and cultivating of prejudice against me, but many of the stories are so absurd that it required a morbid state of opinion to receive them.

"Dobbin" [Preston Johnston] always was sterling; his father and his mother were pure gold. Tell him how gratefully I recognize his care for my children. On the whole, it must be more comfortable to be the deceived than the deceiver. Sometimes I feel that there is a real compliment in the trust displayed by some of my slanderers, to whom it must occur that with a single breath, I could topple over the miserable fabric their selfishness is making.

Farewell, my dear Wife. If as appears to be indicated I am turned over to the civil authorities the chance to see you and to prepare for my defense by intercourse with counsel will probably be better than now. May God bless me again with the sight of you, and may He guide and protect you.

Ever affectionately, your Husband
Jeffn. Davis

Varina Davis to Jefferson Davis

The members of a secret revolutionary brotherhood, the Fenian Society, established in New York about 1858 for the purpose of freeing Ireland from England, were agitating in Montreal, and Davis was disturbed about his children's welfare and schooling.

[*The beginning and end of the letter are missing.*]

[Dec. 14, 1865]

The letter I send you from our darling Pollie is my best comfort in the course I thought myself obliged to adopt with regard to the children. At the time they left me, I did not sleep an hour in the night, and I was so frantically nervous that the sound of the little boys crying the Newspaper extras nearly made me faint, and I was not a proper guardian for them. I could not bear them to speak aloud. Do not fear that she will not be developed. The nuns, I think, just suit her temperament. They would have suited me in the affluence of love by which they control through gratitude. Jeff needed a little hard rubbing, but as usual he is a favorite with his teacher. The Bishop of Halifax's offers to Jeff remain to me a great comfort, because a certainty of education for him.

Dec. 18th. I am so happy I have yours of the 7th too. You ask me about the shirts. They were not stolen, Robert took them. I suppose in that same way that he took all your thick clothes, and such like things, not secretly, but announcing that he would be better with them and you could get more. I expect the fact was he did not like to ask for money from Ma's scanty store to buy himself such things, and desired to dress on his European tour. Mr Benjamin writes me that he saw Robert in Paris with Mr Jewett —"dressed quite like a gentleman in handsome clothes, kid gloves, etc—otherwise unchanged in his quiet respectful demeanor."

I think the Fenian affair is of very little importance viewed as bearing upon our children, though I have taken precautions. Lennoxville and Sault au Récollet are both so far from Montreal that they would probably be uninterrupted, and where could I find for the poor hunted creatures an asylum so near to me? Their lives were saved by a gentleman's coming up unexpectedly to their aid in Savannah, else a negro Sentinel would have shot Jeff. I think like you that there is imminent danger of an insurrection here. The negroes speak of it openly. So that I hope helpless women and children may be protected. I shall go in town either to Athens or to Augusta for the holidays.

I have been every day hoping for leave to go to my children or to you, as Mr President Johnson stated that there was no purpose to torture me, but so far have heard nothing, and counselled by my best friends in the North that an effort to relieve my maternal anxiety or perform my maternal duties will bring upon my head dire punishment. I do not know what—some say a termination to my leave to correspond with you, my dearest and my first object. Here am I. Here will I remain until the great end of the constitutional government of a great and free country be answered by my restriction like yourself. It is possible for me to be reticent of complaint—if it is obligatory, nay, necessary, to bear, but I bleed inwardly. By the division of our household, of course, my scanty means are further depleted. Then you know how necessary I am to our family in the matter of a balance wheel—though your motive power is better than mine.

Varina Davis to Jefferson Davis

Dr. Charles Minnegerode, Rector of St. Paul's in Richmond, had been allowed to administer Holy Communion to Davis in prison on December 11.

The "little man" was Joseph Evan Davis, aged five, who fell to his death from a balcony at the Executive Mansion in Richmond in April, 1864.

Prospect Hill, Georgia
Dec. 25th 1865

My dear suffering Husband,

May this day be filled with spiritual comfort, may the eye of faith be granted to you by which you can see the past glories which were opened to us by the birth of the little child who 1865 years ago "All meanly wrapt in Swathing bands, And in a manger laid."

Thank God that Mr. Minnegerode administered to you the blessed

Sacrament of his body and blood from which you have been so long debarred—and I humbly pray that it has proven to you that support & comfort which is promised to those who let it to their salvation. How my heart yearns over you! How far above the Jewels and kingdoms would I treasure the permission to kiss your dear hands even through the prison bars this day. It goes hard to be denied access to my children and to my Husband too. Yet while you love me, while you exist, nothing is too hard to bear. But if any thing happens to you—I cannot, I cannot— May God have mercy upon me, and guard you safely for me. I am nervous, I suppose—so I will wait until I can write calmly.

Last Christmas we had a home, a country, and our children— and yet we would not be comforted, for our "little man" was not. [*Tears have made a sentence scarcely legible.*]

You tell me you think I do not understand the kind of forgiveness which we are to exercise. I do not if it is required of me to pray for those who despitefully use you. For those who willingly afflict you and *torture you with bee stings,* with petty malignity, because you are in their power, I cannot find in my heart a prayer. I pray God that some change in the disposition of the forces may relieve you of those who desire to do you harm. If not, I do not want the person so annoying you to go to Heaven—and I cannot help saying so even if it is not religious. It is a great sorrow to hate, and a very intense feeling when the object so detested is powerful and the sufferer powerless. You have ere this seen that Christmas away from you has depressed me so that I will try to write more pleasantly for fear that you may share my feelings.

Temporarily I have left Mr Schley's house in the abundance of my caution. His brightest and most accomplished daughter, the only one with administrative capacity, went to Baltimore upon a visit, took scarlet fever and died in four days illness. This frightened me, as young Dr Schley was on his way home with his bride and would bring the corpse with him, so I moved over to the next neighbors, Mr J. S. Wright's house—there to remain until I go to Athens. I am a good deal at Mill View in the evenings, because it seems to comfort the poor stricken Father to see me.

Dec. 28th. My friend Mr Schley talks of going in a few weeks to New Orleans en route to Texas and going to settle there. His daughters are very averse to going, but really nothing could be worse than this country is. A youth, a son of one of Mr Schley's cousins, was found by his Father murdered in his store. Gentlemen are shot down all over the country by the colored soldiers. Murder and theft are rampant. Every man sleeps upon his arms. I went to town a few days ago, and as the carriage passed a negro orderly who was passing on the side of the road caught my eye, and deliberately made a mocking gesture and a face at me. The merchants who are bringing goods here, and beginning the world anew with great hopes of success, have stopped work, afraid to risk a stock of goods. Imagination cannot conceive out of the Fiji Islands a more insecure tenure for life or property.

I thank God on my knees for the cloud which directed me the day I sent my poor little boys away from danger. A quarrel with a negro child caused by the negro snatching a toy from its hand, which the white child's Father reclaimed from the negro, brought to the rescue two negro soldiers, who, finding that the white man had help, desisted, but came back with twenty more at night and were only prevented from murdering him by his barring his doors and sending secretly for the police, whom the negroes mistook for the colored guard from the arsenal and ran away. Every day there is a fight somewhere—every night several robberies. And now that it has been decided the helpless and the infirm shall not be removed from the plantations until their relations decide that they can support them, the planters think of leaving them the plantations. Freedom may be a good thing, but its bark sails on a sea of blood and tears, to say nothing of treasure over which this flood rolls.

I hesitated about going in to town for safety, but the country seems safer. Of course I shall go to Canada whenever I can get permission to do so, but that seems as far off as ever.

I have a late letter from Mr Benjamin in which he speaks so kindly of you.

I enclose you a letter from poor little Jeffy D. He was passing quietly through Portland when he was arrested, and thrown into Fort Warren, without any covering except one blanket to keep him warm. The poor child is brave-hearted though wretched as you see. He does not know what he has done, but he does know that those who arrested him robbed him of every thing on earth he had except the suit on his back.

The children and Ma are now quite well. Robert has returned to New York, and will, I hope, be soon with me.

Do try to eat—to sleep—for my sake. Do you want a shade made for your eyes to keep the light from them? Perhaps I can invent one.

But I lose my sense and reason when I think of you in prison. May the lord bless and keep you safe from harm and make me in some measure worthy of your great virtues is the prayer of your devoted—

Wife

Jefferson Davis to Varina Davis

Fortress Monroe 30th Dec. 1865

My dear Wife,

Yours of the 14 Inst. enclosing that of our little Daughter reached me yesterday.

The Preference you express for mythical symbols over your own idealities masks a happy state of realization which I cannot communicate. Indeed one of the difficulties usually met when I attempt to express an opinion on a metaphysical subject, is the inappropriateness of language drawn from material objects to describe spiritual things; so much the more is this the case in regard to pictorial representations. The artist in his working nature mingles with my contemplation of his study. Living souls devoutly offering praise to God present spirituality supreme over matter; and it is perhaps therefore that the simple singing of an excited congregation of Methodists has stirred in my heart a deeper devotional feeling than the noble ceremonial of the High Mass with all the brilliant surroundings which in the richly endowed Cathedrals are associated with it. All modes of Christian worship are in themselves good, they are the different kind of roads suited to the great variety of travellers, and why not to the different faiths?

I am glad under any restraints to be able to write to you, and it is for me only to accept the terms which are imposed and leave others to judge whether they are properly observed. I should write more freely if I knew that the Atty. Genl. *only* inspected my letters, but as I send them open and don't know how they are forwarded, and do know that objections have been made here to the contents of a letter enclosed to the Atty. Genl., I have to conclude that they are read before they reach him and may be stopped on the way.

Write as I may, or if not at all, you will still know how truly I am, as these many years I have been, affectionately

Your Husband
Jeffn. Davis

THE PRISON LETTERS,
1866

Jefferson Davis to Varina Davis

Fortress Monroe, Va.
16th Janry. 1866

My dear Wife,

I have this day received your letter of the 25th with enclosure. It does not surprise me that you were sad on the anniversary of a Day which with peculiar force brought to mind the separation of our family and the sad causes which had led to it. Let us train our hearts to feel that these are afflictions given us to direct us in the way to eternal life. Though, of course, we may not with joy accept the severe discipline, we may at least bear it with resignation.

I will be glad when you are removed beyond the reach of the brutal cruelty of such statements and suggestions as those which have so disturbed you. They are crosses which you cannot bear and I have seen in your letters their evil as well as painful effect upon you. By dwelling on them they grow into more than their real importance.

I have feared that our negroes would be disturbed by the introduction of others among them, but could not have imagined that they would be driven away from their home by those pretending to be their especial advocates. What a beast he must have been who turned old Uncle Bob out of his house, to find where he could a shelter for the infirmities of more than a hundred winters. That claim was manifest. Of the truth, fidelity, the piety which had so long secured him the respect of all who knew him, a stranger might plead ignorance.

17th. I have been suffering from neuralgia in the head, and the usual effect upon the eyes causes me to write at intervals. Indeed, considering the circumstances, it is rather to be wondered at that I am not worse. Once a day it is still permitted to me to walk in the open air; and, though the time is brief, the result is beneficial.

In my isolation a daily experience enables me to realize the heart-warming influence of little Winnie's presence with you.

Farewell, dear Wife, there is a great satisfaction in feeling that you know most of that which I *would* write, but do not. May He that will not break a bruised reed guide and comfort you. Your loneliest hour will not be alone, for there is no emotion that does not send my spirit to hover about the object of its dearest affection.

Your Husband
Jeffn. Davis

Varina Davis to Jefferson Davis

This letter is blotted with tears. In spite of her resolutions to write calmly, Varina's emotions would often overcome her.

Prospect Hill, Ga.
Jan 22nd 1866

My very dear Husband,

I see by the papers that you are again in solitary confinement because of a supposed plot on foot to rescue you from Fortress Monroe! Pie and I hoped to rescue you from its gloom if permission had come to go to you—but we are not men of might, though loving perhaps as strongly as such men could fight.

I go in a few days to Athens for an indefinite time. The dear family with whom I am now staying are very kind, very lovely, but I feel since they will take no board that they are too poor to be burthened.

I am expecting Dobbin here daily—he will tell me all I desire to know, and upon his report I will decide as to my future course. No news from our children directly, but indirectly I hear they are well. I am so hungry for their little faces, but what do I feel for yours! If I could be with you once more in freedom or even in imprisonment, I could be happy even leaving them in Canada. The

Lover of my early youth is only less dear than the old Husband of my tortured, bereaved middle age. I can see no way out of our troubles, the vista is so long, the distance makes it so dim. But perhaps I may yet be permitted to see you. I know Mr Speed feels sorry for us, and will beg for me—at least I will believe so—and so hoping will take it for my comfort in the sleepless hours of the night when with Pie's little hand in mine I lie.

God has greatly blessed me with dreams for the last three weeks. When I do get to sleep I dream of sitting by you and counselling with you in our common troubles. I had a queer dream some days ago—I thought that there was a war of the U.S. with England, indeed with all the world, and that we were in Canada, and desperately poor, and that a man came and offered you a command on the English side, and that you rejected it, and that when he went away I asked you to tell me what you felt, and you said I will never be goaded by want into performing the part of a Swiss or Hessian. It was so plain, and I felt so proud and happy to see that no circumstance could debase you. Sometimes these dreams strengthen me—comfort me—and I forget for an hour that I am alone.

I have read nothing since I wrote but the Bible. I can read no History save that of the Jews. It is only in fiction that virtue is rewarded. In History, "virtue is its own reward"—quite a different thing. This is a town of traders, they do not read, they do not care for books consequently there is no book store of even tolerable availability.

Dear Husband, if I have ever offended you, and I have been often willful and irritable, oh forgive your poor old wife for her great love's sake. It is such a comfort to me to tell you that I beg your pardon for everything I have ever done wrong or disagreeable to you—and how grateful I am to God that I am your wife, and may love as much as I please. All my words seem so faint when I express my love in them. All my prayers seem so weak when I strive with God. But I become incoherent, and do not tell how the torrent of loving memory sweeps away all restraints and barriers between us. A lingering longing, loving farewell to you, my precious good Husband.

W

Excuse these tear blots and love them—

Jefferson Davis to Varina Davis

F. Monroe Va. 28 Jany 66

My dear Wife

Yours of the 17th Inst with the photograph is received. I am grateful for both, though I cannot say that the likeness is satisfactory. There is another one which is not carried in the pocket, not to be seen of others and of fadeless tints, which is better than all of these. That one can neither be destroyed or stolen, it shines by its own light, is always present and visible.

Mrs. Clay is still here and, as I learn, daily visits her Husband. I am indebted to her for several kind attentions in the way of comestibles and for a photograph of herself in evening wrap. The fact of her husband's continued stay here shows the failure of her main purpose in visiting Washington. But her visit is said to have benefitted her Husband.

Trying as it may be, you will have to make the effort to leave me, for the present, out of all your plans; and may our Heavenly Father strengthen your heart for the difficult task of filling the place of both parents to our children.

29th. Oh, that the law-makers had facts instead of suggestions on which to base their action in regard to the Southern States. Fear not what man can do; it is God disposes. Now I am shut up and slander runs riot to destroy my fair repute, but any investigation must redeem my character and leave it for an inheritance to my children, which in after-times they will not be the worse for possessing. The treatment I have received will be compared with my treatment of others, and it will be the reverse of the picture my enemies have drawn. Conscious rectitude is a great support to the sufferer, whatever may be the form or the end of the afflictions.

Farewell my much long loved Wife. Every hope, every pain, every speculative thought whether of organic or inorganic bodies brings to me the want of your presence.

Do not lose the advantage you have of communion with others to turn your thoughts from the sad memory of our separation.

Once more, dearest Winnie, farewell. All of love unspoken your

heart will suggest as felt by mine. Ever affectionately praying for
our reunion in peace and safety, I am

Your Husband
Jeffn. Davis

Varina Davis to Jefferson Davis

Mrs. Davis has received permission to visit her children in Canada.

Perhaps Varina is referring to her childish anguish when she caused
her grandmother Kempe's home to be burned to the ground by fearfully
putting a flaming broom into a clothes closet after she had accidentally
set it afire when sweeping a hearth. Her father had early begun deplet-
ing her mother's inheritance by business ventures that proved ruinous.
In 1848, '49, and '50, the young Varina quarreled with Joseph E. Davis,
the brother Jefferson idolized, and she was uncertain whether her
husband would side with her or his old brother.

Feb 2nd 1866, Ga.

My darling Husband,

Your two letters of 16th and 26th reached me within a day of
each other—the latest first. The account of your suffering touched
me to the soul. Are you restricted in a greater degree than heretofore as to food? What do you get? Tell me exactly how cooked. I
know kind Mr. Speed will do what he can for me. I believe to him
is due a permit to go to Canada, which I received through him three
days ago.

Until to-day I have been very very anxious about the children
only because I knew nothing about them, and Dobbin spoke in
mystical language, and hinted at things of which he wished to talk.
My excited fancy, the silence, induced my interpretation I presume.
Ma's letter is very pleasant. Margaret never writes. This is bitter
to me—but I presume it is the thoughtlessness of youth—at least
I will not complain. May the good Lord never so afflict her that
she will repentantly and unavailingly revert to my long vigils of
unnecessary doubts and fears with keen regret. Hers has been a
very sheltered, unchecked life. The adversity and anguish of my
youth was good for me. I thank God that I can see it so. In
looking back from my present "winter of discontent" over the gulf
between me and my clouded youth, especially the winter and

summer of 48 & 49 & 50, I find that I do not suffer so fiercely and keenly—now that I am certain the possessor of that doubt of which I then despaired in my own right. Every hour I thank God for its possession. Dearly beloved, protector of my youth, joy of all the sentient years of my life, be not "bowed down by anxiety for your wife and children."

My darling Husband, you know that I can bear up in trouble, that I have a heart single to you. You must remember that I have suffered when weak and untrained, young and alone, deeper anguish and did not faint by the wayside. I shall not now. I will try to do what is right even though it slay me, and God will strengthen me to do it aright.

So far my health is very much improved. I am about now as well as usual to me, though not as strong from the want of exercise which it is hard to take now, because the country is so unsettled that ladies are afraid to walk in the woods or paths or even in the public roads because of the vagrant lawless negroes—unless in the broad sunlight, or with a gentleman.

After very mature deliberation I have determined to go to New Orleans first, thence to Vicksburg, and Jackson, and from the river by way of Louisville on North. I shall thus be on the spot in consultation with Brother Joe, who will explain all his views to me, and hear mine.

In starting on this journey alone "I feel not the least alarm." No son of our soil "will offer me harm." I shall call on any man of our people to help me, confident of answering action. I have a very trusty man engaged to go with me—a negro—he used to be upon Genl Beauregard's personal staff—and says he "saw and greatly admired" you at your last visit to the army of the West. He is a negro of the tall, straight, muscular race of Ham—a very accomplished servant and begs of me not to consider wages, "for Madam, if you never get your rights I shall have had the great pleasure of serving you and I know you will pay me then if you get them." His name is Frederick McGinnis. Nothing from Robert either by letter or otherwise.

I will make your eye-shade tomorrow, I have no blue cambric now. I will make you two and send them to you and one will be for night, the other for day. I could not bear to keep you waiting for the letter until I could get the shade done.

May the Lord bless you, darling, and keep you. May God keep my precious treasure. My Lover, Husband, benefactor, guide, strength and honor, my only love, farewell.

Your own
Winnie

Jefferson Davis to Varina Davis

Fortress Monroe, Va.
February 3, 1866

My dear Wife,

Men turn to the judgment of posterity for the reversal of the decree of their contemporaries.

The newspapers will have informed you of the petition in my behalf by seven thousand ladies of Richmond and vicinity. It was not ineffectual; it refreshed my burdened heart as the shower revives a parched field.

Like you, I feel sorry for the negroes. What has been done would gradually and measurably be corrected by the operation of the ordinary laws governing the relation of labor to capital, if they were let alone. But interference by those who have a theory to maintain by the manufacture of facts, must result in evil, evil only and continually.

At every renewal of the assertion that the Southern people hate the negroes, my surprise is renewed; but a hostility, not now or heretofore existing, between the races may be engendered by just such influences as are indicated.

On the night of the 13th I was sitting before the fire, because I could not sleep, and had a startling optical illusion, such you know as were common to me in fever; but to my vision, I saw little Pollie walk across the floor and kneel down between me and the fire in the attitude of prayer. I moved from consequent excitement and the sweet vision melted away. I have not called it a dream, because not conscious of being asleep, but sleep has many stages, and that only is perfect sleep which we call Death.

To use your expressive phrase, I am hungry for the children's little faces, and have habitually to resist the power of tender feelings which may not be gratified. I look only to those hopes of which man cannot deprive me, and to such relief as a record may afford.

Farewell, my much loved wife. Affectionately,

Your Husband
Jeffn. Davis

Varina Davis to Jefferson Davis

The eyeshade, in which the eyes were masked and the only holes were for the nostrils, proved a boon indeed; for the lamp still burned all night in Davis's prison room.

Feb. 8th 1866

My darling Husband

I am so triumphant about my shades for your eyes. I have succeeded in making you a cloth mask for night which if you adjust the nostrils aright, excludes *every ray* of light so that you may lie down in it in the day. The other, day-shade, I covered with cambric because I feared the silk would stain your forehead, and I made it as light as I could—the strings of the mask must be crossed behind and tied in front of your head. Would to God that I could so cover your "defenseless head." It has been such a pleasure to me to contrive them. If they suit I shall thank God for my success.

I was wretched about you, the reports of your rapidly failing health make my blood stand still. Husband, anything but this—I cannot bear this. Even Heaven does not console me for the prospect. Dear beloved, saintly Husband, hope—and expect—as I do. If I could come to you my sensibilities would be so deadened by joy that I should see everything pleasant; because you were there. In my day before yesterday's letter I told you that I could go now—and every thing else.

Harrison is released, and they telegraphed me to know if I would meet him in Washington or here. I telegraphed him that I should go to Missi first and desired him to come to go with me—shall hear tomorrow the result.

I am in constant penance because I see that I have distressed you. Dobbin says upon the whole the children are well taken care of. His first letter nearly drove me wild because it seemed to me to be full of hints of evil which he could tell me when he saw me, and then express fully. He used to wring me up just so about

Congress and I ought to have remembered it, but got to crying, and walking up and down with "itty Paie" and then wrote to you, my rock of defence and haven of refuge.

I shall leave here to go South and do what I can there, and then go to the children, take apartments at Lennoxville or at Sault au Recollet—as at present advised.

I enclose you a letter from Mrs. Cobb—to warm your heart as it did mine. I shall go by Athens, stop two days and tell Mr Cobb my affairs, and take advice.

This month brings to my heart many delightful though sad memories, the long walks in the Hurricane garden with their rose borders—and mockingbirds—and your sweet voice in my ear as we walked, and talked of our future when we should be married, and at home—and how I sneered at old married people when they told me I should even love you better than then—and how I used to see you dash by the carriage so free and strong and think you the strongest and most helpful of men.

Now I know you are the dearest, the purest and best of men—and love you so much better than then that it seems to me wonderful to compare that feverish childish passion with this waking certainty.

God bless you and good bye.

Devotedly your prayerful wife,

W.

Jefferson Davis to Varina Davis

Lize Mitchell is the granddaughter of Joseph Davis. In later life she preferred "Lise" to "Lize."

Ft. Monroe, Va. 17th Feby. '66

My dear Wife,

My last letter to you was directed to Macon and this will be addressed to the same place as the time of your movements is not so definitely stated as to enable me to select another place as more likely to be appropriate. I am very glad to have my big boy's likeness and that of my dear little Lize, dear to me as if she were my own daughter and nearer to me if that be possible than heretofore by the sad traces which care has left on her childlike face.

The suffering of all nearest and dearest to me deadens the pain I should otherwise feel because of my own condition. Oftentimes the question occurs to me, would the spirit of vengeance be satiated by my sacrifice so that my family and countrymen would then be left in peace. If so, I trust my past life will bring others to the conclusion that is embodied in the mental answer I have so often made, and that those who would mourn me longest would least expect or desire me to shrink from the purchase.

You will know how to tell my Brother of my anxieties for him, and constant affection.

Sometimes the mind becomes diseased by long dwelling on a given subject, sometimes shut out from observation it turns inwards with a force before unknown and sees more in darkness than it did in light.

Kiss my baby. You cannot write as much as I wish to have of her sayings and doings. Say to my dear relatives and friends somewhat of those things I have written in various letters. I hope you will in meeting find some relief from the isolation you have so worthily borne. May the protector of the defenseless, the refuge of the oppressed, be with you always.

Farewell, dearest Winnie. Nerve your heart to life's trials as you have to its duties, and let us hopefully wait and pray. Again Farewell

Ever devotedly your Husband
Jeffn. Davis

P.S. If Mr Harrison is with you give him my sincere regard, with regret that his faith to me should have brought him so much evil.

Varina Davis to Jefferson Davis

"Burrow" is the pet family name for General Howell Cobb, who had been a United States Senator. Burton Harrison has come to accompany Mrs. Davis to Mississippi and to visit his mother in Oxford.

Macon, Georgia, Feb. 23rd 66

My beloved Husband,

Your dear letter enclosing your hair reached me safely upon my arrival here and cheered me at the threshold even more than the loving reception of my dear friends the Cobbs. They were however affectionate enough to have satisfied the most depressed and unreasonable people. I seemed to feel quite at home once more. My route to Atlanta was marked by no incident. At Atlanta I found our friend here had telegraphed his brother-in-law Col. Glenn to meet me, and I was taken to the Atlanta House where I met the proprietor—he was very attentive. Then a negro man would take nothing for porterage, said tell your good gentleman for me that I have admired him ever since I knowed him, like my Father, as a fine gentleman, and that I would work for you all, but dont want pay. I could not force money upon him.

Since I have been here in Macon we have been very quiet, but all the citizens have called, and they are really a charming class of people, cultured and refined.

Little children come to me to kiss Pie and ask for "dear, dear Mr Davis" and not infrequently their little voices falter, and tears course down their cheeks. This is my comfort—that never man was so beloved, so admired in his sorrow.

I have put off telling you a very painful thing but must do so—my dear Friend Mr Schley is no more. He had returned from Texas, and was not pleased with the country as a residence, had had a chill on the cars. He was very like my dear Father in his faith in men and his habitually soft and kind manner. At his funeral the sobs of his negroes, present in a body, almost drowned the voice of the minister, and the voice of one swelled over the general wail into the exclamation "never one hard word—never one hard word—my best and my only friend is gone—Lord have mercy upon us poor negroes." But I am really unable to write of him quietly. I am sorely grieved at his death.

Speaking of this dear deceased friend and protector brings me to dear Burrow—and to his generous kindness. He scarcely will let me go from him without money—urges it with tears coursing down his face—says "Do let me comfort myself so." But I do not now need it. My wants are few, and my means exceed them. My simple mourning dress and linen collars would not be relinquished if I had Queen Elizabeth's wardrobe—therefore it is useless to accumulate obligations under which I now stagger.

Mr. Harrison has arrived looking quite well, and though he suffered much in his early imprisonment, has recruited under a kind commandant's care. He tells many touching, and many funny stories of Preston Johnston and Governor Lubbock. The former wrote poetry all over the walls of his cell—the latter darned his socks, and cleaned his room, and looked as gentlemanly as he could. *When I see you* I shall tell you many of them. Harrison is a dear, enthusiastic boy—and had decided that he cannot settle down until I am safe in Canada. So he goes South with me the morning of the 27th, and then I shall go to Canada. Every where on the railways we have free passage—so that it costs but little to travel. *I do not despair of seeing you*—after I have seen the children. May the Lord have you in his holy keeping until then.

Varina

Varina Davis to Jefferson Davis

26th Feb. '66

This, my only love, is our wedding day—the saddest and gladdest day of my life contrasted does not leave me so full of cheering thoughts to send you in your deprivaties and restraints. But I can at least thank you for all the high and honorable lustre which you have shed upon me—all the support and love showered upon my family, and how shall I characterise the shield of loving, generous, manly devotion, which has prevented me from feeling the bitter blasts of this hard, stormy world, "commixed and contending." May the church unite our souls in heaven, if man has put us asunder on earth. I thank you every hour of my life for your love—for your bright example, as the source of all temporal happiness to me. In looking back over these last twenty-two years of my life it seems that they absorb the whole brightness and sweetness of my existence. With love unspeakable, dear, beloved Husband, with prayers immeasurable your wife's heart throbs, and thanks God that it is her privilege to suffer and love you.

Devotedly and gratefully
Your wife

Maggie Davis to Her Father

> Sault au Récollet
> Sacred Heart
> March 2nd 1866

My Precious Father

The Bishop came here the other day and he confirmed some of my little companions and it looked so pretty for they were all dressed in white and nice veils on also, and the Bishop had on beautiful cloths which consisted of a nice silk vestment worked in gold thread—on the back was a pretty heart set around with Emeralds and if not Emeralds they were some kind of Precious stones and what was more surprising to me was that he had on a large Mitre made of the same kind of things as the dress and he also had a large gold Pastoral staff in his hand and after he had given us an instruction he put it down and confirmed the girls. He put some ointment on their heads and after that the Mother Superior put a bandage on their heads. They went to their seats and not long after they received communion and then their confirmation was finished. Precious Father, we are all very well and happy and Jeff has gone back to school as well and happy as ever and I hope with the good intention of trying to learn as much as possible and I am of the same intention, Precious Father. I must now tell you Good bye and hoping to meet soon again and by most fervent prayer to our heavenly Father, I hope we may obtain that grace. I remain your most affectionate little Pollie

> Maggie H. Davis

Child of the Sacred Heart

Varina Davis to Jefferson Davis

Varina is visiting Jefferson Davis's nephew, Joseph R. Davis, in Canton, Mississippi. L. Q. C. Lamar, admiring friend of Jefferson Davis and former prominent Confederate, was to become a Justice of the United States Supreme Court.

[*The beginning of the letter is missing.*]

Canton, Miss.

March, 1866

Spring is declared here—the grass is "springing fresh and gay" and "the lark sings high in air"—and I feel weak, and chilly as I always do in this climate, and thirsty like chills. It is not imagination, it is the real fact that the Southern climate does render me unfit for anything but tears and chills. The freedmen are working very well on Joe's place and he has no difficulties with them at all. The house servants are all the same that they were, except that Bob is not with them.

The night before I left Macon I was invited to dine with Mrs Whittle. I desired to refuse, but Mr Cobb thought it would be better not, and so I went with him and his wife and Harrison. Among others there was Genl Jackson, who was once a member of Congress, and his handsome, fleshy wife. I was quite taken aback by the velvet dresses, and headdresses, for I had on that time-honored poplin which I wore to Mary Lyons' wedding, and the same plain linen collar and sleeves which I had worn all day. As the splendor dawned upon me, I felt blacker, and plainer, and more separated from other women, and choked up and went blind—and plucked up heart of grace, and won the palm for impassibility, I have no doubt. At dinner I sat near Col Whittle's brother, whose empty sleeve was buttoned to his coat—a grave quiet young man of thirty I suppose, whose other strong arm and brawny shoulders and determined eyes seemed to say all which might have been possible to him had not his youth been blighted—and he tread so softly and reverently over the grave of our cause. Tears arose in his eyes, and his hand and lips trembled when a silent toast was drunk, that I should have been glad to shake hands with him, and cry outright for both. I would not go through it again for a great many rewards. I am so differently constituted from others—I cannot be distracted from trouble by such things—a contrary temper I presume.

After dinner about fifty pretty well-dressed women came, and a good many gentlemen. They were very pleasant, and two of them sang charmingly. I there met for the second or third time Mr— —well, I think my mind is failing for I cannot remember his name.

He upon this occasion brought his wife to present her little boy to me, upon whose head your "hand had rested." The boy said "I hope, dear Mrs Davis, I shall be good enough to deserve it hereafter. I pray for him, we all do." I choked, and said nothing—they did not seem to expect it.

Early in the morning, wished God Speed by our dear friends and all their family, we started for Atlanta, where Mr Mackey met me again, profuse in hospitality. We were joined before we got there by "Bill Arp," so-called, Major Smith, who let me into the pretences which had been used by Alexander Stephens and his friends to delude the Ga. people. I listened to the whole thing, and then stated to him exactly the circumstances of the whole matter of the peace propositions and referred him to the gentleman who would confirm these things. And he did certainly say things which I could not say, but which delighted me extremely. He is a quiet, serious gentleman and a member of the Ga. Senate—a great admirer of yours.

On the cars from Chattanooga to Grand Junction many people came and spoke lovingly of you and kissed our baby. I felt that at liberty in the enjoyment of your rights, you would have passed unnoticed—it was not only of old that the blood of the martyrs could become the seed of the church. The feeling is bitter about your imprisonment.

I have just been interrupted by pretty ittie Paie coming in to beg me come out and "hear sing." I went and heard mocking birds. Between the borders of jonquils and hyacinths, blue, yellow, and white, and over the dry leaves and ground powdered with plum blossom petals, for the trees have bloomed and shed their blossoms. The spireas are all in bloom, the periwinkles and the violets. Every one but me seems to be looking forward to something sweet and bright.

Where was I on my journey at Grand Junction? Well—the place was so dreadfully dirty that we got upon a freight train, and went down to Holley Springs. I thought Pie looked rather ragged, and found upon inquiry that some federal officers had cut the buttons off her little dress to take to their children as mementoes. They treated me with the most marked courtesy, and one of them brought some of my personal luggage from one car to the other. Pie took an immense fancy to them—she is a friendly little thing. At Holley Springs Harrison left me at my request, so as not to lose time in seeing his Mother at Oxford, and then the citizens who knew you came to see me—warm and devoted as ever. The town is nearly destroyed but pretty still. A number of ladies and gentlemen met me at the cars.

At Oxford the students came to the cars, as did Mrs Harrison and her daughter, but I barely got time to speak to them, and then left H. there. When we reached Coffeeville Mr and Mrs L. Q. C. Lamar came down to see me—and urged my going to them, and after a few minutes stay *he* decided to go to Canton with me. And in Lamar's woeful account of his difficulties I forgot for a time my griefs, and laughed heartily. He stayed one day at Joe's and then went back. He has had a return of his attacks, but they are slight. He sent you so much love, and sympathy & wants to write. Shall leave here on the Sunday's train, rejoined as I shall be then by Harrison, who goes with me to New Orleans.

Don't eat any pork meat, dear—I hear this shocking German disease Trichinia is spreading here in this country. Keep well for your old wife who so dotes upon you and beseeches heaven for your safety. I never should have known how inexpressibly dear you are to me if your misfortunes had not been so great. I thank God it is I who share them with you—

> Devotedly and with my whole heart,
> Your own wife

Jefferson Davis to Varina Davis

Many Southerners, finding Northern dominance too distasteful, are leaving the United States to take up residence in Brazil, Mexico, and other Latin-American countries.

> Fortress Monroe, Va.
> March 13, 1866

My dear Wife,

Your reception at Macon was such as I anticipated from my own experience, and it is so much the more valuable because those friends have little demonstrativeness and no insincerity. The kind manifestations mentioned by you as made by the negro servants are not less touching than those of more cultivated people. I liked them, and am gratified by their friendly remembrance. Whatever may be the result of the present experiment, the former relation of the races was one which could only incite to harshness a very brutal nature.

I hope the reports of growing despondence, because of political action leading to organizations for expatriation, have been exaggerated. All cannot go, and those who must stay will need the help of all who can go away. *The night may seem long, but it is the part of fidelity to watch and wait for morning.*

Warned by a sad experience against such calculations as would make hope sanguine and expectation swift, I will yet hope, though in patience, and strive to find adequate protection beneath the shield of the conviction that all things are ordered in wisdom and mercy and love.

In all the affairs of life we are reduced to choosing between evils, every situation having disadvantages. You recollect the instructive satire of Horace on the desire for change.

If my letter seems disjointed and obscure, do not infer any physical ill as the cause. The tramping and creaking of the sentinel's boots disturb me so as to render it difficult to write at all.

March 14. In the selections for the morning service of this Sunday I have found comforting promises.

The weather is warm for the season, the buds of the willows are swelling and all this suggests the fear that you will find the crowded cabin of a steam boat in your journey to and from N.O. uncomfortable, if not unhealthy. Mr. Harrison will I know do all in his power to provide for your comfort, and I feel great confidence both in his head and his heart. I once hoped to have been of service to him and much regret that the reverse has been the result of his connection with me. You will probably see "Dobbin" in Canada and you know with what confidence and affection I regard him.

Farewell, dear Winnie. To Divine guidance trust your steps.

Ever most affectionately and trustingly, your Husband
Jeffn. Davis

Maggie Davis to Her Father

"Little Pollie"
Sault au Récollet, Mar 14 1866

My Precious Father
Grandma came here the other day and gave me such news as made me jump for joy, for she said that Mother was on her way

here and would be here sometime this week. It may be that you know it but as I did not know I thought that I would tell you. Precious Father, so as to recall your joy, I have applied myself so well to my Arithmitic and other studies that my Mistress says that she is very much pleased with me and she also told Grandma, and I now know so much French that I mean to make a little surprise to Mother when she arrives by speaking French to her and also playing a nice Waltz which I know will give her very great Pleasure. Precious Father I always shall believe firmly hereafter that what ever I ask our Heavenly Father He will grant it to me, for I have had reason to think so, for I have prayed every night and every morning for Precious Mother and you and that we might all meet soon again and He has granted that I should see Mother if not you, but as I will continue to pray I hope that he will also grant that you may come to see us and live in happiness and harmony all our days together.

Goodbye my Precious Father. I remain your most affectionate little Pollie

Maggie Davis

Child of the Sacred Heart

Varina Davis to Jefferson Davis

New Orleans
March 18th 1866

My Precious old Husband,

I have been so constantly occupied since your last letter met me here that I have not had time to write—for when I go to my room for the night my little tyrant can't have a light so I must grope my way in the dark, lest she may choose to awaken, and make a night of it. She is well, and the brightest thing I ever saw.

It is impossible to tell you the love which has been expressed here for you—the tenderness of feeling for you. People sit and cry until I am almost choked with effort to be quiet. But it is a great consolation to know that a nation is mourning your suffering with me and to be told hourly how far above reproach you are—how fair is your fame. The Confederates are nearly all here. Genl Longstreet is in a commission business, as is Genl Wheeler—so, I may say, are all the ex-generals. I have seen Genls Ferguson, Wheeler and Maury. This last night Maury sent you a message full of love and respect. All sent you grateful messages of kindness, but none so warmly as he—Genl Hampton, Preston, Robinson and the Owens, both, Mr Tom Byrnes, Mr Payne, Mr Soulé in very warm terms of which I will tell you. It seems to me that I never saw so many old friends in one place before. Dick Taylor looks well, has leased the canal here at a large sum, and expects to make a large amount by it. He is a warm hearted man. But I will tell you all about this when I see you. My precious Husband, I hope a little now that I may be permitted to do so.

I am overwhelmed by the love which every thing of your name attracts. But for your vigorous imprisonment I fear you would never have been believed. At least people would not have found out as your poor old wife knows—all your noble nature. My dear suffering love, I cannot tell my pride and gratification. That your food is better is a great source of gratification to me, and of thanks to Dr Cooper. He will like you I know. I hope to come to you before very long, and perhaps I may succeed in getting you a longer period in the open air. Perhaps I may get a parole for you to walk with me alone—only one sentinel—I cannot say—but I can try.

My health is very good now—iron, and treatment during the spring have set me quite up again. I am better than I have been for many many months, indeed very well again. I shall write you from Vicksburg and indeed from all available points.

God bless you, dear precious Love. I pray for you—long for you —and love you more "hour by hour." Joe Davis joins me in dearest love. Harrison speaks of you like a Father and seems absorbed in your welfare. Again, with love unspeakable, Farewell—

Varina

Jefferson Davis to Varina Davis

Fortress Monroe, Va
22 March 1866

My dear Wife
I am in the condition to give the highest value to quiet, it being the thing never allowed to me by day or night.

The spring is slowly appearing and, as well as the calendar, reminds me of the many months during which I have been closely confined without any legal proceeding, or even informal notice of the charges and evidence on which I am held as a "state prisoner." So I strive to possess my soul in patience, and by every means attainable to preserve my health against undermining circumstances. The officers of the guard treat me with all the consideration compatible with their position.

My dear Wife, though I cannot expect you to feel less anxious about me, let me beg you to address all your energies to the heavy task imposed on you in having sole charge of the children. You cannot effect anything for me and would probably meet wounding repulse in any attempt to do so. If it be so that I can go to you it will involve little delay to reach you wherever you may be. Until then seek in making the best practicable arrangement to find the most agreeable employment for you.

Farewell, my dear Wife. May the peace of the Holy Comforter be with you, ever prays with all the fervor of devoted love, Your Husband

Jeffn. Davis

Jefferson Davis to Varina Davis

Fortress Monroe, Va.
8 April 1866

My dear Wife. Your letter from N.O. with its enclosures came safely to hand. The newspapers have announced you as passing Memphis on the 31st, and by this date I hope you have joined our dear little ones in their place of refuge. The colder and drier air will, I am assured, be beneficial to you. You need rest both for body and mind and your new situation should enable you to make such arrangements.

Next to the consciousness of rectitude, it is to me the greatest of earthly consolations to know that those for whom I acted and suffer, approved and sympathize. It is common in cases of public calamity, for those who feel the infliction, to seek for some object on which to throw the blame, and rarely has it happened that the selection has been justly or generously made.

I feel deeply indebted to Dr. Craven and the ladies of his family for a benevolence which had much to suppress, and nothing selfish to excite it, and but for which my captivity would soon have ended in death.

Your trip has been through so many degrees of latitude that I had hoped the spring would have opened before your journey was closed. The sententious Roman claimed that man might at least be allowed the wisdom of a migratory bird, and therein, I think, committed the error of claiming for reason more of certainty than belongs to instinct. Greater extension it has, but within its narrow and special channel instinct seems to me more unerring. The rod of the water-seeker may dip where there is no vein, except that of wonderful credulity, but the roots of the willow will run towards the water.

I prayed that you would not be exposed to the prying curiosity and heartless vulgarity of the scavengers of the press, who cater to the unmanly malice which has so long and unscrupulously assailed me.

Kiss our children for me. My love is ever with you, devotedly clinging to the happy memories of our younger days and assuring me of one thing which though earthly is unchanging. Farewell, yr. Husband

Jeffn. Davis

Varina Davis to Jefferson Davis

New York Hotel
April 12, 1866

My dearest husband

Strange as it may seem to you I have not written to you since I left New Orleans—though I stayed there fifteen days. I only wrote to you once for two reasons—for one, I never had a half hour to myself during the whole day from nine until eleven at night. I could not then write because the baby is your child and every thing must be pitch dark, and quiet as silence and sleep can make or she wakes, and cries piteously.

I went up to Vicksburg on the "Stonewall," a very good St. Louis boat. Every boat which either left, or ever expected to leave, invited me to go in the most flattering and kind manner. Toward the last of my stay I saw any number of my old schoolmates, and friends—and they were all so affectionate to me. It would have been delightful if my heart had been at ease—but still God bless them for the comfort they gave me. Genl Maury spoke of you in a manner alike honorable to him and precious to me, as did every one in the different degrees of graceful power of expression which each possessed.

On the boat were a large number of Negroes (discharged soldiers) "going to Davis Bend" with pistols, trinkets and calico to sell there. We passed our home in the night. When I arrived at Vicksburg it was just as day broke. I put Pie and Mary in a room in the Prentiss House still kept by McMakin, and walked up to see Brother Joe. No one was up, but the birds were "singing blythe and gay" in the garden, where the lilacs, yellow jasmine, hyacinths, and violets were in full blossom—and sweet as if a civil rights bill had been passed for their protection. Lize looked very well and bright—her spirits are good and she seemed overflowing with love for you, her "dear good gentle Uncle." Then came in Brother Joe—changed in that his hair has grown whiter—but otherwise about as well as any old gentleman of his age that I ever saw and as bright. He does not even lie down in the day now. He has a rockaway and two mules in which Jack drives him to and fro—he likes the excitement of being in a little town, and goes around a good deal. He would have long since received back his property, but he refused to pay the blackmail which a Genl Thomas of the freedmen's bureau offered to levy upon him. He said he would not be accessory to a bribe, so he can not get it until a court is assembled upon his charges against the Genl—which he hopes will be soon. He tells me that the Negroes are doing very well there. I sent Ben Montgomery twenty dollars to provide for old Uncle Bob who is quite well, but suffering for comforts, which I ordered Ben to give him. I saw William C, Tom, Grandisen and Jack A, also George Green—they were very glad to see me—but talked like proprietors of the land. William told me they are getting along very well—"but twas n't like old times." *But they have all changed.*

You have every reason to feel happy about Brother Joe's health. I begged him to come to me in Canada in the summer, and stay with me which he promised to do—when I trust in God you may see him. He was quite out of money and I gave him four hundred dollars—and your Griffith dressing gown as he had none. He was very affectionate and begged me to stay with him longer. I read the largest part of your letters to him, and he seemed delighted and comforted and very grateful—full of love for you. But who of our people is not excepting only Joe Johnston, Beauregard and Jordan—the meanest and basest of mankind.

We got on the "Virginia" and came up safely, without expense to St. Louis. We reached Louisville to find Preston Johnston and his wife awaiting us at his house—and we staid with them two days. Genl William Preston came down to see me, delighted, begged as if for life to get Jeff to educate, and offered everything but was kindly refused—he is a noble man. Johnston's account of our children was in the main satisfactory. We got on the mail boat and went to Cincinnati very safely—still perforce guests. The superintendent of the line sent us on by the new English railway, and the Erie broad gauge road. We had sleeping cars, and every comfort until finally we arrived here safely—were very kindly received. Malie Brodhead joined me yesterday and we have had a nice cosy time. I have seen Dr. Craven and Anne and his dear wife. God bless and keep them, for all they have done for you in your hour of extreme agony. I have seen Mr. O'Conor and am well satisfied with his course. Dick Taylor has also been affectionate as a brother & son.

I am kept in the parlor until twelve at night from ten in the morning—so that it is now late. Make yourself easy, my dearest, about the permission to go to you. I have no fears, because I will have from the President, or from the considerate and kind Atty Genl, an exact permit as to what I may, or may not do. Keep heart, dear love—look forward. We will be happy yet, so very happy.

It is one o'clock, yet I cannot bear to stop but must do so—as I have a few notes to write of civility. Mr. Harrison is all in the world to me that a grown son could be, and is very thoughtful and affectionate—full of love and care for you. May the Lord bless and keep you safe is the prayer of devotedly, your poor old Wife.

Varina Davis to Jefferson Davis

Though written April 14, 1866, this letter was not received by Mr. Davis until May 18, 1866, when his wife was with him at Fort Monroe.

Montreal
St. Lawrence Hall, C.E.
April 14, 1866

My dearest Husband,

Very tired, but otherwise not uncomfortable, we arrived here safely. I drove immediately round to Ma's boarding house hoping to find rooms in it, but there were none. Upon going up stairs, the first person I met was Margaret, delighted to see me beyond anything which I can express. Then our beautiful Billy—immensely grown—fat as a little possum—and so sweet and loving to his "Mudder." Put both his little hands on my face, and with his same old baby gesture, said immediately, "where is Fader—is we agoing to see Fader, say Moder, say." Then our little Maggie, fat, but not rosy. She talks often of you, and always sweetly. Jeff was not in from school. I will send for him to morrow. Ma has been very ill with a severe attack of bronchitis, and is very weak and looks dreadfully—still confined to her bed. Very much depressed, I do not wonder that she is so, for the house in which she lives is a shocking place—the air is laden with odors of things cooking, and things unclean—and the family is so large that I cannot see how we are to get lodgings together of a better class. Margaret is very much out of health, has no appetite, and cries if she hears a loud noise. The Dr. says it is only some nervous shock which has upset her. However my general health is now very good, and I think I can bring order out of chaos.

April 16th. Jeff came in to day—Jeffy D brought him into us. He is a little boisterous, but otherwise unchanged, except that he is very healthy, and much grown. The only change I see is that he has learned to fight. He fought a boy sixteen for pretending to believe that you were in petticoats at your capture—I understand the boy did not intend to hurt him, but only to make him show his spirit. I told him your last message, and he seated himself in a chair, covered his face, and sobbed out, "the dear dear fellow, will I ever see him again?" He has a number of English expressions —this "dear fellow" is one. He has just come to say "do tell my darlin' Father that your ownself heard me read a piece in my spellin' book."

Harrison will remain with us a very few days, and then return to New York. He is a dear, warmhearted boy—full of generosity, and love for you. With warmest love and brightest hopes, my beloved Husband, I am devotedly, your Wife.

Jefferson Davis to Varina Davis

In January, Dr. George E. Cooper, a Republican, had replaced the sympathetic Dr. Craven as State Prisoner Davis's physician. General Miles considered him politically "sounder" and better suited to handle Davis's case. But Cooper proved to be a man of good heart, and he was soon attracted by the prisoner's rare qualities. In May, after Varina's arrival at Fort Monroe, Cooper succeeded in stopping the maddening tramp of sentinels, which had not ceased, night and day, for twelve months.

Ft. Monroe, 21st April 1866

My dear Wife. Your welcome and anxiously looked for letter reached me on the 18th by which time according to the newspapers you had reached Montreal. In the joy of your reunion with the children I rejoice, finding in the event your common happiness and welfare.

Of myself I have little to say. The happiest event for me which has occurred here was the release of my friend and fellow sufferer Mr. Clay. He was not allowed to take leave of me, and his Wife was unable to obtain the permission she sought to visit me. Dr. Minnegerode visited me a few days since, full of the Christian and humane love which my sufferings have led him to make more manifest than in the time of my prosperity. Do not be distressed about my health, there is no cause for alarm, as there is no active disease and change is so slow that I expect to be on hand like Micawber.

The young soldier who saw you in the cars at Binghampton reported the interview, and described how bright and wide-awake little Winnie was. It was a great pleasure to me to hear an eyewitness.

The weather is quite warm, the earth is clothed in her bright robes of promise, the birds sing joyously, and I will not complain that they are so tuneful while "I so weary fu' o' care." Though not the voice I long to hear, I draw from it the pleasure it was designed to give by the bounteous Creator, who did not mean that man's happiness should be at the mercy of man, and therefore formed him for companionship with nature, and endowed his soul with capacity to feed on hopes which live beyond this fleeting life.

Often has it occurred in the world's history that fidelity has been treated as a crime, and true faith punished as treason. So it cannot be before the Judge to whom all hearts are open, from whom no secrets are hid. Dr. Cooper has just been here to visit me, he says all which is needful for me is air and exercise. But I do not hold that it is man's wisdom to equal the swallow, but man's dignity to bear up against trials under which the lower animals would sink. Resolution of will may not, according to Father Timon, prolong indefinitely our earthly existence, but it will do much to sustain the tottering machine beyond the observer's calculation.

You can imagine how one, shut out from all direct communication with his friends, dwells upon every shadow and longs for light.

Tell me as much as you can of the sayings, doings and looks of the children. Let not anxiety for the absent cloud the joy which your reunion is capable of bringing to you and to them. It is no misfortune to you that care and responsibility for others will occupy you, and in useful effort may the Lord give you comfort.

Yesterday my walk was extended to two hours, and I hope for the continuance of the extension, as the good doctor has urged the necessity for more air and exercise.

Give my most affectionate remembrances to all our family and receive the warmest aspirations of the heart which is devotedly yours as it has been these many years. Your Husband

Jeffn. Davis

Dr. George E. Cooper to Varina Davis

Mrs. Davis had finally been granted permission to come to Fort Monroe and had arrived with the baby Winnie and Frederick Maginnis in early May. Distressed at the condition in which she found her husband, she immediately began to try to secure for him the parole of the fort. She was allotted quarters in which to set up housekeeping and permitted to see her husband certain hours of the day and to walk with him on the ramparts.

Fort Monroe, Va.
May 23d, 1866

Madam,

I am in receipt of your communication of date in which you ask of me "how the health of your husband can be recruited, as you see him growing weaker and sinking daily."

I have done all in my power to keep his health up, but I must own I see him becoming more and more weak day by day. He has been well cared for in the matter of food; the tramp of the sentinels he no longer hears. He has exercise one hour in the morning and as much as he wishes for after four in the afternoon.

Notwithstanding he fails and the only thing left is to give him mental and bodily rest and exercise at will.

This can be only by having the Parole of the Fort with permission to remain with his family now residing there.

He will then probably recuperate.

Your Obet. Svt.

Geo. E. Cooper,

Surgeon U.S.A.

Mrs. Robert E. Lee to Jefferson Davis

When it became known that State Prisoner Davis was permitted to receive a few letters from friends, one of the first to arrive was from Mary Custis Lee. The body of the letter had been written a year before, in late May of 1865. Enclosed in the envelope she sent a copy of her favorite hymn—all six verses transcribed by her arthritic fingers. She boldly addressed the envelope to "Ex-President Jefferson Davis."

June 6, 1866

My heart has prompted me, my dear friend, ever since I knew of the failure of our glorious cause to write to you & express my deep sympathy how much more since I learned your captivity, your separation from your beloved family & your incarceration in a solitary dungeon. If you knew how many prayers & tears had been sent to Heaven for you & yours, you could realize that you were not forgotten. We did so long to hear that you could reach in safety some foreign clime where you could enjoy the repose & consideration which seems to be denied you in your own country. Oh why did you delay & fall into the hands of those whose only desire is to humiliate & destroy you? The only consolation I can now offer you besides our deep attachment & remembrance of you, is contained in the words of my favorite hymn which I have transcribed for you. As a Christian I feel confident that you have fortitude "to bear the cross & *despise* the shame" & even to *pray* for your persecutors.

As I know not if this letter will be allowed to reach you I will not say more—you can imagine all we would say & feel & know that one sentiment animates the hearts of your true friends & among them, believe, there is no one truer than

Yours, Mary C. Lee

If you are allowed to write let me know if you receive this, where your family have gone & if I can do anything for them. You don't know how I value *the chair* you sent me.

6th June 1866 I do not know that I can write anything more expressive of my feelings towards you than this letter penned a few days after I heard of your imprisonment, so I send it now with the love & prayers of all my family.

Varina Davis to Jefferson Davis

After three months at Fort Monroe, Mrs. Davis, feeling that not enough was being done to secure her husband's release, left for New York to see if she could effect some action.

Charles O'Conor, the attorney in charge of Davis's case, thought that Davis would be given parole within ten days. Attorney General Stanbery was in favor of Davis's release from prison. "J." is President Andrew Johnson, who would have given Davis a parole earlier if he had dared risk the wrath of certain Northern politicians.

Lake George
Thursday—Aug. 17th 1866

My dear old Ban,

You will be astonished to see the caption, Lake George, but let me tell you first the news. Mr O'Conor is here, and says that he thinks ten days at the utmost is the extent. He had a most satisfactory interview with a man he considers very satisfactory—Mr Stanbery. Stanbery and "J." are our friends. Now that I have relieved your mind on more important topics, I will tell you of the way I came here. When I found, as I did after I wrote to you, that Mr O'C. was not in New York I felt such a sinking horror that I decided to come the eight hours farther to Lake George. Mr Hopkins offered and insisted upon going with me, and I came up very safely and pleasantly. Mr O'Conor got on the cars at Saratoga, not knowing that I was on them, and came up with us in the stage.

When I found that I was not quite eight hours from the children I decided to go to Montreal for two days, so I shall go there to-morrow, look at them, and come back to you Thursday morning, thus being no longer absent than I had expected, but I do feel so hopeful—so young and happy.

It is cold as November here—but it is the most beautiful place I have ever imagined.

Devotedly your old
Winnie

Varina Davis to Horace Greeley

Greeley, abolitionist editor of the New York *Tribune*, had first taken the position that the Confederate States had a right to withdraw from the Union. Because of his onetime high admiration of Jefferson Davis and his attempt to bring about peace in 1864, Mrs. Davis makes a touching appeal for his help.

Fortress Monroe, Va.
Sep. 2nd, 1866

Private and Confidential
My dear Mr. Greeley,

May I come to you again in the bitterness of my sorrow, the black uncertainty of our future, for light and help. For thirteen months, I have prayed and tried to cheerfully grope through the mist to find the end, and now it seems no nearer. I see my Husband patiently, uncomplainingly fading away, and cannot help him. Those who represent him as being well, and about as strong as he used to be, stay a few moments and are deceived by his *spirited self-controlled bearing*. A slight illness would kill him, for he is fetched up by the most excessive care both upon his part and mine. He does not gather strength, but rather loses it.

Our children are in need of my care, and of that of their Father, yet in our present position I cannot bring them to him. And I am I confess not equal to the self-sacrifice of leaving him for their sakes. I hoped much from the exposure of the suborned testimony against him, but it brought no fruits. And now I appeal to you who always sympathise with the weak to help me. *Will you not procure signa-*

tures enough to that paper which Mr. Shea has, to arrest Mr. Johnson's attention?

I cannot, my dear kind Sir, tell you all my sorrows growing out of this arbitrary imprisonment of my Husband. They are legion. But I have enlisted you I am sure when I say that I am utterly helpless and well nigh broken hearted. If a victim's tears could wash out venom, then mine ought to have cleansed many a heart filled with the lust for vengeance—and for blood. May God give you success, for I know you will labor to assist me. I am dear Sir,

Gratefully and most sincerely yours,
Varina Davis

Varina Davis to Her Mother

Mr. Davis has been given new housekeeping quarters where his wife and child can be with him.

Fort Monroe
Oct. 18th 1866

My dear Mother,

Your kind and cheerful letter came to day and gave me some comfort in my forlorn, discouraged condition. Malie is with me, and in our trouble we compare notes helplessly by the hour without seeing our way out. Jeff grows hourly weaker, more exhausted; he has now to cling to the banister, and to use his stick in descending the steps—and staggers much in walking. This decision of Mr. Johnson that he must be left to the Republicans, that he can do nothing for him seems to promise that his life will be spent in prison. It is in the power of the judge to postpone his trial from one time to another and this they have done. I am too grieved, too agonised to talk of this. God knows what we shall do—what we can do. That the children get on moderately well is my only hope & comfort. As long as I can maintain them at school I shall not be perfectly hopeless.

I do so long to come to Canada to see you all but Jeff suffers so much when I go, is so wretchedly lonely. Malie is kind in staying here, for it is a wretchedly dull place.

Thank God my dear Mother for your improved health. May He preserve you long to us.

Believe me devotedly your child
Varina Davis

Varina Davis to Horace Greeley

In a telling editorial in the New York *Tribune* of November 9, Greeley had urged Davis's immediate release from prison. And he had taken Johnson sharply to task for not publicly retracting his absurd charge that Davis was involved in Lincoln's assassination.

Fortress Monroe, Va.
Nov. 21st, 1866

My dear Mr. Greeley.

Allow me to thank you for the article in the *Tribune* in which I thought I received the fulfilment of your kind expressions contained in your letter to me. But everything seems to fall pointless which is essayed in Mr. Davis' behalf. This last nineteen months that I have been part of the time a prisoner in Georgia and part of the time a voluntary exile from my poor little children has quite unhinged me, and I feel unable to bear further torture. Can you not, will you not get some such pressing recommendations for my Husband's release as will move Mr. Johnson? We are totally broken up in fortune, and he in health, the only things left to us are our Children, and they are growing up without our influence. If he is to languish here all winter, the summer will deprive me of him. I make no apology for thus urging upon you my petition for help, because I know you have a sympathetic heart and can understand what these many weary months must have cost us. And now to look forward to so many more is a cruel suffering to inflict. To sentence a man to a year's close and nearly thirteen months solitary confinement, groaning at the same time under the affluence of observation which is not sympathy, would be a dreadful punishment if proven guilty—but to be chained, starved, kept awake systematically, almost blinded by light and tortured by the ingenuity of a cruel and irresponsible jailor in small constantly varied annoyances, before one has been tried, is cruel indeed. I am hungry for a sight of my little children, and our finances are so narrow as to render it requisite that I should be with them so as to enable me to husband the little I have left. Yet I cannot leave this Father to languish out his days here. You are powerful with your party. Can you not restore us, dear Mr. Greeley, to our little ones?

Excuse this entirely personal appeal, and believe me
very grateful for your sympathy, and sincerely yours,
Varina Davis

Varina Davis to Jefferson Davis

Mary Stamps, whose husband, Captain Isaac Stamps, a nephew of Jefferson Davis, had been killed at Gettysburg, had come from Mississippi to Fort Monroe to see her "beloved Uncle." She had also been charged by Joseph Davis to get his imprisoned brother's permission for him to sell Brierfield plantation along with his own Hurricane to their former slaves, Ben Montgomery and his sons. Mrs. Davis takes this opportunity of leaving her husband with Mary's congenial companionship to go to Canada to see her children. She is struggling hard to secure her husband's release from Fort Monroe. Numerous Northerners offer their services. *The Black Crook* was a somewhat notorious extravaganza and burlesque, a British importation with gorgeous scenic effects and girls in tights.

New York Hotel
Sat. Dec. 8th 1866

My dear old Banny,

I arrived here yesterday evening very safely, and had a quiet journey here, safe from intrusion, still less rudeness. Malie Brodhead and her daughter Camilla were here waiting for me with Judge Packer. So you see I am not alone. I saw Mr O'Conor today, and he looks dreadfully, says he has been quite unwell. He thinks I had best go to Washington before the bitterness of party strife begins, and thinks I may do some good, therefore I am going down to Baltimore Monday evening, and spend the night with Charlotte Gittings, and on to Washington in the morning after an interview with Governor Pratt, who I think can make suggestions as to my course. I do not know my dearest, most precious love, that I can do any thing, but Mr O'Conor thinks there is a chance of getting some Republicans to recommend your release. Genl Preston will go down to Baltimore with me, and then I think Gov Pratt will go to Washington. I feel confident I can do you no harm, perhaps some good. It is but deferring my visit to the children a few days.

I went to see The Black Crook after finding that respectable people all went. The play is a series of exquisite scenic effects, interspersed with some very pretty ballet dancing and poor dialogue.

I hope our darling Pie is well. Tell Mary Ahern please to watch that she does not get into the backyard.

Tell Mary Stamps I went out to look for her children's books today, and found that they cost nearly twenty dollars, and decided to get them in Canada. You cannot open a store door without spending money, so I have bought nothing. I ought to go away from home sometimes to know how rich I am. You seem a thousand feet high compared with the rest of the world. I seem to feel sanctified by our last long kiss as we parted and the memory of your love gives me confidence to do anything *except risk your displeasure.*

How do you and Mary get on I wonder. I think I can see you strolling around the Ramparts, and then sitting around the lamp shade ("mine own contrive") to read. Do give my best love to Mary. Malie is going to bring both the boys and come to us Christmas, but she cannot go to Canada, though she will go to Washington with me.

Pray for us, and for my success. Farewell dearest. Again and again I love you.

                                   Your devoted Wife

Varina Davis to Jefferson Davis

Varina is planning for a big Christmas in Fort Monroe. She is bringing Margaret Howell back with her and hopes to bring little Billy. But his father vetoes the latter as he does not want his children to have remembrance of him in prison. Davis had greatly enjoyed the calm society of Mary Stamps and regards the intimation of Christmas excitements with some misgivings. Becket Howell had been a junior officer on the famous *Alabama.*

Montreal
Sunday Evening
(Dec. 16, 1866)

My precious Husband,

At last my longing arms have embraced all our children. Jeff reached here yesterday quite well. He is very much improved in manners, and full as ever of tenderness for his parents. When he saw the prayer book he shed tears, and said "this book will be worth all the world to me." Billy I hope to show you. He has a great many old fashioned ways. His health I think would be strengthened by a change of climate, his digestion seems weak. Margaret is decidedly in bad health and I think to bring them to us is the lesser of the two evils. Still I shall cheerfully abide by your decision in the matter and be guided by a telegram.

I have received but one letter from home since my departure from you, and that was the most hurried and unsatisfactory of notes from Mary Ahern in which she only speaks of my Winnie Anne incidentally, and I am impatient to be gone. We will leave on Tuesday next, which will land us at the Fort on Sunday. Malie is coming down to us Christmas with her two boys.

Will you please tell Frederick to get one of the downstairs rooms cleaned up and to see if he can get a bed and a few things put in it for the chance company. It will be too late when we get there. And will you please tell Frederick to send to Norfolk and get five pounds of raisins, ditto, currants, a barrel of apples, to make Julia store the raisins and wash the currants well, and chopping the raisins very fine to put into a stone jar with the currants and chop seven pounds of peeled & cored apples *very* fine and mix with them —and to engage some suet against I come—tell Julia to make a pound and a sponge cake and ice them—and to make a batch of potatoe pies—and tell Frederick to lay by some eggs. I feel ashamed of troubling you dear Banny about such trifles, but I feel very anxious to have things a little nice.

If Mary Stamps has not left you, which I fear she has, do give my best love, and thanks to her. Just at this moment there is a cart passing, and the ground sings like a piano at a distance. There is no snow on the ground, but it is hard frozen. The people are wrapped up like grisly bears in their furs.

Becket seems about the same boy you knew, very willing to a

physical exertion & exceedingly anxious to work—I have seen no evidence of intemperance about him. Jeffy D. is a very good boy and steady. Becket gives me some queer items about the *Alabama* prize money which will astonish you. But of this I cannot speak safely now.

I think every little while of you in your solitude, and our Winnie Anne, and liberty does me no good. I feel as if nothing could ever induce me to leave you again.

God bless you my precious old Ban, and keep you safely for your devoted Wife—

Winnie

THE PRISON LETTERS,
1867

Varina Davis to Mary Stamps

Mary Stamps's father, Governor Humphreys of Mississippi, did not approve of his daughter's making her own living by teaching school in New Orleans. To force her to live with him and her amiable young stepmother he refused to release her share of her dead mother's estate, or help her in any way. Her little girls, great-nieces of Jefferson Davis, are currently with their grandmother, Lucinda Davis Stamps, at Woodville. The Southern States have been put under martial law, which was to last for some nine years.

Fortress Monroe
Feb. 17th 1867

My dear little Mary, I know I have been more than remiss, I have been culpable in not writing sooner, but it has not been for want of thought of and for you. Your Father's letter enclosed in yours to Jeff convinced me that for the present at least you have nothing to hope from him, but it is a sad conviction for me, for I felt sure he would aid you. It seems to me, however, that you take to yourself too little sleep, too many hours of labor for your health. Get the children with you by all means. It is better to do so than to leave them anywhere. At their grandmother's they have not the educational advantages that they have with you, otherwise it might do there.

Did you get a locket that I sent you? We could never find yours, but I bought you one in Canada, and had my hair and your Uncle's put in it, and sent it to you by young Barksdale. I do hope you have it—for I think it is a pretty little thing and I wanted you to wear it always.

I found the children well, but oh what agony it was to part from them. I went out of Canada with the bitterness of death in my heart.

The newspapers turn me sick with terror. We suppose from all we can gather that the Southern States were last night, Saturday, under martial law, restored to the condition of territories, and civil law abrogated. If so the night will be long and dark for this generation, and for how many others? Plunder will destroy the land, and life be sighed out in military prisons by more suffering, for by the provisions of this new bill the military commanders over the districts have the power to condemn and execute by court martials.

We can see Mr. Davis's future no plainer now than when you were with us. Indeed it seems to grow darker in the little distance into which I am permitted to look. God surely intends to let me enter into the joys of eternity, as I have the punishments which ought to purify.

Pie is every day growing sweeter and brighter and talks all the time. Maggie Howell is very weak, and anything but cheerful. I had such an accumulation of cake and candy from Christmas that I invited the children in the Fort to a little tea party with Pie.

My dear little Motherless widow, remember that you can always turn to us for love. You will always be welcome, and dear to us— longed for in absence, cherished when near us. Therefore trust and love us as we do you, let us serve you if we can and above all let our love shelter you a little from the cold. Your Uncle speaks often and very confidingly and tenderly of you. Your visit gave him great pleasure. He says "give her my tenderest love."

With much love from Maggie and more from me than I can tell, I am devotedly your friend,

Varina Davis

Joseph E. Davis to Jefferson Davis

[*The first page is missing.*]

[Vicksburg, March, 1867]

I feel unwilling to express the pitiful evasions that mark those in power and lawlessness of officials.

After I have the contract with Ben I will write you and I may feel able to write more coherently than this.

Lize is with me & well. Joe Mitchell has lately returned from Texas with his father who is attempting to cultivate his old place in Madison Parish. I wrote to him that he would be overflowed & he had better move, but he is still there.

Most persons that attempted to plant last year were ruined—usually northern men; some borrowed money and gave mortgages on their land & lost all.

I had sold land to about seventy thousand dollars—the purchasers are either dead or broke—I get back the land, but it is unsaleable.

Accept my prayers for you & yours,

Your Brother

Varina Davis to Jefferson Davis

Mrs. Davis has gone to Baltimore to stir renewed interest in her husband's release and to have some dental work done. She is staying with old friends, John and Charlotte Gittings. The Reverend Mr. W. F. Brand runs an Episcopal boys' school. Hettie Cary, the acknowledged most beautiful girl in Richmond during the war and the widow of Brigadier General John Pegram, helps her mother conduct an exclusive girls' school. Mrs. Yulee is the wife of the former Senator from Florida, at whose house Davis's trunk of personal belongings and papers was stored in hiding. Yulee, fearing incrimination, had it taken to the railway station where the Federal authorities found it and shipped it to the War Department in Washington.

Baltimore
March 15th 1867

My dear Husband,

I arrived here yesterday and had a very safe journey, and quite a pleasant one. Mr. Robinson, he who is Presdt of the Seaboard, was on the boat, and he took express care of me. I found Charlotte Gittings at breakfast and overjoyed to see me. Mr. Brand had just arrived in town, and came, as did Hettie Cary and her Mother, full of love and anxiety to see me and talk of you. They made an offer to take our Maggie and teach her—and Hettie said she would look after her herself. I have diligently enquired here of the school, and this is what I heard, that Mrs Cary had never had an unruly scholar, or a difficulty, that she had seemed to "win her girls to gentleness," that she had the best masters, and that some of the best women in Baltimore had been educated by her. Her school is not large, has few small girls, and these few are all of the best families—they dine with the girls, and live with them. Hettie is sadly changed, though still beautiful. She cried all the time nearly she sat with me, and said if I could only kiss Mr Davis's hand and look at him it would comfort me.

Governor Pratt will be here tomorrow, and then I will go to Washington perhaps about Tuesday. It was thought better for me to spend Sunday here on account of not being able to do anything there on that day.

The dentists here are numerous, and engaged every hour it seems to me, but I shall know to day when my time will come—Volk is said to be very good and I think I shall take him.

Mrs. Yulee is here exhorting the Southern women "to submit and be placid, and have pleasure." Her dress on these occasions is a grass green bonnet & dress of the same color, with a splendid cloak of velvet. She goes to parties every night, and enjoys herself. She attacked Mrs Clay to me as not possessed of the proper spirit, "too fierce, not submissive enough." I said, but she is very polite and gentle to the Yankees, and is quite inoffensive to them when she is thrown in their way. "Yes, but she is not submissive enough, she ought to have pleasure." I could not stand this, so I said, "The widows and orphans all over the land send up a wail of mourning, and want and poverty goad them always, and their dear country lies prostrate before them, and how can we be comforted when they are not?" In fact I grew eloquent, and found I had my audience, fourteen or fifteen ladies with me, for they cried, and she settled down in her double chin, and said nothing but asked me when I hoped you would be released. I said I did not know; so, said she, God keeps him there for some good purpose—to influence your character, and when you please Him He will change his condition. So I quietly said that God did not always chasten his outcasts or his enemies, but I thought chastened whom he loved, and I could wait as could you. So much for pharisaical talk from a really good selfish woman.

Kiss my dear Pie.

Devotedly, dear, dear Husband

Your Winnie

Varina Davis to Jefferson Davis

Baltimore
March 18, 1867

My dear Husband,

At last I am on my way to the Dentist, pale with fright, but plucky to all outside appearances.

Gov. Pratt called yesterday and went over this morning to see the ground, and I trust that we may know what can be done tonight. Dick Taylor is in New York, and hourly expected. I thought he might possibly help a little. Rest assured I shall not stay an hour here for pleasure—for I long to get home. Quiet is more acceptable to me than this compassion of ever polite and sympathetic faces. Invitations have poured in upon me, but I have been nowhere. However I shall go to see Mrs. Cary's school before I leave.

I went to church twice yesterday, and once I went with Mr Brand alone—we walked after church, and had a long talk about our children's prospects.

Kiss my precious children for me.

Devotedly
Your Wife

Callers begin before breakfast is over and continue until ten o'clock at night.

Joseph E. Davis to Jefferson Davis

Vicksburg, Mar. 26th 1867

My Brother

I have closed the contract with Ben. This was delayed by an act of the State Legislature forbidding the purchase or sale of real estate by Negroes. I before stated the conditions of the contract. Nine years credit with six percent per annum interest payable the

1st of Jany of each year. The debt bound by Mortgage of the property sold. Few expect the contract will be complied with. I trust it will if Ben lives. He is ambitious to be a rich man, and will control the labor.

The prospect of a general overflow the present year will add to the distress of the Country and this is I fear inevitable. A few places may escape. I hope the Bend may escape, upon it depends the payment of the interest for the present year.

By the work done by officers of the Freedman Bureau they have succeeded in cutting off the bend and it is now the main channel of the River, the effect has been to raise the water at Woods about one foot.

I feel much anxiety to know how you are, it is a long time since we heard directly.

Our friends are well or rather are not worse since I wrote you. I hope soon to hear.

Yr Brother

Varina Davis to Jefferson Davis

During April Mrs. Davis was extremely active in contacting strategic men who might help secure her husband's release on bail. President Johnson would have been more than willing to release Davis, if he had dared. Best of all she won the sympathetic interest of John W. Garrett, President of the Baltimore and Ohio Railroad, to whom Secretary of War Stanton was under obligation. Garrett went to Washington and virtually browbeat the implacable Stanton until he finally declared he would not object to the Attorney General's arranging for the state prisoner's release.

Baltimore, Md.
Sunday, April 9, 1867

My dear Banny,

At last I can see some little way into the millstone which weighs us down—Mr. Garrett seems to think that the Sec. of War is now favorably inclined to your release, and to hope much—in which hope all your friends seem to share, but more of this when we meet.

I am to go with Prof Smith tomorrow and have seven or eight

teeth extracted by the use of chloroform to give me courage. Now if the operation is not successful you shall not receive this letter—if so, I will leave it at the office on my return home—after taking it. So don't be uneasy.

I am devotedly your wife,
Varina Davis

Dear Banny, I have returned after quite a suffering time but the most of my decayed teeth are out, and I live to tell this wondrous tale. Will be down on Wednesday morning, God willing.

Varina Davis to Jefferson Davis

William B. Reed, the Philadelphia lawyer sympathetic to Davis's case, had joined forces with Charles O'Conor of New York as chief counsel for the prisoner.

Charles Wilson, Senator from Massachusetts, had made a motion for Davis's release from prison.

Baltimore, April 25th 1867

My dear old Banny

I had fondly hoped today would finish for the present Mr. Volk's work upon my teeth, but the last operation, pulling seven teeth, was a very severe one and our advisers seemed to think I must wait until Congress adjourned before I put myself hors de combat. Now Mr. Reed telegraphs me that he will be here on Wednesday, and I must surely remain and await his coming. I never was so tired in my life or so anxious. No one can tell effect of Mr. Wilson's motion, but people seem to agree on your immediate release. It has been thought better for me to refrain from going down to Washington. A very potential man went there today, but I have not seen him of course yet. Everyone seems very sanguine. Dick Taylor and I failed to meet by the accident of Sunday stopping his letter to know if I was here, and that delaying the answer until he had gone to New York. I have had so many disappointments that I am greatly stirred up but not hopeful, where others seem to feel certain. There never was anything like the love and anxiety people seem to have about you here. It seems as if they could not do enough for me. But I am awfully, awfully tired. Everybody seems garish in the brightness of prosperity and freedom.

Kiss my darlings for me and tell them to make you understand how devotedly I am

Your own wife—

Varina's persuasion of John W. Garrett to intercede with Secretary of War Stanton resulted in the discharge of Jefferson Davis from Fort Monroe to the civil court in Richmond where, it was hoped, he would be released on bail.

On Saturday, May 11, the Davises, accompanied by General Henry S. Burton, Dr. Cooper, and Burton Harrison, left stony Fort Monroe, boarded the *John Sylvester,* and sailed up the James to Richmond. At the little landings on the river, clusters of people gathered with flowers to pay their respects to their former President. In Richmond men lined the streets with bared heads and women waved handkerchiefs from windows. Friends overflowed the Spotswood Hotel suite and almost overwhelmed the Davises with attentions.

On Monday in the tense court room, Horace Greeley, Gerrit Smith and other prominent Northerners signed Davis's bail bond, set at $100,000. Then the marshal directed the court to release the prisoner. The crowds inside and out and along the streets went wild with exultation, and later there was rejoicing and celebration all through the South.

Davis's open carriage, in which Dr. Minnegerode, the Rector of St. Paul's, and Burton Harrison sat with him, had difficulty in getting through the felicitating throng. But when they reached the Spotswood with the jam-packed mass before it, the men were silent, too moved to shout. As Davis rose to leave the carriage, a deep voice commanded, "Hats off, Virginians." "Five thousand uncovered men did homage to him who had suffered for them." Davis entered the hotel in this tribute of emotional silence. Joyous friends rushed into the Davis apartment to enfold him in grateful embraces. Because the excitement was so wearing on him, Burton Harrison got the family aboard a steamer bound for New York that very night.

Burton Harrison to Constance Cary

The fiancée of Davis's devoted young private secretary is with her mother in Paris, where Harrison had visited her briefly after his release from a torturous imprisonment, during the first five weeks of which he was kept in an eight-by-four cell in total darkness. In commenting on this letter Constance Cary wrote: "No one could read this loyal outpouring of a young man's enthusiasm for a fallen chief with any doubt that his friendship and heart's desire to serve Mr. Davis continued always—but the course of their lives, diverging at this point, never ran in parallel lines again."

Richmond, Va., May 13, 1867

My Darling:

Tomorrow's papers may inform the far-off world of Paris that our great chieftain has been finally liberated on bail. But we may yet be disappointed, and may be called upon to conduct Mr. Davis again to a dungeon. We are very anxious of course—feverishly so.

On Friday I went down to the Fortress and there spent, with him, the last night of his sojourn in the bastille. It was the second anniversary of our capture. Next day we came up the river. General Burton was as courteous to his prisoner as he could be, subjected him to no restraint, brought no guards.

We were brought to the Spotswood Hotel, and Mr. and Mrs. Davis occupy the same rooms they used in 1861, when they first came to Richmond under such different circumstances. The Northern proprietor of the house has caught the zeal of the entire community and actually turned his own family out of that apartment.

There are no sentinels, no guards. No stranger would suppose the quiet gentleman who receives his visitors with such peaceful dignity is the State prisoner around whose dungeon so many battalions have been marshalled for two years, and whose trial for treason against a mighty government, to-day excites the interest of mankind.

Everyone has called, bringing flowers and bright faces of welcome to him who has suffered vicariously for the millions.

A mighty army of counsel is here. O'Conor is towering in his supremacy over all lesser personages and looked like a demi-god of antiquity, yesterday, when we gathered a few of us around Mr. Davis to explain the details of his arrangements.

I am called. More soon.

Your devoted Burton

Joseph E. Davis to Jefferson Davis

Joseph Davis has received the telegram from Richmond announcing Jefferson's release from prison.

Vicksburg May 14th 1867

My dear Brother,

Your gratifying dispatch of yesterday is rec'd, I will not attempt to tell you how much we are relieved and gratified at the intelligence & how anxiously we look for your letter from N'York. I enclose you a letter from Ben, though gloomy in its character I know you would be anxious to hear anything and everything from home.

Your Brother

Jefferson Davis to Varina Davis

To get Davis away from the New York crowds and the persons trying to see him, Burton Harrison had whisked him off to the privacy of Charles O'Conor's estate at Fort Washington. In a few days Davis considered himself strong enough to go on to Montreal to be with his children.

On the Hudson
New York State
Saturday Evening
May, 1867

My dear Wife

I have spent a very quiet and pleasant day. Mrs. O'Conor has been hoping to see you with such expectation as caused her to start whenever the wheels of a carriage were heard. Mr. O'Conor and lady urge that instead of going in to-morrow morning that all of you should come out. I wish to see you and Joe Davis and, if he is with you, Chas. Brodhead for business talk. Need I say I wish to see you and Winnie & Maggie & Mary for love. I have agreed to write this and to wait for answer in the morning. If you cannot come, I will go in to town.

Mrs. O'Conor is earnest and says she had dinner enough for twenty.

As ever affectionately
Your Husband

Franklin Pierce to Varina Davis

For weeks after the release from prison, letters of felicitation came to both Mr. and Mrs. Davis from a host of strangers and friends. This letter reveals the continued devoted friendship between Franklin Pierce and Jefferson Davis, dating from before the War with Mexico.

Concord, N.H.
May 14, 1867

My dear Mrs. Davis—

I reached home last evening and found the telegraphic announcement that the Govt. declined to proceed with the trial of Genl. Davis and that he had been released upon bail. I do not know whether this will reach you at Richmond, but send it at a venture; to the care of Gov. Wise, who will know how to change the direction, if you have left. I infer from a remark of Genl. D. that you may all, in the first instance, proceed to Canada to see your boys. I would not influence your husband with regard to his movements, but I am strongly impressed with the convictions, that his state of health, if no other consideration, should settle the question of his remaining at the North during the summer months now near at hand. My Cottage at Little Boon's Head will be ready to receive all your family by the middle of August. The latter part of that month and the whole of Sept. is usually delightful there. The place will be as quiet as could be desired—to make everything agreeable to you. Pray write and let me know how I shall direct letters to you and what I may expect. I think, upon reflection that this note had better be directed to the care of Judge Lyon as Gov. Wise may be absent on professional engagements.

The package of books will be committed to the express tomorrow.

Always and truly yours,

Franklin Pierce

P.S. One of the photographs of dear Mrs. Pierce was taken during the last year of her life when she was very feeble.

James Murray Mason to Jefferson Davis

Virginia's James Murray Mason had been the Confederate Commissioner in England during the war. Now he is living with his family as a refugee in Canada, where the ex-President is shortly to spend a reviving week with him among refugee friends of prominence.

Toronto

May 14th, 1867

My dear Sir:

It has been a great relief to me to learn that you were at last at liberty, and under circumstances in which I confidently rely that you will not again be molested. Whilst in England, where I remained for more than a year after the sad reverse in our fortunes, I wrote from time to time to *Mr. O'Conor,* and who I found was allowed to have interviews with you as counsel, on matters that would be interesting to you in the perils that seemed to surround you, and I hope he made known to you the character of our correspondence. It is needless to go into now, but I should be gratified that you were kept informed of the interest felt in your safety by those who were beyond the reach of the enemy—and that such interest was not of mere barren sympathy. I venture the hope that you may come for the present to Canada. I see little prospect at present of my getting back to Virginia, and of all things I should desire once more to be with you and to talk over what may be the future of our unhappy country. I have with me my wife and daughters, and fortunately from some remnant of my wife's property beyond the reach of the enemy, have the means at present of living without want. We spent last Summer in the Town of Niagara, at the confluence of that river with the lake, about twelve miles below the Falls—it is a very healthy and cheap country, and being immediately on the frontier, and thus accessible to any friends who may come from the South, have thought it might be an agreeable residence for you. Should your health require the invigoration of mineral baths, there is the Town of St. Catherine's not far distant, the waters of which have great celebrity, and the Town itself an agreeable residence. But above all, I have thought it might be to you, as it was to me a matter of some moment, to be and remain in a country freed from the *tyranny* and brutality now dominant, at our once happy homes. When you have leisure pray let me hear from you, if only by a brief note, and tell me of your plans so far as formed.

You will I know be harassed with letters, and I will therefore trespass on you no further, than to express my sincere and un-qualified appreciation of all that marked your career in our late noble struggle, and with most respectful regards to Mrs. Davis to subscribe,

Most truly and affectionately yours,
J. M. Mason

John H. Reagan to Jefferson Davis

Fort Houston
near Palestine, Texas
May 21st 1867

My dear Friend:

My gratification is great indeed at hearing of your release from prison life, after the two weary and desolate years at Fortress Monroe. No statement has yet reached me of the condition of your health. But I sincerely trust it may be such as to enable you to enjoy the little freedom which is allowed you. You can hardly know what a source of gratification it would be to me to see you again. And if my means would permit it I should come to Richmond, or wherever you be, for that purpose. I sought the privilege of communicating with you, when at Washington City, on my way home but was not allowed to do so.

The feeling of relief and joy, on account of your release, is universal and strong here; and all feel that both justice and good policy required that this feeling should have been allowed to be perfect by your unconditional release. Intense as your labors and great as your trials were during the war, and cruel as your sufferings have been since, it will no doubt be a great consolation to you to know that the great mass of our people regarded you as suffering in your own person for and on account of them, and that no patriot, or statesman, or soldier, enjoying the highest honors of success and good fortune, was ever honored by stronger sympathy and more earnest affection from the people he represented or served than you have received from our people during your period of misfortune. Success might have left you, for this generation at least, the usual allotment of friends and enemies; but misfortune has embalmed you in the sincere and earnest affection of all our people. And you can at least enjoy this pleasing reflection, amidst the general wreck of liberty and of fortune, that you served a people and suffer for a people who love and venerate you more as your and their misfortunes and sorrows are greater. I have not ceased to pray, and to teach my little children to pray, for your health and safety, and for your final restoration to liberty and happiness again.

> Very truly your friend & sevt.
> John H. Reagan

Robert E. Lee to Jefferson Davis

> Lexington, Va.
> 1 June 1867

My dear Mr. Davis,

You can conceive better than I can express the misery which your friends have suffered from your long imprisonment and the other afflictions incident thereto. To none has this been more painful than to me, and the impossibility of affording relief has added to my distress. Your release has lifted a load from my heart which I have not words to tell, and my daily prayer to the great Ruler of the World is that He may shield you from all future harm, guard you from all evil and give you that peace which the world cannot take away.

That the rest of your days may be triumphantly happy, is the sincere and earnest wish of your most obt. faithful friend and sevt.

R. E. Lee

PART II

REFUGE IN CANADA

THE TREASON TRIAL POSTPONED

WHEN JEFFERSON DAVIS reached Montreal, he had an affecting reunion with his children, his mother-in-law, Margaret Howell, and his wife's three youngest brothers. Though outwardly calm, he was in such a weakened condition from his prison experiences that the city noises tormented him and he could hardly bear the voices of his own exuberant offspring. The Howells were living in a cheap, smelly boarding house.

Davis fell into such a lassitude that he was shortly persuaded to go for a visit with James Murray Mason, summering with his family in Niagara. There, surrounded by a group of refugee Confederate friends, who manifested their love and admiration, he rallied. On his return to Montreal, a wealthy Canadian publisher, John A. Lovell, rescued the Davises from their dismal lodgings and brought all of them, including Mrs. Howell, Margaret, and two servants, into his great mansion opposite Christ Church Cathedral Square.

Subsequently a well-appointed furnished house was found for the Davises at 1181 Mountain Street, the rent paid by anonymous Confederate sympathizers. To stir her husband, who declined all dinner invitations, Mrs. Davis got the President's letter book and other documents from the vault of the Bank of Montreal in the hope of interesting him in writing his history of the Confederacy. But he pushed them aside, saying in a constricted voice, "I cannot speak of my dead so soon." It was to be eleven years before he actually began to write the book.

With a trial still hanging over him, Davis wrote Colonel C. J. McRae, the former Confederate business agent yet abroad, of his hope of forming a business connection in Liverpool, by which a subsistence might be earned to support his family. "Here there is nothing for me to do," he said, "and until the pending prosecution of me is settled, it would be impossible for me to engage in any regular pursuit in our country." Later his interest was aroused in a Canadian copper mine with probable profitable employment in selling shares in England. With a spark of hope he went to inspect the mine and found the prospects encouraging.

With the problem of his children's schooling coming up in September, the Davises decided to move to the village of Lennoxville in eastern Quebec province, where young Jeff was already in school. So the family took up residence in the humble hostelry called Clark's Hotel. In the town itself Davis found some pleasant companionship in two cultured English families and in the faculty of the renowned Bishop's College, where many Confederate boys were enrolled. His trial in Richmond was now set for late November and his interim stay in Lennoxville was troubled by warning letters from several persons revealing a purported plot that he was to be murdered by two Negro barbers when he re-entered the United States.

Robert E. Lee was to be tried with Davis on the charge of treason, since the United States Government had given up the ridiculous fiction that Davis had conspired in the assassination of Lincoln. But James Murray Mason declared that the Government would never dare actually bring Davis to trial on a treason charge, because Chief Justice Chase, despite his character defects, had a certain honor in regard to the law. "With the world looking on," Mason wrote, "the Chief Justice cannot rule that to be law which he knows is *not* law."

Joseph E. Davis to Jefferson Davis

The first letters from Mississippi to reach Jefferson Davis in Canada were anything but cheering.

Ben Montgomery and his sons, who bought both the Davises' plantations on mortgage, have little expectation of paying any interest because of the devastating floods.

Vicksburg
June, 1867

My Brother,

I find it difficult to write to you, as there is so little encouraging in the present state of affairs. I am inclined to think that our

Military governor is the best of the set, so far as his conduct has developed any thing. Registration is going on here, principally for the negroes. From the imperfect view I have, I would prefer the Military government to anything which we are likely to obtain under the reconstruction act.

The Mississippi is subsiding slowly, still over a large portion of the bottom lands. The people have planted as far as the water would permit, and seem more hopeful than under the circumstances would be expected. At Hurricane and Brierfield they are said to have planted about 800 acres, mostly in cotton. Ben, who was here a few days ago, said they had been able to supply those who remained with provisions, to do which they had incurred a debt of $8,000, but hoped they would be able to pay their expenses. I believe I informed you that I had thought it proper to release them from the payment of their interest for this year. I have been looking anxiously for a letter from you when you should have reached Canada. I hope you found the children as well as you expected, and I share in your joy in seeing them. Lise unites with me in love to you, Varina and the children.

As ever affectionately,
Your Brother

[*Enclosure:*]

Ben Montgomery to Joseph E. Davis

Hurricane May 30 1867

Kind Sir:

I have nothing encouraging to report. The excessive rains and cut worms are damaging the cotton. In so many places the worms have destroyed the stand entirely although seed had been planted this spring. We are still replanting and following up the water. A few of the people have planted some corn, but not much.

Our mule case will come up for trial again in June term—I do not know what time.

The health of the people generally good. I am constantly advising them to live as economical as possible in both provision & clothing so that they may be able to save a little of what they do make. Still hope to make expenses.

Your obt servt
Ben

J. M. Mason to Jefferson Davis

Niagara—Canada, West—
June 7th, 1867

My dear Sir:

I hope you had a safe and pleasant run down the Lake, and found all well in Mountain Street—how unfortunate that you left us so soon, had you remained till now, you would better have understood the early summer climate of Western Canada—the thermometer at 11 A.M. today, stood in the verandah at my front door in the shade though facing the sun, at 81°. Then again I brought with me from Toronto a supply of fishing tackle, and yesterday and today, in an hour or two, caught herrings enough to supply my table for a week— Ah! what you have lost by the perverse habit of having your own way—I hope however that indulging the like inclination, you will soon come back with Mrs. Davis and your family, to remain for the Summer.

Do write me of anything that may interest you, and more especially of anything in which I can serve you. With kindest regards from my household to yours

Yours my dear Sir
Most cordially and truly
J. M. Mason

Jefferson Davis to Maggie Davis

Maggie is at school in Montreal. Mrs. Davis has gone to Bennington, Vermont, because her mother became seriously ill while visiting an old friend. Mr. Davis had to leave for his trial in Richmond without his wife. His mother-in-law died in Montreal on November 24.

Lennoxville, Canada
28th Oct 1867

My dear Daughter,

I have lately received a letter from my Brother in which he mentions his disappointment at not receiving a letter from you. I had last summer notified him of your purpose to write to him.

We are all well here, Billy, and Winnie Anne much stouter than when they came to this place. Jeff is often with us, though his school hours do not give him much leisure.

Nurse Mary has been sick and is still unable to attend to the children, which is a great inconvenience, especially during the absence of your Mother.

I will be glad to have a letter from you and to hear fully of your daily occupation and of whatever interests you.

This is a very quiet residence, therefore pleasant to me. The weather has been fine for outdoor exercise and we have taken advantage of it.

Good night, my dear Little Pollie, may you be as happy and as good as your Father's prayers would have you.

Ever affectionately,
Your Father

Charles Minnegerode to Jefferson Davis

Richmond, Va.
5 Nov. 1867

My dear and honored Sir:

It is but natural that my mind always faithful in its remembrance of you, should turn to you more than ever, now as the time is coming on when we shall see you here—and God grant, under such circumstances as may be overruled into consistency with truth and justice.

My desire was to ask you, to make my humble home your residence while you are here—and I would be only too glad, if this agreed with your views.

My own judgment, I am sorry to confess, has been convinced by others that it will be more expedient for you to stay where you were before, at the Spotswood Hotel. Mr. Milward is your old host and personally devoted to you. It is at his earnest request, that I now write to you and endorse his own invitation which he sent you in two different letters.

Your former rooms are ready for you, and any other accommodation at your disposal that may be desirable.

If you are not to stay with me, I would like for you to be near us; and I believe you could not be made more comfortable anywhere, nor would you be so convenient to the attendance to any thing connected with your stay here, at any other house.

I abstain from enlarging on all I feel and hope for you and yours. You know how I have you in my heart and remember you in my prayers. I will only add my kindest regards and best love to Mrs. Davis and all your household—and most earnestly invoking God's blessing upon you, I remain

Yours faithfully and affectionately
Chs. Minnegerode

In Richmond at the November trial, the old friends, Jefferson Davis and Robert E. Lee, met for the first time since the surrender. Lee was questioned for two hours by a mixed jury of Negroes and whites about military movements of which the whole world already knew. His story was considered proof of "armed insurrection against the authority of the United States." Davis, whose nerves were keyed up to his defense and eager to speak, was not even called to the stand, for Chief Justice Chase did not appear as scheduled and the United States Government assigned a new trial for late March. Again Davis was reprieved but not free. Mrs. Davis joined him in Baltimore, and at a physician's charge, he decided to avoid the harsh Canadian winter by staying with various Davis relations in Mississippi until the next trial. They sailed for Havana to see about some funds that had been deposited there for the Davis children's education by the former Confederate agent. In Mississippi Davis witnessed the destruction wrought by the Federal troops. The drastic change from the comfortable living of many friends to dire poverty and makeshift depressed him greatly. Varina had expected the stay with devoted relatives to recruit his health. But the plight of the South under the heel of Reconstruction made him—in private —more dispirited than when he had been in Lennoxville.

Maggie Davis to Her Father

Maggie is now almost thirteen.

Lennoxville, Canada
Dec 26th 1867

My darling Father

Don't think that I have neglected writing to you and Mother, for I have written five or six letters to you both but I did not expect you to get them as you were travelling about so much. I hope you are well and also darling Mother, and that you have been treated kindly and have been very happy, as happy as you could be with so much weighing on your darling head, that head that no other is like or ever could be like to me.

I have not been very well but am improving greatly. The doctor ordered porter for me and as I cannot drink a whole bottle every day Aunty helps me, as the doctor ordered it for her too. I think that it is doing her a great deal of good and I know it is me.

Darling Father, I have written to Uncle Joe, as I knew it would be the best Christmas Jeff and I could offer you.

You have no idea what a nice time I have here, for I do snowshoeing and sledding and tobogganing and also go for midnight drives and we have such fun, for you know all the little girls in the village come too.

Hoping you are all well and wishing you a happy New Year and with much love from all I must say adieu.

I remain your most affectionate little daughter
"Polly"

Jefferson Davis to George H. Young

Davis declined to stay with any of his old friends, who sent him pressing invitations, lest they suffer open or concealed reprisals by the Federal soldiers or carpetbaggers who had swarmed into the state. This fragment of a letter in answer to an invitation reveals the state of Davis's mind and a degree of his melancholy. Colonel Young lived at Waverly plantation near Columbus, Mississippi.

Vicksburg
February 25, 1868

Dear Friend,

The desolation of our country had made my visit sad, but the heroic fortitude with which our people bear privation, injustice and persistent oppression fills my heart with pride. It cannot be that so noble a race and so fine a country can be left permanently subject and a desert.

The belief that I might embarrass my friends by visiting them, has caused me to restrict my trip to the amount of travel necessary to reach the home of my nearest relatives.

I start this morning for Richmond, but it is probable the trial will be again postponed. Having robbed me of everything I had, my enemies do not now allow me the poor privilege of going to work. [*The rest is lost.*]

The trial was again postponed—until May. On March 30 the trustees of Randolph-Macon College at Ashland, Virginia, sent a committee to meet Davis in Baltimore and offer him the presidency. Regretfully he explained that he was still a prisoner though released on bail, and he felt that he could not risk the fortunes of an institution until the odium cast upon him was removed.

After his return to Canada, Davis's plight was made worse now by the impeachment trial of Andrew Johnson. If the President was convicted the vengeful Radicals would be in complete control; so Davis's attorney, Charles O'Conor, wrote him to prepare to flee to Europe. But the single vote of Senator Edmund G. Ross of Kansas brought about Johnson's acquital. And a few days later Davis's treason trial was postponed until "some day in October agreeable to the court."

However, as James Murray Mason had predicted, Chief Justice Chase did not dare bring Jefferson Davis to trial on a treason charge, for it might prove patent to the world that the Southern States had the Constitutional right to secede and the North would stand convicted of an unjustifiable war. On December 5, 1868, the Chief Justice put himself on record as saying that the indictment against Davis should be quashed. Though the case was to be left dangling, O'Conor assured his client that he would never be troubled further. And by President Johnson's general amnesty proclamation of Christmas Day, 1868, Jefferson Davis was no longer a prisoner on bail. In the meantime he remained in Lennoxville until late July when he took his family to England.

Jefferson Davis Howell to Jefferson Davis

Davis has secured a position on a ship for his namesake brother-in-law, who likes the sea and has already had a voyage to Brazil.

Oporto, Portugal
June 28th, 1868

My dear Brother—

We had a very pleasant passage out, & in my new capacity as 2nd Mate I have given satisfaction. I have been studying navigation & now I think can navigate pretty well, but if you get me on the why's and wherefore's like you used to do on Algebra, I don't know how I would manage. I have wished for you often to be near me to give me an explanation of difficult passages, and when I meet you will call on you.

Accept my sincere thanks for your kind wishes, Sir. My best love & kisses to all the children & Sister, for the latter you will please find enclosed a letter, & Believe me to be as ever, Sir,

Your affectionate Bro.
Jeff. D. Howell

Jefferson Davis to Howell Cobb

Toward the end of June Jefferson Davis suffered a serious accident in the Lennoxville hotel where the family was staying. Carrying the baby Winnie downstairs one day, he missed his footing on the top step and plunged to the bottom into the lobby, severely injuring his head and breaking two ribs. (He had the presence of mind to drop the little girl on a landing.) His physician was gravely worried and recommended a sea voyage. Some English friends were sailing from Quebec to Liverpool on July 25 and urged the Davises to go with them. In despair of finding suitable employment in America and technically a prisoner under parole and still to be tried, Davis decided to look into a business connection in England that had been offered him. Still incapacitated, with Mrs. Davis acting as his amanuensis, he dictated a letter to Howell Cobb in Georgia.

Lennoxville, C.E. July 6th 1868

My dear Sir,

The proceedings against me having left a longer interval in which to cast about for some employment by which to support myself and family, I have decided to go to Liverpool to see what may be done in establishing a commission house, especially for cotton and tobacco. An Englishman of very high character and social position who has been extensively engaged in the India trade as a commission merchant has proposed to me a partnership under the belief that I could obtain assurance of the shipments of the staple of our own country, with such assurance I would be willing to attempt a new pursuit confident that if the business was strictly that of commissions my friends would incur no risk, and I might hope for an increasing income. I write to you to inquire what may be expected in regard to shipments by your friends and neighbors.

I expect to take passage the 25th from Quebec, consequently your answer would not reach me later than the 24.

Mrs. Davis is my amanuensis, as I had the misfortune to fall and break two of my ribs ten days ago, and am quite feeble from the effects of the fall.

With kind regards to Mrs. Cobb and the family, believe me

Very sincerely
Your friend,
Jeffn. Davis

[*Postscript from Mrs. Davis:*]
P.S. Dear Burrow, I trust at last that we see our way clear if the guarantees of cotton to be sent reach us before we go to Liverpool, or soon after our arrival there, to be raised above the wretched sense of idle dependence which has so galled us. I am sorry to say that Mr. Davis' health has not improved, he looks wretchedly, and I think much of his indisposition is induced by his despair of getting some employment which will enable him to educate our children. There were many things in our visit to the South which convinces me that for a year or more, until at least civil law prevails, Mr. Davis could not quietly remain there. Then if it should please God that we should ever meet I will tell you. Until then I shall as ever remain,
Yours affectionately,   V. Davis

WELCOMING ARMS
ABROAD

Judah P. Benjamin to Jefferson Davis

On the ocean voyage Davis improved, and on arrival in Liverpool the ex-President was greeted by a host of well-wishers, some from as far away as Glasgow, inviting the family to stay with them. Among those pressing for an immediate visit was Alexander James Beresford-Hope, Conservative member of Parliament. Among the stack of welcoming notes was the following one from Judah P. Benjamin, who was now practicing law in London and had an important case pending. Unable to meet the ship on its arrival, he came a few days later.

> Temple Building, London
> 6th Augt 1868

My dear friend

I shall have the extreme gratification of pressing yr hand again, (after all that has passed since we separated) on Tuesday next, but I could not wait till then before saying how much I rejoice at the prospect of seeing you once again, surrounded by your family and greeted by friends—

With best memories to dear Mrs. Davis and the little ones, I remain very truly your friend,

> J. P. Benjamin

Jefferson Davis to Varina Davis

Davis is the house guest of the Earl of Shrewsbury.

Alton Towers
4th Sept. 1868

My dear Wife,

I arrived safely at Buxton and stayed all night. The next morning as there was no public conveyance by which to go to Alton I hired a "Fly" and went over the highlands of Derbyshire to Leek and thence by rail to Alton. The day of the floral exhibition was the 3d, Thursday—so I had time to spare.

I regretted much your absence from the fête. The gardens and grounds are very extensive and more beautiful than any thing I could have imagined.

Lord Shrewsbury, with his Wife, three daughters and little son, came to the fête and we returned last night.

They are very cordial and earnest in the wish that I would stay and write to you to join me.

I intend to go to-morrow to London, but may stay till Monday morning.

Every thing is on a scale of great magnificence, but the people do not seem to feel their grandeur, so I am quite at ease. Kiss my dear children and accept the constant love of your Husband.

Jefferson Davis to Varina Davis

Davis is hoping to sell interests in a Canadian copper mine. His family has settled in Leamington for the autumn.

The Junior Athenaeum
London
Sunday, 22nd Nov. 1868

My dear Wife,

I found the head of the House from which favorable results were expected was out of town and would not return before Thursday. The prospect of a direct sale is not encouraging, but there is a chance and there is also reason to expect some important papers from Canada, so that if I were to go on to France it would involve a very prompt return; and therefore I have decided to return to Leamington on Tuesday.

I tried to get hair put in the locket, but it being Saturday I failed, and so gave up the locket and the loose hair.

I am at the Club marked on this sheet to dine with Mr. Benjamin.

This morning I went to Westminister Abbey for the service and if I were good at description I would not hope to give you an idea of its grandeur.

Kiss the children for me. It is very sad to be separated from you, but as I cannot cheer you I will not give you a reflection of the gloom of this dismal London day.

May God bless and protect you all is ever the prayer of your affectionate

Husband

Jefferson Davis to Varina Davis

Shortly after Christmas, responding to repeated invitations, the Davises went to Paris where they were warmly entertained by expatriate Confederates like John Slidell, ex-Senator William McKendree Gwin, and Emily Mason, the estimable sister of James Murray Mason. When Mrs. Davis returned to England, her husband stayed on for a while as the guest of A. Dudley Mann, and in the hope that he might get rid of a persistent cough acquired in the English damp he went to Switzerland for a fortnight.

Paris 17 Bld. de Madeleine
27 Jany 1869

My dear Wife,

By the caption of this you will see that I have left Rue Dupliots. Col. Mann insisted on giving me his room and fitted up the adjoining one for himself. We are quite well but for the gloomy, wet day which has not allowed me to get out.

Your friends came in early and in battalion to see whether all was gone and the rooms in your absence seemed so desolate to me that I could realize their fear of flight or disaster.

The concierge wanted to know when I announced my departure if *I* left because of the rooms, or deficient service or what. I endeavored to satisfy him that we had no complaint and paid his bill.

Nobody offers to go to Switzerland or Italy with me and it has been suggested that there may be difficulty about a passport, as I cannot of course apply to the U.S. Minister. So it may be that I will not do all the fine things contemplated, but return sooner than you expected to London. Please keep me fully and exactly advised. I long to have my dear children once more in my arms and to hear their sweet voices breathing the affection which is sweetest to the least happy.

It is sad to me to recollect how little I saw of Jeff in his holiday. May God bless and guide him.

Farewell, may the Lord preserve and bless you is the earnest prayer

of your Husband
Jeffn Davis

Jefferson Davis to Varina Davis

With the thought of settling for a time in France, Davis has been "house hunting." Dudley Mann has a country place, Mont Po, near Chantilly.

Paris, 7th Feb. 1869

My dear Wife

Since you left I have been again to Mont Po. The day was bright, the roads dry, and everything appeared to better advantage than when we visited the place together.

The drives through the forest are very pleasant. Col. Mann, with the approaching prospect of a sale, renews his arguments in favor of it for you and the children. I have not entertained his propositions, but have reminded him of your decided opinion, and of the equally fixed decision on my part to endeavor to arrange matters so as most nearly to meet your wishes.

I went to see the house you looked at near to Capt. Morris' residence. It did not impress favorably. The amount of progressing excavation in that neighborhood and new buildings are unfavorable to health.

The objection of our friends here to my going to Switzerland on account of the necessity for travelling by night, has delayed my starting; but I think the cough is now less than it was when you left, and it is my purpose to start to-morrow evening, unless there should be an unfavorable change in the weather. Possibly I may find something in the trip which may be freer from objections than any thing I have seen here.

My opinion of Paris as a place for education has not changed for the better, but rather for the worse. The tone cannot be delicate where living objects and inanimate representations so glaringly offend against decency; and it is to be doubted whether the many advantages found here for intellectual cultivation counterbalance the demoralizing influences which co-exist. I know we cannot expect to command every thing which is desirable, and am prepared to make the best of a hard case; but in my estimation a butterfly that has lost the down of its wing is not in a worse plight than a girl who has been disrobed of her modesty. The shops have been unusually brilliant in their windows of late, as Lent approaches, and crowds of men and women are gathered in places where prints and toys are exhibited, and occasional observation has taught me that whereon the number of gazers is great one may expect the presence of prints of nude women and toys expressive of amorous passions. The population which remunerates for such work and the exhibition of such types of general sentiment cannot be favorable to the cultivation or preservation of *modesty*. This would no doubt be regarded here as fantastic or rustic, perhaps barbarous; but I am thankful my wife was reared beyond the contact of these "refinements," and many others of which I forbear to make mention to you.

I made the projected trip to the cemetery, Père Lachaise, and found in the names on the vaults much to excite historic memories and sad reflections. The grounds are very extensive and from the hill the view of the city is very impressive. There is a tomb of Abélard and Héloïse. Their effigies are on the tomb which bears an inscription announcing that the remains of Abélard and Héloïse are reunited in this tomb. It is covered by a dome supported on graceful columns, the whole being built of material brought from the convent founded by Abélard and of which Héloïse was Abbess.

I became uneasy at not hearing from you and went to learn if Mdme d'Erlanger had news of you, she had not heard directly, but the dressmaker said you were coming back, which I was prone to believe even on that authority, then I sought Mdme Brelaz who informed me that she had received a letter from her Sister who reported all well.

Miss Emily Mason and Mrs. Tyson have been here, both asked about Maggie's coming and whether you would be with her. Mrs. Tyson offered her services in a very acceptable manner.

It was late before I began to write and as it gets colder as it grows later several reminders warn me to go to bed.

My dear Winnie, I have missed you in all ways and at all times. It seems to me now that my entreaties against your departure were fuller of regrets than you supposed, as else you had not gone. Well, well, let us pray it will all be well until it is better.

Good night, good bye, God bless & preserve you,

Ever affectionately
Your Husband

John Slidell to Jefferson Davis

John Slidell, former Confederate Commissioner in France, has been very attentive to the ex-President and often entertains him.

Paris
February 12, 1869

My dear Mr. Davis

I suppose that you will have profited by the fine weather & gone to Chantilly. I send you a letter which was enclosed to me from London. Also a permission to visit the Polytechnic School. I am most happy to accompany you thither, unless you state preference to go Incognito.

Ever faithfully
Yr Servant
John Slidell

A. Dudley Mann to Varina Davis

Davis had paid a long visit to Mann after Mrs. Davis's return to London. Mann now gently reproaches her for neglecting to write thank-you notes to persons who had entertained her in Paris.

17 Boulevard de la Madeleine
March 15, 1869

Dear and good Friend:—

My little home has been cheerless ever since the President left me. The enchantment which he imparted to it will I fear, never return; certainly never unless he brings it back and brings yourself along to grace our enjoyments. I often, when alone, laugh immoderately at your amicable mimicry of your *two* friends, and in that connection I have something to tell you that is excessively amusing.

Of our friends: The Slidells first—they seem to be as happy as they well could be, Madame d'Erlanger included. Mr. S. is as regular as ever in his fortnightly visits, and in his general bearing there are indications of *satisfaction* at the genial way in which the world moves. He is more of a philosopher than I formerly supposed him to be. The McGruders, I fancy, were smartly chagrined that no acknowledgment of the visit of the Abingers was manifested by yourself or the President. Miss Emily Mason was *wondering* why she has not received a letter from you, or answer to hers. Good lady, as she is, I have succeeded in consoling her. Mrs. Acoste is your earnest friend, but perhaps she would have been a little bit better pleased if she had received a card from you. The Perkinses, though they say nothing to myself of their fancied neglect, are outspoken, almost clamorous to others. Mr. Duncan and Mrs. Thames have nothing but friendly regards for you both. The foregoing was scarcely worthy of sketching, still I thought it might not be without interest to you.

I was at Mont Po last Saturday. The day turned out to be cold. I never beheld a more beautiful spectacle than I witnessed from its window of the Oak Room:—a snow storm which would have graced Siberia; the sun shining brightly all the while and its rays forcing themselves with dazzling splendor through the thickest of the descending flakes.

Grant has made a *grand start!* The reconstruction of his cabinet clearly indicates that he is "mere clay in the Potter's hands."

With sentiments of affectionate esteem for every one of yours.

A. Dudley Mann

Jefferson Davis to A. Dudley Mann

When Davis returned to Dudley Mann's Paris flat after his sojourn in Switzerland, his plaguing cough was entirely gone. Now in London, Mrs. Davis and he have decided to send fourteen-year-old Maggie to the convent school recommended by Emily Mason. Toinette is Mann's jewel of a servant.

                                        18 Upper Gloucester Place
                                        19th April 1869

Dear friend

My daughter Maggie is to leave us this afternoon and will hand you this on her arrival in Paris. I am very reluctant to see her start and though it is not possible for me to overcome the fears which arise from the separation, I find much consolation in the fact that she will be near to you and be under your supervision. My purpose has been from day to day postponed to write to you fully, but around my past there are so many sad memories, and over my future such forbidding clouds that it must be when I feel more collected, that the task will be performed.

The quiet days passed with you remain to me the one happy appreciation of recent years. God grant that they may not be our last together, but when the happy reunion may occur it is for chance to determine. When you see our friends the Corbins and Acostes and the others of my obliging acquaintance in Paris, please make my kindest salutation. Present me to Mr. Slidell, who I hope makes his daily call on you as formerly, remember me to Toinette and the noble cat Tammy, and believe me ever cordially

                                        Yours
                                        Jeffn. Davis

P.S. I send you two photographs taken in the clothes I wore when captured. The same hat, coat, waistcoat, trousers and boots; the spurs I had were lost. J. D.

Jefferson Davis to Cora Semmes Ives

Colonel Joseph Ives was a handsome New York–born West Pointer of considerable charm, who married Cora Semmes of Baltimore. He joined the Confederacy, and became first a secretarial aide of Robert E. Lee and then an aide-de-camp of President Davis. Since Mrs. Ives was rich and had taken a large house, the Iveses did much entertaining for the Davises and often housed distinguished foreign visitors. Though Ives was a favorite of both President Davis and General Lee, who had complete confidence in his loyalty, because of undoubted leakage to the enemy of coming events, some suspected Ives of betrayal. Even sharp-eyed Mary Chesnut, whose husband was also a Presidential aide, had her doubts about Ives, and reminded her husband that Ives often opened direct communications of Lee to Davis and even Mrs. Davis's private letters as well, which no other aide dared to do. Her husband pooh-poohed her suspicions. After the surrender there was desultory talk of Ives's treachery, but Jefferson Davis had no belief in it.

Mrs. Ives, like her distinguished relative Admiral Raphael Semmes, was a devout Catholic. She now lives in Warrenton, Virginia. In this letter Davis attempts to console her over the death of Colonel Ives early in 1869, and to reassure her about her husband's loyalty.

> 18 Upper Gloucester Place
> Dorset Square, London
> 25th April 1869

My dear Mrs. Ives,

As Mrs. Davis wrote to you immediately after the receipt of your letter, I have delayed to answer in the hope that it might be in my power to see the Revd. Father O'Reilly and give you a message from him. This hope has not been fulfilled and I am unwilling to delay longer.

My regard and esteem for your Husband was formed long before the War began, and you will perhaps remember that my confidence as to the course he would pursue was expressed to you before we had heard of his leaving California. The trust was not destroyed by the reports to which you allude, and the assurance I expressed to you when we met last in Baltimore, that those reports were untrue, rested on facts known to me, and which were sufficient for my own thorough conviction as to his fidelity; though the corroborating evidence you have obtained had never come to the light. I rejoice however that you possess such testimony as you have found.

It is a blessed consolation to know that our friend died in the full faith and with the consolations of the Christian Church. You can but grieve long and deeply over your loss; but looking as you do, on this world as but a pilgrimage to another and better state, your sorrow is tempered by the hope, the assurance, that after a brief day you will rejoin your Husband where the wicked cease from troubling and the weary are at rest.

I hope when it may again be my fortune to return to our country, that it will be permitted to me to see you and your dear children. Pray teach them ever to regard me as the friend of their Father who never doubted his honorable fidelity, and will ever love them for his sake.

My daughter Maggie is at school at the Convent of the Assumption near to Paris, France. My son Jefferson is at school near to Liverpool. The younger children, William and Varina, are here.

Mrs. Davis and Miss Howell speak of you often and always affectionately. Of myself there is nothing pleasant to communicate and I have too many proofs of your sympathy to justify me in telling you of my anxieties and disappointments.

That God may in his own good way bind up your wounds, and lighten the burthens you have so meekly yet so bravely borne, is the earnest prayer of your sincere friend,

Jefferson Davis

Maggie Davis to Her Father

From the Convent of the Assumption in Paris, where her mother had sent her "to acquire a good French accent," Maggie writes she is being well cared for.

April 30th 1869
Monastre de l'Assomption

My darling Father,

I received your sweet letter today and thought I would answer it today as I had fewer lessons to learn. Mr. Mann brought it and he said he had been ill ever since he came to see me. Mrs. Slidell came yesterday with Miss Slidell and they wanted me to go out with them, but Madame Walburge said she could not let me without a written permission from home. Mrs. Tyson took Carrie and me out to the Bois de Boulougne on Sunday and I enjoyed it very much. She also took us to the Arc de Triomphe, which I enjoyed even more than the Bois. This Sunday we are going to walk out to the Bois. When I was there last there was a consert there, although it was Sunday, and the people were buying things to eat. Madame Walburge is so good to me, she calls me her "dear little baby," comes every night to see if I am comfortable and every morning to know if I have a head ache and if I would like to sleep longer, and if I am asleep always tells the nun not to wake me till I wake of myself and comes three or four times a day to see if I am awake and continues to come till I do.

I must close my letter with much love and many kisses to you darling Father. Give my love to all the Blandys and all our other friends.

Adieu, my precious father,
Your loving "Pollie"

Jefferson Davis to Maggie Davis

London
10 May, 1869

My dear Pollie,

If any thing could entirely console me for your absence it would be found in your cheerful brave resolution to avail yourself of present advantages to acquire the means of future usefulness.

I cannot express my gratitude to dear Mrs. Tyson and the kind Nuns for their goodness to you, in the hour of your desolation, at least what would have been desolate if they had left you to brood over all from which you had been so lately separated without giving to you anything to take the vacant place.

Billy has returned to Mdme. de Zastro and is reported to be quite happy among his school fellows. The poor little fellow, despite his anxiety to return to school, broke down at the moment of parting and was a sad & weeping boy.

Winnie is well, loving and interesting as usual. Your Mother is now as well as usual, but as she is writing to you, I will let her speak for herself.

My plans have been interrupted and my departure may be consequently delayed until the hot weather in Missi. is over, so as to enable me to go there in safety.

God bless you, my darling daughter, ever prays

Your Father
Jefferson Davis

Alexander James Beresford-Hope to Jefferson Davis

The Beresford-Hopes had shown the Davises many courtesies.

Arklow House
Connaught Place (London)
July 4, 1869

My dear Mr. Davis:

I am very sorry that you should have for one moment thought of the conventional hour for visiting—for we are always glad to have the pleasure of seeing one for whom we have so high an admiration & regard. It was a great regret to Lady Mildred not to have been able to have seen you the other day. But she was really very ill. She begs to thank you much for your kind sympathy.

I have been particularly anxious to see you to settle the details of the visit which you & Mrs. Davis & Miss Howell & such of your family as may be at home have promised to pay us at Bedgebury. Parliament will be out in a month & in the latter week of July Lady Mildred (if well enough) wishes to go for a short time to Scotland to take part in the coming of age of her nephew Mr. Balfour & to see her sister there. So let us plan for the second week in August— sometime about the 8th or 10th & we expect a *good* visit. We are, as you know, very accessible from London.

Many thanks for your news of James Murray Mason. It will be a great comfort for him if he can settle in peace in his own Virginia.

Lady Mildred begs to join me in kindest regards to Mrs. Davis & Miss Howell.

Believe me
Yours very sincerely
A Beresford-Hope

Jefferson Davis to Varina Davis

On the last Saturday of July, 1869, Jefferson Davis sailed from London for Edinburgh with Charles Mackay, the Scotch poet and onetime editor of the London *Illustrated News*. Mackay had visited Richmond during the war and had come to admire the Confederate President. Now Davis is to have a month of relaxing travel through the land of Walter Scott and Robert Burns without the incumbrance of wife and children. It proved to be the most delightful and revivifying trip of his life. Mackay was the foster-father—some authorities say the real father—of Marie Corelli, a girl of fourteen in 1869, who was to become a best-selling novelist. For four days the male companions were to be house guests of John Blackwood, editor of the famous *Blackwood's Magazine,* and they spent a few days each with James Smith in Glasgow and Lord Abinger at Inverlochy Castle.

THE ROYAL HOTEL, EDINBURGH
July 27, 1869

Dear Wife,

We arrived safely last night and this morning I had to prepare in haste for breakfast and then was borne off to see sights so that my purpose to announce my arrival here has been delayed until afternoon.

From the Tweed northward we have been rarely out of sight of some place of historical association. The Towers of Tantallon and the rock where Ravenswood comes down to the sea were under close observation. The Bass-rock, too, by our obliging Captain was brought so close to us that we could see the remaining portions of the old prison and the myriads of gulls sticking to the sides of the rock, so little acquainted with the obstructive tendencies of "civilized" man that they to a great extent remained sedentary, though the boat whistle screamed while we were passing. We have been to the castle, to the Holy Rood, to the old Parliament House and to Jno. Knox's residence, the latter not open to-day.

The fog hangs over King Arthur's seat and we have postponed the ascent for a brighter day. We are pressed to go hence to visit a gentleman who lived near to Melrose Abbey and to Abbotsford; if we do so it will be next week before we reach Glasgow. And so I think it will be. The sea was very smooth and the voyage quite pleasant.

Give my love to Maggie and the children. I shall hope to hear from you and them when I arrive at Glasgow.

May God have you all in His holy keeping ever prays your ever affectionate Husband

J. Davis

Jefferson Davis to Varina Davis

Ettrickbank
Selkirk
30th July 1869

Dear Wife,

I have been turned aside from a direct journey to Glasgow, and am now at a pretty country house on the bank of the Ettrick.

Yesterday I visited the ruins of Melrose Abbey, those of the Dryburgh Monastery, the place where Sir Walter Scott was buried, and then drove to Abbotsford. The present proprietor, Mr. Hope Scott, received us very kindly and showed us many relics not seen usually by visitors.

The original manuscripts of several novels, Scott's diary, and some portions of his autobiography were to me the most interesting.

The country about the Tweed, the Ettrick and the Yarrow is the best combination of the beautiful, the useful, and the grand that I have beheld. There is in the people the warmest hospitality and cheerful greeting. Many ask for you and regret your absence.

I send you a few sprigs only of interest because of the localities where they were gathered. The little daisy was plucked from the ground near the depository of the Heart of Bruce. The Harebell grew near to the Tomb of Scott. Another, the smallest, from Arthur's seat. The little white flower from the plain where Lord Marmion is described as pausing enraptured with the beauties of the Firth of Forth and the plains of Down Edin. But I won't force you to read more of the talk so like a guide book.

I propose to-morrow to go to the house of Mr. Blackwood at St. Andrew's and thence either through the Trossachs or direct to Glasgow.

I will write soon a letter to meet Maggie on her arrival from Paris for her vacation. Tell my big boy that if he leaves before my return I will see him soon in Waterloo, D.V. I write in haste as the carriage is ready for a drive up the Tweed. God preserve you all, is the constant prayer of your Husband,

Jeffers. Davis

Jefferson Davis to Varina Davis

Mrs. Gerald Porter, the daughter of John Blackwood, who was a young girl at the time of Jefferson Davis's visit to Strathtyrum, wrote in 1898 in her memoirs of her father: "We felt that it was quite like entertaining royalty. . . . Any one who had the privilege of knowing Mr. Davis personally could not fail to be attracted by the straightforward manly uprightness of his character, which was apparent in everything, and withal the charm of his manner, a mixture of dignity and simplicity, that compelled a certain respect which his kindly courtesy only made more impressive."

> Strathtyrum
> St. Andrews
> 2nd Aug., 1869

Dear Wife

I am at this old Cathedral and sea-bathing town, now St. Andrew's, formerly St. Rule's, and am the guest of Mr. Blackwood, the proprietor of your favorite magazine.

The great feature of the place is the ruin of the Cathedral, said to have had the largest chapel in the Kingdom. It was built about 700 years ago and of such good material that it might have lasted twice as many centuries more, but for the infuriated mob which, under the excitement created by a sermon of John Knox, assailed and to a great extent demolished it.

Mr. & Mrs. Blackwood are accomplished and very agreeable. They have both often expressed their regret at your absence.

On the ground dedicated to the "Royal game of Golf" I picked three Harebells, one white, one blue and the other a color between the two, they are also enclosed.

In two days I expect to reach Glasgow and there to receive news of you and them. We go hence to the Trossachs, and Loch Lomond, and when I come back to London will give you as much recital of my wanderings and doings as you wish to have.

May God have you all in His holy keeping ever prays

> Your Husband
> Jefferson Davis

Jefferson Davis to Maggie Davis

Fourteen-year-old Maggie, who has just returned from a convent school near Paris, was well acquainted with *The Lady of the Lake*, for her father had read and recited it to her when she was a little girl.

Callander, Scotland
6th Aug. 1869

My dear Daughter,

Your Mother will probably have explained to you the circumstances which have caused me to be absent at the time of your return. I have been passing through much of the most lovely scenery of the Lowlands and am now at what is often called the Gate of the Highlands of Scotland. The mountain of Ben Ledi is in full view from the window of my room, you will recollect it in connection with the description in the "Lady of the Lake" of scene when Roderick Dhu showed his men to Fitz James.

This is the scenery described in the first canto of the Poem, and it is with special pride that the course taken by the stag is pointed out to visitors.

It is wonderful to remark how thoroughly Scott's descriptions have entered into the minds of the people hereabouts as History. At Stirling Castle I saw the room in which King James stabbed Earl Douglas and the window is pointed out from which the body of the murdered Earl is said to have been thrown, beneath that window I picked the two white flowers enclosed.

The leaves of Box and the Harebell were gathered at the little garden shown as that of Queen Mary when she was a child and placed for safety on the Island of Luchmahorne in Loch Ard. The chapel and palace are in ruin. The Island has no other occupant than a small flock of sheep, but the grand chesnuts and the humble box remain as mementos of the unhappy Queen of Scotland.

God bless and preserve you, my darling Pollie.

Your Father

Jefferson Davis to Varina Davis

The well-to-do James Smith, prominent businessman of Glasgow, had gone to Liverpool to meet Jefferson Davis on his arrival in August, 1868. He had invited the entire family to stay with him at his home, "Benvue," in fashionable Dowanhill Gardens. After almost a year Davis was able to enjoy his invitation. Smith, an ardent pro-Confederate, had made a small fortune on a Mississippi plantation in the 1840's and retired to his native land after the death of his first wife.

Mrs. Davis and the girls liked to receive pressed flowers in letters. She plans to go to Yarmouth, the English seaside resort.

> Glasgow
> 9th Aug. 1869

Dear Wife,

We reached here this afternoon and found your three letters waiting for me. We went to the Lochs made familiar by Scott's "Lady of the Lake." The descriptions are wonderfully true to nature but the beauty and grandeur of the scenery can only be realized by visiting it. I have a copy of that great Poem for you, and you find your wish for photographic scenes anticipated to some extent by its illustrations. I picked some leaves and flowers on "Ellen's Isle," as even the boatmen on Loch Katrine call it; they grew at the spot where once a hut stood & which is assumed to have been the home of Roderick Dhu. The moss was pulled from a rock beneath the oak where Duncan's widow stood when her "husband's dirk gleamed in her hand." I will send them with "The Lady of the Lake" by Book-post.

At the head of Loch Earn we saw the grave of Rob Roy, and there I gathered the little wild flowers, which I will try to enclose in this. The good people of the Highlands have shown me much genuine hospitality. Mr. & Mrs. Smith have welcomed me most cordially and seem truly to regret your absence. We propose to leave here on Thursday for Oban and the western Islands. The weather is cool today and the air invigorating. I have improved rapidly.

In the old Cathedral of the ruins of Dunfermline Castle, I saw the most beautiful effigy in marble, erected to the late Lieut. Genl. Bruce. It is something larger than life, is recumbent and a veiled figure representing his Wife bends over that of the Genl. so as to bring the two faces into close proximity. On the head stone is inscribed "The Lord watch between me and thee when we are absent one from another."

I hope you will find the sea shore pleasant and beneficial to you all. Kiss my dear children and share with them the love I bear to you all in sufficient quantities to supply each.

Affectionately
Your Husband

Jefferson Davis to Varina Davis

Benvue, Dowanhill Gardens
Glasgow
11th Aug. 1869

Dear Wife,

For any future shortcomings in the matter of letter writing you should give me credit in the excess of my present attention.

I write by a fire though the day is clear and the sun is shining with unusual splendor for this "land of mist."

We leave early tomorrow for Oban & the Isle of Mull.

My stay here has been very pleasant, and I have met with most cordial attention from many beside the kind family with whom we are staying.

The only cathedral of the olden time which is not a ruin is in Glasgow. I purchased two views but they give a faint idea of the grandeur and beauty of the structure. The crypt built in 1175 is in perfect preservation, except the stained glass which has been renewed, and for modern manufacture is the best I have seen, but fears are expressed as to the durability of the colors.

You may have your impression as to the appearance of Mr. Blackwood corrected by fulfilling a promise I made—which was to send to Mrs. Blackwood a photograph of myself, and if you choose to do so and to ask for one of her husband, she will no doubt comply and be gratified by the request.

Today some books and the leaves and flowers from Ellen's Isle go by book post.

My tenderest love,

Your Husband

Jefferson Davis to Varina Davis

Lord Abinger was married to a niece of the Confederate General John
B. Magruder, who had been a cadet at West Point with Jefferson Davis.

> Inverlochy Castle
> Kingussie, N.B.
> 17th Aug. 1869

Dear Wife,

At "Oban" I received your letter informing of Lord Abinger's
movements. By a mere accident we met at Greenock and came on
to Oban together. Dr. Mackay and I stopped at Oban and went
around the Island of Mull visiting Fingal's cave and the ruins of
Iona, where in the dark ages Christianity found a nursing mother.
I picked up some relics and views which I will bring to you.

From Oban we came to this, the residence of Lord Abinger. We
have been most hospitably entertained, and Lord Abinger insists
upon my staying in the Highlands and sending for you and the
children. Lady Abinger is still an invalid, has to be carried in a
sedan chair up and down stairs, but says she is improving and
speaks so affectionately of you, manifesting so sincere a wish to
have you here that I am quite charmed with her. The scenery
about here is the grandest of all the sublime spectacles I have met
in Scotland. You would find a wide field for your imagination in
the mists & changing lights & shades which characterize the Scottish
mountains.

We leave here to-morrow and go by the Caledonia canals & lochs
to intersect the Rail Road from Inverness to Edinboro and expect
to be in London in five or six days.

The weather here is so cool that fires are burned daily and the
air is bracing and most tonic. I tried Salmon fishing yesterday and
go out Grouse shooting to day—with such evidence you will be
relieved of anxiety for my health. I hope you find the sea shore
pleasant and beneficial to yourself and the children.

> Farewell, affectionately
> Your Husband

Jefferson Davis to Varina Davis

J. B. Jennings has been endeavoring to make a suitable connection for Jefferson Davis, and now the ex-President is thinking of business in London.

> Dochfour House, Inverness
> 22d Aug. 1869

Dear Wife,

We came to this terminus of the Caledonia Canal and propose to leave tomorrow Monday by rail for Edinboro and thence after a short delay to proceed to London. The last letter I have was from London and from its contents I suppose you are at Yarmouth. Yesterday I went to the field of Culloden and to the Fairy's Mountain. I send you some heather from the first named and harebell from the last.

I hope to reach London by Wednesday and there to learn of you enough to direct my further movements.

I have not heard lately from Mr. Jennings and may have some delay in London but will not let it be long.

With kisses for you and the children, I am as ever affectionately,

> Your Husband
> Jefferson Davis

Jefferson Davis to Varina Davis

Davis had returned to London from his month in Scotland—the best trip of his life—and again faces reality: the attempt to find a worthwhile business connection.

> London
> 26th Aug. 1869

Dear Wife,

I find that there is no steamer hence to Yarmouth tomorrow and that I must remain until Saturday morning. At that time I expect to leave by Boat to meet you.

The heat and smoke and dust of London seem all the worse as compared to the pure and cool air of the Scottish highlands.

It was a great relief to me to learn that the children were improving in the Sea air, and I hope that it has been of benefit to you.

I went to the City this morning, but found the matter still hanging and was disposed to consider it a matter for somebody else who had more years to work, but was requested to wait until evening when I should see what I should see.

Tell Winnie I have a flower, Folks or Fox glove, picked for her at the mountain on which the Folks or Fairies are said to dance; they were not dancing when I was there. I am very anxious to see my own little Pollie.

Ever affectionately
Your Husband
Jeffn. Davis

Jefferson Davis to Varina Davis

Jefferson Davis is returning to the States to see about a position with an insurance company in Memphis. His family remains in England until his business affairs are settled. After Mrs. Davis bade her husband goodbye at the London railway station, he wrote her the next morning from Southampton. Maggie did not return to the Paris convent.

South Hampton
25th Sept. 1869

Dear Wife

We arrived at the Hotel about midnight found it crowded and so little comfortable that I had cause to be content at your not having accompanied me thus far. I wished as you walked off to run after you and see you in the cab, for in your failure to look back I had the evidence of the struggle you had made to suppress the manifestation of your emotion. Poor little Billy looked so confused that I could imagine his asking you, what will happen next?

I have been on board the Steamer, there are few passengers and everything looks well. The Captain is a sturdy German and seemed disposed to be civil. We are to sail at one o'clock today and before this reaches you my eyes will have turned with longing looks to the place where my treasure is. Let us hope that the separation will be brief and that it will enure to our common good.

I will send with this a note which you can use at your discretion. Do not place yourself in matters of business on the footing of one expecting favor, but for equal or greater advantage it may be better to divide our deposits, as, if the interest is not increased, the safety may be.

I enclose a letter which may be of service to our good friend Charles Mackay, and which as a letter of civility I ought to have written before starting, so I prefer that it should be mailed at London. Give my tenderest love to all our children. When I awoke this morning the sorrowful realization that I could not have their morning kiss came upon me with a force which belongs so specially to the waking hour.

You will know how to order all things for Maggie's mental and physical good. She was nervous from her infancy and a mistake in her treatment would be to us a crowning misfortune. I would not have been willing for her to go back to the convent had it not been that you were to go with her.

Billy will I hope be happy at school and be able when I see him to read for me. My sensible little darlings will learn enough without urging and be to you a constant source of joy and pride.

You must all write to me often and fully. The daily incidents of little worth to you will be very precious to me.

Farewell, dear Winnie, and that God may guide and protect you is the most fervent prayer of

Your Husband

RETURN TO AMERICA
AND A DIFFERENT KIND OF
PRESIDENCY

Varina Davis to Jefferson Davis

My dear Husband,

I trust that tomorrow or the next day will see you safe in Harbor some where near about Fortress Monroe. Until you are safe on Land, nothing seems to me to be certain but storms. We are about as usual, but we have had a sad set back in our plans. Just as I had made ready all things for Paris, Dr. Davis came and brought Dr. Jackson to examine Maggie's back. They vetoed her going, not because of a developed disease but because they did not know at what time the spine might "rotate" and show a tendency to curvature. They pronounce the Convent of all things the worst for her. Dr. Jackson insists upon a rowing chair which will give the action of rowing a boat to straighten her shoulders & develop her chest, but, says I may make it enjoyable to her by letting her row in the Serpentine in Regent's Park as often as it is fine weather. She is the happiest thing you ever saw at the prospect of staying with her "darling Mother," flies at me, and kisses me a dozen times a day.

I have hopes of getting a daily governess at sixty pounds a year from ten until two for her—and will myself give her music lessons. We will give up the dining room from ten until two, and excuse ourselves to visitors so as to leave the drawing room quiet for her. I hope I have met your views in all that I have done thus far. You are generally most generous in your silence when you disapprove if you do so, but in this instance as it is such a thorough change of plans I do not know quite if I have done what you would like. All that perfect regularity and close attention can do, rest assured will be done. God will do the rest in answer to our prayers. Maggie is very lively & hopeful of her governess being a nice, youngish person. As soon as I have decided according to the best lights I can obtain I will write to you quite fully.

I heard from Jeff a day or two since, he was quite well. And full of tenderness for you as usual . . . [*The rest is lost.*]

Jefferson Davis to Varina Davis

Davis reached Baltimore on October 10, 1869. He was, not unnaturally, somewhat apprehensive when the agent for the insurance company who had come to meet him had "lost the papers."

Davis has the fervent hope of being offered an executive position with the Southern Pacific Railroad, for he had had a strong penchant for railroads since their invention and he believed in their great value for developing the country.

Baltimore
Barnum's Hotel
11th Oct. 1869

Dear Wife:

I arrived here last night after a very rough voyage. Found Brother Joe and Lize waiting for my arrival, and both of them in better health than when we saw them in Vicksburg.

Capt. Dukeheart called to invite me to sail with him on Friday and but for small reasons I would do so. The agent of the insurance company met me here with full powers to negotiate for my connection with the company, but with very little of the information which was needful to determine the propriety of joining the company. He says he lost his satchel which had the papers showing the condition of the company and its mode of transacting business, that he expects to recover it and them.

Brother Joe seems to think the offer made by the company a good chance. I do not feel quite satisfied with the signs, but may as the view opens regard them more favorably.

No answer to my letter about the Southern Pacific R.R.

If you have forgotten it, as I did, let me remind you that the chemists bill down in Praed Street was not paid. The bootmaker in New Street had not sent in his bill when I left. The Tailor Burmeister, you will remember, and those were I believe the only incumbrances I left. [*The rest is lost.*]

Jefferson Davis to Varina Davis

Baltimore
15 Oct. 1869

Dear Wife,

Your letter reached me here and gave me great joy, for it seemed very long since we parted and I could hardly hope that you would realize my anxiety to hear from and of you. Brother Joe is so feeble that I wish to save him from the fatigue of a journey by land, and we sail in a few hours on the *Cuba* for New Orleans.

Your friends by the battalion have called and inquired for you.

My friends here are anxious to do something for us, and don't like the idea of my going into business, but you know my feelings and can judge of replies. I will go soon after reaching Miss. to Memphis and confer with the insurance co. on their proposition. The railroad which was offered to me in La. has been sold under execution and bought by a New York man. [*The rest is lost.*]

Varina Davis to Jefferson Davis

Miss Hatchard is Maggie's more than satisfactory part-time governess. George Campbell, who has a Virginia wife, has got rich with his importing business and shipping interests.

London
Oct 16th 1869

My dear Husband,

We were all rendered more content by seeing your arrival noted in the telegrams from America. I felt comforted on Sunday when I heard the prayers of the congregation asked for you, for I felt sure some one was praying for you among the many good people present.

We are very happy here in the improved health and perfect teachability of Maggie. She has improved wonderfully in her health —is almost one inch larger than when she came from Paris, and perfectly happy with her governess, who is very strict, but manages to hide it in an affectionate kind of exhortation which delights Maggie beyond expression. If I had searched the country over I could not have done better. Both the governess and I give Maggie lessons in music and in French. We are very very happy together.

It is beginning to be very cool here—so much so that I have had fire to-day. The draining of the Serpentine has created a good deal of trouble here, and the public indignation is divided between the new Bishop of Carlisle, and the Commissioner of Public Works Mr. Layard. Lord Derby lies dying from gout in the stomach. There seems to be a great deal of sympathy for him.

Mrs. George Campbell is very anxious for us all to spend our Christmas with her. I should have done so but for the expense of going there, and that I do not wish to give Maggie more than two weeks at Christmas, because I am afraid she will get out of gear. The nuns in Paris took the ten pounds, which I sent over to them you remember. I wrote to thank them for all their kindness to Maggie and sent them Dr. Davis's note. I have no late news from our Boys, and hope that no news is good news.

I own to being very anxious to hear from the insurance office matter. It seems to promise more of a home than anything else.

With dear love to Lize and the family, as ever your affectionate wife

Varina Davis

Jefferson Davis to Varina Davis

Hugh Davis is the son of Lucinda Stamps by her first marriage. Jefferson Davis has been to see his two sisters, one at Bayou Sara, Louisiana, the other at Woodville, Mississippi.

Vicksburg
9th Nov. 1869

Dear Wife:

I stopped in at Bayou Sara and after visiting Sister Anne and Joe Smith went to see Sister Lucinda at Rosemont, thence went with Hugh to Konnochetto and the next day to Natchez, where I took a boat for this place. Sister Anne is quite feeble but walks better than when you saw her. Sister Lucinda is unchanged. Mr. Stamps is much the same as two years ago. They all spoke of you with warmest affection and Hugh seemed ready to start at once for you and the children.

Many friends in New Orleans wished me to settle there and spoke of good things in the future for me, but all contingent, yet they generally deprecated my connection with life insurance business. If I had fewer necessities or more means I would in deference to their sentiments decline the offer of the Co. But soberly, indeed sadly, looking at my needs as well as those of others near and dear to me, I am inclined to "gather grass by every mile that's justified by honor."

A letter from the President of the Co. was waiting for me here, asking to meet them on the day in the afternoon of which I arrived.

There is a desire to serve me and benefit themselves by so doing on the part of several companies. [*The rest is lost.*]

Jefferson Davis to Mary Stamps

Mississippi's Governor Benjamin Humphreys, Mary Stamps's father, had been forcibly ejected from the Executive Mansion in Jackson by a carpetbagger with Federal troops. Certain prominent Southerners have become scalawags.

Vicksburg, 10th Nov. 1869

Dearest Molly,

I did not write to you from any cause you may choose to assign except that of neglectful forgetfulness.

Our relatives in Wilkinson were in their usual health and made many affectionate inquiries for you. Brother Joe and Lize came on direct to this place and on my arrival they were at home and received me as their guest. Letters which were waiting for me at this place require me to go on to Memphis and may prevent me from returning to New Orleans, as was hoped when we parted.

If you do not see me or hear from me in a fortnight, please write to me at Baltimore care of Peyton and Starke.

Your father called on me yesterday, he was well, but not pleased with the political condition of the state, of which I will only say it could hardly be worse.

I am waiting for a dispatch from Memphis which will decide whether I go at once to that town or wait until the latter part of the week.

To me there is something very sad in this tone to which I see a proud, honorable people reduced. I have lived for the fame of our people and looked in the darkest hour to posterity to right the wrongs to which we were coerced to yield; if we consent, thus becoming parties to our own degradation I shall die hoping that our posterity spurn the example and pass over our memory to that of a more worthy era.

I have thought of you without intermission for years. You have been remembered as you wished in the pause of my prayers, where the chosen are spiritually assembled, and as you will be in the future.

Kiss the dear children for their Uncle and believe me, ever faithfully and affectionately

Yours
Jefferson Davis

Maggie Davis to Her Father

19 Upper Gloucester Place
Dorset Sqr.
14th Nov. 1869

My darling Father,

Your very welcome letter arrived last night, to relieve our anxieties concerning your safety on your second ocean journey. You must have seen in Mother's letter that I was at home. I am so much better and happier at home and I have such a sweet young lady for a governess. She is so gentle and kind, and she says I am improving so fast. She teaches Winnie for an hour every day and she is so fond of her. We are living very quietly now and see very few visitors, but my studies are so interesting and fill up the time so nicely that I do not mind it. Winnie, at five, can tell you any place on the European map and is learning to write and read. We

are all going down to Liverpool to spend the Christmas holidays
with Mrs. Campbell. Aunty has gone on before us and is enjoying
herself very much. It is getting dark, my darling Father, and I have
exhausted my stock of news, so I must say the adieu, my darling
Father, of a loving daughter

"Your little Pollie"

Jefferson Davis to Varina Davis

The offer from the Southern Pacific did not come through. So Davis
perforce became President of the Carolina Life Insurance Company.

Memphis, Tenn.
23 Nov. 1869

Dear Wife:

The point of delicacy was quietly removed and being satisfied
of the solidity of the institution and the character of the Directors
I placed myself at their disposal and withdrew. The result was
soon afterwards communicated to me that I had been unanimously
elected President of the Co. with a salary of twelve thousand dollars
per annum and travelling expenses.

I have entered on the duties of the office and will try to extend
the operations of the company to the eastward so as to increase
the income as well as the security of it.

A residence in Memphis will probably not be agreeable to you,
but it gives me the prospect of means which will enable you to
live elsewhere until all things may combine to give us a less restrained choice. It is possible that after a year it may be found
desirable to transfer the parent institution to Baltimore as a larger
monetary and commercial centre, but this will depend upon the
success of the Co. here and the prospects of business in the Atlantic
states.

I am now at the "Peabody Hotel," a good house kept by an acquaintance of former years, and would be comfortably situated if
there were more quiet. Joseph R. Davis came up to see me from
his present home in Bolivar County and stayed several days. I miss
him greatly now. He spoke most affectionately of you and the
children.

Genl. Wade Hampton with his wife and three youngest children have been here for several days.

The political condition of Tenn. is so good that no further trouble is anticipated, and this winter it is said all the obnoxious legislation of the Radicals when in possession of the state government will be repealed. The negroes here about are said to be quiet and the security from thieving and violence to be about the same as in former years. You know *that* was not equal to the safety in England or France.

Tell Winnie Anne I am trying to get "a good home and to stop wandering about" as she advised, and that the kiss she sent to me will help me to work until I make one fit for her.

I dreamed you were by me darning my socks and asked me what I expected to do without your assistance. I do try to do what is before me. I find it more pleasant to look to the future than to the past.

Kiss the dear children and in each response take one for yourself.

Affectionately,
Your Husband

Jefferson Davis to Varina Davis

It came somewhat hard for Jefferson Davis, who had been a President, a Cabinet Minister, a Senator, a successful planter and a soldier of renown, to enter an insurance business, even as its head. As he says, he "compounded with his pride for the material interest of his family."

[*The beginning and end are missing.*]

[Memphis, November, 1869]

Your ideas of the desirableness of a residence which would secure to our children associations beneficial to them are fully concurred in; but if you forget, others will not fail to remember the difference between a man of business and a Soldier, or a Planter, or a Senator, or a Cabinet minister, or a President, or even an exiled representative of an oppressed people. The difference between these classes would be greater in London than in Liverpool than in Baltimore, in Baltimore than in Memphis.

I have compounded with my pride for the material interest of my family, and am ready to go on to the end as may best promote their happiness. So now having laid down the premises, let us proceed with the conclusion.

You can remain in Europe and give the children the advantage of the Schools there for some time to come, or you can when the season is favorable to crossing the ocean come to Maryland and put the boys with Mr Brand and Maggie at school in Baltimore, where you will find a pleasant residence; or you may leave the boys at Mr Brand's and come here with the girls to stay with me for all except the Summer Months.

You can judge better than myself as to the probable suitableness of this climate for yourself and Margaret and Maggie and Winnie and that should be the ruling consideration in the selection of a home.

While I live, there is reason to believe the money necessary for an economical mode of living will be at my command, and subject to your order. So choose freely.

Varina Davis to Jefferson Davis

Davis has entered upon his duties as President of the Carolina Life Insurance Company. Mrs. Davis is loath to return home while the South is in the throes of Reconstruction. She feels that many Southerners have become, as she calls them in her despair, "mere temporising people of expedients." Winnie is now five years old.

Dec. 3d, 1869
18 Upper Gloucester Pl.
Dorset Square, London

My dear Husband,

A few days ago I felt a sheet of paper and wrote you a scrawl which I could not read, but today am up again after a week's confinement to my room. I never saw anything like this prevalent influenza. Our whole family have had it more or less violently. Maggie and I were the only ones who had fever with it. She, poor child, is still in bed with an eruption yclept shingles, which is annoying but of no consequence.

I was sitting in the horsehair chair in the dining room and asked Winnie "Who does this chair remind you of?" "Of Father, he seems sitting in it ever, and taking me on his knee to tell me stories." I promised to take her on my knee after a while, but in the mean time Mary came for her for bed and Winnie burst out with, so you mean to break your promise! No, said I, get up in my arms—so she seated herself, then gave way to paroxysm of tears. "Oh, do go, Maimy, do go—can any child sit in her Mother's lap with any sort of satisfaction with you waiting, her very nurse waiting to carry her to bed?" Mary and I were so amused that she saw the humor herself, and Mary went off to await Winnie's convenience.

The children are nervously alert about our trip to Liverpool. I confess I would prefer to remain at home as the time draws near to go. How soon solitude and the habit of isolation becomes a pleasing vice. I miss my friends too when not with them. After our last visit to Liverpool I really grieved to be withdrawn from daily association with the Walkers and the Campbells. Now it seems like a cold plunge to go among those who are happy and at home with a tolerably certain future before them—if indeed one may apply such a description to any one in trade.

I dread the return to America as a country in which we are to live and die, more for you, and for our children than for myself. I think I can get up an interest in something or other anywhere, but a future is beyond my power, and it is this I think of for our Boys, and I turn sick with the thoughts of what you will undergo while you see the ideal people of your life's long love change into a mere temporising people of expedients. This death in life is the most harrowing of all sorrows. May God give you strength to bear it. I have loved the people of our country through sympathy with you, but have not partaken thoroughly of all your expectations if I have of your enthusiasms. I thought I saw a woeful change when we were in New Orleans.

You will receive this about Christmas I suppose, and with the tenderest of good wishes. More than half my life I have lived with you, and in our early life we were seldom together at this season, but it has always awakened tender thoughts of you in my heart. Anniversaries have a peculiar effect upon me—I suppose because they were observed in poverty & even in grief by my Parents. This is what Christmas brings back to me. I cannot tell you the strange mixture of sorrow and joy I feel over these memories, but I will not give way to the distressing course of thought in which I was about to indulge, but try to be sensible.

It has never been Christmas before without my giving you a trifling gift—now you are too far away for me to send it to you. God knows how to give good gifts to his children, and will not forget you. May He keep you safely, and do all for you which in these long years I have blindly & madly tried to do, and send his ministering angels to bear you up under your many trials. Weariness endureth for a night, but joy cometh in the morning. May many Christmases bring renewed assurances to your soul that Christ is indeed with you, or has sent his comforter to your weary heart.

Receive my tenderest sympathy, and most fervent prayers, and believe me as ever your affectionate wife,

V. Davis

Jefferson Davis to Varina Davis

In letters Davis does not often indulge in sad reflections on the miserable political situation of the South. Judge Louis Dent, brother-in-law of President Ulysses Grant, had recently moved from Washington to Mississippi and run for Governor on a newly created moderate National Republican ticket against the radical J. L. Alcorn. Grant not only refused to support Dent's candidacy but repudiated it in an historic letter of July, 1869. There were many more Negroes on Alcorn's ticket than on Dent's.

Memphis, Tenn.
4 Dec. 1869

Dear Wife:

I have been not a little annoyed by some kind friends whose zeal outrunning their discretion have engaged in soliciting contributions for an endowment for myself and family. It came to my knowledge by Col. Geo. H. Young writing to me that he had collected three hundred dollars and asking how it should be remitted. I thanked him for his good intentions and, assuring him that my salary would suffice for my wants, requested him to desist from his labors.

The election in Mississippi has gone for the radicals. The true men of the state to a great extent declined to vote, holding Dent to be little if any better than Alcorn and the fact of Negroes being on both tickets, a sufficient reason for refusing to support either.

If that had been the only issue they might have maintained their positions, but the real question within their control was the choice of legislators and that was the vital point. All is lost, and a long dark night settles on our beloved state. I have not been so depressed by any public event which has transpired since the surrender of the Confederate Armies.

When I was in New Orleans, Mary Stamps showed me her black shawl torn into pieces by a servant whom she had discharged, and I told her I would write to you to get her another one like it. In default of such memory on your part, I can only say it seemed quite long and pointed. I think she called it Lama lace, but it did not look like wool, nor quite like lace.

I fear from your account of Winnie Anne's extraordinary conversations that her brain has been too much excited. She is too old for her years, pray keep her back that her constitution may be such as to bear study when she can better profit by it.

Do not misunderstand me, the sole purpose is to secure your greatest contentment and comfort, and therefore I abstained from expressing any personal desire of my own about a residence.

Mrs. Howell Cobb wrote to me on the 30th Nov. She mentions you as her "dearest friend," and asks me to give you her earnest regards and to say that your letters "were as balm to her crushed and bleeding heart, and were unanswered because she was completely unfitted for mental exercise."

The interruptions are so frequent by visitors at the hours when I am not engaged at the office that it is difficult to write connectedly.

Affectionately,
Your Husband

Charles Mackay to Varina Davis

Charles Mackay had been Davis's traveling companion on "the trip of his life" through Scotland.

Fern Dell Cottage,
Boxhill, Surrey.
Dec 21 1869

My dear Mrs. Davis,

Mrs. Mackay, who has been, & still is, unwell, desires me to write to you, to express how sorry she was, when in London a few weeks ago, not to have been able to call upon you. We have received two or three papers from Mr Davis from Memphis, from which we learn that that city is to be his future residence, and that you are likely soon to cross the Atlantic to join him. We both hope sincerely, if this be true that we shall have an opportunity to seeing you before your departure.

I should like very much to know, if Mr. Davis's health continues mending; and if the undoubted improvement in it, which took place in Scotland, has been confirmed since his return to America.

When you write to him, will you convey to him the expression of my warmest regard and friendship? I admired and esteemed him before we travelled together in my native Scotland; but every sentiment which I before felt for him was strengthened during that pleasant & too short period.

Wishes for all health & happiness at this festive season—and every other, We remain,

Ever yours most sincerely,
Charles & Ellen Mackay

Jefferson Davis to Varina Davis

Among those pressing Jefferson Davis to accept the Presidency of the University at Sewanee was Bishop Henry Green, the Chancellor, a man renowned for his character and his spirituality. Davis would have found the position most congenial, but the salary was only $2,000 per annum, and he could not support his family and educate his four children on that amount.

Memphis, T.
25 Dec 1869

Dear Wife—

On the anniversary so differently associated with childhood's memories yet dear to every Christian, I send you my greeting.

I have been very anxious about my Brother. He fell in getting out of his carriage and dislocated his shoulder. Just before I left town Lize informed me that he was much better, was sitting up and free from pain; but on my return her later account informs me that the shoulder has not been replaced and that there is also a fracture of the arm.

My occupation here has confined me more than I expected. My associates of the Co. are correct, pleasant men, and if I had been trained to such employment it would no doubt be more congenial. As it is, however, I get on pretty well.

Several letters have come to me urging me to take the Vice Chancellorship, that is the Presidency of the University of the South at Sewanee, the college Bishop Polk labored to establish. There are some strong inducements but one stronger objection, they are too poor to pay a salary which would support us. Genl Gorgas is a professor there.

Very many people are so anxious to serve me that their zeal is sometimes quite disagreeable, not to say offensive. And yet it is evidence of a regard for which I am grateful & may well be proud. [*The rest is lost.*]

Varina Davis to Jefferson Davis

Lord Campbell had long admired Jefferson Davis, and, at a rally in Manchester in February, 1864, had eulogized him as "one of the bravest and noblest minds which Providence has formed." Lord Campbell often called on the Davises in London. Jefferson Davis had stayed with Lord Abinger at Inverlochy Castle in Scotland the preceding August.

Ella Magruder was Abinger's sister-in-law and niece of the Confederate General John Bankhead Magruder.

18 Upper Gloucester Pl.
Dec. 22 and 25, 1869

My dear Husband,

Your kind letter with its enclosures is before me. It found me in bed with a bilious neuralgic attack. Winnie with a fine crop of chicken pox. She is in bed singing and laughing with her bed full of play things. The Boys are well and hopeful of seeing us at Christmas, but tomorrow I must send them their presents, and go to them in New Year's week, as though Winnie is free of disease, she is not of infection, so I must remain here for fear of giving the disease to Mrs. Campbell's children, and Billy and Margaret, who have never had it.

Winnie is certainly a most charming child, and entertains me as much as an old person. This Christmas an excellent "Child's Bible" has been published profusely illustrated in wood cuts from fine pictures, with the old and new testament both in it, only the former expurgated. Yet all that there is in the Bible which a girl of sixteen might read is there given in the very words. She never rested from the moment she heard of the book. "I will give up a doll house, my tea set, my Christmas candies, every thing, only let me have the Bible." She has not seen it, but I have it for her, *and* a tea set.

I have a canary bird, a gift which touches me much, for I longed so for one. It is quite unexpected. I found it hanging up in the dining room. So much for Xmas.

I do not remember Mary Stamps' shawl in the least, but have purchased one for her of Lama lace—they are expensive things, and now not much worn. Shall I send it to her, or what shall I do with it?

Before this reaches you, you will have received my letter in answer to yours inquiring what I desire to do in the future, and you will know that I have begged you to choose for me. Only whatever you decide, do it soon, and do not leave me in doubt as to your wishes. I will not decide a question in which your happiness is so much involved, and whatever will render you the happiest, will be the most acceptable to me.

Xmas. The children greatly enjoyed their Christmas. Winnie is in ecstasies with her Bible & playhouse. I have not heard from the boys yet. Maggie and I went to the Blandys' on Christmas Eve and saw their tree. They all talked much of you and drank your health very lovingly, making many allusions to last year when you were there.

Every Sunday after Church Lord Campbell comes in, grave as an owl, but it is astonishing how very much he improves on acquaintance. He stays sometimes two or three hours, and talks very nicely about literary subjects, only he does talk about lighter subjects very much as Winnie's mock Turtle in her Alice's wandering in Dreamland. He often speaks kindly of you, and several times enthusiastically. Lord Abinger has been to inquire for you, as well as Ella Magruder. Dr. Mackay has written to inquire as well.

I can only wish you every happiness, and that God may in his goodness direct you how to choose for us so as to insure the greatest amount of happiness to you and good to your children, and having accomplished this end, you will do the most agreeable thing for me, no matter what your decision may be. Believe that, absent or present, you are always remembered in the prayers of

Your affectionate Wife

Jefferson Davis to Lise Mitchell

Robert Brown, President Davis's body servant at the Executive Mansion in Richmond, remained devoted through the tearing vicissitudes that followed the fall of the Confederacy. Brown was to live with Davis at Beauvoir in the later '70's and '80's. At the ex-President's funeral in New Orleans in 1889, he was to sit beside the driver of the carriage that bore Mrs. Davis and Maggie Davis Hayes and to stand with the family at the cemetery service.

Memphis, Tenn.
30th Dec. 1869

Dear Daughter Lize,

I am truly thankful to you for your kind consideration. My anxiety for my Brother is so great that it makes me imagine the worst cause for any failure to write. It is true that I could do no good if with you, and that my presence is just now peculiarly needful here, but I trust that it will not be long before we may meet.

Jack has disappointed me. That he should not have been prevented from leaving by the illness of his Master is worse than could have been expected. My old servant Robert is in New Orleans. He had one fault, or failing, a fondness for drink; with that exception his capacity and faith are great. He is expert as driver and groom and never drank when he was traveling with me. He never seemed to have any fellowship with his own race, but was grateful & affectionate to his former owner, as well as myself. I intended to take him as soon as I had a place for him, & told him to keep Mary Stamps informed of his whereabouts. If you want him Mary can probably find him & I think he will be true to you for my sake.

Give my tenderest love to my Brother.

Ever most lovingly,
Your Uncle, Jefferson Davis

Jefferson Davis to Josiah Gorgas

General Gorgas, the Confederacy's able Chief of Ordnance, wanted Davis to be President of the University of the South at Sewanee, where he himself was on the faculty.

Jefferson Davis, President   CAROLINA LIFE INSURANCE COMPANY
No. 291 Main Street
Memphis, Tenn., 6th Jany, 1870

My dear Genl.

It was with the most cordial pleasure that I received your kind letter and read the expression of wishes so fully my own. This official paper will convey to you my present position. I left England with undefined objects and without a home to come to or the means to get a new one. Under these circumstances it was deemed best to leave my Wife and Children in England, until my affairs were in a more settled condition. Maggie and the Boys are at school and progressing favorably. Mrs. Davis spends most of her time in London, which after various experiments we found to be the most economical place for herself and our little daughters.

I am grateful to you and the others who thought of me, as you mention, in connection with the "University."

The necessity for an income was such as to require me to consider the question of salary as the important feature in any proposition which was made to me. This Company was the first to invite me to join it and offered the largest compensation for my services. The Directors are very agreeable and worthy men, and my relations with them pleasant. Their conduct towards me has been so generous and considerate that in any future action I may wish to take it will be incumbent on me to consider their interest as well as my own.

The position you desire me to have would be more congenial to my tastes than that now occupied; but it would be with great distrust that I would assume its duties, if indeed your confidence and a like kind trust by others could induce me to hope such results as you indicate.

I desire my sons to have a home education and wish to be near them. There are few places in the South which are well calculated for the physical development of youth, and yours, my good friend Bishop Polk assured me, was one of that few.

Please give my affectionate remembrance to your Wife, whom I hope to see often and whose companionship would be very precious to my Wife. That we and our families may be near to each other is the sincere wish of

Your friend
Jefferson Davis

FAMILY REUNION

Mrs. Howell Cobb to Varina Davis

Mrs. Cobb is grieving over the death of her "beauteous, auburn-haired" daughter. Because of the sad state of affairs in the South, she urges Mrs. Davis to stay longer in England.

Athens, Georgia
Feb. 26th, 1870

My dearest Friend

I have made an unconditional surrender of my child to God. While I look forward and keep the eye of faith upon Christ's reconciled face, I am calm, resigned, and my will is to stand just there. With God's help, I *know* I will stand.

May He comfort you in yr loneliness and separation from yr husband. *As long* as you can bear the separation, *remain in England.* You know not what may be in store for you and yr children in this country in the present state of political affairs. You, of course, know best—but from my standpoint and looking only to yr safety and peace, I would say stay away as long as possible. There will be no peace to the country during the Radical rule, and there is much cause for apprehension that things will grow worse than better. Georgia has fared better than many States in the South, but vast efforts are being made here and at Washington to remove her back to military rule, declaring her out of the Union and under a provisional Govt. Our Gov. was before the war an express driver (for New England), afterwards Express Agent (during the war) at Augusta. Other States have recently imported Govrs from Northern & Western States.

I thank you for your long letter.

Devotedly,
Mary Ann Cobb

Varina Davis to Jefferson Davis

Margaret Howell is engaged to Karl Stoess, a native of Alsace, in an import-export business in Liverpool. His name was sometimes written Carl de Stoëss.

London
March 4th 1870

Dear Husband

I wrote to you a long letter a day or two ago, and told you of Margaret's engagement, but now, probably by the same steamer, I write to say that I have seen them. She returned yesterday, and he with her. He is twenty years her senior, but seems younger than this—his manners are very good, his morals irreproachable, he neither drinks, smokes nor gambles. He has, I believe, means sufficient to support her completely—a moderately nice house. He is an importing merchant and an exporting merchant of the wholesale kind. He thinks he is sure of maintaining Margaret at the least, in great comfort. He seems devoted to her, and deems it a great privilege to marry her &, knowing her to have no money, can never sufficiently express his gratitude for the privilege of being her Husband. Mr. Campbell has made many inquiries about him, and says that they have all been most favorably answered. Socially his position is exceptionally good. His wife died at the birth of her first child seventeen years ago—& since that time he has lived with the child & taken care of him as well as in his power. (The boy is very good, and gentlemanly.) What I know of him I like very much.

He says that his business will not admit of his leaving Liverpool except in April. He desires to leave there for a little tour when his marriage takes place, and therefore desires to be married at Easter. They seem both anxious to be married in your presence & with your expressed consent. If you can come over, as he begs in any event, will you telegraph him or me—first your consent—then the time of your probable coming. Then will you add simply a number to show me what I must expend in *pounds* for Margaret's trousseau. I think she is very happy in her prospects. Now I feel bound to say I could not be so. Having married young I suppose I idealised more

than she does. I do not think there is any romance in her connection
with him.

Farewell—Pray telegraph as soon as you receive this letter. The
children all send dear love—

Believe me with prayers for your welfare—

Yrs.

V. D.

Margaret Howell to Jefferson Davis

London

March 4, 1870

My very dear Brother

I have only time before the mail closes to write you a line in
order that I may tell you myself of my great happiness in my
engagement to Mr. Stoess, and to beg that you will give me one
more of your numerous proofs of love and affection to your "poor
little daughter," and give me your consent to my marriage and if it
is possible be present at it. Sister has written you fully, and am
sure, my dearest brother, you will believe that your eldest child
desires to show you all the love and affection that a life of love
and kindness to her would imagine her to show. With many kisses
and again begging you to come, I am devotedly yours

Sister

Varina Davis to Jefferson Davis

Mrs. Davis is disappointed that her sister has made no better match.
But at least Jefferson Davis will no longer have to support her. The
Marquess of Hartington became the eighth Duke of Devonshire.

March 28th 1870

17 Upper Gloucester Place

Dorset Square, London

Dear Husband

Your telegram has been received safely, and Mr. Stoess and
Margaret seem both very happy over it. They have set the 28th

of April for the day, and I asked that Mr. Lambeth should perform the ceremony. Mr. Stoess went to see him, and he was more than kind and promised to make all the crooked paths to matrimony in England strait for them. The whole affair nearly drives me mad. I could as soon love a —— however, I will not say—the memory of having written the words would arise hereafter to preclude my being fond of him if I could ever change. He is, however, I will say, a very honorable, upright man, and more humble to her than one man in ten thousand would be.

Rely upon it, it is head work with her, and flattered vanity. I am more and more wretched as the day nears. I have decided to give her away and I do not know who will walk up the Aisle with me—somebody I suppose; if not, I shall go with Jeff, and I rather think I would prefer this. I wish most heartily that you had named the amount which you were willing to spend. I will try to keep within five hundred dollars, but do not know if I can. On Saturday we will go to Paris—she and I, and remain a few days to get the trousseau, which rely upon it shall not be an extravagant one, and then we will return home. I should have gone to Paris tomorrow but that I foolishly accepted an invitation to dine with Mrs. Bushy, the Mother of the gentleman who came over with Lord Hartington to the Confederacy. He showed me the five cent piece which he still wears on his watch, and which I gave him then. [*The rest is lost.*]

Jefferson Davis to Varina Davis

Davis has still not given up all hope in the business of the Canadian copper mine.

Memphis, Tenn.
April 3, 1870

Dear Wife,

The news in regard to the copper mine is better, but my expectations have not risen to the level they had when I left Canada.

Of my health you need not feel any immediate anxiety. It will probably be in my power to leave here before the sickly season begins, and I am quite as fleshy now as when we parted. The decay of age is unmistakeably felt, but not so as to interfere with ordinary transactions or to indicate any visible decline. Indeed I am often congratulated on my good condition.

I am glad you see Lord Campbell, for whom I retain a very high regard. And this suggests to me the memory of Scotland and the thought that, as you do not think Maggie should return to Paris this summer, it might be well and probably very pleasant for you to go with the children to Scotland. Travelling to a great extent by water you will see the most attractive portion of the country and at the least expense.

I am faithfully yours,
J. D.

Jefferson Davis to Varina Davis

Memphis, Tenn.
17th May, 1870

My dear Wife,

Your notice of Maggie's wedding reached me in due course of mail. I wish you could have had Mr. Mann with you, otherwise it was probably best that you should bear the embarrassment of giving Maggie away yourself. God grant that she may be happy in her marriage.

The weather here has been alternately hot and cool; in the latter state it was also damp, and thus my old enemy neuralgia was aided in an assault.

I sent to Mr. Payne the last payment of the principal of the debt due to his house, a balance created by supplies sent to the negroes during the War, which you recollect was three thousand dollars. So if he does not bring in an account for interest I am now out of debt. The Smith place was sold and paid for itself, that is the remainder of the purchase money.

Ever faithfully and affectionately,
Jefferson Davis

Lord Lytton to Varina Davis

Besides the Earl of Shrewsbury and Lord Abinger with whom Mr. Davis stayed, other Britishers of title who sent the Davises invitations were the Duke of Northumberland, Lord Lothian, Lord Campbell, the Marquess of Westminster, the Duke of Sutherland, and Lady Eardley, who offered them her London house at 4 Lancaster Square for a season, although they did not accept.

June 2, 1870
12 Grosvenor Sq.

Dear Mrs. Jefferson Davis

Captain & Mrs. Hamilton are coming to dine here quietly next Sunday ¼ to 8 & I should be much flattered if you will do me the honor to meet them. It cannot be called a party as I only expect 2 or 3 other friends.

Yrs truly
Lytton

Varina Davis to Jefferson Davis

The first Baron Lytton, Edward George Earle Bulwer-Lytton (1803–1873), novelist, was the father of Edward Robert Bulwer-Lytton, first Earl of Lytton, English statesman and poet who wrote under the pseudonym of Owen Meredith (1831–1891). It is the younger Lytton who frequently sends invitations to Mrs. Davis.

London
June 22nd, 1870

My dearest—

Your letter written on your birthday was received this evening, and I thank you very much for remembering to write to me then.

Do not regret the comb & case, it answered the purpose of giving you pleasure, and if I can see again I will make you another with quite as great a desire to serve you as I had then, one that tears will not drop on & spoil the leather, and cause me to work new ones before one is done.

I shall dine at Mrs. Dallas' again on Thursday, and dined a few days ago with Lord Lytton & many other people. Lytton is handsome, & has eyes like yours were when your miniature was painted & more than agreeable, though much spoiled. He is very anxious for me to go to Knebworth, but I do not think I shall go & so wrote him. The children require me more than Robert Browning or Owen Meredith or any other of the great people I should meet there, for they are a swarm in these small rooms, my fine young ones, what with the educational rumpus going on from morning until night & their reflecting thrown in at random between their music lessons.

May the Lord keep you, with the most anxious and affectionate hopes that could agitate the heart of one so alone as I am in the world.

Believe me yours, Varina

Jefferson Davis to Winnie Davis

Davis's youngest child is now six years old.

Memphis, Tenn.
27th June 1870

My dear Daughter:

This is the day that brought to me a source of unchanging comfort and joy, in that it gave birth to my Winnie Anne.

You have not such oppressive heat in England as we have here. The sun today blazes and burns so as to make exposure to it for even a few minutes, not merely uncomfortable but positively sickening. Old animals do not bear heat as well as young ones and perhaps it is for that reason that I find this summer more oppressive than southern summers used to be to me.

Yesterday the Stockholders of our company had their annual meeting, day after tomorrow the Board of Directors newly elected are to meet and elect the officers of the Company for the ensuing twelve months. Then I shall arrange to leave as soon as practicable, and passing through Georgia and the Carolinas go on to Baltimore. I long to see you all, it seems to me very long since I saw you and my heart is weary of isolation. The people here have been very civil to me and I have reason to be grateful for their kind efforts to make me feel at home. At an earlier period of my life the society would no doubt have been very charming to me; and so I hope your Mother and all of you children will find it.

While your dear Mother suffers from inflammation of her eyes it will especially devolve upon her daughters to entertain her and relieve her from every thing which taxes her sight.

God bless you, my dear Baby, and keep you from every evil is the fervent prayer of your loving Father.

Jefferson Davis

Jefferson Davis to Varina Davis

On his way to England to fetch his family home, Davis spends a few days in the Virginia mountains.

White Sulphur Springs, Va.
1st Aug. 1870

Dear Wife,

The intense heat in Memphis so affected me as to make it necessary to go to the nearest cool place, which was Lookout Mountain near to Chattanooga. Thence I went after five days to Richmond and found, though well on the mountain, that the same difficulty felt in Memphis returned, and so I came here. In two days I intend to go to Baltimore and after attending to some company business there which will occupy three or four days will have probably to go on to New York to get a vessel to sail for Liverpool.

Many of your friends are here among whom I mention as the most cordial, Mrs. Chesnut.

The Company here consists of about five hundred, and the delicious air, shade and greensward would render it charming to me if you and the children were here. Brother Joe & Lize did not get ready to leave with me and wrote that they might join me in Baltimore. He is very feeble and can scarcely hear or see to read. I wished much that they should go with me and thought he would be better, if removed from the disturbing causes now about him.

My early and cherished love, I pray ever that the Lord will guard and guide you. Dr. Brand is here and talks much of you.

Affectionately your
Husband

Jefferson Davis to Mary Stamps

At Sea
Aug 1870

Ever dear Molly,

As distance is magnified between us my thoughts draw closer to you. I hoped to have received a letter from you before I left, in default of which the newspapers had to serve as comforter in so far as they pronounced the city healthy. You were greatly missed after your sudden departure. Where nature inflicts a six months night she gives us an equally long day. As age bears more heavily upon me I feel more the want of my tried and loved friends. But fate has ordered otherwise and each year instead of bringing reunion increases the separation. It is well for us in these days of sorrow and disappointment that we have too many demands on our time for much of retrospect. On ship board one has an enforced leisure and availing of it my memory has summoned the past, so that I have seemed to be living much of it over again. It is however the happy quality of my memory to preserve the pleasant more readily than the painful; and among the stores it has brought none were sweeter than those to which you have so largely contributed. Conferring happiness amid the horrors of a prison you excelled nature's busy little chemist which extracts honey from the bitter leaf.

My dear little Molly, I hope we may see happier days and that it may be my good fortune to return to you a fractional part of the joys you have bestowed upon me. I trust we may meet early in the fall, as it is my purpose to return very promptly to America and at the approach of cold weather to make a tour in the Gulf States. Next time you come to Memphis you must visit me even if I should be in a hotel.

Think of me always as your own property and whenever I can serve you be assured of the pleasure it will give me in any and every way to show you how devotedly and lovingly I am your uncle.

Jefferson Davis to Lise Mitchell

Joseph E. Davis has died in Vicksburg. Jefferson Davis received a telegram shortly before taking ship for America.

Mrs. Davis could not get ready in time to return on October 6 with her husband, who had to be back for business. He arrived in Baltimore alone. When Mrs. Davis finally arrived on a later ship she put the two boys in a private school and eventually reached Memphis where the Davises were to live temporarily at a hotel.

Baltimore, Md.
24th Oct. 1870

My dear Niece,

Your kind though sad letter reached me in London. Notwithstanding the warning you gave and the sad foreboding with which I left my beloved Brother in the heat of Vicksburg, my heart refused to surrender hope, and I crossed the Atlantic hopeful of being able again to embrace my mentor and greatest benefactor. You, who better than any other can sympathise with me in this sad bereavement, will appreciate how bitter are the waters in which I am overwhelmed.

I will come to see you as soon as possible. Some duties here and elsewhere connected with my office will detain me for awhile, how long I cannot exactly say. After arriving at Memphis you shall be more definitely informed.

My dear Lize, I feel how vain it would be to offer consolation to you, but it must be a great satisfaction to you that you rendered the last days of him most dear to us both, as happy as it was possible to make them.

Your sweet and exemplary devotion to your aged grandparent has long commanded my admiration and warmest thanks.

May God reward you, and keep you ever under His guardian care. For awhile, I trust a little while only, farewell.

Lovingly,
Your uncle
Jefferson Davis

Varina Davis to Jefferson Davis

Mrs. Davis tried hard to adjust herself to hotel living in Memphis and she made a most pleasant impression on the local "society." But her continued ill-health troubled her husband, and when hot weather came in May he sent her to the supposedly cooler clime of Baltimore, where she had numerous interesting friends.

June 3rd, 1871
Barnum's Hotel
Baltimore

Dear Husband,

Please accept my congratulations upon another birthday, which has dawned upon you today. May God prolong your life many years, and bless your efforts in all that you undertake or desire to accomplish.

The children one and all send much love, and indeed they had a kind of a plan to send you a roundrobin of congratulations, but it fell through, I think, owing to the heat. It has been the most intense heat that I have ever felt—a boiling, suffocating heat that leaves one no energy to look out, or even to brush off the flies. As usual in cities in the most intense day of all, the Germans got up a demonstration & the negroes another—the former had some German name—"kinderfest" will do as well as another. The negroes' festival has the "fifteenth commandment" as the servants at the table called it. A part of the procession carried each the others arms round the neck like a yoke—some carried the U.S. flag like a blanket ready to toss a delinquent. Then there were carts, full of negro girls with long mohair switches of hair hid in their wool & hanging down. It was a rare show.

Your speech at Augusta created quite an excitement here. The commentaries upon it are very various. It must have been flattering to you to be met so cordially by your own people—but it was hot work, was it not?

I enclose you a note from poor little Mary Stamps. The crack has I fear come before I thought it would. It is very sad. I am afraid that nothing under three thousand dollars would help her—

still I do so long to do something for her in her trouble. Poor child, I do not think that she or I would ever succeed in business.

I have been busy for some time sewing—so that I can hardly see. Excuse mistakes and believe me

Ever affectionately
Your Wife

Jefferson Davis to Varina Davis

Davis is continually being called upon by nieces for financial help. Lucy Boyle is the daughter of his sister Anna, and inherited Locust Grove plantation at St. Francisville, Louisiana.

Memphis Tenn.
7th June 1871

Dear Wife,

I have just received yours of the 3d Inst. It came just in time to prevent me from sending a telegram to inquire how you all were.

It is quite wrong to employ yourself so constantly in sewing. By hiring as far as our means will permit and limiting the amount of clothing to that margin, you may surely avoid a tax which your eyes cannot bear.

I am truly grieved at the unfair assessment of Mary Stamps, if as you seem to conclude the sale of the house means the failure of her enterprise. Do you think we could relieve her? You say "I am afraid that nothing under three thousand dollars would help her, still I do so long to do something for her in her trouble." I can wish, but what can I venture in the face of our wants and uncertainties?

Mr. Payne has written to me that Lucy Boyle had overdrawn the amount for which he sold her small crop until the Clerk of the House in the absence of the partners stopped paying her drafts: that she had written to him in some trouble about her unpaid bills and taxes yet due, and he asks me what he shall do. This because I requested him to try and arrange her mortgage on the Locust Grove place so as to save their home, and that I would sustain him in the event of loss to him. So I have replied to him that my ability was smaller than my good will.

To urge economy seemed idle in view of their experience and

apprehensions, but now it appears their little crop was all and more than expended before it was sold, leaving even the taxes due and their debts increased. I suppose every thing purchased was needed but needs should be measured by one's means. Poor thing, I am sad and perplexed about her. I do not suppose without the sale of land which at this season is next to impossible, she could now be relieved by less than twelve thousand dollars, and next year the sum requisite will be greater, if the creditors wait that long. I can work and fast and wear shabby clothes and walk wherever I have to go, but this does not furnish a fund sufficient for the half it would please me to do for others.

If it be as hot in Balto. as here, it will be a severe trial for Maggie to walk to Mrs. Cary's daily. Billy in his second letter explains what he wants to buy with the dollar and seventy five cents—an axe—but I fear he is too small to use one with safety to himself.

Kiss the children for me and ask them to kiss you back again for their Father.

Ever affectionately
Your Husband

Jefferson Davis to William L. Davis

Strangers were continually writing Jefferson Davis for advice. Occasionally he would answer with special care, as in this letter to a young businessman in New York.

Memphis Tenn. 12th June 1871

Dear Sir,

Your's of the 1st Inst is received. Your remarks in regard to the absorbing pursuit of mammon in New York is probably true of all commercial centers. Your observation may teach you what to shun, without disqualifying you for the contest in which you have engaged, and I hope you may be able to acquire wealth without impairing your regard for principle.

I have paid little attention to political affairs for some years and know little of the recent organization or purpose of party men. In a recent trip which was purely undertaken in the interest of the Company with which I am connected, it became necessary as an act of courtesy to acknowledge manifestation of good will made by the people at several places, where I had stopped to see agents of the Company for which I am acting. The knowledge that whatever I said would be misrepresented caused me to say very little. You seem so well aware of the absence of any disposition on the part of the South to make organized forcible resistance to usurpation and oppression that it would be superfluous to say anything to you in regard to the falsehoods to which you refer. I leave to younger men the work of restoring to the country its liberties as guaranteed and defined by the Constitution of '87. I hope you may live to see the government such as it was at your birth, and with my best wishes for your prosperity and happiness, I am

Respectfully yours,
Jefferson Davis

Varina Davis to Jefferson Davis

Baltimore
June 16th, 1871

My dear Husband,

It is very good of you to write so often to me. I am more than gratified that you knew I would write on the third. This is the pleasure of anniversaries to me—they are mortgages on one's friends, if they have long been observed, and are pretty sure to be renewed from year to year. I not only wrote to you, but dreamed that I walked with you and we talked of love & I felt old & you seemed young & so you are to me—ever young and beautiful and beloved. But I will not get off on this strain again, for I am ashamed of a letter I wrote you a few days ago, and beg you to believe that I had been awake and anxious until I had forgotten everything, even my dread of critical analysis and your astonishment at a seeming mad letter full of highstrikes. However I erred on the side of love & you will the more readily excuse me. I know when I think of it that I should not have been inconsiderate about poor Mary Stamps—I only felt wretched about her. Poor child, I do not think any amount of help would build her up for long, but still I feel so sorry. Of course I knew that three thousand dollars you could not give.

I have less sympathy with Lucy's course, because she has known for a long time these difficulties, and ought to have refrained from many expenses she has incurred & yet I am so poor an economist, so unequal to many of the really grand acts of self-denial that she has practiced that I am the last person to throw a stone. My idea is that the more you do in her case the more you may do, for I think a fortune could be swamped on their affairs & then they would be involved.

We have not had helpful families on either side, have we? And you dear old love, how faithfully you helped my people in every way. The Lord has a blessing for you for all that you have done for others. [*The rest is lost.*]

Jefferson Davis to Maggie Davis

Memphis
29th June, 1871

Dear Daughter:
Your sweet letter was duly received and I am glad to know that you are so well. The condition of your Mother's eyes gives me great anxiety and it is a comfort to me to remember that you are with her and able in so many ways to relieve of such labor as would tax her sight.

This has been an unusually busy week with me and I have been prevented from writing to you as soon as I wished. The weather has been intensely hot, but yesterday and today the rains have made it much cooler. I hope you have not been in like manner a sufferer from the heat of the season. The people here are leaving for the summer and I hope to get away in a week or so.

Some of my friends at Sewanee, the "University of the South," have urged me to visit them on the 12th of July, their commencement day, and if it should be practicable I will do so and go thence to Md.

Give my love to your Mother and Winnie and to Jeffie and Billy. With earnest prayers for your welfare and happiness I am affectionately

Your Father

To my little Pollie

Jefferson Davis to Varina Davis

Davis did go to Sewanee and gave the commencement address.

Memphis, Tenn.
30th June, 1871

Dear Wife:

Yours of the 24th inst reached me yesterday. You do not tell me how your dear eyes are, and the heat and bright sun we have had here render me fearful as to their effect upon you.

We have reelected the Board of Directors with some improvement in the personnel of Board and Committees.

I left the board when they were about to elect officers and was soon hunted up and on my return to the office was informed that I had been unanimously elected Presdt.

I thanked the board, the more because my annual report pointed out what I regarded as the defective policy and practice of the Co. and suggested changes which might have offended their amour propre.

Genl & Mrs. Hampton left here this morning for Carolina. They both asked to be remembered to you.

Bishop Green has written, sent me an urgent request to attend the commencement at Sewanee on the 12th proximo, if I can get away in time I will go.

Our Hotel has run down very low; but for the good room I have I would go elsewhere.

Thank Winnanne for her drawings. I hope she will soon pass on to more pleasant literature than the spelling book.

Kiss the dear Children for me, I have missed you dreadfully and wish we had a quiet home. With many kisses and all my love, I am, dearest Winnie, your

Banny

Jefferson Davis to Varina Davis

While Mrs. Davis is spending the summer in Baltimore, Davis has been traveling on insurance-company business. He has stopped in Lexington to see the Lees. Jeff, Jr., is with his father looking over prospective colleges.

Lexington, Va.
Saturday, 2nd Sept. 71

Dear Wife,

We arrived here safely. Mrs. Lee and Genl. Custis Lee have made many friendly inquiries for you. Custis invites Jeff to stay with him, but he expresses a preference for going with me and I propose to leave this morning for the White Sulphur Springs.

The weather here is cool and the scenery very grand and beautiful. We are now within 17 miles of the Natural Bridge and were it not for my engagement to be at the Springs this week I would not lose the opportunity to see that wonder of the world. Perhaps it is reserved, that we may see it together.

Jeff is captivated by the Cadets and announces his desire to come to the "Institute."

Ever affectionately and with earnest solicitude for your welfare and happiness, I am

Your Husband

Jefferson Davis to Mary Stamps

Mrs. Davis has stopped in Richmond to try to buy back some of the family furniture sold or left in the President's mansion in 1865. Davis is again alone in the dull Memphis hotel.

At Christmas, 1871, all of the Jefferson Davis family were finally "settled under one roof" at 129 Court Street, in a rented house.

Memphis, Tenn.
8th Nov. 1871

My dearest Mollie,

It has been long since I received a line from you, yet, as you are constantly in my thoughts, it is not tolerable for me to suppose you have not been thinking of me, though you have said nothing.

In your last letter, long, long ago, you spoke of changing your residence. Where are you, and how are you situated? Beloved, all which concerns you interests me and you should not leave me in darkness, lest I famish without hope. In the time when I was most dreary you came to me as a good angel and the memory of your loving kindness is ever with me. Though I have thanked you for your goodness heretofore, "from the fullness of the heart the mouth speaketh," and again I thank and bless you for the comfort you gave me in many ways and times. Always, too, remembering that you have not grown weary in well doing, but have lost no opportunity to add to my obligations and swell the memory of happy hours. So I am expectant, whenever it may be my good fortune to see you, that you will be my good angel again.

Do not, my own sweet Mollie, take up the burden of life so gravely as not to write sometimes to one who loves you so well that he is not willing to see you cover the light within you by that awful bushel: the routine of business. Have you not a life apart from the throng with which you move along?

Give my love to Lucy and little Mollie, and believe me ever with tenderest affection

Your uncle Jeff

William Stamps to Jefferson Davis

This letter from William Stamps, Davis's brother-in-law and second husband of his sister Lucinda, had considerable influence in a lawsuit over Brierfield a few years later. Jefferson Davis had been appointed one of the four executors of Joseph Davis's will in which he had left $20,000 to each of Jefferson's four children. But there was no mention of Jefferson's owning Brierfield, which was still legally in the possession of Joseph Davis though mortgaged now to the Montgomery Negroes. There was no cash in the estate to pay the children's legacies. It seems that Jefferson is considering establishing his ownership of Brierfield which his brother had given him in 1835. But since this move would entail a lawsuit against Joseph's grandchildren and since his current salary of $12,000 a year was adequate for his family needs, rather than risk a quarrel with his relatives, Davis drops the matter.

Robert Davis (no relation) had married Mary, the youngest Davis girl.

Rosemont
near Woodville, Miss.
Nov. 10, 1871

Dear Jefferson

In the year 1822 your Brother Joe bought of your Father his plantation near Woodville—for which he was to give him the sum

of Five Thousand Dollars, out of which he was to pay John Brown
something over Two Thousand Dollars, which your father owed
Brown for the place. At the time Joe did not pay your father but
500 Dollars of the purchase money. Your Father gave Brother Joe
a Bill of Sale for all his negroes, for which he never paid one dime.
The negroes were Bob and his wife Sarah, Charles, Jim Pemberton,
Samson and Charity, which negroes would have sold in the open
market for about $5000. It may be unpleasant to you to know that
the sale of the land and negroes to your Brother Joe was in consequence of your Father's liability as security for Robert Davis for
a considerable amount. As to your Father or yourself being dependent on your Brother, the idea is absurd to all who knew your
Father would assert.

Your Brother Joe never assumed ownership over the negroes
until after the death of your Father. Your Father had the negroes
in the crop with your Brother Samuel in 1824, when some mis-
understanding between your Father and your Brother Samuel, he
took his negroes to Vicksburg, bought a boat and shipped them
with himself to your Brother Joe's plantation—then managed by
your Brother Isaac. Your father took the fever on the River and
died within five or six days after landing. Nothing was ever done
after by anyone of the Family, all conceding that whatever he had
belonged to Jefferson Davis, his son, who was off at school.

I had several conversations with your Brother Joe in regard to
Brierfield, in which he asserted that it was yours emphatically, and
one of the considerations for it was his getting you to resign your
commission in the army of the United States, that he wished you
to reside near him.

Under all considerations I do not think Brierfield as you settled
it in the woods a full compensation for what I think was the value
of your father's claim upon him at the time you settled the same.

Your Brother told me several times you had purchased so many
negroes—that you bought them with your own means.

I am very feeble and cannot last much longer. My love to your
family.

Your Brother
Wm Stamps

William B. Reed to Jefferson Davis

William B. Reed, a distinguished Philadelphia lawyer and onetime Minister to China, admired Jefferson Davis and had offered his professional services in his trial. With Charles O'Conor of New York he eventually secured his release on bail.

Ward Lamon, Lincoln's law partner in Springfield, who had accompanied the disguised Lincoln on his secret journey to Washington for his inauguration and who had been on the most intimate terms with him, had produced what he called "a frank and truthful picture" of the man.

New York
129 Fifth Avenue
June 3, 1872

My dear Sir:

Owing to my change of residence from New Jersey to this city your most welcome letter of the 11th ult. has been a long time reaching me. I had indeed almost despaired of ever hearing from you, so often have I written to you. Your kind letter removes all the misgivings and I am glad my little review of Mr. Crittenden's life brought me back to you. I wrote it rapidly and chiefly to gratify Mrs. Crittenden and his daughters. It is as such premature biographies—imprudent. The oddest book of the day, let me note in passing, is the new life of Lincoln by Lamon. It professes to be the true life and I should think it so—but there is a secret history about it which is very curious and which if you and I ever meet I shall tell you. It cannot be written. I have read but part of the book.

And now, my dear Sir, let me ask as I have done perhaps impatiently in every letter I have written. Is your record and the record of the Confederacy never to be written—and is it too late or too early to begin it? I have heard your confidential archives survive and are accessible. I cannot tell you how much pleasure it would give me to assist in such a work. Here is the great centre, and here you could work better and less interruptedly than anywhere. Do think of it, for all our sakes!

Give my kindest regards to Mrs. Davis.

Yr Faithful friend,
W. B. Reed

Jefferson Davis to Varina Davis

Barnum's
Baltimore
29th Sept. 1872

My dear Wife,

Though I have been here longer than anticipated, my work is not done. Whatever has been done or commenced by others was much worse than nothing. There is a fatal weakness in most men, that of conceding too much for the sake of avoiding controversy or offense. Thence comes my present difficulties and will flow drafts on the Company, the question being how far I may diminish them.

Mrs. Hampton is confined to her room. In the mean time it cripples her Husband as an Agent.

With love to the Children and a double portion to yourself, I am, as ever your affectionate

Husband
Jefferson Davis

Mrs. Robert E. Lee to Varina Davis

The Davises had been in their Court Street house less than a year when bright, gay-hearted William Howell (Billie) Davis died suddenly of diphtheria in October, 1872. Jefferson Davis had now lost three of his four sons. (Only one, Jeff, Jr., the least promising, was left alive.) Letters of condolence by the hundreds poured into the Davis household. This one from Mrs. Robert E. Lee is selected as characteristic. "Robbie" is Robert E. Lee, Jr., the youngest of her three sons. Mrs. Lee herself was to die in November of the next year.

Lexington, 18th Novr 1872

The papers informed us, my dear Mrs. Davis, of your great sorrow in the loss of your noble boy & I have wished ever since to write & express my deep sympathy tho' I feel that Mr. Davis & yourself must both know the interest we take in all that concerns you both of joy & grief. That gracious God "who doth not willingly grieve or afflict the children of men" can alone give you true consolation & on Him can we lean with trust & confidence. I, too, lost a lovely little grandchild last Xmas, but He has sent me another, born, too, in my house the past summer. The only one of your children I have seen since the war has been Jeff & he has grown & improved so much I should scarcely have known him. Maggie must be now quite a young lady grown. You must give our love to them all & to Mr. Davis, in which Custis begs especially to participate. He is just the same, quiet & grave, & I have almost relinquished the hope of ever seeing him married. Indeed none of my family seem inclined that way. Mary is now in Paris enjoying herself extremely & hopes to pass part of the winter in Rome. Her friends have been so kind & she has had so many invitations from them that I hope her funds will hold out & enable her to see all she wishes before her return which will probably not be before next autumn.

We are all quite isolated now in consequence of the horse epidemic which has stopped our canal boats & I fear may soon hinder the stages from running. Our hopes of a RRoad are also postponed for another season which is a grievous disappointment, but if ever it is completed you must all come & *make us a visit as I shall never be able to visit you.* I am much better since my tour to the Hot Springs this summer but never expect to walk again. You have no doubt heard that Robbie lost his sweet young wife about 9 months after their marriage & before the house preparing for their reception could be completed. It is a sad cloud upon his life, but youth is elastic & is rarely crushed save for a time by any sorrow. I pray that God may preserve us & all dear to us both now & forever.

Yours most truly & affectionately,
Mary Custis Lee

THE PANIC YEAR
OF 1873

Jefferson Davis to Lucinda Stamps

The "bereavement" refers to the death of Billie. Dr. Joe Smith is the son of Davis's sister Anna.

Memphis 4th Jany '73

My dear Sister,

I have not written to you for some time and mainly because of the hope of being able to visit you. Business engagements and illness in my family at other times have detained me here. Varina has for a long time suffered from a numbness in her limbs and the mental depression caused by our domestic bereavement has increased both the frequency and the violence of the attacks. The doctors seem powerless, and only advise cheerfulness.

I shall have to go very soon to Vicksburg on account of the unsatisfactory reports from Ben to whom our Brother sold the Hurricane and Brierfield. Perhaps it may be practicable for me to go on to see you, if so I will do it. Winnie often speaks of her happiness when with you and wishes again to see "the deep, deep woods" and be in the garden where she was allowed to pull as many flowers as she pleased.

I hope to meet Dr. Joe Smith in Vicksburg and to learn from him full news of you all.

Give my love to Brother Stamps and each of the family, and accept for yourself the full measure of the love and reverence with which you have always been regarded by

Your Brother Jeff.

Jefferson Davis, Jr., to His Mother

Sixteen-year-old Jeff, Jr., and his older sister Margaret are spending the summer in Lexington, boarding with William Preston Johnston, who is a Professor of History at Washington and Lee University. Custis Lee has his father's place as President. General Smith is at Virginia Military Institute where Jeff will be enrolled as a cadet.

Lexington, Va.
June 19th, 1873

My dear Mother

I was so sorry to hear of your sickness. I do long to be back with you. I received Father's letter and will answer it soon. Maggie has gone to a party with the Miss Prestons and Johnstons, but she looked just twice as well, only she has been sitting up so late of late that her eyes did not look as bright as usual. She is enjoying herself very much. There was great excitement here over some gypseys, everybody went to see them and they turned out to be Irish people. Has Father gone to Iuka yet? How are the puppies & the shades in the kitchen?

I went to see Genl Smith, he was very kind. I also saw Genl Lee. I will not report for duty at the Institute for some time yet, but as soon as I do I will have my picture taken and send you. I am going to tell you something, please don't say any thing about it—When I was over at the Institute I heard one cadet say to another, "Who is that?" Ans. "Jeff Davis's son." "Well damn if he aint got a fine figure that will get him a corp," meaning a corporal.

I must stop now, with much love to Father and Winnie and more than I can express in words for my dear dear Mother

I remain as ever your affectionate Son
Jefferson Davis Jr

Jefferson Davis to Varina Davis

The Carolina Insurance Company is threatened with failure. Jefferson Davis is in New York to try to borrow money to save the faltering company, but the panic of 1873 is in full swing and money is hard to get. Many banking firms were closing their doors and the New York Stock Exchange temporarily stopped operations.

Mrs. Davis, with Winnie and her white nurse, Mary Ahern, has gone to Canada to avoid the Southern "sickly season."

New York Hotel
12th July 1873

Dear Wife,

Yours of the 9th has just arrived and finds me preparing to leave. I have had a vexatious time here and all to no purpose. The great number of deaths at the South during the last year has alarmed the Insurance men. They fear the rate will continue, and rightly conclude that if it does, the business there must be ruinous in the end. I have done every thing except ask for money as a personal favor; that I have been urged to do, and have, as you will anticipate, refused to consider. It is a sad hour and however unjustly must be seriously damaging to my future prospects for business.

I go hence to Baltimore, will be there one or two days, may go to Richmond, Va. but expect in any event to be in Memphis in say ten days and shall hope to hear from you there. Kiss dear Winnie for her Father. Remember me affectionately to Mary. God grant you may all soon be well and comfortable.

I sent a telegram to you to the Galt House, Louisville, and wrote to you to the Rossin House, Toronto.

Ever affectionately
Your Husband
Jefferson Davis

Jefferson Davis to Varina Davis

Memphis
23 July 1873

Dear Wife,

I arrived here yesterday, found Harriet & Susie in possession of our house. The health of the City seems to be quite good for the season. I am now making another attempt to wind up our affairs, but have not such prospect as would enable me to say when or how it may be done. To save those for whom we acted and to get out creditably is my object. Loss of my investment as well as my past labor is probable. To feel secure of exemption from blame is something to one who values his self-respect above the popular praise. That something is likely to be all we shall retain.

As soon as there is anything which will enable me to forecast our approximate future I will advise you. Nothing has been done about St. Lazarus, and there seems to have been no inquiry for a successor to the Rectorship.

As ever affectionately

Your Husband
Jefferson Davis

Winnie Davis to Her Father

Winnie has just passed her ninth birthday. In Montreal she and her nurse, Mary Ahern, were guests at the convent Maggie had attended while her father was a state prisoner at Fort Monroe.

Niagara, Canada
July the 29 1873

My dear Father

I want to see you so much. I hope I will find you well. thare are so meny frat trains standing at the dopo, that you could not count them. I want you to be here when the man is going to walk over the Niagara River, they hav a musiam here it is a good one, but not as good a one as the British Museum, there is a Beawtiful garden, in the fountin thare is a Ball that plais in the water, sometimes it fals but the water catchs it again. Last satarda I slept in the convent in a nunns room Maimai slept in a nunns Bed, the Rev Mother sed that maby she wowld get a Vocation. I slept in a crib & slept very well. We had a splendid Breakfast, in a littel room ol to our selvs. pleas send me five dolors. Mather wont give me eny monie hardley. I remain your afectionate dawghter

Winnie Davis

P.S. Maimy sends her regards

Jefferson Davis to Varina Davis

Davis had again been sent to Richmond with a new plan for saving the insurance company, but while he was en route the directors wrecked the arrangements.

Joe Davis, who fell to his death from a balcony of the Executive Mansion in Richmond in April, 1864, was buried in Hollywood Cemetery.

Richmond Va
12th Aug. 73

Dear Wife,

I am about to leave for Memphis, but propose to go out to Lexington and see the children.

As soon as I left Memphis the evil genius of the Carolina took possession of it and before my arrival here, they had destroyed all for which my trip was made. By telegram I was informed here of doings there.

Hampton met me here and is sadly cast down by the interruption to a promising arrangement we had commenced.

Here, it's thought to be a trick. I think it a blunder, & a scare.

I went to Hollywood Cemetery yesterday and send you some sprigs of grass gathered on the spot.

God bless you, ever prays your Husband

Jefferson Davis to Varina Davis

Davis takes time to send his wife more details about the unfortunate manipulations of the insurance company's directors.

Memphis, Tenn., 24th Aug. 1873

My dear Wife,

Your very welcome letter of the 1st Inst. was forwarded and received while I was in Richmond Va. I went thence to see the children in Lexington. Maggie appeared to be in better health than when she left us and quite happy with the Johnstons. Jeff was very well and looked improved by his military dress and training.

I was sent by our Board to make arrangements in Richmond or elsewhere for the relief of the Carolina.

The seed sown when I was in New York had germinated and there was assurance that I could soon get $150,000 of new stock taken on the condition of taking out a charter in Md. and removing the parent office from Memphis to Balto. Thus the debts of the Carolina would have been paid at once, the old stock would have been absorbed in the new company, the Piedmont and Arlington, and we should have gone on with our present organization and a Capital of $350 or 400 thousand as a basis for future work.

But the day after I left here, under the influence of panic, negotiations were opened with the Southern Life of Memphis and I was arrested in my negotiations by a telegram announcing that the Carolina had been transferred to the "Southern Life." I find since my return that the matter was most loosely and unwisely conducted; that the managers of the So. Life have got every advantage, and the debts of the Ca. are only to be paid as its means shall furnish the money. Boyle alone resisted, and his appeal for delay until my return was unheeded. I am distressed on account of outstanding claims of our Co. and embarrassed by the necessity of paying the notes which stood against my stock, viz. $5,650.00. The Company owes me a part of that amount, the rest I must raise on some Fire & mining stocks which I have.

The only thing which is perceptible of indirection is the evident desire to keep the business in Memphis, for local advantage. The rest I believe was due to panic, ignorance and want of due caution. Here I am alone in this big house, with furniture too valuable to sacrifice. No definite object is in view from which to derive the income we require and the little we have will be little indeed if it all be saved for you and the children. But a truce to gloomy forebodings, and let us hope that in this little family world of ours, as in the great world of which we are a part, the darkest hour is that which next preceded the dawn.

It is probable that either by closing up or quitting the connection, I will be free to leave here in a week from this time, and, if there is nothing to prevent it, then join you in Canada, and go wherever there is a prospect of getting something to do.

Kiss my dear baby for her Father, remember me kindly to Mary, and take immeasurable love for his Waafe from

her Husband

Jefferson Davis to Varina Davis

CAROLINA LIFE INSURANCE COMPANY
No. 42 Madison Street

Memphis, Tenn., 26th Aug 1873

Dear Wife,

With a heart full of love and therefore not bowed down by trouble, I propose to send to you a business letter.

Left to solitary meditation on Sunday, I calmly reviewed the action taken by the Board of the Carolina while I was absent, and concluded that our obligations as Trustees for the widows and orphans of deceased Policy holders, as well as for surviving Policy holders and Stock holders of the Co. had not been properly fulfilled, but that the case was irremediable. Therefore not to be responsible for it and to avoid the necessity of going before the public in the language of censure, I yesterday sent in my resignation as President, briefly stating my reasons & today the resignation has been accepted. I will wind up my affairs as rapidly as possible, & hope something else may soon be offered to me. My salary of course stopped yesterday. For the month of July it was $750.00, for a part of Aug. $625. Total receipts since you left $1,375.00

I will tell you by way of consolation that Bowmar reports favorably of the crop on Hurricane & Brierfield and expects to get some money from Ben, this fall.

It is hot and the air feels poisonous. I often rejoice that you are not here. You know I can go at an hour's notice, if there should be an epidemic, and intend to go very soon anyhow.

I am glad that you have agreeable people and possible accommodations. There is no need to look for cheap places on thoroughfares. The rates of supplies must in such places approach the average, and diminished prices for board be at the expense of the comfort needful for health of body and mind. Kiss my precious baby for her Father. Remember me kindly to Mary. Lovingly your Husband.

Jefferson Davis to Varina Davis

The Davises are again in the sad condition of "floating uprooted." Davis is without a position. Uppermost in his mind now is his purpose to write his book on the Confederate Government.

Memphis
28th Aug. 73

Dear Wife,

It was my purpose to join you in Canada, but if you think it better not to stay there after this month, it would perhaps be better that you should not wait for me but move to a more southern point for our reunion. At Louisville or Baltimore or elsewhere as might be most agreeable and beneficial to you, I would join you with Maggie or go with you to get Maggie in Lexington and see Jefferson "a wearing of the gray."

I have been working hard to bring up my correspondence, and yesterday afternoon had the assistance of Mr. Clark in answering complimentary invitations to all sorts of Fall meetings, with numerous applications for the delivery of public addresses.

In the absence of any business offer it is hard to select a future residence. Mississippi is politically speaking going rapidly from worse to worst and is out of the question for me and mine. Kentucky, if we had means to buy and stock a small farm, might do very well.

In view of the purpose to write on the causes and events of the War some place easy of access and central in location would be desirable. Our means without some remunerative occupation would not support us in Baltimore. I have thought of Warrenton, Va. or of Charlottesville, Va; but know only that a number of Confederate Genls. are at & near the first place, and the University Library is at the second.

The Thermometer yesterday 93° and night before last it was too hot to lie in bed, and the mosquitoes were too active to let one stay outside of the bar. My dear Wife must not risk the loss of the little she has gained by a cool climate. I wish you would send me a telegram on the receipt of this, by which I will know whether you wish me to join you in Canada or at some other named place. Give my tenderest love to little Winnie and take a boundless measure of the same for dear old Waafe—from her loving

Husband

Jefferson Davis to Varina Davis

At the lowest ebb of his fortune, Davis gets more bad news about other investments from which he expected to raise cash.

Memphis
Sunday 7th Sept. 1873

Dear Wife,

I propose to leave to-morrow for Louisville and to send you by the most speedy method practicable two hundred dollars, that you may pay off your bills, make the small purchases you desire, and join me at the Galt House. We will then confer as to what shall be done next.

The tide of my fortune is at lowest ebb. Every thing is adverse. This morning Judge Clayton informed me by letter that the coal & iron Co. in which on his recommendation I had taken stock, is under a cloud and that his ill health had induced him to resign the Presidency of it and sell out his interest at a heavy loss.

I have no proposition for any business engagement as yet; though Maj. Goodman, who has just returned, called yesterday and mentioned that when in New York he heard several persons speak with friendly concern about my future.

It is not possible to look complacently on the treatment I have received from the Directors, yet generally I believe they did not wish to injure me, but were too selfish to view the case properly— some of them I am sure are friendly.

It may be that in Louisville something will be discovered for future occupation, a few days will suffice for observation.

Do not despond. Though seriously injured as a business man by my connection with the Carolina, I think there will be opportunities to earn the worth of my labor and that we shall not suffer.

If any sensible disposition had been made of the business and property of the Carolina I should have got nearly all the value of my stock; & if any care is exercised there will be, say, three fourths of it paid for a while. In the meantime we can dispose of a portion of our furniture here, and raise some money in that way.

Many persons express regret at the prospect of losing us from Memphis.

You surely did not understand me as complaining of your want of economy. I intended to show you only the danger of having bills, which are sprung upon us after our money has been used for current demands. Jno. Randolph once startled the Ho. of Reps. by announcing he had "found the Philosopher's Stone," and explained "it is to pay as you go."

Kiss my dear baby for me, and tell her to kiss you for me in return. I am very anxious to see you both, and most concerned to have you out of the cold nights on account of the disease which still lingers about you.

May God bless and preserve you, and soon reunite us, is the fervent and loving wish of your Husband.

Jefferson Davis to Varina Davis

Now for the first time in his manifold vicissitudes Jefferson Davis confesses to deep depression and the fact that he sees no cheering light ahead.

Louisville
10th Sept. 1873

Dear Wife,

I sent to you a telegram of this date saying come to Louisville. So much time has elapsed that I suppose it will be cool enough when you reach here to go on to Memphis and close our affairs there. It is an object to get rid of the rent and incidental charges, and when people are preparing for the winter the furniture will probably bring the best price.

There are many things on which I shall consult you when we meet, but it would be worse than useless to write of them.

If I do not go for Maggie before you get here, I will try to meet you on your way, say at Cincinatti. I am much depressed and see no light ahead, but am ever as lovingly devoted to you as in the day of prosperity.

Your Husband
Jefferson Davis

Jefferson Davis to Varina Davis

Davis had left his wife in Louisville while he went to Baltimore to consult with Wade Hampton about the insurance company. Apparently he had decided to make no claim to his Brierfield plantation until after the failure of the Carolina, when he was without the means of subsistence. Now he has come to the unhappy conclusion that it is his duty to attempt to recover his Brierfield property. Judge Thomas Farrar of Vicksburg was a lawyer and friend of the Davis family.

Barnum's, Baltimore
10th Nov. 1873

My dear Wife,

Yours of the 6th Inst. received this morning, and you do not tell me of that which most concerns me, your health.

Judge Farrar writes that it would appear we could recover the Brierfield if prompt measures be taken, but that in 1875 the action would be barred by limitation. He and a Missi. Lawyer he consulted attach no importance to the oral agreement with Ben, for the return of the place on my demand. For all these reasons I thought it important for me to go to Memphis and Vicksburg.

Since we parted my health has rapidly improved.

You will have heard of the death of Mrs. Lee. Johnston told me she seemed to sink after the death of her daughter Agnes, and was not expected to recover when he left Lexington.

With love to my dear children I am affectionately, your old Bann.

Jefferson Davis to Varina Davis

As no offer for a business connection came the family had been forced to return to Memphis. Davis has gone to Vicksburg to see about the Brierfield lawsuit and other affairs. Earlier in the year Davis's sister

Lucinda Stamps had died at Rosemont, the old family home near Woodville.

Vicksburg
31st Dec. 1873

Dear Waafe,

On this the last day of the year I write to wish you and the children a happy new year and to offer to good Mary the like greeting.

Accept my thanks for your full and interesting account of Christmas doings. That day I went to Church and heard Dr. Lord preach a beautiful sermon, so good that I asked him if he did not intend to use it on a future occasion, to give it to me for you. He promised to do so, but said he must write it out.

You ask for my condition. Though wearied and worried, I am no worse than when we parted, perhaps better as to the cough, and the swelling of the feet only a little increased by an unusual amount of exercise on foot.

Jeff. writes that he's despairing of the receipt of his Xmas box, and sends love to all, from his sorrowful "penitentiary." I will write to him quite soon. This scrawl is written in a noisy office and amid many interruptions, through and over all which my love reigns undisturbed, though poor may be the expression of it.

I will go by Boat to N.O. Now it is vain to go to Woodville. The last link that bound me to happy childhood is broken.

God bless and preserve you is the warmest prayer of my heart.

Farewell
Your Husband

AGAIN ACROSS THE OCEAN

BRIERFIELD LITIGATION

"Poor old Sister" is Amanda Davis Bradford, the last living sister of Jefferson Davis. The "rest" are chiefly Joe Mitchell, Lise's brother, and her husband, M. E. Hamer.

Memphis, Tenn.
Jan. 1st, 1874

My own dear Husband,

Many many happier returns to you of this day. May you be happier yet nearer to me than you are today. I am so anxious for the promised letter & trust I shall receive one tomorrow telling me about your dear feet, and everything concerning yourself.

I am delighted with our new servant, and she seems to think the work nothing, and to be always gay & kind.

The rumor tonight is that the negro candidate has defeated Mrs. Moodie's brother-in-law for Wharf Master, and that the whole radical ticket has been elected. A most ludicrous scene took place at the preliminary meeting when they hired the room but found no lights. McRae protested he could not speak without light & they jeered him & the negro explained & mollified the crowd. One cannot say how are the mighty fallen because McR. was never that, but he used to be a Confederate soldier & a white man. The negroes are rampant & very proud of the wharf master.

2nd Jan. I have your dear letter. I trust that you saw poor old sister and Lize before you left; the rest are wretches & I do not care for them. Ben Montgomery has got off easily, but I know you did your best with him. Don't you wish we could get waited upon so? I will send the receipts, or I should say orders, to Mr.

375

Pittman tomorrow when I can get some one to open the box. There are very many of them.

Maggie & Winnie received your messages with loving gratification, but I wore your dear letter near my heart as I used to do. Your loving letters do me so much good I feel better & happier and more kind to the outer world.

Good night, sweet dear love—good night—

Believe me devotedly your old

Waafe

Jefferson Davis to Varina Davis

Davis is in New Orleans considering a sea voyage as a remedial venture. His nephew General Joe Davis has accompanied him from Vicksburg. Edgar Farrar, a cousin of Varina's, married Mary Stamps's daughter Lucy.

New Orleans
5th Jany 1874

My dear Wife

I arrived here this forenoon and found your sweet letter waiting for me. You cannot realize my anxiety about your health or you would not write so briefly concerning it.

No letter for me from Liverpool. Dr. Blackburn has written to me to urge the propriety of a sea voyage, but it seems to me a serious thing unless there is money to be gained by it. As soon as there is better opportunity and means I will write more fully of that and other things.

I am now at Mary Stamps'! Joe Davis preferred not to go to a Hotel but to take a room and eat at a restaurant, so I came here. Your cousin Edgar Farrar is here and quite a well-informed, intellectual young man.

I am as well as when we parted, perhaps better of the cough. The feet much the same. No cause for present solicitude about either. So pray rely on it that you shall have timely information of any important change and let your mind in the mean time be at rest.

Kiss my sweet children and give them immeasurable love from their Father. A kiss for dear old Waafe from her Husband.

Jefferson Davis to Varina Davis

William Howell, married to Minnie Leacock, daughter of an Episcopal clergyman, had been unable to make a living for his family. Now estranged, he has gone to California to find employment. Jeffy D. Howell is captain of a merchant ship in the Pacific. Becket was trying to farm under great difficulties.

"R." is one of the young Charleston Rhetts of the family linked with the newspaper that hounded Jefferson Davis unmercifully during the war.

New Orleans
8th Jany 1874

My dear Wife,

Your very interesting & loving letter of the 3rd was received this morning. Minnie Howell called when I was out. This evening I went to see her at the Leacock's. Your brother William is in California, and Mrs. Leacock wishes all the family to go there. Lena, a very beautiful, well-behaved girl made many inquiries about you and the children. She told me Becket was in the country at the same place where he had been for several years and that her Father had gone on a voyage with Jeff.

The trunk has arrived, and your sweet note and solicitous care in sending the prescription were not the least valuable of its contents. Please give my thanks to Mr. Semmes for the cigars, and say kind things to them all as I would if answering for myself.

The lawyers have not yet informed me whether or what form of suit should be brought for Brierfield. I have required that there should be all possible certainty of success or no suit at all. The Revd Mr. Lord was asked why in Latin the word *lex* was feminine; he replied because it was so uncertain. The question was put by a female and the answer was not intended for a reflection on the sex of the inquirer. Unexpectedly propounded, the answer was happy, but in the connection in which I have introduced it not quite encouraging.

It is very painful to me to think of my little Pollie as tolerating the suit of R[hett]. I know little of him personally but what good can come of such a case, or what sensibility and generosity can there be in such a mouth? You will know best how to treat such a case and may the Lord grant you grace to insure success.

Nothing yet from Liverpool. You write as though my voyage was begun, and I feel as if I should not leave you.

J. E. Johnston's book is in the press. The advance sheets exhibit his usual malignity and suppression of the truth when it would affect his side of the case unfavorably. Hood is quite excited and anxious for *others* to fight Johnston. *Says* he will make a reply to the part specially affecting himself. We shall see, what we shall see. Col. Blaine called to see me and told me that during the campaign in Ga. Johnston's family told Mrs. Blaine that J. had all the papers necessary to vindicate his record. From which Mrs. B. drew the just conclusion that his own record more than his country's defense occupied his mind & heart. I send an article which you will see was written by some one in Hood's interest, manifests what Hood avows: a desire to make common cause with me against a common enemy.

I do not want to go across the seas, unless there is money to be made by it, and do wish before doing anything else to see what is to be done about Brierfield.

I hope to hear often from the love of all my mature life, the partner of all my great efforts, and more than equal sharer of all my trials and sorrows. It will be, if made, a severe struggle for me to go further from you. I long to be with you, to take you in my arms and listen to your sweet assurances and wise counsels. But I press down my desires most effectually by the thought that to relieve you of Anxiety concerning me may best contribute to your health.

Tell my dear children I rely on their affection to guard their Mother from painful excitement, and to keep before her cheerful things. [*The rest is lost.*]

Varina Davis to Jefferson Davis

Monday, 12th 1874 January
129 Court Street, Memphis

My own dear Love,

Your sweet and very precious letter written in pencil is before me. How sweet it is to an old broken-hearted woman to be addressed by the love of her youth it is not granted to me to tell you. I do feel from the bottom of my heart that our souls are very near, and that there is no longer any lack of that love which casteth out fear.

But your letter grieved and shocked me, as well as gave pleasure. I thought you had finally determined to go abroad. I will come down to wish you a pleasant voyage, and fold you again in my arms, but do not, oh do not come back, dear love. Do not. You know that a little more enfeeblement may take the water now settled in other parts to your heart. *Now* you are easily curable—then—then what would become of me. Only and dear love, think of this and go—go at once—

You can do nothing in the Carolina affairs but sit, and shudder under the rule of "brass & iron" and see shears made of those metals fleece your friends.

You cannot help the suit of Brierfield just now & above all, you cannot answer Genl Johnston's miserable paltry attacks, until you have recovered your strength and elasticity and then blend proof with commentaries "harmoniously" and I can wager pretty securely that it will have weight with the country & do you honor. Let the public fight him for a time, and you "go a fishing." You will spend no more money abroad than you will here, and then you will be acquiring strength physically and mentally. Now is the accepted time for you—six months later your heart may be involved. I shall nightly go to your side and mingle my dreams with yours. I cannot live without the hope of being with you to my journey's end.

You should take some constant tonic. Take of burr artichoke leaves chopped small enough to fill a whiskey bottle lightly pressed full—then pour in best whiskey and fill it—take at first a teaspoonful three times a day, and increase to a dessert spoonful. It is intensely bitter but is a specific for dropsy. Now, dear, will you get Mary Stamps to get the leaves & chop them & will you take it for me—will you do it because I love you to distraction? Will you do it to remain a protector for our children? Will you not do this as a wedding present for me? Mary can get the leaves from any vegetable garden.

Mr. Rhett is more than spooney about Pollie. But I am on guard—& ready with Excalibar in the shape of ridicule, & of course a hero shrinks before a silhouette cut by an artist.

I am so glad Minnie's child is so pretty. Do see them as often as you can and beg them to write to me. California may suit Billy better than New Orleans. I trust the poor boy may succeed.

My heart & soul are both yours.

With love to all our family, I am, with many kisses your

Own devoted
Winnie

Jefferson Davis to Varina Davis

Mrs. Davis has hunted out several old letters that might bear on the suit for Brierfield.

New Orleans
16th Jany 1874

My own dear Love,

Your very charming letter accompanying the package sent by express was received yesterday. The letters are very well, so far as they were written by my Brother.

I wish to conform to your desire in regard to a sea voyage, as much because of the effect it may have on you as for any other consideration. Mary says she will get the artichoke leaves and I will use your remedy, by which you assure me you will be made happier.

The S.S. *Alabama* is in port. She is said to be the finest ship sailing from this port to Liverpool and is to leave this week, say Saturday. The Agent has invited me to go with him this morning to see the vessel. I will probably go on her, but if it were not for your anxiety I would stay until our affairs here are more satisfactorily arranged before putting the wide wide sea between me and them.

I went to consult Dr. Choppin, he made a patient examination of my heart, said there was no organic defect. Attributes the swelling to some functional derangement, probably of the liver. Says the head swelling has no connection with any thing else, and as it has increased rapidly of late, proposes to draw off the water, and by an irritant restore the natural condition which he says in three or four days can be done, without doubt, or possible effect on *any other organ.*

Joe Davis has just come in and sends his love to you. The hour is at hand when by appointment I am to go to the ship so without having written but a small part of what I have to say, it is necessary to stop. Dearest, for a little while farewell. With boundless love for my dear old Waafe I am

Your Husband

Varina Davis to Jefferson Davis

Davis is still extremely reluctant to make the sea voyage for his health's sake, but his wife pleads with him to go, for she rightly believes that nothing else will relieve his prostration.

Memphis
January 17th 1874

My dear Husband. I was so glad & sad at receiving your letter written in Mr Payne's office. I am afraid you do not improve.

I have sent the cheques to Mr Pittman. I have not much expectation of a favorable result of the Brierfield suit—still you & they know best. I said nothing when you wrote to me about Helen Keary's mishap but in thinking it over, I feel it is due to you that I should say how I feel. I think that every dollar we spend is throwing the hatchet after the helve—in Lucy's & Helen's case, & really I think it is a sinking fund in the literal sense, and as pecuniary embarrassment now bears upon your health I am not willing to continue at such sacrifice.

Why can you not await your business letters in Havana instead of New Orleans? I am perfectly wretched about you—oh, do go— please do not linger. It seems to me I could emulate the labors of Hercules to insure your success in re-establishing your health—infinitely dear as you are to me & necessary to my life. You will see on this that I am anxious & frightened about you—when you are at sea I will be braver. If I could only go with you—if I only could, God would be very merciful to me.

The children send you dear love. I can not send that which you have. Dear love, farewell. Your devoted

Winnie

Jefferson Davis to Varina Davis

New Orleans
18th Jany 1874

Beloved Wife

The operation of which I made mention in my last letter was performed yesterday morning by Dr. Choppin. The amount of water drawn off was about seven ounces. From the injection of iodine there has been irritation and consequent soreness, which keeps me undressed, but the Dr. says it will disappear to-morrow or next day, and that all is well in the case. So, my dear Winnie, consider me as relieved of a trouble which was rapidly increasing, and as in no possible danger in consequence of the operation. The *Alabama* is to sail on Saturday morning and I will, if nothing detains of a business nature, go out in her.

I hope thus to remove one of your anxieties, and am sorry so little is in my power for the fulfilment of my obligation to bear your burdens. Joe Davis is still here and is now with me. He said he would write to you. Mary Stamps proposes to write to you inviting you to come here. I explained to her the difficulties in the way, and my unwillingness for you to travel alone. Would that I could see you as the ship moves away and bear your last blessing with me; but it will not be long before I hope to fold you again in my arms, and perhaps bring you news of brighter prospects in our worldy affairs.

Kiss my dear children for me many times, and tell them to give you a double portion of like expressions of my love.

Farewell for the present. Soon I will write fully on finances of J. & V. Davis, and again express what is ever felt, by day and by night, the love and admiration with which I am your

Husband

Jefferson Davis to Varina Davis

New Orleans
21st Jany. 1874

My own darling Wife,

Joe Davis brought me your letter of the 17th this morning. I lay awake last night revolving all the joy your presence would bring, mingled with the fears lest some harm should come to you from the fatigue of the trip, or some evil befall our dear ones in your absence. You were right not to risk coming, though I see by your letter our hearts were one in their longings. I will sail, D.V., in the "Alabama" on Saturday morning for Liverpool direct. I will possess Joe. with my views and wishes in regard to the suit for the Brierfield. Like yourself, I am not sanguine, and unless the Lawyers are confident, do not intend a suit to be instituted. Ben's statement satisfied the wish to establish my Brother's purpose to allow me to reclaim the place at my pleasure. So much for the sentiment.

I have long since ceased to expect anything immediate from the Carolina, and fear there will be nothing ultimately.

You are probably right as to Helen and Lucy. It was useless to take the mules from Helen, as that would have rendered it impossible to make another crop, and there was nothing else to take, unless she were to be turned out of her home.

As soon as anything is decided I will notify you and let us hope it may be in our power to reside where we shall be more comfortable and be more permanent than we have been since the war.

Your wish to have me on salt water will be gratified perhaps by the time you read this. You said you would be happier if I notified you that I had begun to take the extract of artichoke. I have been taking it— [*The rest is torn off.*]

Jefferson Davis to Varina Davis

After all, Varina came to New Orleans to see her husband off for England. She is the guest of Mary Stamps. Since the financial misfortunes of the panic year of 1873, with Davis's sharp decline in health in the fall, husband and wife have become perhaps closer than at any other period in their life.

SS Alabama
26th Jany 1874

Dear Wife,

We are this morning at the Bar and how soon we may get to sea is problematical. With the hope that we shall pass out in a few hours I write now to take another farewell. If we get out this will go to you, if not I will write again before the Pilot leaves us.

I have made friends with the slippers, for they served so well when my feet got cold last night that I was compelled to recognize your wisdom in making them instead of looking over papers which I was to leave with you. Waafe is always right where my welfare is involved.

The ship is quite comfortable and the officers very pleasant.

Lingering in your neighborhood is subject to the regret that I should not have been permitted to remain with you, until the unwelcome separation was necessary. I would prefer to get on a tow boat which is near us and go back to my treasures.

It is hard to leave all which is near and dear to me without definite purpose, for notwithstanding the concurrence of the Doctors I think I could have got well at home. Where there are hearts there is home, even though it be under the rule of "brass and iron."

Kiss my own little Pollie and my dear little sunbeam Winnanne. Love to Mary Stamps and her Daughters and to dear Joe, for to me he is very dear and much honored. With another kiss and another and another, I must perforce say again good-bye.

Your Husband

Jefferson Davis to Varina Davis

S.S. Alabama
15th Feb. 1874

Dear Wife

We have entered the Irish channel and expect to reach Liverpool on the evening tide. That I may send to you the earliest news I write on the ship under the disadvantages of much motion and little light, for the day is dark, rainy and windy. During the long interval in our correspondence my heart has been sad for want of its only sunshine and my fears have been busy in regard to you. God grant that I may find in Liverpool a letter with comforting assurances.

Long and wistfully did I look after you when the carriage bore you from my sight, and wish, vain wishes, as the poor may, who have little left to them save the power to feel and to regret.

We have had a rough voyage even for the winter, but it has been beneficial to me, at least so my increased strength and appetite indicate. Even along the trackless sea there were things to remind me of you and our journeying together.

Yesterday we passed in full view of the harbor of Queenstown, this morning through rain and mist we saw "Holy Head" and are now near to the great Ormes Head. The loneliness of the ship suits me so well that I am not anxious to reach the port.

Give much, very much love to my dear Pollie & Winnanne. When the circumstances are more favorable I will write to them, and look forward hopefully to the letters which I expect they have written to me.

I write between the rolls of the ship, and if I had the gift of descriptive narrative it could not be manifested. Don't take this as an intimation that I ever hope to be a model letter writer; that talent, if it was confided to me, has laid so long in the napkin that it cannot be made productive. Farewell dear Winnie, across the seas I send you immeasurable kisses and oceans of love.

Your Husband

Jefferson Davis to Varina Davis

Norman Stewart Walker, a Virginian, had been sent by President Davis in November, 1862, to Europe with $2,000,000 in bonds for Major Caleb Huse, Confederate purchasing agent. He returned to Bermuda as a resident disbursing agent. Then in August, 1864, he was sent to England on Confederate Government business. He and his wife Georgiana stayed in England after the collapse of the Confederacy. By August, 1867, Walker had moved from London to Liverpool, where he found considerable profit in an export-import concern, and where he remained until 1878. Both Walkers had been at the dock when the Davis family arrived on August 4, 1868, from Canada. And now Walker was there to greet the ex-President when he arrived in February, 1874.

Mrs. Davis was deeply hurt because Margaret Stoess sent her no line of sympathy at the death of Billie Davis in Memphis.

James D. Bulloch had been the chief Confederate Naval Agent in England.

> 19 Abercromby Square
> Liverpool
> 17th Feb. 1874

My dear Wife,

I wrote to you on ship board just before we reached the Mersey. We did not get into dock as soon as expected and I remained on board until the custom officers came down yesterday morning. Maj. Walker was expecting me and said Mrs. Walker claimed me as her guest. We went to the office of Mr. Stoess, but he had gone to look for me. Not finding me at the Hotel to which I had sent my luggage, the Adelphi, he left a note from Maggie telling me she had a room ready for me, but in the meantime I had accepted Maj. Walker's invitation.

After luncheon Mrs. Walker went with me to see Maggie. The dear child was disappointed, and it pained me that I was the cause. We arranged that I should hereafter go to her. She is not looking well and seems troubled like Martha. She has very fine children. The boy is large and stout, and both bear strong resemblance to their Mother.

Your letter has just come and I have anticipated the request for news of Maggie and her children. You need not have qualified your message of love to her; poor child could not repress tears when she spoke of you and her longing desire to see you. She said she had forborne to write for want of cheerful things to communicate.

Mrs. Walker made many loving inquiries about you. My little friend Georgie W.[alker] was overjoyed to meet me, and so seemed the other children. Capt. Bulloch is in some employment in South America, but is expected here daily for a visit.

Gladstone has sent in his resignation and it is thought that Disraeli will be asked to form a ministry, and if that fails the invitation will then be given to Lord Derby. So much for news.

It is cold and rainy, and I have stayed in doors, and you have herein the work of the morning. [*The rest is lost.*]

Jefferson Davis to Maggie Davis

The Davises had rented an apartment with the Blandy family in London in 1868–69. Davis had been the guest of James Smith in Glasgow in August, 1869.

> Liverpool, England
> 24th Feb. 1874

My dear Daughter,

Since I wrote to your Mother I have removed from Major Walker's to Mr. Stoess's, and your Aunt does all which is possible to make me feel at home. The weather is chilly and damp, and my thoughts ever turning to the land which holds my heart's treasure, brings often to remembrance the sunny days of our own land. Though you all cried out with one voice in denunciation of Tom Paine's love for America, it is not possible for me to find elsewhere "so fair a land."

I propose to go to London about the last of this week, unless some business development should detain me here. At present there is no prospect of such good fortune & in either event my address will remain the same.

Dr. Blandy has written a most affectionate letter requesting me to come to him and be healed. Mr. Smith has written in like manner, save & except the healing clause, asking me to come to him at Glasgow.

When I have any definite view your Mother will be advised of it. My acquaintances here pronounce my appearance more robust than at our departure from this country. Which may assure you that I have improved since leaving Memphis.

Dear Pollie, strive by gentleness and compliance to protect your Mother from agitation, she is most needful to us all.

Give my love to your dear Mother and Sister, and remember me kindly to Mary. Ever solicitously and affectionately,

> Your Father
> Jefferson Davis

Jefferson Davis to Varina Davis

Davis learns more forcibly than in 1868 that the Northern animosity against him individually is so great that British firms fear to give him a position.

Liverpool
26th Feb. 1874

Dearest Winnie,

On this day my heart uncontrolled turns most longingly to you. Many years and very many sorrows lie between this day and that which made you mine in law.

I will not now enter on recitals which may wait for tomorrow. On Saturday I hope the steamer will be in and bring me a letter from you. None has arrived since you left New Orleans, and you need not be told that my anxiety is great to know how you are.

27th Feb. Mrs. Van Arnim gave a dinner yesterday for me, but I was not well enough to go. Maggie and Mr. Stoess went, and I had the luxury of being alone with my love and living over the happiest of our married days. They came back about midnight and were surprised to find me up. The time had flowed with rapid current bearing along reminiscences of what had been, thoughts of what might have been, and speculations of what is to be, so that it did not appear to me late, and the comfortable sofa on which I lay before the fire saved me from weariness of body. The dinner was reported unusually good and my absence to have been much regretted.

So be not disturbed with unwarranted apprehensions, but the rather continue to hope for my return in restored health.

28th Feb. No letter from my dearest and now I must wait until Tuesday's steamer. This is the last day of our month, and here I am still in Liverpool. Maggie is very attentive and most unwilling to hear me speak of leaving her while any care is to be taken in matter salutary. If nothing intervenes my purpose is to go to London early in the next week.

Now for the "Royal Insurance Co.," Walker said he had written to me that upon inquiry he was assured that the reason for the inconsistency in the correspondence with me was, that the agent of the Co. in New York had the superintendence of the Southern branches and that the Directors doubted the wisdom of establishing a separate and distinct agency for the South. I called on the "Manager," who said the agent of the Co. in New York who was English had been asked if my appointment to control the business of the South would affect their operations at the North and he had replied that the animosity at the North was so great against *me individually* that my appointment would imperiously affect their business in the North.

How far dread of the Yankees may render it impossible for me to get any thing in this country is doubtful. I cannot run round begging for employment, less still can I promise to conciliate the meanest, basest, but not the wisest of mankind. I could hunt or fish or chop and hoe, but could not in that way make enough to support our wants. God guards the sparrow, and will I pray keep watch over my dear Wife and children. The world keeps pace with fiction and so the liars rule.

Kiss my dear children, and take mountains of love from

Your devoted Husband

Varina Davis to Jefferson Davis

Address 98 Court Street
next letter

March 8th 1874
129 Court Street

My dear Husband,

An unusual time has elapsed since I have written to you because I have been both uncertain and anxious about my future course of conduct until your return. I have been canvassing the pros and cons of boarding houses and such other matters, and not been able to tell what was the most economical, and proper thing to do until now. At last I settled down upon the house which is one of three on the other side of the street. I have taken at sixty dollars a month until the end of November, when perhaps the furniture can be sold. Heretofore it has rented for $150 a month & it was something of a joke my offering to take it at sixty & I was surprised at the assent.

We can eat & sleep for fifty dollars a month, and that makes our living come to $110 a month. The house is very large but we will live in a small part of it. I do hope that you will know without my telling you how I have striven to do right in this matter. I move next week to be out by the 20th of this month. We shall clean all this coming week, and scrub etc. My little household are very cheerful over their coming labors—and willing to do their best.

I heard the most magnificent sermon from dear old Dr White today on the garden of Gethsemane—I wished you could have been here to hear it, but it would be a real grief to me if you were to come home until your health is re-established perfectly, which I have not a doubt it can be by plenty of sunlight, fresh air, generous food, and exercise.

I went to Dr Maury and had my heart examined critically. He told me that he could find no disease of that organ. He inclined to the belief that my nervous organization had sustained so many severe shocks that it had succumbed to a serious extent, etc. etc. So he gave powders, and I shall trust in Providence & keep my powder dry.

Winnie is getting fat as a little pig, and is so sweet to me. We talk of you every night, as we sit cheek by jowl alone. I was reading her *The Tempest* and at the scene between Miranda and Ferdinand, "Oh me," sighed she, "I hardly think that women take as naturally to men as she did."

I am glad that you have consented to go to Margaret's. I supposed she would expect it of you and be hurt if you did not go to her. She is, as I always knew, utterly selfish, and I do not think has much to distress her which she does not make. Her forgetfulness of me in my sorrow is a thing I can readily forgive, but not forget. Poor child, I hope her children may do all she desires them to do, but I should in her place dread that the measure she has meted might be returned to her again. Give my love to her, because that I cannot withold, but do not ask her to write. I am not well enough to write letters except in answer to heart confidences & of these we have none together unless she wants to use me for her own purposes. I have worked for them all, prayed, and denied myself the joys, the best of youth, and sacrificed the little vanities of life to them every one and not one thinks of me, and I am done, I am done. I ceased to hope & then to care, and then to wish—How bitter this has been to me I can scarcely say even to you.

I may say how I long to see you & how I wish you every day a happy day & good appetite, and warm feet, and good friends and everything but forgetfulness. I do not think I would have longed for, or used, the water of Lethe—Memory is truly possession some-times, and I possess your dear smile in the memory of it, and your sweet voice is in my ears. Stay away until autumn & then we may feel as if we have a future together. Do not, please, do not cut short your visit—& do not stay to hear Margaret fret & fume. You have gone away for relief of spirit & health—do not deprive me of the reward of my self-sacrifice by staying with her. I think our friends the Walkers have a right to a visit from you. *She* is more of a sister in thought and deed than Margaret.

Good bye, my dear old precious darling blessed Bannie. I am, as ever devotedly, your own Winnie.

Jefferson Davis to Varina Davis

Davis has almost despaired of a British business connection. Having had no letter from home, he is filled with anxiety. He does not receive a letter until April 1.

47, Prince's Square,
Bayswater, London
15th March, 1874

My dear Wife,

I have delayed writing for several days in the hope of being able to tell you something satisfactory of pending business arrange-ments. Now I shrink from the recital of disappointments which I know will be sad to you, but you have always shared my troubles so bravely that you have an unquestioned right to fullest confidence.

After the equivocation of the "Royal" Insurance Co. and the final acknowledgement that their course had been decided by the fear of detriment *from the animosity felt towards me by the Northern people,* I felt less sanguine than before, but still was resolved to see what could be done in London, yet not willing to go round soliciting employment, I had to employ an intermediary. Mr. Jennings very kindly undertook the task of learning whether any of the strong Cos. wished to engage in American business, of those Cos. not having an American agency. He has approached several and been uniformly told that the matter had been considered and that the conclusion was not to enter on insurance in America. It was therefore unnecessary to mention my name and he assures me that he has not done so. There is but one chance he says left, and the past leaves little to expect. The financial and political condition of the U.S. causes distrust of connections there generally and *of Southern connections especially.*

Mr. & Mrs. Campbell with whom I am staying speak very affectionately of you.

My health has improved in London and Dr. Davis says my condition is better than when he first saw us. He finds now as then weak action of the heart, but says it results from debility and will end with improvement of the general health. So as you saw me recover from the former prostration you may expect more certainly now a like result.

A letter from Mary Stamps has informed me of your departure from New Orleans, and I have with painful anxiety looked for a letter from you. So little is there for which I can hope, so many and so bitter have been my sorrows that it is but natural that dread of evil should most readily present itself. Sweet Wife, I long to see you, to have your counsel, to be near you if you are ill, to be happy with you if you are well, and am so lost without you that it seems like an instinctive warning must have caused the extreme reluctance with which I came away.

God grant you may be well and that no harm has come to my dear children. I could not bear another great misfortune.

I intended to write about the pageant lately seen here on the arrival of the Duke & Duchess of Edinburgh, but this letter is so long that it may be postponed.

Kiss my dear daughters, of whom I think constantly, lovingly.

I am interrupted and you are spared another page. Blessings ever attend you dear Waafe ever prays your old Bann

Jefferson Davis

Jefferson Davis to Varina Davis

Colonel F. R. Lubbock, ex-Governor of Texas, who had joined Davis in London, now accompanied him to Paris. Except that the Tuileries

Palace had been burned by the Communards, Davis saw few traces of the recent uprisings in Paris. He was amazed at the political passion displayed in the Chamber of Deputies.

Emily Mason, sister of James Murray Mason, conducts a fashionable school in Paris. Mary Lee, the daughter of Robert E. Lee, is spending some months in Europe. The Baroness Erlanger and Mme. St. Romain are the daughters of John Slidell.

Paris

29th March '74

My dear Wife,

On this day of rest how sadly does our separation oppress me. With Mr. Mann and Gov. Lubbock read the morning service, and then with Gov. L. went to the chapel of the hospital of the invalids. You have seen the building, therefore I need say nothing of that. The veterans in many stages of decay and disability came in, each bearing a smart tricolor and many with military orders on their breasts. An old officer led them and gave commands from time to time and in different parts of the service they were required to raise their flags or to rest the butt of the staff on the floor. Quite a number of boys with drums constituted the band. They are said to be the sons of gallant soldiers. It was a spectacle which could but painfully remind me of our neglected braves and their unprovided orphans. It is well that virtue is its own reward, for sometimes it would otherwise be without compensation.

Last Friday I went to Versailles. The debate involved the power of the Deputies to decide on their form of government for France. A more stormy meeting I have not seen, even when the assembly was not called deliberative. To my mind the present government has no rightful claim to more than an ad interim existence, but the President avows his intention to hold office for seven years, and it may be that the people are so weary of strife that they will permit him to do so. I thought the French were especially logical, but their present condition does not justify the belief.

30th March. I have seen, of your friends, Emily Mason and Sarah Wood, who is with her, and Mary Lee who is with Mrs. Buckeler, and Matilde Erlanger and Rossine St. Romain. Afternoon by special invitation I went to luncheon with Dr. Buckeler, Mrs. B. asked for you with affectionate seeming, as also did Miss Lee.

On leaving London I gave my Paris address to Mr. Jennings that he might inform me of it, if any thing should occur to open a prospect for a good business connection. He has not written which of course meant nothing for me. You could not readily conceive how much the recent action of the Southern States on the question of the bonds issued by the carpetbaggers has increased the distrust and created a reluctance to engage in further affairs. It is not always possible to be good natured under the remarks which ignorance and cupidity dictate to the men of the English Exchange.

One sees little trace of the seige here. The destruction of the Tuileries was you remember the work of the communists. They said as long as the nest remained the bird of prey would return, so to destroy the monarchy they burned the Palace. The Orléans Princes have gone to reside near to Chantilly, and Mr. Mann says Mont Po would now be a pleasant residence for you. So impossible is it for our best friends to comprehend the measure of our requirements.

Dear Winnie, I reproach myself with the trouble you are bearing alone. I have shared your joys and profited by your care and wish ever to divide your sorrows and your burdens. Could I have foreseen the course events have taken I would have gone back from Liverpool. I have, however, done as you wished and trust it may prove well for us both. Good night, beloved, honored, trusted, sweet, sweet wife.

April 1st. This morning I am happy in the receipt of yours of the 8th of March. The arrangement you have made about the house is as no doubt the best you could do and in these days of our hard fortune, we must consent to be submissionists. When we can we will try to find a more congenial home than Memphis. I have met disappointment in all my business attempts. The English seem to think every thing in our country is dependent on New York and therefore want their branch offices in that city. I try to look hopefully on the future but, with my wishes for you and the children, it is hard to avoid melancholy.

Dear Mr. Mann is full of projects to have me resident in France. The last is to turn his country place into a farm to breed horses. There is, I think, about seven acres of land on it. What a wild herd we could have on that domain! *Afternoon.* I have been to the Bois de Boulogne, this being the day called Longchamps. Am now interrupted, but ask time for a line more. Take, my dearest, a thousand kisses and all the best wishes of your Husband's heart. I have little hope of doing anything over here, if I had *no* hope I would return at once.

The preparations for Easter appear everywhere in the shop windows and at each stop the sad want of money is brought to remembrance. God bless and keep you all ever prays your devoted
Husband

Jefferson Davis to Varina Davis

Paris, France
13th April, 1874

My dear Wife,

I have been delayed here longer than was expected by propositions to organize a land company to aid our people and to secure emigration to the South.

Tomorrow I propose to go to London, where it is thought the organization can be effected.

My health has much improved; the swelling in the feet has not entirely disappeared, but is less. But for disappointments and anxiety for those ever dearest to me, I believe I should be very well.

No needless delay shall prevent me from being restored to my own dear Waafe.

Devotedly
Your Husband

Jefferson Davis to Varina Davis

Senator Benjamin Hill of Georgia was Davis's ardent supporter throughout his Presidency, and did all that he could to counteract the backstabbing and disruptive tactics of Vice-President Stephens and Georgia's Governor Joseph E. Brown. After the war, Hill continued to uphold the honor of the South. Joseph E. Johnston's recently released book on the war was largely a defense of his own actions and an attack on Davis's administration. Johnston's disaffection came in the summer of 1861, when

President Davis named Robert E. Lee to rank him, as Lee already had in the Army of Virginia. Frank Alfriend, onetime editor of the *Southern Literary Messenger,* had produced a favorable biography of Davis in 1867.

London
47 Prince's Square
Bayswater
26th April, '74

My dear wife:

I have lingered here for a week past under invitations to meet committees and men of business, but all the prospects thus opened have only been vague if not delusive. The ignorance of our section is truly astonishing and I have felt at every step that there was *a secret dread of displeasing the Yankees* which presents an obstacle to my success in any effort for my personal benefit. From each overthrow of a hope, I rise proud in the consciousness that my sin is the love of my country and may it be added that my suffering is for virtue's sake. Well I have been treated with consideration and am now asked to wait until Tuesday, day after tomorrow, for another conference with a Co. which contemplates transactions with Southern land owners, by advances on real estate and the sale of lands to emigrants. Perhaps I may effect something for our people if not for myself. There is a difficulty in my case growing out of what I owe to our people if not to myself, which is that the dignity conferred upon me does not permit as another might to ask employment by personal application.

Dear old wife, I hear you say—we can fast, we can toil in secret, but *we can not crawl in public.* The season is near at hand when you and the children must leave for a more healthy place and I am impatient to join you. If nothing prevents, that is to say if nothing offers a sufficient reason for delay I propose to leave here on next Wednesday for Liverpool, perhaps may go to Glasgow and hope to be with you in the next month.

The copies you sent to me of Senator Hill's speech have both reached me. He has again done a good work in presenting to the public a bold arraignment of our enemies and a spirited call on the South for the maintenance of this cause by the assertion of truth. I am glad you thanked him for his notice of us.

I have seen the appeal to which you refer, and think if Johnston paid much for it, he did not get an equivalent. His plaint on the subject of rank is without any just foundation, and is easily answered. His attempt at correction of Alfriend is only excusable on the score of his ignorance of the closing events of the battle.

Johnston has more effectively than another could shown his selfishness and his malignity. He is skillful in suppression and his memory is very convenient. For instance he does not remember that he did not leave the U.S. Army to enter the C.S. Army, but that he entered the Army of Virginia and when Va. joined the Confederacy came to the C.S.; also that in the Va. Army he was the subordinate of Lee, and that they were nominated to our provisional congress, at the same time and with the same relative rank they had in Va. [*The rest is lost.*]

Jefferson Davis Howell to Varina Davis

The youngest of Varina's brothers had been in command of a ship that ran to the Hawaiian Islands (originally known as the Sandwich Islands). Seventeen-year-old Jeff Davis, Jr., has discovered that he has little taste for study or V.M.I. discipline. Former Senator and Mrs. William McKendree Gwin returned to California after a several years' sojourn in Paris. Captain William H. Parker had once been Superintendent of the Confederate Naval Academy.

> S.S. Pelican
> At Sea, May 17, 1874

My dearest Old Sis:

I fully understood, or thought I did, the reason of your silence & assure you, you had my heartfelt sympathy. I did not hear of your bereavement for some time after the occurrence, but wrote you as soon thereafter as possible.

How many, many times do those scenes in Montreal to which you refer, present themselves to me, I fancy I see poor Ma as she stood in the door the day I left, and said, "I'll not say Good bye, my son, but God Bless you! Come back soon!" Until then I had not realized fully what I had undertaken, or how many trials, troubles, and privations lay before me in my fight with the world. I had looked upon going to sea as a life of adventure; in fact, a careless, romantic sort of Existence, the contemplation of which, when compared with the life I led in Montreal, viz—that of idleness and dependence—

fascinated me, and I determined to go. It was a sore trial to me, Sis, to put up with the taunts and insults from those above me while at sea, and many times have I had to ram my hands in my pockets, and biting my tongue & lips, run away to some other part of the ship, fearing to remain in their company lest with my mild (?) temper I should do some act of violence upon my tormentors. However, it is all over now, and well have I been rewarded, but God forbid that I should ever have to do it over again. I am so glad to hear what dear old Bro Jeff says about me, and grateful that I have lived long enough to prove to him that all the trouble and expense he was put to for me in my earlier years and for which I will ever be thankful has not been entirely thrown away.

Lordy! I'd give ten years of my life to see you all again, it seems like centuries since we met. I sometimes wonder if you would know me in case I ran across you accidentally. Do you think you would take a hard-looking, weather-beaten, wrinkled cuss for the girlish looking boy you saw 7 years ago to be one and the same person? I don't.

I had a good hearty roar, one that Ma used to say sounded like an empty barrel with the bung out, when I came to the description of Jeff. I never thought he'd be hung for beauty, but he used to show evidence of something more to be desired by far, i.e. a big, honest heart. Encourage him in the idea of coming to me, if he ever runs away. You know it runs in our blood and he might do just such a thing sometime. If he does I guarantee he will be glad to return and promise to "sin no more"—in that line at least.

I saw the Gwins last evening and set up to Larrie the whole evening, talking about old times in Washington. She is very clever and bright, but oh! Sis! she is so ugly and passes for 24! Mrs. G. still goes to parties and occasionally sports a low necked dress. The doctor looks the same as ever, in fact not a bit changed.

Mrs. Parker and Capt P. are still here and often speak of you sending much love upon all occasions. Capt P. says "Jeff, tell Mr. Davis that I am still devoted to our lost cause, and look upon him as the Representative man of our people."

My dear old Sis, if you had only come out last summer when I was commanding the Sandwich Island Steamer I could have shewn you a glorious time. The present King of that place Lunalilo I is a great chum of mine, and has frequently taken me out hunting. [*The rest is lost.*]

Jefferson Davis to Mrs. S. A. Ayres

Jefferson Davis had returned to Memphis in the summer with restored health, but with no business connection. He now answers numerous letters from old friends. This typical one is to a lady in Keokuk, Iowa. Davis had paid a second visit to James Smith in Scotland.

Memphis, Tenn.
19th Aug. 1874

My good and dear Friend,

Your kind and most welcome letter was duly received. It was truly cheering to my care worn heart to have your congratulations on my safe return. Though it was for the benefit to be expected from a sea voyage that I went abroad, my stay on shore was pleasant and beneficial to my health. You ask me how I was received elsewhere than in England, and I answer one must have been in Scotland to know the full import of "a Highland welcome." Among the many pleasant memories left to me, is my ramble in the land of Burns. The white thorn was in bloom, the fields were gaudy with the furze "unprofitably gay" and the modest crimson-tipped daisy clustered with the gowans, buttercups, and wild hyacinths. The cottage in which Burns was born is neatly kept for show, and Kirk Alloway, now quite a ruin, unfit even for the witches' dance, still stands to remind of Tam O'Shanter's ride. The Landlady of the tavern where Tam and Souter Johnny had their drinking bout courteously invited me to sit in the chair Tam occupied on that night made famous by Burns. The "auld Brig" across the bonny Doon yet stands though severely marked by time, but beneath it runs the sparkling river bright and fresh as ever, reminding us of Tennyson's brook.

The Ruins one meets in Europe, and sometimes buildings in good repair, which were constructed before Columbus sailed on his voyage of discovery, most forcibly reminds one of our country how new we are.

And what reflection could be more sad than that which one finds in our moral decadence. But you did not ask for reflections on our own land & times. I found every thing quiet and prosperous in France. Paris inside of the fortifications had suffered little damage by the war, and the people seemed comfortable and happy. They are nominally Republican and though you might deny their right to be so called, it probably means so much as that monarchy, if re-established, will be of short duration.

I am truly obliged to you for the offer of one of your ancient coins, but must decline it, because the loss of everything I had collected, by the events of the war, discourages me at my advanced age from attempting to renew the work; further it may be added that my residence is not sufficiently permanent to give the proper security to so valuable a relic as that which you offer.

You ask if I would accept the buttons you offer and I assure you as a token of your friendship they would be gladly received, the more so, however, if you would instead of the proposed initials, combine the letters so as to indicate as well the donor as the receiver.

It will always give me true pleasure to hear from you, and with the hope that we may meet again in this world, I am, faithfully and most respectfully,

Yours
Jefferson Davis

Jefferson Davis Howell to Varina Davis

Jeffy D. has lost his position because he had been a teen-aged cadet at the Confederate Naval Academy during the war.

Occidental Hotel
San Francisco
Sept. 28, 1874

My darling Old Fat Sis,

Applied for a command in the P.M.S.S. Co., which I was fortunate enough to obtain over the heads of some 75 or 100 applicants. I had no influence or anything to help me, simply stating my ability for the position and announcing myself ready to be examined and compete for the command with others. Sufficient, I as before stated, took the ship. Owing to this, these men who were disappointed, made a petition to the Managing Director, setting forth that I had been a "Rebel" serving in the "Rebel Navy" and they had been loyal to Union throughout the war, and they thought it hard that I should be appointed over them. Had I not been a confiding fool I might have put a stop to this, but fancying myself secure in my position as long as I conducted myself in a proper manner, paid no attention to it. The result was that after two voyages to Panama, I was placed on waiting orders without pay—giving me as a reason that on arrival at Panama my ship was dirty, none other. This was an absolute lie, but nothing compared to what was subsequently told on me.

At first I felt like giving up all hopes and sliding down the hill, this infernal world was doing its best to kill me, but thanks to my native stubbornness, I am still clinging tooth and toenail.

My friends here, God bless them! have stood by me through thick and thin. Everyone who has ever known me is indignant at the manner in which I have been treated, and many have openly gone to the Agents and expressed their indignation in the plainest terms. Senator Jones (I.P. of Nevada) had gone so far as to write a letter to Mr. Hatch, protesting against the injustice making my speedy reinstatement a personal favor to himself—this from a U.S. Senator and a man with $19,000,000. Capital will I think have some weight.

When I look back on my tussle with the world since the time I went in the *Lord B.*, for then my persecutions commenced, I tremble for poor little Jeff, when he comes to encounter the rude buffets of life. [*The rest is lost.*]

Jefferson Davis to Varina Davis

Davis now turns his attention to the unhappy business of the lawsuit to recover his plantation, Brierfield.

Vicksburg
23d October 1874

Dear Wife,

I arrived here safely yesterday. The trip was much longer than expected, yet nothing was lost, as Ben was not here, and Joe Smith arrived this morning.

I found that Lize and Joe Mitchell had filed an answer to my bill, and by bold statements and by seeking advantage of my kindness heretofore shown to them, have denied my claims and pleaded an estoppel.

Maj. Pittman attaches much importance to the letter of Brother Joe, proposing to buy the Brierfield and the personal property on it, also to the conversation with you in regard to the sale of the Brierfield when I was in prison. He wants you to write to him fully as to your recollections of the letter proposing to buy, and of the subsequent coversation with you when you were on your way to the North. His object is, after receiving your letter, for a basis to form interrogatories and send them to you for your deposition. He thinks that the establishment of the proposition to buy will be conclusive, and that the letter being lost its contents can be proved orally.

Any other fact known to you which bears upon the question of ownership of the Brierfield you will please state and Pittman will know whether it is necessary to include it in your deposition or not. I had hoped to keep you out of the controversy and had the other party been fair & truthful it would not have been necessary to introduce you as a witness. Even now I say that if you prefer not to testify you are free to decline and I will be satisfied that you have good & sufficient reasons for your decision.

Give my love to my dear daughters. The weather here is quite warm and the streets very dusty.

Your Husband

Jefferson Davis, Jr., to His Father

Jeff is still a cadet at V.M.I. and a member of Kappa Sigma Fraternity. He enjoys the drill field, but is doing poorly in his studies. His warm-hearted, happy nature, however, is revealed between the lines of this letter.

V.M.I.
Nov 2nd 1874

My dear Father

I received your kind letter and you can not tell how glad I was to get it. I would have answered it before but as I did not have time to write any but a hurried one I concluded to wait until my return when I could write you a full account of our trip. You will be astonished to learn that the Corps has been to Richmond and back since you heard from me. It was so sudden that I did not have time to notify you of it, in fact, we did not know ourselves until a few days before we started. Then we drilled four hours a day in Battalion drill which, as you know is, the hardest of all drill. When we arrived at R. to our supprise after the 1st Va Reg. saw Dress parade they refused to drill against us. The papers were all inquiring how it was that we moved as though we were on springs and nearly every boy in Richmond wants to come to the Institute. When we arrived at R. we were quartered about the city among the citizens. For your sake I was invited to stay with several of your old friends among whom were Judge Lyons and Mr. Ould and Gen Anderson, but I stayed at the Grants who invited me very kindly before I left Lex.

I took dinner with Judge Lyons who told me to give his love to you and ask you to write to him for he loved you very dearly. I called on all of your old friends whom I knew. All sent a great deal of love to you and said they longed to welcome you back to R. I have often heard of kissing a man for his Mother but just think— Miss Mattie Ould, the belle of R., kissed me for my Father, but you may judge I was very glad to get it under any circumstances & particularly as it was for your sake. We arrived last night and of course are very tired, but I am never so weary that I can not think of and write to my dear Father. I am very much obliged to you for the stamps you sent me—I did not have them. Is it true that you have accepted a position as Pres. of a line of Steamers? I heard so in Richmond.

Please write and tell me all about yourself for you know *that* interests me more than anything else. Hoping this letter may find you well, my own dear Father, I remain as ever

Your loving
Boy
Jeff

SPEECHMAKING
AND A NEW UNDERTAKING

Jefferson Davis to Varina Davis

Still attempting to find means to support his family, Davis went to inspect some remote property in Arkansas that was thought to hold minerals of value.

Kellog Mines, Arkansas
22d Feb. 1875

Dear Wife,

We reached Little Rock at 2½ o'clock A.M. and after an early breakfast started in a buggy for this place, where we arrived in safety in the forenoon. From such examination as I have been able to make my conclusion is that the deposits are irregular in the shale, below which no shaft has been sunk. The deposit of metal is mixed, there being more lead than silver, zinc or copper, all of which exist in the same deposit. The exterior indications are favorable to the existence of a metallic vein, but to reach it much deeper exploration needs to be made. The lien I learn is in several hands. The country hereabout is very rugged and often plainly shows volcanic eruptions.

Tomorrow we will make a prospecting tour and perhaps find something which will cost little & may prove of great value.

If no opportunity occurs to send this to the P.O. in the morning I will add the result of the prospecting.

Affectionately your
Husband

23d Feb. 75

The morning was cloudy and threatening rain, nevertheless we started on horseback and soon the weather made good its threat.

The Engineer, a good Confederate soldier, furnished me with a rubber overcoat and the rain did not much affect me. We found at least one knob which appeared as good as the place where the work is now going on. It is thought that it may be purchased for five dollars an acre or less.

Today finer specimens have been obtained than heretofore, but they are not sufficiently numerous to change my belief that the deposits are small i.e. not a vein or what is in strictness of language a mine.

Not being a practical miner I am at a loss to decide on the character of some of the material taken out.

Capt. Cobb, such is the name and style of the Engineer, is a frank, sober and studious man. He lives in a log cabin, and we are his guests. The country about here is very poor and the few inhabitants are as poor as the country. There ought to be mineral as there is surely nothing else.

Tomorrow we expect to leave for Little Rock and the next day hope to be with you.

Your Husband

Jefferson Davis to Varina Davis

The papers had announced that Jefferson Davis was to appear at a State Fair in Houston, Texas, even before he had actually accepted the invitation. He has been besieged with invitations. He leaves Vicksburg in the midst of preparations for the presentation of his lawsuit. In a sense it was well that Joseph Davis had kept Brierfield in his own name, for the property of the Confederate President might have been confiscated by the Federal Government.

Jackson, Mississippi
6th May 1875

Dear Wife,

The letters and telegrams have been so many and so pressing that in conjunction with the fact that the press of Texas has announced me as coming to the Fair, I have started to Houston.

The gentle fair relations of ours in Vicksburg are industriously trying to show that I never had any thing and that the house on

Brierfield was built by Brother Joe and paid for by the Bradford place.

The deed to *that* place in favor of Marcy and Zeigler bears date 1852 and the price was $2500. You will see that the date and price neither correspond with the time or the amount proper.

This trip is very disagreeable to me as well because of the interruption as the fatigue. The hot weather here is oppressive.

One of the attempts is to prove that by general repute Brother Joe owned Brierfield. If you can, find the newspaper slip noticing the death of Brother Joe, where he is represented as taking care of my property and thus saving me from the common fate of politicians. I wish you would send it to Pittman. It is I think in a small bundle with other similar things.

As ever, with a heart full of devotion,

Your Husband

Jefferson Davis to Varina Davis

Davis received a real "Texas welcome" with rousing cheers and a military escort. A Houston newspaper declared that "thousands of warm hearts in our midst are beating with joy and yearn to pay reverence to him they honor and love so well." He was accorded ovations at the Fair and all along the way. A private train was put at his disposal.

Houston, Texas
15th May, 1875

Dear Wife,

I have been so strongly urged to go to Austin and Dallas that I have consented to do so and propose thence to proceed by way of Fulton and Little Rock to Memphis.

The people here have been more than kind, and in general terms express a wish to make it my interest to remain with them. Some propose the Presidency of the Agricultural and Mechanical College, which is immediate; others, the Presidency of a Rail Road to the Pacific, which is prospective. But I have declined the first and nobody has power to offer the second. The route from Austin to, Dallas passes by Bryan, the site of the College, and gives an opportunity to see it.

Numerous inquiries have been made for you and regrets expressed that you did not come with me. Mrs. Lubbock sends you many good wishes and friendly remembrances.

I wished to leave this evening, but the Mayor and City Council make a point of having me to dine with them on Saturday night. A special train is being put at my command. My stay will be very brief at the two places where I will stop and my arrival will be earlier than it would have been by way of New Orleans & Vicksburg.

The weather here is hot, in the sun. The country is beautiful, abounding in flowers. There is a refined society, a goodly number of old Mississippians and their descendants. The people have a robust, healthy look, and are cheerful and confident of their future. I send you two newspaper slips in regard to *us*. My hostess Mrs. Franklin is the Daughter of my boyhood's acquaintance Ben Hadley and she is very cordial & cultivated.

Too much attention has made me weary, the novelty of being a people's guest has its painful memories mixed with the gratification.

Kiss my dear children and tell them I expect them to make their Mother as happy as she can be.

Ever with sincere devotion,

Your Husband

Varina Davis to Jefferson Davis

Mrs. Davis has heard from her husband, who is on court business in Vicksburg. She is saddened on his sixty-seventh birthday by the thought of their going to live in Texas. Davis has been offered the Presidency of the new Texas Agricultural and Mechanical College at Bryan, but he has not accepted the position, despite the newspapers' reports. In the end, he did not accept.

June 3d 1875
98 Court St.
Memphis, Tenn

My dear Husband,

This is your birthday, and I write, not to remind you, but show that I have not entirely forgotten the day. How very sad anniversaries become. They are for the young and hopeful and for the very old and hopeless. A spark of expectation reveals the gloomy, weary waste. But I am deeply grateful to God who spared you "from the Lions" as the Psalmist says. You and I have lived long enough to know that "other refuge have we none"—and when I find myself looking forward with dread to our Texas hegira I feel some times that our times are short and that I need not care when the evening of my days closes, just so it is calm and finds my day's work done. But I only meant to ask God's blessings upon another year on which you have entered, and to moralize is an offence.

We are as well as usual. Little Winnie said the "Wreck of the Hesperus" this evening at Mrs. Meredith's commencement and did well, and looked lovely and aristocratic in the extreme. I felt out of sorts and sad.

Good night, and goodbye. Take care of yourself & do not expose yourself.

Affectionately
Your Wife

Jefferson Davis to Varina Davis

Davis has gone to Florida Davis McCaleb's plantation, Diamond Place. Perkins was once a family friend. Cox is a former plantation manager.

Vicksburg
5th June 1875

My dear Wife,

I found all at the Diamond Place in their usual condition and many affectionate inquiries were made concerning you and each of the children.

Florida has none of the letters written to her from Hurricane except those of her Father in regard to her own affairs. She expressed willingness to testify in our case, and said she remembered to have seen two wills of an old date in one of which I was mentioned as an heir in common with Brother Joe's children. She scoffed at the idea of her Father having built the residence at Brierfield for me. I have told Pittman to have interrogatories prepared for her.

I have been shown interrogatories for Jno. Perkins. One of the questions regards a conversation between P. & Brother Joe, in which P. was told he was to be an Executor, and that it was decided not to give a deed to Brierfield, lest I should die and the place pass into the hands of my wife's family. Whether the scoundrel ever heard so or not, it is to be inferred that he will so answer.

Cox came over and his testimony is quite satisfactory. Lize is, I learn, to testify orally on Monday next. It will be unpleasant to meet in hostility, but if she romances she must be exposed.

The weather is intensely hot and I feel the effect of the Sun more than ever before. I shall be detained here for some days and will then decide whether to go to N.O. or return to you.

Kiss my children for their loving Father. Tell Jeff. to go to bed at 10 o'clock P.M. and get up at six A.M. Tell Maggie to walk in the cool of the morning & evening. Tell Winnie to keep out of the Sun and to avoid excitement.

With love and urgent entreaties that you will take good care of yourself I am ever devotedly

Your Husband

Jefferson Davis to Varina Davis

Vicksburg
9th June '75

My dear Wife

Your letter of the 3d Inst. was received before your telegram. Thank you for your commemoration of my birthday, however sad the event may be regarded it is pleasant to know that those nearest to us do not consider it as a day of fast or one to be ignored. I was on that day at the Diamond Place, and they honored it in due form, with new corn as well.

The dodgers seem to think my presence a formidable incident and so evade taking testimony. So I am yet here and may be for the rest of this week. Cox wrote to me that if I could not come to see him at Clinton that he would come here. I answered that I wanted to see him in the presence of Bowman & Pittman and asked him to come to-day.

Florida agrees to tell all she knows, and will I think be a valuable witness for us.

Our enemy is trying to prove that the legacies to our children was in compensation for Brierfield and I told Pittman let them do so, *it is an admission of my ownership.* If Lize is relied on to prove a purpose to strike at you, the attempt must fail, or if it succeed be but the addition of insult to injury and in no case affect our legal and equitable rights. I have instructed Pittman to ask Lize about the relations between you and Brother Joe, at the time you saw him here. Did she hear his avowal of a wish to live with us even in a log cabin?

With tenderest love to the children, I am affectionately

Your Husband

Jefferson Davis to Varina Davis

Lise Mitchell maintained that her grandfather failed to give Jefferson Davis a deed to Brierfield because of hostility to Mrs. Davis and because he abhorred the idea of the property falling into the hands of the Howells, whom he regarded as undeserving. Though Varina had quarreled with Joseph and his family before the war, on her last visits with Joseph in Vicksburg in 1866 and 1867 their relations were friendly, and on two occasions she gave him several hundred dollars from her small store.

Vicksburg
14th June 1875

My dear Wife,

The cross interrogatories do not I suppose require a statement of the painful controversy in which your Ma was involved, but only the fact of an alienation and such bitter feeling as no doubt did, when excited by artful fanning, render my Brother unjust to you and me. If Lize or Lucy Mitchell would tell the truth they would say that Brother Joe, after being irritated by remarks about you when I came to Vicksburg after leaving you in England, did then most emphatically deny any hostility to you and so speak as to compel me to relent.

But "in my wrath I said they are all liars" cried the Psalmist, and the world has not I fear much improved.

Do not fear for me. I will, under God's protection, fulfill my mission and if care will suffice to render duty safe, shall come back to you as surely as does a bad penny.

Thank Maggie for her letter which shall be answered promptly, but I felt it needful to guard you against probing old wounds to your hurt and so have written in haste. With love to all, I say good bye for a little while.

Your Husband

Varina Davis to Jefferson Davis

Samuel Davis was buried in Washington; Joseph, in Richmond; William, in Memphis. The Davises were deeply touched to know that there were still persons in Washington who remembered to decorate the grave of the baby Samuel who had died in 1854 during the Pierce administration when Davis was Secretary of War.

June 18, 1875
Memphis

My dear Banny,

I enclose a letter which speaks for itself. God seems to keep green the memory of our solitary little dead children—whether they lie on the hillside in the midst of enemies or sleep in the earth their Father defended and prayed for strength to keep inviolate. May God bless the gentlewomen who have turned from the clamorous to decorate my child in death— The past is inexpressibly bitter, is it not?

Our Jeff is very loving to me, and I find I can keep him very well in hand. He says he will write to you tomorrow. I feel constant anxiety on your account, and hope for the best with fear & trembling—

As ever believe me

Affectionately
Your Wife

[*Enclosure:*]

Washington D.C.
June 11th 1875

Mrs. Davis

Dear Madam

I am sure you will be gratified to learn of a delicate tribute of affection offered to yourself and Mr. Davis on the 1st inst. I met accidentally a young girl and her servant loaded with flowers going to "Oak Hill." We were strangers, but she invited me to join the committee which I did, something unusual for me who rarely leaves the house since my severe afflictions. A dozen ladies met at the Presidential house, where flowers in great profusion were heaped all over the rooms. One exquisite cross of rarest flowers was handed to me & we proceeded in our sad errand; at the Cemetery we met a fine gentleman & commenced decorating the graves, about ten or twelve. Near the close, we came to a *quiet nook*, & I was requested to place the cross "on the *grave of Mrs. Davis' child*," soon the little mound was covered with choice bouquets. Two lovely children pushed eagerly forward crying "Mama, Mama, I want to put some, ah, let me!" They held each a basket of cut flowers which they emptied, in a most graceful manner—filling the atmosphere for a distance with sweetest fragrance—I have never seen in one mass so many flowers.

A short prayer was offered by a Clergyman who was present, and we left as quietly as possible, the absence of an oration rather adding to the solemnity.

Very respectfully
M. Morse

Jefferson Davis to Varina Davis

In early September Davis left Memphis on a speaking tour in Missouri to work up interest in a newly formed Mississippi Valley Association designed to create direct trade between the river states and England and South America. The New York *Times* of September 11, 1875, carried seven columns of extracts from Davis's speech at an Agricultural Fair at De Soto, Missouri. The aim of the International Chamber of Commerce and Mississippi Valley Society was to build up trade through the port of New Orleans, linking European ports directly with North and South American interests. Ships to be built in England were to bring about an interchange of commodities. The entire Mississippi Valley area was to benefit. But again Davis's ideas for assisting the States that bordered on the Mississippi River was doomed to failure. British capital after all was not attracted to build the ships. It feared to offend New York, the commercial and shipping center of the North.

Jeff, Jr., who had been withdrawn from V.M.I., accompanied his father. They proceeded to Colorado to inspect some mines.

Executive Mansion
Jefferson City, 12th Sept. 1875

My dear Wife

I am here tired and a little hoarse from speaking in the open air and talking in the cars. Otherwise better than when we parted. The papers will have told you of our meetings &c.

Jeff. is quite well and hardly remembers any thing as far back as Memphis. We leave here tonight for Kansas City and thence to Colorado.

Just now a committee are coming for me. With best love I am devotedly

Your Husband

Jefferson Davis to Varina Davis

Kansas City
16th Sept. 75

My dear Wife

We leave in the morning for Denver. The light is so dim that I can only write to say that my health has improved and there is every arrangement to make the trip comfortable. It is now after midnight. Jeff has dozed off and may not be ready to start in the morning.

With love to all the household, I am ever lovingly

Your Husband

Jefferson Davis to Varina Davis

Clear Creek Canyon
Colorado, 21st Sept. 75

Dear Wife

I am here among mountains covered with snow and the air so cold as to keep one hovering around the stove.

Yesterday I went with Wilkins Glenn to look at his mine situated 10,500 feet above the sea. He has many troubles but seems confident of great results. We drove down the canyon yesterday in a severe snow storm and in the discomfort of it remembered your preference for cold weather, and, as I have done under all circumstances, wished you were with me.

We leave this morning for Denver where, as we shall be on a lower level, I hope we shall have warmer weather, if so may go down to the Manitou Springs for a day or two, if not, will hasten back to Missouri on the way to you. Jeff has been very joyous, and at Kansas City Jeff. Griffith joined us and they have been boon companions.

I am quite well—much better than when we parted. The stage is ready and with much love I must stop this talk.

J. D.

Jefferson Davis to Varina Davis

Manitou House
Manitou, Colorado,
23 Sept. 1875

My dear Wife,

Your telegram reached me here yesterday and I replied by the same means. I will hasten back to St Louis where it may be the Agent Griffin will meet me, and where after reading the proposition it may be desirable to confer with the Directors of the Branch of the Missi Valley Association.

Jeff. is very well, and my own health has decidedly improved.

We are here deep in the Rocky Mountains at a favorite resort for asthmatic and consumptive patients. One of the springs boils violently and is richly impregnated with soda. The Indians believed it to be supernatural and hence the name, which means Great Spirit.

Every day and almost every hour my regret is renewed that you did not come with me. You would enjoy the scenery, the wild flowers & the *cold* air I am sure.

Take good care of your dear self for my sake as well as that of others and believe me devotedly your

Husband

Jefferson Davis to Varina Davis

Before his return home, on urgent invitation Davis stops to visit his birthplace in southwestern Kentucky.

Fairview, Kentucky
9th Oct. 1875

Dear Wife:

I had expected to leave this morning to visit my birthplace and then to go on to Clarksville and take the train to rejoin you. But the "plans of man," etc., and under pressure I agreed to remain here until Monday and now I find that it was designed to make a demonstration at Fairview and that I cannot reach Clarksville in time for the Monday train, that is cannot get there Monday night. Now I am called for to go to the Fair grounds—

10th October

The reception here has surpassed anything I could have expected. Many say "I wish your Wife had come" and that you might have witnessed an enthusiasm and cordiality—a wild burst of affection—exceeding anything I ever had before. I do sadly regret your absence.

Women who have lost and suffered and bearded men who have served in battle, melt into tears and vainly try to express their love.

With love to each and all of our household, I am ever devotedly,

Your Husband

Jefferson Davis to Varina Davis

After his return from Kentucky, Davis had to proceed to Vicksburg on the lawsuit business. Negroes from both plantations, Hurricane and Brierfield, were brought to town to testify.

Vicksburg
22d Oct. 1875

My dear Wife

I have been here these many days for very little purpose. Today some negroes summoned at Hamer's instance have arrived, and

Little Hagar and Big Sam for whom I wrote are here also. Hagar made many affectionate inquiries about you and the children. Sam also showed like interest.

Their evidence will be to the point of the clearing and improvement of the Brierfield and to the purchase of the first lot of negroes. The Pittmans are confident and seem to be well prepared.

Your deposition has arrived and they say is *the best instrument of the kind they ever saw.* So much for a poor old Waafe, who might in happier days and better relations have been a writer whose name would have gone down to future ages.

I told the negroes that my children would be glad to see them and that their Mistress had often expressed a wish to revisit the Brierfield. The poor things seemed delighted at the remembrance of them. They hate Ben Montgomery, and I fear he has been unjust to those in whose special interest the places were sold to him. Well, well, the world is unjust.

Hagar has come in and says tell Mistress howdy for me and all the old folks. Sam says, "and me too."

Love, ardent love to the children and all that heart can offer for yourself from your devoted

Husband

Jefferson Davis to Varina Davis

New Orleans
7th Nov. 1875

My dear Wife

Your welcome letter of the 6th Inst. has just been delivered by the Postman. I am deeply grieved that you should have such physical suffering and domestic troubles, and I not there to share if not to relieve them. Would that I could even send to you a cheering letter, but woe is me, for I have a story of disappointments to tell.

The letter from the Valley Society was not satisfactory, said nothing about the modifications of the Regulations which I had proposed but made a difficulty about the money to be advanced for the first year's operations and salaries. Griffin offered his own guarantee that all my suggestions would be adopted if I would take charge of the American branches. I declined to accept before assured by the London Committee, and he sent a dispatch by cable, to which no answer has been received. If the reply is favorable I will go to work but there will be no money for me until it is earned.

Helen Keary writes that she has discovered that back taxes were due on the land, so that postpones yet further any payment from that quarter and, as Mr. Payne only advances to her on my account, it may be that if her crop only pays part of the sum due for the year's supply and these back taxes that I will have to pay the rest.

My stay here depends upon others and may be for a week, but shall be as brief as I can make it.

Kiss my dear children for me.

With tenderest love and solicitude I am

Your Husband

Jefferson Davis to Varina Davis

In November of the troubled year of 1875 came another great sorrow to the Davises. A San Francisco news dispatch announced the sinking of the steamship *Pacific,* which ran between that city and Seattle and which had been rammed by a large sailing vessel in a dense fog. The dispatch stated that its Captain, Jefferson Davis Howell, was lost. The news was to prove true. Only twenty-eight, this youngest of Varina's brothers was the most promising and the only one who achieved even the slightest success. After Captain Howell had seen his three hundred passengers safely removed from the sinking vessel, he stripped to his underclothes and swam to a raft with an old lady clinging to him. After three days and four nights of hunger and exposure to cold, Jeffy D. slipped off the raft and was swallowed up by the sea. Davis was as grieved as his wife, for he regarded him as a son.

New Orleans
11th Nov. 1875

My dear Wife,

I have deferred writing you under the hope that an answer would come to a telegram I sent to William Howell in San Francisco asking for reliable information in regard to Brother Jefferson.

Though grievously anxious I am not despondent. The sailor picked up from the pilot house was by his own story a deserter, who with another of the crew cut loose a life boat to save themselves, in disregard of their duty to the passengers. Such a man is unworthy of belief, and would make up a story to cover his own infamy.

Our dear boy was strong in body and in heart, he was skillful in all which was needful in case of a wreck. Too true to his trust to leave his ship while there was anything for the Capt. to do, he would see the danger and provide for it by constructing a raft which would live in ordinary weather for many days. His physical and moral strength would endure much, and in the thoroughfare of ships would be probably rescued. God grant that my hopes may soon be fulfilled and our sorrow turned to rejoicing. For you my dear Wife, my heart is sore, and I long to be with you in this day of trial.

The pride I felt in the gallantry and success of our boy as a Sailor is both humbled and rebuked. Of all the earth you alone suffer as I do, and you I hope will feel the trust which supports me.

With love to our children and all a heart can feel of devotion to you I am affectionately

Your Husband

Jefferson Davis to Varina Davis

From a business trip to Montgomery, Alabama, Jefferson Davis went down to the Gulf Coast to see the lots bought in the summer of 1857 for a home when he would retire from the United States Senate. Mrs. Dorsey, whom he and Varina had known intimately, owned several plantations. Beauvoir was one of her residences.

Mississippi City
Wednesday—Nov. 18, 1875

Dear Wife,

I left Montgomery on Monday morning and came to this place during the night of the same day. In the early morning I got up and the moaning of the winds among the pines and the rolling waves of the Gulf on the beach gave to me a sense of rest and peace which made me wish to lay me down and be at home until this trial is past.

After breakfast I rode down the coast to the lots you long ago selected for our home and found the fence so entirely gone and the bushes so thick that I could but doubt whether the work we paid for had ever been done.

I then went on to Mrs. Dorsey's, but she had left for their plantation last Saturday. Beauvoir is a fine place, large and beautiful house, and many orange trees yet full of fruit.

I then went to Handsboro. The heaviness of the sand had worn down the horses so much that I had to put off 'till the morrow to go out to the Bayou Bernard and see what kind of a sheep walk the children & I could make there.

I have gone to the Turkey Creek bridge, travelled up the Bayou until the water ceased to be salty and wound through the pine forest over to the Pass Christian road and thence back to the Hotel of Col. Nixon, who has made kind inquiries for you.

Everything is to me like an ignis fatuus, save that my pursuit does not bring me to a relieving precipice.

For the time and forever affectionately

Your Husband

Jefferson Davis to Varina Davis

On January 1, 1876, Maggie Davis, who had cohorts of suitors, was married at St. Lazarus Episcopal Church to J. Addison Hayes, a young bank cashier in Memphis of excellent North Carolinian antecedents, but no wealth. Slim, with a golden moustache, he proved to be the perfect husband and the perfect son-in-law. The marriage was a national news item. The couple went to St. Louis for the honeymoon. Davis, who adored his "sweet little Pollie" was not altogether happy at losing her to another man's "authority" at twenty-one. But he grew to admire his son-in-law more with each year and to love him as a son.

The Reconstruction still bound the Deep South and the Chancellor of the Court was not disposed to be fair to the ex-President of the Confederacy.

Vicksburg
11th January, 1876

My dear Wife,

The Chancellor decided against us, on the ground of estoppel, but nevertheless argued the merits of the case in such manner as to suggest either bribery or political consideration. He misstated testimony and omitted every fact in our favor. I have not yet seen the Pittmans, but take it for granted they are prepared to take the case to the Supreme Court, where unless our *luck* runs heretofore we may expect the decree of the Chancellor to be reversed.

I propose to leave this evening for New Orleans to confer with the members of Missi. Valley Society there, in regard to the new development. Judge Farrar, the Presdt. of the branch here, is desirous that I should accept the proposition of the Vicksburg Branch, to go to London without delay, funds for necessary expenses to be furnished by the Branch. I have preferred to wait until after reaching N.O. before making a definite reply.

The Montgomerys are here and those who know less of the Mitchells and the negroes than I do think that a final and equitable settlement will be reached to-day. I am weary of their trickery & vacillation and will not renew discussion with them, as I have stated to their lawyers.

I am glad that Maggie enjoyed her trip to Saint Louis and bears to you on her return evidence of future happiness.

Genl. Adams prefers for me if I go to England the route by rail to N.Y. and thence by sea. My own inclination is towards the route from N.O. by sea, as one avoids the cold weather as well on land as off the northern Atlantic coast.

I am pressed for time to do all cut out for the day's work, so with earnest wishes for your health, I am ever lovingly
                                        Your Husband

Jefferson Davis to Maggie Davis Hayes

                                        New Orleans
                                        19th Jany. '76
My darling Pollie:
Your very welcome letter of the 14th was duly received and I was led to hope that your Mother was coming to join me here; but on the same day a letter from her dispelled the hopes which yours had created.

It is probable that I may go to London very soon, and have

written to your Mother suggesting in that event that she should go with me. The conduct of the owners of the house we occupy is illiberal and the more annoying because of the uncertainty as to my future residence, and the length of time we should wish to keep the house.

I am glad you had a pleasant visit to Saint Louis. It is a great city and probably destined to be the largest interior town of this continent.

Until this morning the weather here has been bright and warm. The orange trees are in bloom, and fears were entertained of disaster to the next crop of fruit.

It is a long lane which never turns, says the proverb, thus far the lane of my ill fortune holds its course, but as proverbs are said to be ever true, if this does not, like the oracles, speak so as to deceive, I may look out for the suggested change of direction.

My dear daughter, it is quite as strange to me as it can be to you, to think of any authority having come between us.

Mr. Hayes' last words to me were in promise to take good care of you and I do not doubt he will faithfully keep that pledge. May God bless you both.

Give my love to each and all of our family, which now, of course, includes Mr. Hayes, and accept the fondest wishes for your welfare & happiness from

Your loving Father

Jefferson Davis to Varina Davis

New Orleans
31st Jany 76

My dear Wife,

I have been elected by the members here to be President of the American Department of the Missi. Valley Society, office at New Orleans. Today I have, as requested, presented a Constitution and Regulations. If adopted as drawn by me it will impose most of the work here on an Executive Committee and devolve on me much travel, including an early voyage to England.

The salary is not yet fixed, you may expect it to be six thousand dollars and travelling expenses.

You shall do as you like about a residence, and therefore I have done nothing to restrict your choice as to house or place.

My preference is that you should go across seas and my hope has been that your health would be improved.

But I will get a house here, or on the sea shore, or in Memphis, or take our lodgings from day to day as may best please you. If, however, there should be anything disturbing you in your present residence just tell the owner to go over Jordan or wait until it suits my convenience to come.

With fondest affection I am

Your Husband

Jefferson Davis to Varina Davis

Davis felt that he could not afford a hotel room and he declined his friend J. U. Payne's pressing invitation to stay as a guest at his house.

New Orleans
15th March, 1876

My dear Wife

I have taken a parlor and chamber on the first floor of a house on Bourbon Street, two squares below Canal Street. The house was once the residence of our friend Mr. Gaskett, is now kept as a lodging house by an old mulatto woman. She does not furnish meals, and says since the war she cannot get along with servants. From her remarks she must have owned them formerly.

On the opposite side of the street there is a family restaurant, at which is offered a small neat room entirely private and board at $1.50 per day, or $2, if sent to lodgings. So whenever it will be agreeable to you I am ready to receive you, and you will not have to ask or confer favors on any body. The Society is waiting for answers from the Branches and all is as when I last wrote to you on that subject.

Give my tenderest love to each of the children and take boundless oceans of the same for yourself.

Your Husband

Jefferson Davis to Varina Davis

Davis had invested a little money in a machine for making ice, but in the end it was not profitable.

New Orleans
22nd March 1876

My dear Wife

Your two letters of the 19th & 20th Insts. have just been received. The symptoms you describe all belong to the effect on the nervous system produced by a severe concussion on its centre, and clearly indicate the propriety of both bodily and mental rest.

There is a faintly manifested wish that I should go out to promote the organization of Branches before sailing for Europe, Texas has been specially mentioned. Tomorrow the Executive Committee is to meet me and if any thing decisive is done I will write to you about it.

Last night I went with Mary Stamps to see Miss Mary Anderson, a Kentucky girl of sixteen, who is the theatrical star of the day. She is untrained and awkward, but has a fine deep voice, is tall, good looking, and when excited shows great power. My mind ran back when looking at her in high passion to what Fanny Kemble was in her youth. There is a wide difference however in the cultivation and in the intellectual expression. This being the only "lark" I have been on, has therefore been described.

The Montgomerys have again failed to pay the drafts, which were taken in settlement last winter. Thornton came to see me yesterday and said they had given Hamer & Mitchell mules and supplies to cover what was due to them, but that he could not get money for us, and that their Commission Merchant here would not accept their drafts, but that he would go to Vicksburg & try to get the house there to accept drafts payable in September.

When what would be satisfactory cannot be had it only remains to take the best which is attainable. The low price of cotton is the excuse and no doubt partially accounts for the failure.

Our Machine has made a little ice and Fixary makes great promises of things you shall see when something else is done.

My dear, dear Winnie, be patient. You have heard there is luck in leisure, perhaps by taking the latter we may gain the former.

Kiss our beloved children and receive many with a heart's best love from

Your Husband

Jefferson Davis to Varina Davis

INTERNATIONAL CHAMBER OF COMMERCE AND
MISSISSIPPI VALLEY SOCIETY

European Department	Office American Department
Office, London, England,	38 Camp St., New Orleans
Hon. John Crossley, President	Hon. Jefferson Davis, President

New Orleans   25th March   1876

My dear Wife,

I have nothing definite to report and am getting quite restless in my anxiety to be with you during your illness. Though my presence would be little worth save as it might serve to beguile your weary hours, love is not to be measured by the rules of logic.

Yesterday I received an unsatisfactory letter from the London office, written by the chairman of the Executive Committee, who is I think a schemer seeking to put money in his purse.

I referred the letter to our Executive Committee and they have just written to me requesting me to address the President of the Society in London. This involves a free criticism of his committee, and it is thought here will lead to reformatory proceedings there. If it does not I shall not confide further in the parent society, as I have done, and then we shall see what we shall see. The American Society could do much without their cooperation, but not as much as with it.

Mr. Payne and his Wife are ever pressing me to go *there* and make me confess that my comfort was not promoted by the change, and are good enough to say they are losers by it. I, however, am well enough, only going to my lodgings at night and leaving before breakfast. With tenderest love to each of our children and boundless quantities of the same for you, I am ever devotedly

Your Husband

Jefferson Davis to Varina Davis

[*The first page of this letter is missing.*]

New Orleans
April 22, 1876

Pittman is sanguine of the decision by the Supreme Court. We have Chalmers in the place of the Yankee Tarbell, and Campbell in place of the Radical Peyton, and may hope for *justice*, if there be such thing in this world to those who have only the right for their might.

I am quite well, and pray that you and Winnie are better. Jeff. informs me that his engagement ends with this month. Had you not better let him accompany you and Winnie to N.O.? Dear boy, I am very anxious about him. With oceans of love to the children, and boundless lands and seas of the same to you, I am ever truly

Your Husband

Jefferson Davis to Maggie Hayes

Shortly before Davis was to sail for England on International Chamber of Commerce business, Mrs. Davis decided to accompany him and to put eleven-year-old Winnie in some European school. On May 24, the three Davises sailed from New Orleans on the *S.S. Memphis* bound for Liverpool. With them was Winnie's little friend Pinnie Meredith. Again the Davises are, in Varina's phrase of 1868, "floating uprooted." Nineteen-year-old Jeff, Jr., remains in Memphis with Addison and Maggie Hayes.

On board the *S.S. Memphis*
25th May 1876

My dear Daughter,

We are outside of the bar and taking in coal to sail for Liverpool.

Your Mother from fatigue and the excitement of leaving you and Jeff. was suffering very much yesterday and last night. She is better today but extremely weak. I offered to return with her but she declined, on the condition of my going abroad without her.

I hope when we meet the cool air of the Sea she will improve, as the neuralgia which is the main feature of her case has no doubt been increased by the heat.

May God preserve my children and restore us in due time to each other. It was hard to leave you both, but fate has left me little power to do as I would.

To you and my Son Addison is intrusted the watchful care of my younger son. A Father's prayers will be fervently offered for you all.

Your Father
Jefferson Davis

NORTHERN ANIMOSITY LINGERS

WINNIE IN CARLSRUHE

ENGLAND WAS AT the climax of bloom when the Davises arrived in June of 1876 and went to stay with the George Campbells at their country place in Surrey. Campbell had been highly successful in business and Davis needed his counsel before meeting with the London members of the International Chamber of Commerce. Campbell hinted at probable disappointments. And when Davis did meet with the members he was not reassured. British capital was now hesitant to invest in the building of the merchant ships for the organization. And Northern interests frowned menacingly on any plan that might divert trade from New York to New Orleans. Though Davis was to remain until November attempting to right matters, he realized in late July that his dream of bringing prosperity to the Mississippi Valley was doomed to failure. With this final blow, after an accumulation of shocks and disappointments, Mrs. Davis collapsed and remained painfully ill for weeks. The family had settled temporarily in a furnished apartment in Kensington. Dr. Maurice Davis came and went and brought other doctors, who said this and that. But Davis had an inkling that his wife was suffering from that most corrosive disease: despair. For six weeks he rarely left his wife's bedside. But the problem of Winnie's schooling had to be decided immediately. So, accompanied by her friend Pinnie Meredith, she was sent to a boarding school operated by the Misses Friedlander in Carlsruhe, Germany. Because of Mrs. Davis's nervous breakdown and her husband's necessitous nursing, Davis had to let the girls go to Carlsruhe in the care of a friend and to say goodbye at the London railway station. He answers Winnie's first letter "home" on September 21 from the new address, 78 Gloucester Place.

433

Jefferson Davis to Winnie Davis

Twelve-year-old Winnie is now a resident of the exclusive Friedlander girls' school in Carlsruhe, Germany, which is under the patronage of the Grand Duchess Luise of Baden, whose palace is not far from the school.

> 78 Upper Gloucester Place
> Dorset Square London W.
> 21st Sept 1876

My dear Daughter,

Your Mother received the letters of dear Pinnie and yourself last night. It was a great comfort to her and for a time relieved her of the physical pain from which she still suffers too acutely to write to our little children.

We moved to this Mrs. Williams' house on Monday evening and your Mother finds the air drier and purer than that of Kensington.

I yet see your sad little face as you sat crouching in the corner of the R. R. carriage, too absorbed in your grief to notice my last salutation. The house seemed funereal when we no longer heard the voices of our little ones, and your Mother said she was ever expecting one of you to come in. It is true, but not pleasant that duty demands self-sacrifice. Yet it is the highest attribute of humanity to be able to give to a sense of duty, that which it costs pain to surrender. The great exemplar of goodness and greatness lived for others, died for the salvation of those who rejected and despitefully used him. I hope the pain of separation from you will be rewarded by the fulfilment of our anxious and ambitious hopes, the one for your physical and the other for your intellectual development. In the German system, there is the marked difference from others, that they put the physical consideration first, and most justly, for not only would it be impossible for a valetudinarian to learn much, but it would be equally impossible to apply what was learned, as it might be done by one of robust constitution.

It was very kind of Miss Friedlander to go to the station for you, and I trust the love you conceived for her at first sight will grow with your growth and strength with knowledge of the world.

Your Mother bids me to write that she will go to you as soon as she is able to travel, and the Doctor assures us, that time is not distant.

I have not left for an hour since your departure and shall remain with her until she is well enough to enable me to leave her without anxiety. When I may, I will visit you, for I long to have my baby in my hand.

Give my tenderest love to dear little Pinnie. Present my most respectful regard to Miss Friedlander.

May God watch over you and shield you from all harm ever prays your loving Father.

Jefferson Davis

Jefferson Davis to Varina Davis

While in Chantilly visiting Dudley Mann, Davis received a letter from Bowmar urging his immediate return to Mississippi because of a development in the Brierfield lawsuit. Davis is on his way to Carlsruhe to visit Winnie at her school before returning to America.

Hotel d'Orient, Paris
Saturday Morning—Oct. 29, 1876

My dear Wife,

Your letter reached me this morning, having been forwarded from Chantilly. I am most happy to learn that you are better, and will start for Carlsruhe this evening, and should arrive at C. to-morrow at 11 A.M. It is my purpose to leave there on Monday and hope to be with you on Tuesday.

Mr. Mann did not come with me, because the damp air was he feared likely to injure him. I left him with reluctance and he evinced deep feeling at the parting. He wishes to go to London to attend to his interests in the Va. bonds as an avowed purpose but no doubt his desire to see you enters largely into his plans. I persuaded him to return to America and he said if he could sell his place and move to one where we lived, he would do it. Please write to him. He is solitary and lives in the past.

Miss Mason called to see me and went to the Bon Marché & got the opera glasses for Winnie as you directed. I will talk to Miss Friedlander about Pinnie & if I have to save it by abstinence from smoking, I will see that the child shall stay where she is and is paid for. The dear little girl must be put at rest and freed from any mortification.

It is today bright but still cold, if the wind changes it will probably be warmer on the road and in Germany.

I came to this Hotel because you had been here. The house is full of some Yankees, one of whom addressed me & said he was a friend of the South. He did not pretend to know who I was and was not told by me.

Thrown by adverse currents on the sands and left to be beaten but not lifted by rising tides I can if hopeless yet I trust calmly look upon the changes which are seen & foreseen.

With tenderest love to Margaret and her children and a heart's full measure of the same for you I am

Your Husband

Jefferson Davis to Varina Davis

Carlsruhe
Monday, 31st Oct. 1876

My dear Wife,

I arrived here yesterday before noon, and having taken breakfast and warmed myself, called at Misses Friedlanders'. The children are both well and heavier than when they left us. Miss Friedlander insisted upon giving me a room in her house and thus I spent the evening in the midst of the pupils. The girls are very genteel and show to each other the most affectionate consideration. The moving of the trains is such that I shall not be able to reach London before Wednesday. Winnie has come to give me a morning kiss and says give my love to mother and tell her I will write to her tomorrow. She was with me yesterday and that is the reason why she did not write then. Mrs. Meredith has written to Pinnie as she did to you. Miss Friedlander has a high and just appreciation of the child and is not at all disposed to give her up. So you may consider the matter settled and I will tell you all about it when we meet. You need not be anxious for me. I am better than when we parted and can see no reason for any apprehension. With love to Maggie Stoess and the children I am ever

Lovingly
Your Husband

Jefferson Davis to Varina Davis

Davis had sailed for America in mid-November and left Varina with her sister, Margaret Stoess, in Liverpool.

S.S. Adriatic
25th Nov. 1876

My dear Wife,

We are nearing our destination and I write on the rolling ship, because it is probable that we shall be in time for the evening train, and if so I shall go immediately on, so as to see the children in Memphis and be in Vicksburg by the appointed day, 1st Dec.

The weather has been so cold and wet as to keep me generally in the cabins and the time has been quite suited to light reading.

I have fulfilled my promise, to reread *The Newcomes*. The pleasure was not a little diminished by the realization of those hateful persons, Barnes Newcome and Mrs. Mackenzie. I think it a more powerful but less agreeable work than *Pendennis*.

I hope you will as you should, on account of others, give all possible care to your health. If it be entirely restored, the sun, the earth and its products will all be fairer to you.

When waiting for the ship to be level, the train of thought is interrupted and this even more than the scratching writing warns me to be brief. Leave to me the cares of our family, and keep me advised of your own wants and wishes.

I can't, like dear Ma, be sure that Providence will bring all things right, but I can count on earnest work to restore our shattered fortunes.

Give my tenderest love to Maggie and the babies and kind Mr. Stoess.

Devotedly & admiringly
Your Husband

Winnie Davis to Her Mother

Winnie went with her schoolmates to a concert at the Palace in Carlsruhe. The "good-natured-looking" little Princess Victoria became the Queen of Sweden and the mother of the present King Gustaf VI Adolf.

Carlsruhe
December, 1876

My dear Mother

In this letter I am going to tell you all about the consert last night which I went to and thought it beautiful. The Grand Dutches was their and the Princess and the Princes, but the Grand Duke was not. I am very sorry to say that I thought of the Grand Dutches more than the music at first, but luckley she came in good time and then all the People rose and I did too. She was dressed in pea green silk and white over it and white flowers in her hair and looked so nice, and the Princess was a littel girl of about 12 or 13 and was dressed in pink silk and I cant say I thought she was pretty but she looked good natured. I think the littel Princes were very odenery boys. The musick was beautiful one piece of Mendelson one of Shueberts and of Batehoven.

When the consert was over the Grand Dutches came up to the comander of the band and then to Genral V., the great German Genral, and then she left, and as she passed we must bow and you aught to see Pinnie—she looked like she was going to but me down as I was just behind her, but she did it well by the way. When I bowed I was so scherd with my hair all up, I sepose it stuck on end. It is a wonder if it did not.

Pinnie and I are very Angels to each other and we live in constant expectation of that box. Auntie Friedlander received notice that it has arrived safe at Hamburg and we hope to get it in 2 or 3 days. I think I shall write more letters than in all my life when I have my new Desk and shall be always arranging my gloves in the box.

The flowes that I will send you will see come from Charlsrue and Heidelberg—the moss from Charlsrue and the violets from Heidelberg. I am in a feaver of expectation for the box, and almost wish that it was tusday. With much love to all and maney kisses for your self I remain your affectionate daughter

Win Anne

P.S. which rute did Father go by?

Jefferson Davis to Varina Davis

After attending to estate matters in Vicksburg, Davis reports to the Mississippi Valley board.

St. Charles Hotel
9th Dec. 1876

My dear Wife,

I came to New Orleans to report to the Board of the Missi. Valley Society and have just returned from a meeting. They listened to my statement & were disappointed rather than indignant at the tergiversation which I had to relate.

They decided to wait for the Trust & Loan Co. and to see if something would not turn up. The luck is running against us, and Mr. Bowmar has mismanaged affairs at Davis Bend so as to postpone, it may be to lose, a part of what was due there. After a while we shall get something, now *little* if any thing. Boyle will pay just as much as we can force out of him, no more, and nothing can be obtained at present. Now having told you the worst, I have to add "be not dismayed, we will get through," provided you get well and return in cheerfulness.

The excitement over the fraud in counting the vote of Louisiana is intense here, but they have become accustomed to injustice and will suffer long.

I do not know how long will be my stay here and have nothing definite in view unless the Trust & Loan Co. be organized, except to join Maj. Walthall at Mobile and push forward the memoirs.

Good night, with tenderest love and solicitude, I am

Your Husband
Jefferson Davis

Jefferson Davis to Varina Davis

Samuel Tilden, the Democratic candidate for President, was cheated out of the election by the Republicans, and Rutherford B. Hayes became President.

With no business prospects, Davis now determines to write his story of the Confederacy.

New Orleans, La.
24th Dec. 1876

My dear Wife,

This evening of the anniversary when families are wont to be united, ours are scattered far and wide. It is sad to me to realize that an ocean rolls between me and my dear Winnie. God grant that our sacrifice may be blessed by the restoration of your health.

Addison and Maggie and Jeff. have all written to urge me to be with them on Xmas, but I could not consistently leave here until something more definite is reached.

I went last Monday to see our niece, Nannie Smith, at Biloxi. I invested ten dollars in the hire of a negro to clear up our lot, and postponed any further effort, though often pressed to build a house.

Weary of wandering and anxious to get books and papers together for the work always in contemplation, I was tempted to get a small house on the beach, but had before my eyes the fear of your not liking it and so was silent. If Nannie Smith would get a house in a quiet place I might take a room by the year.

Mrs. Dorsey is living in her fine house with her cousin Mrs. Cochran, nee Ogden. I was their guest for a part of the time & was charged to give you the warmest expressions of regard. Mrs. Dorsey was compelled to return from New York, by the death of her Brother-in-law, who had charge of her plantation. He was killed by a wound from the gin.

Two Congressional Committees are here inquiring into the election in La. and the Hotel was thronged by a mongrel multitude so when I returned from the sea shore I came to Mary Stamps. Unless they get again into trouble at Vicksburg, I will go direct from here to Memphis, to attend to the Boyle affairs.

The weather has been cold, but since I returned has been raining. I hope you are relieved of your dreadful pain, and have less need of me than I have of you, so far as nursing is involved.

Of your acquaintances on the Sea shore I believe there remains but one family unmentioned, that of Dr. Hollingsworth. He has been quite successful with oranges, but his Wife had not been so much so with servants. That same is a subject in our country as worn and ever recurring as that of the weather.

I will not weary you with details of our political "muddle" as it is commonly called, but will give you my hopeful opinion i.e. that we shall have a peaceful solution and that Tilden will be the next President. The scenes through which we are passing would be ridiculous if less tragical, and may well induce those who doubt the capacity of man for self government, to say I told you so.

Not knowing where to address you, it is sent to care of Mr. Stoess. With much solicitude and boundless love I am your Husband

Jefferson Davis

A HAVEN
WITHOUT ENCUMBRANCES

Jefferson Davis to Varina Davis

Davis is the guest of Sarah Anne Ellis Dorsey, who owns Beauvoir. She had been a girlhood friend of Varina Davis's in Natchez, as her father had been a friend of Jefferson Davis's, and she was shortly to play a significant and peculiarly beneficent role in Davis's life. Her education had been completed in Europe, where she made friends among the British nobility and prominent literary figures of the day, including Thomas Carlyle and the Rossettis. Her lineage goes back to the Northumberland Percys. Under the *nom de plume* of Filia she has published four books. An attractive, olive-skinned woman, she is a charming and sympathetic hostess, never obtrusive. Yet some of her own sex resent her because she prefers the more serious conversation of men. Mrs. Dorsey is a devout believer in the Confederate cause, and, having followed the career of Jefferson Davis since her youth, she regards him as "the noblest man she had ever met on earth."

Dr. Leacock, former Episcopal rector of New Orleans, has moved to the Mississippi Gulf Coast. His daughter Minnie is the estranged wife of William Howell, Varina's unsuccessful brother, who has gone to California.

> Beauvoir
> Sea Shore of Missi.
> Residence of Mrs. Dorsey
> January, 1877

My dear Wife,

I send to you the greeting of a new year and with my own that of your warm friend Mrs. Dorsey and her cousin Mrs. Cochran.

I have been up and down the coast and looked over and talked over the possible places after the manner of "house hunting," as you have in former times described it. There are two houses for sale, either of which might do.

I am waiting for Dr. Leacock and then propose to go to Mobile enroute to Memphis to look after my lame duck.

God grant that this year may be more productive of good health to you and good fortune to us both than was that which has just expired, and may He give you many, many more.

20th Jany 1877

The last letter from you was dated 30th Nov. and I am very anxious to know *where* and *how* you are. At Memphis I hope to have news of you. If I can get a place here and Jeff does not get into proper business, I think it will be well for him to come here and read under my direction and write for me. But of this it will be easier to judge after I get to Memphis.

Before finishing the above sentence the summons to dinner was received. Col. Saffold did not encourage me as to a Seaside home except in the matter of health. It is very attractive to me when stated after the manner of Dr. Hollingsworth viz. that old men come here to die, and get so strong that they live on to ninety. With love to all our Kith and Kin wherever you may be and an ocean of the same to my dear old Waafe, I am ever your devoted Husband

Jefferson Davis

I asked Mrs. Dorsey if she had a message for you, and she said a message would not do, she wished to write to you.

Jefferson Davis to Maggie Hayes

In January, when Davis had been the house guest of Mrs. Dorsey at Beauvoir, she had offered him her east pavilion cottage and free board—"a refuge without encumbrances"—in which to write his long-postponed book. Davis insisted on paying board for himself and his body servant, Robert Brown. The back gallery of the cottage was enclosed as a bedroom and a dressing room. Pleasant living quarters were found in the neighborhood for Major Walthall, who was collecting documents and material for Davis.

The sons are Jeff, Jr., and Addison Hayes. Maggie is sending Davis's books from Memphis.

Missi. City, P.O.
1st Feby. 1877

My dear Daughter,

I am glad to hear that you are better than when we parted. I found the Carpenter was making the repairs and additions to the cottage rented from Mrs. Dorsey, rather on the scale of what he regarded due to me, than what was suited to the state of my purse. Every thing will be ready by the time the books can get here.

The bed room is 10 by 16 feet, with a dressing room 10 by 10 ft. so that only a single bed could be put in it. There are no closets or furniture. The summer is so warm and the spring so near that a carpet is not desirable. I can get some matting, and, if need, a couple of rugs to lie by the writing desk and the bed.

You will remember that you are not to send any thing which is useful to you, as I can get cheap, second-hand furniture in New Orleans. The table and desk and chairs which Joe Davis offered to me will do for my library, with perhaps the addition of an easy chair. For the chamber and dressing room you will know better than I what is needful, and will understand that you are to send only such articles as are surplus in your house.

Mrs. Dorsey offered to take me as a boarder for fifty dollars a month, the rent of the cottage included, and I accepted the kind proposal for it was offered to relieve me from the embarrassing delay in the original programme. With this is also a room for Robert in the yard. It will, I hope, be beneficial to my health to live in sea air and isolation, and in both respects be better than a residence in Mobile or New Orleans.

This arrangement involves no permanent decision and leaves me at liberty to make any change which may be more satisfactory to your Mother. Though her last letter is less encouraging than that which preceded it, we learned also from the last letter that she was suffering from her recent travel and probably less hopeful than usual. God grant that the dry air of Carlsruhe may have the good effect anticipated by Dr. Davis.

The soft air, here, is delicious.

I will write to each of my sons very soon.

Ever lovingly I am
Your Father
Jefferson Davis

Jefferson Davis to Addison Hayes

Missi. City
2d Feb. 1877

Dear Addison,

I have received yours of the 29 & 31st. Those Yankee lawyers seem resolved to give all the annoyance possible.

I am glad that you have fine weather at last, in Memphis. Here it is very pleasant and the sea breeze quite invigorating.

The cottage I have rented is nearly ready for occupation. Please direct Robert to go to New Orleans by steamboat and thence by rail on the road to Mobile as far as "Beauvoir" switch, which is about midway between Mississippi City and Biloxi. Beauvoir switch is about 400 yards from Mrs. Dorsey's house, which is on the beach.

Give my love to Maggie and Jeff, and believe me yours affectionately,

Jefferson Davis

Winnie Davis and Varina Davis to Jefferson Davis

Mrs. Davis has been for some weeks in the guest room of the Friedlander School. Years before the war Dr. Cartwright had diagnosed her numerous ailments as "misplaced malaise," which she had suffered from since her girlhood.

74 Stephanie Strasse
Carlsruhe
Feb. 18th 1877

My dear Father

I hope that you will write soon for I wrote you so long ago. I have written to Brother Jeff to-day and now will write to my dear Father. We had the ball I spoke of and Pinnie's dress as well as mine were very pretty. Mother is here still but will take lodgeings soon and then I will see her every day, but of course that is nothing like having her here. As a parting remembrance she gave Miss Friedlander a most lovely present and Miss Addie an ivory looking glass which was also very pretty. Are you at Mississippy City yet? If you are, write all about the cottage you live in. Please press me a flower and send it for my book. I have found the ring that you and Mother gave me on my birthday you know I lost it. I have not much more to write except that it had been very nice weather and that spring is returning very rapidly.

My dear Father you know that my hart is always with you, so please write and tell me all about your health and pursuites. Your affectionate daughter, Win Anne

My Husband: I went to church today quite half a mile off & walked back without feeling the exercise much. I am much better last week— I am however afraid to risk travelling yet, so remain near Winnie until I am strong enough to go to England again. There is an hotel near here to which I shall go & take my meals in my room, and get an English-speaking maid to come to me for a little while each day to help me a little. It is not very dear, if I can get to the place I want to go. I found out the price of board here, and remunerated these good ladies by a present as well as I could. In this place, money is the equivalent that they must have, and I found that my illness made me burthensome—but they are quite satisfied now. They have been very kind, and attentive to me—and I have sorely needed their attentions. For the first time I hope to get measurably well again. I think my other pains were what Dr. Cartwright called "misplaced malaise."

Winnie is much better, and I think she is learning very well— and better than all she is learning self-control and fortitude, which is very much for a woman to learn. God grant that she may comfort our old age—our little pink placid baby of eleven years ago—

Good bye, my own old dear love, my precious Banny.

Your devoted Wife

Jefferson Davis to Varina Davis

The upas is a tall tree of Java, the whitish bark of which yields a poisonous milky juice used as arrow poison.

Jeff, Jr., is now twenty and has no prospect of a job, so he is living with his father at Beauvoir. His mother is sad and perplexed about him, for he is like her Howell brothers.

Missi. City
26th Feb. 1877

My dear, Dearest, Wife, Winnie,

On this day long ago, we exchanged vows and became one in the eye of the world and the law; as we have been in our hearts and hopes, our joys and sorrows. Of the last we have drained the goblet to its dregs, but the first has been my solace, and remains my comfort.

The world goes wrong to me, men prove false, business affairs turn in other courses than would subserve my interest, the South my loved country is misrepresented, cheated, & the fetters of oppression riveted upon her. Yet from all these clouds, the shadows of which are worse than the falling dews from the Upas, I turn, and am cheered by the memory of the day when a beautiful, gifted, accomplished girl, gave me her soft hand, and virgin heart, taking me for better or worse; and continues yet to say she has not regretted the compact then made.

Jeff. handed to me your last letter to him; when I returned it to him, he asked if it was not a "fine letter," my answer was a "very sad one." In pain, which you can understand but which he could not, I went to my room in order to be alone, with my sympathy in your wounded love and mortified pride. My dear, we do not understand the boy, and I fear never shall. Let us however hold fast to all which is good in him, and there is much, hoping that experience may make him more like what we would have our Son to be. He stays here, seems contented, and has quit chewing tobacco. Miss Mary Ellis, a very bright and well educated girl, occupies much of his time and does not appear to get tired of him. Her cultivation and habit of reading may be good for him; it is at least better association than the slangy girls of Memphis, and not so apt to be embarrassing, in possible sequences. [*The rest is lost.*]

Jefferson Davis to Winnie Davis

The father gives his little daughter some kindly advice. With the help of Mrs. Dorsey and Major Walthall the work on his book is going well. The cottage at Beauvoir in which he wrote the book is visited by thousands of tourists today.

Mississippi City
17th March 1877

My darling Baby,

I have received your two welcome letters. In the absence of the pleasure of looking at your dear little face and reading in your eyes the expression of your tender love, the greatest consolation is to have frequent letters from you.

Your Mother will probably have left you and Carlsruhe before this reaches you. The parting will be a severe trial for both of you, but she is so well satisfied with your condition and so much pleased with the Misses Friedlander that she will have less anxiety about you, than under any other supposable circumstances. We look hopefully forward to your becoming a well educated young Lady, but most of all to your acquiring systematic habits, to your learning how to study, and last and greatest to the formation of a vigorous, healthy constitution. Your heart I am sure will ever lead you aright, but it requires the head to restrain even good impulses. Knowledge and high aims are to human character what cultivation is to fertile land, the necessary means to keep down noxious weeds. You have an example in Miss Friedlander—who would expect her to be troubled about a ribbon or to engage in gossip & back-biting?

Your Brother Jeff is with me, he reads some French and some medicine, occasionally writes for me, and seems quite contented here. I dictate daily for 3 or 4 hours, for a book of reminiscenses of my public career. Mrs. Dorsey acts sometimes as my amanuensis and Maj. Walthall assists in compiling and hunting up authorities.

The sea air is pleasant, but my ability to take exercise is less than when we parted. Without being sick, I am weak and languid, often sleepless and never hungry. But visitors congratulate me on my apparent health. So there cannot be much the matter with me.

My cottage is a square building, the roof is composed of four triangles meeting in the centre. Originally it had one room and galleries all around it, but one of the galleries has been closed so as to make a chamber & dressing room. So that now the original room with shelves is my library and office. Robert is with me and sleeps in the dressing room.

The grounds are extensive and shaded by live oaks, magnolias, cedars, &c, &c. The sea is immediately in front, and an extensive orange orchard is near. Beyond that is one of those clear brooks, common to the pine woods, its banks lined with a tangled wood of sweet bay, wild olive and vines. Then comes a vineyard, than a railroad, and then stretching far far away a forest of stately long-leaved pine. By night I hear the murmur of the sea rolling on to the beach, by day a short walk brings one to where the winds sigh through the pines, a sad yet soothing sound. I send in this letter three of the wood flowers—azalea, yellow jasmine, and a variety of wild olive.

Give my cordial love to dear Pinnie and my respectful regard to the Misses Friedlander.

With fondest love your Father

Jefferson Davis

Jefferson Davis to Winnie Davis

Maggie Hayes has given birth to a boy child named for his grand-father.

Mississippi City P.O.
Harrison   County, Missi.
24th April 1877

My darling Daughter,

The last letter to me from your Mother informed me that you were well and gave a good account of your progress in your studies, for both I was thankful.

My hopes of improvement in her health were not realized, she however proposed soon to leave and turn her face homeward, it is therefore probable that when you receive this she will have left you. It is a great consolation to me to know that Misses Friedlander are fond of you and that we have their affection as well as their sense of duty to assure us of good care of you. From your letters I perceive that you are very fond of them and this too gratifies me greatly. That you should be happy and healthy are requisites to your becoming well educated, and in these are contained the measure of your power to render your parents happy when we shall be united. Your nephew is said to be a very fine boy. It has not been practicable for me to go to Memphis, since his birth; but I hope soon to do so, and then I'll write to you about the boy.

The climate here is very mild and the sea breeze has been beneficial to me.

I send enclosed an orange bloom. The orange grove here is quite extensive and the flowers perfume the air for some distance from the trees. If you and Pinnie were here with me, and your dear Mother also, we should have a much better time than is possible for me so far from those dearest to me.

Well, well, when you children come back with three languages you will be expected to talk three times as much as you did formerly. If it be possible for me, I will go to New York to meet your Mother when she lands.

Give my tenderest love to dear Pinnie, take oceans of the same for yourself from

Your Father
Jefferson Davis

Jefferson Davis to Varina Davis

Davis's routine is so peaceful and productive at Beauvoir that he suggests a summer in Scotland for Varina.

Mississippi City, 1st May 1877

My darling Wife,

I have just received yours of the 8th ulto. and my grief of your feeble health is increased by perceiving that you are needlessly anxious about me. Persons who come here say I am looking unusually well. I think this climate and the quiet which pervades the place, so beneficial that I dread to go into the bustle, the dust, and much talking of other places to which business compels me soon to visit. Jeff. is noisy as usual, but always affectionate and anxious to serve. Mrs. Dorsey is kind and constantly attentive. She speaks often of you and her hope to have you for a guest. Jeff. and she are boon comrades. Our Grandson is reported as doing very well. I hope soon to see him.

I will send this to Liverpool as you write of a speedy departure from Carlsruhe. You cannot be more anxious to be with us than I am to have you here, but my love which passeth my power of expression bids me to ask you not to embark until you feel able to bear the journey by sea and by land. It would be pleasant for you to take Winnie up to Scotland, and the summer there might do you more good than even the joy of being again with your own. Obey your *judgment* and tell what is to be done by me. Mr. Smith's family would be joyful in having you all and from Glasgow you could conveniently go to the most beautiful and interesting parts of Scotland, at a very small cost.

You dread the heat and insects. Here I am writing by a fire, and sleep without a bar. But, darling, I am not a fixture and you shall live where you will and I can.

You are probably right in the supposition that the work on the "Reminiscences" has been productive of exhaustion, for the last week I have been only reading and am better perhaps therefore.

I expect to be in Memphis by the middle of this month, a telegram to Addison stating the date on which you sail and the ship, may enable me to meet you at the landing and "convey ye home"; if I can I will, & would go "across" if not so poor, but I may go to New York to meet you. Our case has been argued before the Supreme Court of Missi. & Pittman expects a favorable judgment.

Dearest, Waafe, love of many years, partner of hopes and disappointments, of joys and sorrows from youth to age, take care of yourself for your devoted Husband

Jefferson Davis

Jefferson Davis, Jr., to His Mother

Beauvoir
May 7, 1877

My darling Mother,

Father is well, interested in the task of writing his book. He is looking better than I ever saw him although very anxious about our darling Mother.

Mother, if I had known then how long we were to be parted I don't believe I could have borne to see the "Memphis" float away without at least trying to go with you.

I am reading law and expect to study hard & be a pleasure to my darling Mother, who becomes more and more dear to me every day.

Father's letter will tell you all about our business and in fact everything except my love for you, and that I intended to tell you myself but I find I am like the girl at the Centennial who tried to write & just wound up with "Oh! Oh!! Oh!!!" She like myself became too "full for utterance." Indeed, Mother, my heart does become so full that I can't express half that I feel or that I know you already know so well.

The other day I longed for you to be behind the door when my Father was talking about you—he told me that you were a woman worthy the worship of any son. I felt just like picking him up and kissing him.

So good night, my all in all, and believe me that I am more affectionate & devotedly than any other son was before, Your Boy
Jefferson Davis, Jr.

Maggie Hayes to Her Mother

Memphis, Tenn.
Saturday, 9th June, 1877.
My own more than precious Mother,

Your dear letter came this morning & though I understand how you feel about my not having written to you still I think my explanations will satisfy you.

My baby was very thin when he was born & every one discouraged me about him. I felt so very helpless & miserable. I longed so to nurse him & tried so hard & I think I would have had enough if I had not been so much disheartened. Now my milk is nearly gone & I have to use condensed milk. It agrees with him splendidly & he weighs more. Now I have nursed him into a pretty fat little baby every one admires him. He is named Jefferson Davis and called Jeffie D.

Father has gained his suit about Brierfield *in every particular* & writes that he is in Vicksburg & will be with us in a few days. He says he is well.

Your room is ready & waiting to receive you. I have made my

house look as near like the old Court Street house as I can so that you may feel at home.

Your devoted
Daughter

P.S. Father arrived Sunday looking very well.

Addison, June 11th

Jefferson Davis to Varina Davis

Davis has gone to Memphis to see his new namesake. Mrs. Davis is annoyed because a magazine article reported that Mrs. Dorsey was helping her husband with his book, and she has refused to reply to Mrs. Dorsey's cordial invitations to come and stay at Beauvoir. Although Davis has won the Brierfield suit, Lise Hamer and her brother Joe Mitchell are having it "reviewed."

Memphis, Tenn., June 11, 1877

My dear Winnie,

Our Grand Son is a bright and beautiful child. Is getting plump as a partridge. Maggie, though a slave to her boy, is not fussy or foolish about him. She is not well for her, though Mr. Hayes says she has been very well until quite lately. The weather is now pleasant, and I shall urge her to leave, with her baby, when the hot and sickly season begins. She has your prejudice against the sea shore, or I would persuade her to go there. In a former letter I gave you the long list of our relatives now residing on the coast.

And while on that subject permit me to correct a misapprehension you have fallen into, about Mrs. Dorsey's invitation to you. She several times spoke of her desire to have you on the coast, but I had told her you had such unfavorable recollections of it, that you had earnestly urged me neither to buy or build there. She thought if you would try it again, your opinion would change, and beginning with only a brief visit in view, you would end by a more permanent stay. The salt air and salt baths have been of service to me generally, especially in stopping the cough, and mitigating the pain in my shoulder & arm.

Had my cases been concluded as was expected, I could now follow the yearning of my heart, and go to you. For not only would my presence here in October have been unnecessary, but the money tied up in the hands of the receiver of Boyle in Bankruptcy, would have been sufficient for that, and other events. You must try your arithmetic and let me know when and what money you must have. Though it is a bitter disappointment to my hopes, for you to remain abroad this summer, it's what my judgment told me you should do. To return to this malarial region before white frost has fallen, would be surely hazardous to you. If we get our own, or half of it, I can come for you next winter, and stay with you until you are strong enough, with me for a nurse, to come back in safety. My own love, I send you the kisses of youth, the love of your devoted

Husband

Varina Davis to Jefferson Davis

Mrs. Davis is staying with her sister, Margaret Stoess, in Liverpool.

Liverpool
July 2nd, 1877.

My dear Husband,

I have been vainly waiting to be able to tell you when I would sail, but one hot day brought on cold skin and pain at once. I do not think I could live through the sea sickness, exhaustion—if I thought I could, I would go to our children at once. Oh how I do long to see the baby and its Mother! Of late, I feel the trouble more in my spine, and am sure that I could not be other than a burden.

I am so glad that you have won your suit, for the moral point gained more than for the income, necessary as the latter is to us.

Mrs. Walker left here yesterday for her new home in or near the place of the Ascot races. It is a lovely old cottage containing 14 rooms, fully furnished at 120 £ a year, with the use of the Duke of Northampton's park included in the rest—& we gave twelve hundred a year for a naked house in Memphis! Where Mrs. Walker is now she will see the best county society in England & they have been very civil in calling to see her already. A trading town is a beastly place—I would not stay a day here if it were not for Margaret's lonely, hysterical condition.

How is our Jeff? Bless my dear boy's heart. Is there any prospect of his getting something to do? He is old enough now for a definite plan, and he should try to concentrate.

With dearest love to my Son & kind remembrances to Robert. I am, dearest love, always

Varina

Jefferson Davis to Varina Davis

Maggie Hayes's baby has died. Mrs. Dorsey has fitted up her west pavilion cottage in the garden as a guest house for the Hayeses and is most courteous in her attentions.

Missi. City
15th July, 1877

My own dear Winnie—

My last letter to you was to announce our loss in the death of our Grandson. Jeff returned, and, as I had proposed, Maggie & Addison came with him. Maggie was both mentally and physically in need of a change of scene and air. She has rallied in spirits and is much improved in bodily health. I will keep her with me if I can until cool weather, and if she will not stay here so long shall insist on her going to the mountains. Mrs. Dorsey at first wished to regard Maggie as a guest, but agreed to keep us all for one hundred dollars per month, which she said was equal to half of her current expenses.

Maggie reads, Addison fishes; they both bathe and drive, and seem to be quite satisfied. Indeed Maggie thinks you would like the sea coast if you would try it *now*. I am well for me, I find work on "our cause" exhausting the more so from want of references.

I suppose our baby's vacation has commenced and that she will soon be with you. If you decide to remain until fall and to go to Scotland, it may I trust be of service to your health and in many ways be of good effect on her. Sometimes I doubt if she had not better return with you, and exchange for the advantages of a German school the wholesome influence of her Mother's association. But of this you must judge by your standard, not mine.

I wrung out of the Montgomerys a payment of $2,500 and shall try to anticipate the shipment of the next crop, so as to get something more in the fall.

My darling Wife, age has not brought us the rest needful in the closing years of life, but misfortune has left us the richest treasure, a love which has grown as all else decayed. Our separation has been hard to bear, but let us hope it is nearly over and will not recur while we both live.

Farewell, with measureless love and innumerable kisses, I am devotedly

Your Husband

Varina Davis to Jefferson Davis

Buxton is a popular English watering resort.

Liverpool
July 22, 1877

My own dear old Husband—

Maggie's great loss, to say nothing of ours, has rendered me more than anxious to get to her, and I had pretty well determined to risk the journey, but I have begun in the last two weeks to swell so much, and do not feel as strong as I did a month ago. This, however, alone did not keep me, but I had not the strength of purpose to leave England two weeks before Winnie came, with the certainty which weighs upon me that when once we part I shall never see her again. I do not think I could bear the journey, yet I cannot bear the separation from all my own.

The darling's death was a sore loss to me, having as I had been doing ever since its birth felt so rich in the possession of a baby in whom was united the tenderest loves of my life—named for the lover of my youth, looking like the idol of my middle age, named in tenderness by the pet name of my child Brother, all wrings my heart so.

You said in your letter that Maggie would not consent to go to the M.S. Coast, so I wrote to her to go to Sewanee, but I am more than glad to hear that she and her dear Husband went to you instead of among strangers. I do want to get well so much, for I do so long to be useful once more, but, dear, I fear I never shall— too late—too late. There does not seem to be anything the matter with me but this swelling and sore spine, but so I am rendered unable to serve myself and others.

Winnie will be here on Monday, or perhaps even Sunday. Margaret intends going to Buxton and implores me to go with her. I tell you frankly I do think she will go mad if she does not get some little let up from the present state of things. It is the most dreadful household that I ever saw. No one comes, no one seems to be on terms. Carl is not so unkind, as he is perfectly uncongenial and tiresome. Every time I speak of going Margaret only sobs and says that she is in solitary confinement but for me, and I feel that the child is so. Carl is quite like a brother to me—and looks forward to Winnie's coming as though she were his own. I do not know what we shall do yet.

I do so thank God for the choice that Maggie has made in life. Her tender, well-principled Husband will I know show her every tenderness that is in his power, stricken as he is with his own grief. Is she staying with Mrs. Dorsey or with our nieces?

The weather here is cold as spring. I go out very little, but always need a shawl when I do.

By the way, both Mr. Campbell and Carl are laboring under immense pecuniary embarrassment, I have been told. So much for trading people. Money takes wings with everybody who invests it in these days.

God bless you, my Husband. I would that I could have lasted on until the end in my natural state, and now I pray unceasingly against becoming useless. Kiss my little bereaved girl for me. What a weary year this has been to me. Farewell Husband. I am as ever affectionately

Your Wife

Varina Davis to Jefferson Davis

Winnie has joined her mother in Liverpool. She has improved immensely under the Misses Friedlanders' tutelage and away from her mother's neurotic attentions.

Liverpool
August 2nd, 1877

My dear Husband,

At last our baby is with me again, and my heart already sinks at the prospect of another and longer parting. She is in much better health and is very much improved in temper and manners too. She is so biddable, and so cheerful, and so considerate. She says that she can speak German ungrammatically. Her mind is now just beginning to learn system, and we may reasonably expect another scholastic year to have good effects. Your suggestion in your letter to bring her home with me has been considered before —but the place where you desire to live seems to render an education of the higher sort impossible there and the humid climate of New Orleans is poison for one of her rheumatic tendency. My heart aches over leaving my ewe lamb who sympathizes with every thought of mine—but God knows I would die away from her for her good more cheerfully than I would live with her to her hurt.

She has grown to be very much taller. She yearns so over her family it is quite touching. She says, "Now let us imagine ourselves a little home." She has already bought a little piece of work for "our home," and is busy over it.

I so often long for that old shackle-down house on Court Street where I had all my children in my own home and they lived as they pleased. I used to tell them then that it was good—if the paper did drop off the walls.

I see by an allusion that you have called your book "Our Cause." I have so often hoped though so far away that you would find it necessary as a matter of sympathy to tell me of its plan and scope, and of its progress—but I know I am very far off—and—"and things."

We go to Buxton as the rheumatism seems to cling about Winnie. I thought, as the water is considered a specific, that we might both be benefitted by the baths. Margaret goes up tomorrow to get lodgings and I pay two-fifths of the expense and she the other three.

The weather here is delightfully cold—quite cold enough for fire and heavy winter wraps.

Kiss my precious little Maggie and tell her three letters in nine months is short allowance for her old Mother.

Farewell, my dear old Husband. May God grant you release from trouble that now environs you, and may He bless and keep you safe is the prayer of

Your Wife

Varina Davis to Jefferson Davis

Varina at fifty-one considers "we must sink to rest so soon," but she lived to eighty. In this letter she makes plain her aversion to boarding at Mrs. Dorsey's until her husband's book is finished. Her letters of discontent take strength from his work. Varina hopes to make him leave Beauvoir, where he has everything to make him comfortable in an atmosphere congenial to his tremendous task, which is progressing favorably. Appleton's, the publishers, have advanced money for Walthall's expenses.

18 Upper Gloucester Place
Dorset Square
9th Sept. 1877

My dear Husband

I brought Winnie here four days ago to prepare for her journey to Carlsruhe. My very soul sinks at the thought of our parting, but Miss Friedlander has worked a great improvement in Winnie's mind in its power of application and concentration, but there is much left to do, and I feel that we must sink to rest so soon that we must not sacrifice our child to our love for her. She is very sweet, very tender, and so loving and strong. Self control she certainly has acquired, and forbearance.

We had a most wretched summer at Buxton—But I will spare you the details. Carl not being there, the legitimate drama was superseded by your two raw recruits—myself and Winnie, and a miserable life we led of it. I had determined to go to Scotland and very much desired to go, but Margaret considered it a great unkindness to her, and I allowed myself to be bullied and begged into going with her. But at present I am here, thank God, and when I leave here, I will go to the ship to go to you. I think I shall embark about the first week in October on the *Spain*.

I am sorry not to have written Mrs. Dorsey—but I do not think I could satisfy you and her if I did & therefore am silent. I do not desire ever to see her house—and cannot say so and therefore have been silent. Nothing on earth would pain me like living in that kind of community in her house. I am grateful for her kindness to you and my children, but do not desire to be under any more obligation to her. When people here ask me what part of your book she is writing, and such like things, I feel aggravated nearly to death. Of course she must have given out the impression, as it could not so generally prevail, no one would have known she wrote at your dictation even, still less would it have come out in the newspapers. I have avoided mentioning her in my letters, for I felt too angry at the last squib in an illustrated paper to be reasonable.

Now do not be annoyed at me because you know I would not have mentioned it now, but for your reminding me that I had not answered her last letter or her first. Please thank her for me for her kindness to you all, and excuse my silence as you will.

Believe me, darling, full of thoughts of you of tenderest love and intense longing to be with my precious old Banny.

Your old Winnie

Jefferson Davis to Maggie Hayes

Addison Hayes had stayed in the sun too long while fishing and had a slight sunstroke.

Missi. City P.O.
15th Oct. 1877

My darling Daughter,

I did not write lately because I supposed you were absent on a trip for the benefit of both your and Addison's health.

I lament the misfortune which hastened your departure from the sea shore.

My last letter from your Mother was of the 9th ulto. She was in London and mentioned her intention to sail on the "Spain." By inquiry in New Orleans I have learned that the "Spain" would sail on the 10th of Oct., D. V. I have several times requested that a telegram should be sent to advise me when your Mother should sail. As no notice has reached me, it is probable that she may have deferred her departure, though it is also very possible that she would sail without giving me notice, for fear of my going to New York to meet her.

Everything goes on as when you were with us. I wish you were back here, the mosquitoes have almost disappeared, the heat has subsided to autumn range; we have fire usually in the morning and evening. Addison could now fish without inconvenience or hazard.

With love to Addison and most earnest wishes for your welfare, I am with devoted affection for my own dear Pollie, her

Father
Jefferson Davis

The orange trees are loaded with golden fruit, good to see.

Jefferson Davis to Addison Hayes

Missi. City P. O.
22d Oct. 1877

My dear Addison,

Mrs. Davis in her last letter wrote that she would sail on the "Spain." That vessel was advertised to leave Liverpool on the 10th Inst. and would be due at New York about the 20th. I telegraphed to B. N. Harrison, Equitable Building, 120 Broadway, requesting him to meet the Spain at her landing and to give to Mrs. Davis any needful attention.

Have received no reply, and suppose the vessel has been detained, as if Mrs. Davis had not been on board, a telegram would probably have been sent to me.

With love to my darling "Pollie,"

Ever affectionately,
Jefferson Davis

VARINA HELPS WITH THE BOOK
—FROM A DISTANCE

MRS. DAVIS DID arrive in New York in late October, 1877, and without communicating with her husband went straight to Maggie Hayes in Memphis. Mr. Davis, with Jeff, Jr., visited his wife the last week in October, but he could not persuade her to come to Beauvoir, where Mrs. Dorsey had prepared rooms for her. Davis stayed several days in Memphis trying to mollify his wife, but she remained resentful, and he returned alone to his writing at Beauvoir. On November 7, Varina wrote sarcastically to Constance Harrison in New York: "In the course of human events I shall probably go down to Mr. Davis's earthly paradise temporarily. He inclines to the 'gentle hermit in the dale' style of old age—so behold we are a tie—and neither achieves the desired end."

However, when Davis requested his wife's help on some portion of his book, she was most co-operative, and with her remarkable memory she was of great assistance by mail.

Varina Davis to Jefferson Davis

In February, 1878, Mrs. Davis is still with the Hayeses, refusing even a short visit to Beauvoir.

In this particular letter Varina reveals a logical clarity of mind and shrewd perceptions. She had never trusted R. M. T. Hunter, the rich Virginia planter and politician, who feared above all else losing his slave property. He proved himself a hypocrite; and now in his old age, thirteen years after the war, in an effort to denigrate Jefferson Davis, he wrote an article accusing Davis of obstructing peace. Judge Campbell, onetime United States Supreme Court Justice, who had got his appointment through the support of Davis, and was later regarded by many

Southerners as a traitor in his post as Assistant Secretary of War of the Confederacy, had attacked Davis in the press during his torturous imprisonment.

William Preston Johnston wrote Davis that Senator Hunter had tried to undermine him in Richmond in the hope of succeeding him as President.

As commissioners to the Hampton Roads Peace Conference in January, 1865, to meet with President Lincoln and Secretary of State Seward, Davis had sent three men most vocal in urging the Confederate President to make peace at once: Vice-President Stephens, Judge John A. Campbell, the Assistant Secretary of War, and Virginia's Senator R. M. T. Hunter. But they failed in their peace negotiations; for the only terms on which Lincoln would treat was an unconditional laying down of arms and a return to the Union.

Memphis
Feb. 4th, 1878

My own old Dear,

The number of the Southern Historical Society Papers which you kindly sent is before me. I did not care for Mr. Hunter, but you did. One could forgive him on the score of defective memory from advancing age, but the thread of truth so deftly twisted through his tissue of false suggestions and travestied truths forbids the assumption. Just such a statement of the peace conference as he makes was made out by Judge Campbell during the time that you lay in prison, and the responsibility was then laid upon you. I sent for him in New Orleans, and he reiterated it to me.

I found that Mr Blair's interview with you had been misrepresented both by him and Judge Campbell & told both of them that you had a verified copy of his propositions to you. And probably with more frankness than politeness I told Judge Campbell that his sense of obligation to you for all your services to him beginning with his nomination to the vacant Judgeship, culminating in procuring the ratification of his appointment by confirmation by the Senate—to say nothing of your having vouched for him in the Confederacy, and kept him from being mobbed, should have restrained his tongue when you were in prison.

I remember that there was a debate over the expression "two countries" and that you settled it by the argument that if there were not two countries, then you had no authority in the matter.

That you could not resign your leadership as commander-in-chief of the Confederate States until your place was filled, or abolished, and could treat in this capacity only with authority from the States, as none other had been conferred. It was to surrender our claim to any consideration at once, to use the words "our common country." Anything more absurd I could not imagine than the claims of Messers. Hunter, Stephens, Campbell, Seward & Lincoln to such a mode of describing the belligerents before a treaty and it would not have been seriously mentioned ten years ago by the three former men. Now centralization has made such inroads upon all vested rights that this country is a vast despotism. You remember that these words "our common country," were believed by every one *then* to be a suggestion of Seward's in order necessarily to defeat the objects of the conference.

It seems to me that Mr Hunter's article is point no point. First, he disapproves of your manner of designating the country—says it was a great obstacle to successful negotiation. He then goes on to prove that it made little difference as absolute submission was required without guarantees. Says he came and told you all was lost, or rather hopeless. Thinks you should have so told the Congress, but says you were afraid of public opinion—owns the soft impeachment himself & says he does not blame you. Acknowledges that you agreed to be guided by the counsels of the most trustworthy Senators—owns that Mr Barnwell dissented from him and agreed with you, and then to crown his inconsistencies, acknowledges that he, believing that the children were to be shot and starved and their mothers made widows and childless in a hopeless fight, went to the African Church to hear his report read which urged *further resistance* as our only hope! Ten thousand times would I rather have your position. You believed and so counselled our people that our independence was not lost. He urged them on to death, certain that it was naught. Did he turn his face to the enemy? Never—he remained in the bomb proof Congress, while you exposed your life on every field near enough to Richmond for you to go. Tomorrow I had rather die crying liberty or death, than "peace at any price."

His account of his conversation with Genl Lee does not surprise me. You, I know, do not believe it, but I do. I never believed Genl Lee meant to fight when the Army moved out of Virginia. Remember a message that Ives brought you from Petersburg which he said Genl Lee did not *exactly send to you*, but predicted upon his remarks to Ives that without food, clothing, and reinforcements his army must evacuate Petersburg & Richmond. You went down to him at once, and he said Ives had mistaken his meaning.

The difference between you and Mr Hunter is that he was a hypocrite to those who believed him true. You, if you were mistaken, acted honestly out of the abundance of a noble faith, and self-sacrifice. I would not answer Mr. Hunter's letter. There is nothing to answer—but dirty little flings—and it is an endless kind of coil. Falsehood, like the ancient symbol of eternity a snake with his tail in his mouth, can roll on to the end of time.

You have not been a conciliatory man in your manners always, and the vain and dishonest men who could not bend you to their wills, do not like you. Controversy will only forestall the material of your book, and open a fire upon you which will obscure its effect. Forgive the advice if you do not like it because I love you.

I send you our baby's letter. I know that Winnie is now safe from excitement, learning to apply herself, and getting into regular habits. She is learning to live with people and to obey strictly & without questioning authority, and the nervously irritable, dreamy child that we left at Carlsruhe, inert, rheumatic, and dyspeptic, is an active, hearty little gay girl reasonably studious and very hungry always. I do so long to take her "in my hand" that I understand how you feel.

Nothing about Brierfield as yet—Alfred Pittman writes most hopefully. I sit here all day, with an occasional let up of an invitation to the theatre—or an hour with one or the other of my dear friends who seem always so cheered by seeing me that I am a little less blue after seeing them.

My Jeff is quite well, and, but for breaking a looking glass, quite happy—he & I are so superstitious.* He talks over the wildest kind of projects & goes to his work the next day.

Addison & Maggie, Jeff and I went to see Fanny Janauschek last night in *Brünnhilde,* a play from Nibelungenlied; also saw her in Catherine the 2nd of Russia. She was however simply an incarnation of lust—true to the life I imagine, but therefore disgusting in the extreme. She is a very great tragic actress, but she is too ugly to take her audience captive.

Her jewels are marvellously fine, $200,000 worth on exhibition

---

* Jeff was to die of yellow fever in October.

here. It has been a feast to one to look at them, I so love the sheen of cunning goldsmith's work, and the shimmer of the dancing lights in the jewels. I do not care to wear them any more than I desire to have a star when I gaze on it admiringly, but I intensely enjoy the sight of the colors, and the forms of the jewels & jewelry. For me, jewels are flowers that winter cannot blight. I am so glad that you are well—all through the day and night the assurance that you are comes to me like "the comforter."

May God keep you, dear Husband, safe from harm and console you in your sorrows as He only can is the prayer of

Your devoted wife

Jefferson Davis to Varina Davis

Missi. City, P.O.
16th Feb. 1878

My darling Wife,

Your precious letters of the 4th and 12th insts. have been received.

Your review of Hunter is very forcible and reminds of something I had forgotten. His inconsistencies are so palpable that any attentive reader would detect his prevarication, and his sophomorean twaddle is beneath notice. The assertion that his confidence was violated and that my aides were used to secretly injure was a falsehood that seemed to me to require exposure, so I wrote to Sidney Johnston, Custis Lee, and Lubbock on that point—the first have answered explicitly denying, and Johnston mentions having been told that Hunter was undermining me and hoped to succeed me. Browne wrote to me, indignant that Hunter should seek to cover his shuffling timidity during the war by bold words in peace, said he had sent for the magazine & would write fully after seeing it. Genl. Early states that Hunter is senile and not worthy of an answer from me. Joe Davis says he is so pointless and notoriously cowardly that no notice of his article is called for. Col. Johnston urges me not to pursue him, so you see your opinion is not singular, but if it stood alone it would be worth more than all the rest in deciding my course. The last time I met Judge Campbell on the street in N.O., he hesitated as if about to speak, I looked over his head and passed on. I want no controversy with any one, but, hating treachery, must repel a traitor.

Mr Mann in a recent letter writes that Miss Emily Mason had been to visit him and had told him that next autumn Winnie would go to Paris. Of you, he always writes with special regard, and in his last expresses the hope that your health has been completely restored. Would that it were so, and that unlike the old men at the rebuilding of the Temple, we could forget the sorrows of the past, and sing our song of triumph unmingled with lamentation. Whether we eat our bread with oil, or moisten it with tears, I am ever your devoted

Husband

Varina Davis to Jefferson Davis

Pope Pius IX, who admired and befriended Jefferson Davis, had died in February, 1878. When the ex-President was in prison His Holiness had sent him a large photograph of himself with a crown of thorns woven by the papal fingers and an inscription in his own hand. The photograph and thorn crown may be seen today in Confederate Memorial Hall in New Orleans.

Addison Hayes has secured for Jeff, Jr., a position in the bank in Memphis.

362 Vance St.
Memphis
March 3rd, 1878

Dear Husband,

Yours of the 26th was received to-day, and please accept my thanks for it. The inscription is "Venite ad me, omnes qui laboratis et ego reficiam vos, dicit Dominus." I could not make out the abbreviations of the Cardinal—the signature however is "Cardinal Barnado—Dec., 1866," who attested to the inscription by the Pope. It will be long before a better man fills the Papal Chair, and I very much regret his death.

Tomorrow is the beginning of the Carnival, & the town is full & stuffed, and the Mardi Gras tickets much in request, and very pretty they are. I sent mine to Winnie, who delights in them. Maggie hopes to go to see the procession, and is keeping quiet for the occasion with all her might. She is much better & I think now is in a fair way to recover her health though it must be through great care. If indulgence and forbearance ever prolonged youth and life, hers ought to be perennial, for Addison is most devoted— I thank God for him daily. Jeff is well, but sits up to all hours of the night & still philanders about Bessie Martin too much for his business. He cannot resist a German to which she is going & she, poor little thing, likes his attentions "immensely."

That God who knows how to give good gifts may give you your "heart's desire," I am, dear Jeff, as ever

Affectionately yours,
V. Davis

Jefferson Davis to the Editor of The Catholic Universe

Jefferson Davis felt impelled to send a personal letter of condolence to the editor of the Catholic magazine on the death of Pope Pius IX.

Beauvoir, Mississippi
March, 1878

Sir:

I grieve with you over the decease of the great and nobly good Pio Nono. In common with all who honor true piety, that which begets universal charity, I feel the loss which the Christian world has sustained in the departure of this grand exemplar. But I have personal obligations added to the common cause for mourning. You have mentioned many characteristic acts of that sublime man. Let me add one, of which you might not otherwise learn, for it was as privately as it was graciously done.

When our war had closed in the defeat of the South, and I was incarcerated with treatment the most needlessly rigorous, if not designedly cruel; when the invention of malignants was taxed to its utmost to fabricate stories to defame and degrade me in the estimation of mankind; when time-servers at home as well as abroad, joined in the cry with which the ignoble ever pursue the victim; a voice came from afar to cheer and console me in my solitary captivity. The Holy Father sent me his likeness, and beneath it was written, by his own hand, the comforting invitation our Lord gives to all who are oppressed, in these words:

"Venite ad me omnes qui laboratis, et ego reficiam vos, dicit Dominus."

That the inscription was autographic was attested by

Al. Cardinal Barnado,
Dec., 1866
(under his seal).

Faithfully yours,
Jefferson Davis

Jefferson Davis to Winnie Davis

Beauvoir
Harrison Co. Mississippi
30th March, 1878

My darling Daughter,

Your Mother has sent to me your last photograph, and after looking at it, address you as daughter instead of baby. Letters from Memphis have given you no doubt all the news of our family there.

My engagements have confined me closely here for some time, but I expect soon to go to Memphis, to see the family and to Vicksburg where business calls me.

Robert has your Xmas present in a frame hanging in his room, and so earnestly asked me for a likeness of you, that I gave him, with much reluctance, the photograph of you as a flower girl. He said it looked as you did when he came to Fortress Monroe, and you ran up to him and called him by his name. He is one of the few of the pattern of old fidelity yet remaining.

This season on the seashore is charming and it would most probably be beneficial to your Mother if she would come here, but her dislike of this coast is so great that she refuses to make it even a short visit. My health has been generally good here, for me, and the absolute quiet is best suited to me. My hostess Mrs. Dorsey talks often of you and has even spoken when her affairs would permit of going to Carlsruhe to see you again, and improve herself in German. You can hardly remember her, she met us in Baltimore.

With her greeting she sends the enclosed bud of the frascata, which I put under press this morning, together with an orange bloom pulled from a tree close by my cottage. Also some illustrations of the doings in our Carnival. The Mystic Crew is composed of highly cultivated gentlemen and their procession & tableaux in the Opera House are annually the subject of admiration by the many thousands who come from all parts of the Union to witness it. This year the subject represented on the Mardi Gras was the Metamorphoses of Ovid.

Give my sincere love to dear little Pinnie. Present my most respectful regard to the Misses Friedlander.

Praying that you may grow in grace and knowledge as rapidly as in stature and years, I am

Most lovingly
Your Father
Jefferson Davis

Varina Davis to Jefferson Davis

Because Margaret Hayes invited a young friend to be her house guest, Varina moved out to Mrs. Allen's boardinghouse. She became dissatisfied there, and writes with cool bitterness. She continues to speak ill of the Gulf Coast, in which she had delighted in the summer of 1857. But she is beginning to give in to the fact that she must live where it is convenient and comfortable for her husband to finish his book.

Mrs. Allen's, Second Street
Memphis
April 7, 1878

Dear Husband—

Many thanks for your kind letter, it found me at Mrs. Allen's, where I still am. Poor little Maggie never sees me without assuring me that if she had known it would disturb me at all in my habits she would have put Eva off indefinitely, of which fact I was perfectly conscious before she assured me of it. But I sleep so badly that I would disturb anyone and I do not like to do so, even to a stranger. I dined with her today and I think as a hygienic measure Eva is good for her.

It is very kind of you to invite me to meet you in New Orleans. I very much desire to have my teeth attended to as they now are stretching my upper lip in a most disfiguring degree, but the expense deterred me from going, as well as my unwillingness to go so near to your home without visiting you at it. And I say that the five months that we have been apart, now verging as it does on to six, and the year that preceded it, broken by ten days of your companionship when you met me here, seem a long absence. If it did not interfere with your other plans I should be more than glad to claim as much of your time as you could conveniently spare—not as a right, but as a tribute to a life spent together in happier years. It grieves me to know that you are not well. I think the Sea Coast one of the most unsafe of places if one seeks to escape bilious attacks. May God restore you soon to health, and inspire those about you with a knowledge in some degree equivalent to my experience of thirty years with you.

I beg that you will write me at once to say how you are—and as well how soon you wish me to come, and where. I prefer going down on the railway, and if you desire to do so, would as soon visit Cousin Florida as not, provided the visit is not so late as to give us chills & fever. Memphis is warm just now, but not oppressingly so. The insects, thank goodness, have not come.

We have on hand a St. Lazarus Ball at the Peabody for the debt of the Church and it promises to be a success. Mr. Brinkley gave us the hotel with the kindest expressions of sympathy in our effort. Everyone has shown a willingness to serve us, and altogether Mrs. Allen's part and mine has been most agreeable—viz., the organization of the ball. The begging we have left to others.

Today is communion Sunday, but I feel such lassitude from the Spring heat that I could not go away out to Grace Church. It is dusty and where the streets are not watered one almost smothers with the clouds raised by the cars.

Jeff is very well, and rebels against his routine life, but improves under it and I think could not be much better off than at present.

Thank you for the frascati and orange blossom. They quite perfumed the letter. The trees are coming out here cautiously. The willow catkins are waving their little greyish plumes, and the vine leaves are pink as roses. The roses are very backward, but the flowering blackberry (a new thing to me) simulates the rose very well. A most absurd thing happened to me—I saw at the nursery garden one of them in bloom, and it is exactly like the bridal rose which used to grow at the Briars, and one of which I wore in my hair when I was married. The tears sprung to my eyes and I began to feel bewildered as usual, when I heard the man say to Mrs. Allen that it was a double flowering blackberry, so I "toned up" and saw the difference.

Well I could write on if I could entertain as easily as I can occupy you, but of illegible scrawl you have probably enough.

With prayers for your welfare and happiness, unceasing, if not efficacious always, I am

Yours affectionately
Varina Davis

Jefferson Davis to Varina Davis

Though Davis offers to leave Beauvoir, Varina knows that it is only a gesture made to please her. After his financial losses in Memphis, she fully understands that they cannot afford to live in a city as she desired.

Anti-Davis articles continued to appear in Northern papers. Crafts J. Wright of Chicago, who had been a cadet at West Point with Davis, wanted to set a record straight. Davis is referring to the incident of his capture in May, 1865, when Federal troops broke into his wife's trunks and appropriated whatever took their fancy, including prayer books, the baby's dresses, and a new hoop skirt which had not yet been worn. Ellen was the colored maidservant.

Missi. City, 10th April '78

My dear Wife,

I have received yours of the 1st & 7th Insts. and delayed answering the 1st because a letter written to you but not received when you wrote contained a proposition on which your decision was desired. Robert several days since picked some strawberries for me, the first of the season, and I made a wish that you would write to me proposing to meet me in New Orleans and so I have waited for your letter with that wish on hand. You should not have delayed so long about your teeth; the poorer we are the more need for teeth and nails to bite and scratch our way through the world.

Write to me when you will leave Memphis and I will go to New Orleans to receive you on your arrival. Mary Stamps has written to me that her landlady could accommodate me and if I came to the City she wished me to stop there. Mary & Lucy now board where they formerly kept house. If you prefer not to go there I will select another place. As to your coming here, you must do as you please & we can talk of that hereafter.

Maggie's ill health and loneliness formed a reason for your stay in Memphis & at her house, as soon as you left her I felt that you should be with me. My circumstances here are well suited to my present engagements, but are not indispensable; so if you will not stay on the coast I have been willing to change my abode until we have a *home*.

My friend & classmate Crafts J. Wright has sent me the newspaper article and the enclosed letter. I replied that you were not with me, at present, so that it was not possible to avail of your recollections & "answer at once." So I wrote to him that I could not state the value of the articles pillaged but knew that it was swift and general. That I had no recollection of such a conversation as Col. Pritchard narrated as having occurred with you & me, but was sure if he had been guilty of such insolence he would remember my reply. That it was not only the general thieving, but especially the stealing several times of the breakfast the servant was preparing for my children which induced the severe language addressed to Lt. Col. P. The liars with many variations continue to assert that I was sent to my tent and confined there, the purpose being to sustain the main falsehood of female attire. I think that instead of returning into the tent, that I went by it to the fire in rear of it; and that Ellen picked up the waterproof & shawl and carried them back from the spot on which I dropped them when the horseman attacked me. If that be so, a statement from her would answer a hundred lies of the many who claim to have been the "leader of the charge."

If you had ever shown an unwillingness to bear a full share of my burthens, I would not trouble you with these harassing matters, which come in swarms upon me.

With love to the children. I am hoping soon to hear when you are coming. Ever affectionately,

Your Husband

Sarah A. Dorsey to A. Dudley Mann

Dudley Mann in France had often spoken of a desire to return to the States and live near Jefferson Davis. Mrs. Dorsey generously invites him to be her guest.

Beauvoir
25th April 1878

My dear Sir:

I have had the great joy and honour of Mr. Davis' society in my house during the past year. You who appreciate him so truly can comprehend what a privilege this is to me. Mr. Davis feels a sort of responsibility towards me from having been so closely connected in the bonds of dearest amity with my father and his family. He has always kept a kind of over-sight of me and now that I am left entirely alone and desolate in the world, he is kinder and more considerate than ever. I hope and think that my house will be, at least, *one* of his homes as long as he lives. I am anxious that he should make use of it exactly as if it was his own and should esteem it a great consolation if I could add in any way to his comfort and happiness. So, dear Sir, if you should really choose to come to America in order to be near him you can come to me, *sans cérémonie*. The first desire of both of us will be to make this noblest of men as happy as we can.

With best wishes,

I am sincerely yours,
Sarah A. Dorsey

W. B. Pittman to Jefferson Davis

Davis has finally gained absolute possession of his plantation, Brierfield.

WESTERN UNION TELEGRAM

Jackson, Miss., May 20, 1878

Your case again decided in your favor. Former decree of Supreme Court stands.

W. B. Pittman

Winnie Davis to Her Mother

Wilhelm I, King of Prussia and Emperor of Germany (1797–1888), the father of Grand Duchess Luise of Baden, was unhurt in an attempted assassination.

May 26 1878
Carlsruhe, Germany

My dear Mother

I received your letter the other day and also the one you sent at the beginning of the week. You cant immagin how happy I am when I get a letter from you in which I hear that you are having a pleasant time.

You asked in your letter how I would like to go to Paris this summer, well I would like it very much and I would like to go to Scotland, too.

I am very glad St Lazarus made so much by the ball. Miss Friedlander found it so funny that there was a *ball for the Church.*

You know that as the Emperor and the Grand-dutches of Baden were riding on the 11 of May and some one shot at them and that the Grand Dutches threw here self over her father to protect him so neither of them were hurt and when she came home, of course, there was a great fuss about her; and the schools went to welcome her home and we went with the rest. Little Mary Heart, a little German girl who is a boarder, gave a basket of red roses prettily arranged to the Grand Dutches, who had forbidden flowers to be thrown. We all made a deep bow as she passed, and then stood silent. The next school threw flowers and cried "ho!" as she passed. (It looked so vulgar when she had forbidden them to throw flowers.) We then went home just in time to see the rabble come up to the castle to sing songs to her.

Please read this to father but, dont tell him my mistakes.

Kisses for Mother. Kisses for Father. With much love I remain as ever your lovin Baby

Winanne

The Reverend Mr. Frank Stringfellow to Jefferson Davis

The Reverend Mr. Frank Stringfellow, an Episcopal clergyman of Virginia—and, incidentally, the grandfather of the well-known Stringfellow Barr—was a secret agent of the Confederate forces and accomplished many daring and courageous missions within the enemy lines. Believing in President Davis's military abilities, at a critical time during the war he had urged him to "take the field." In a reply to Stringfellow's letter of admiration and affection, Davis explains why he could not risk leaving the executive office in such incompetent hands as those of defeatist Alexander Stephens, the Vice-President, or R. M. T. Hunter, the "timid" President of the Senate.

P.O. "Sublett's Tavern," Powhatan Co.
May 22d, 1878

Dear Sir:

I have just returned from a Church Council held in Lynchburg where I met Genl Early. In the course of our conversation I asked for you, and he told me that you had been inquiring for my address. It is not surprising that I should often think of you, Mr. President, but that you should think of me is.

I do not think that our people have forgotten you, and although many seemed to consider it a religious duty to criticise each official act during the time of your administration they are at present very prompt to resent even an insinuation that you were not the very best President in the world.

So far as your reputation abroad is concerned I am sure that success would have been best for you, but so far as the *love* of your own people is concerned you are more beloved today than if you had carried our victorious banners through every Northern State.

Personally I have always been a Davis man, and could see but one blunder in your administration. I told you of it during the war. I wanted you to *take the field.* If you had assumed command of the Southern army the result might have been quite different. I do not mean to say one word against the Generals who commanded them, in turn, for I am sure that each one did his best, and they were good soldiers, but in my admiration for you, and *your peculiar qualifications for a commander,* I was satisfied that our Congress made a blunder in not requesting you to take command of Johnston's army at the time that Sherman began his march, or better still, before his plans were formed.

It is easy to see how things might have been otherwise, but it is hard to see why we did not succeed. I know that we were right, and I know that God permitted our overthrow, but I do not know how to harmonize these facts. I am sure that you have not thought any more on this subject than I have, but doubtless you have thought more *clearly.*

I still have your picture sent me through Mr. Francis Hopkins, when on yr. way to Europe. To give it prominence it hangs alone in my parlor, no other picture is allowed in the room. We often think of you and wish very much that you could come and visit us. You would find many friends in Va. who wd. do every thing to make you happy.

I understand that you are engaged in writing a history of our late war. Many desire to see the political side of the question. All agree that you are able to make a valuable and interesting contribution to the cause. If I can aid you in collecting materials for your book I will do so very cheerfully. I could help you to present a view of warfare wh. has never yet been noticed by any respectable writer, for want of *information* on the subject. I wish that you could come to see us, but if that is not possible I should like to be able to see you, perhaps I could aid you in yr. *undertaking,* or *pecuniarily.*

My wife and little Ida desire to be very kindly remembered. We can make you very comfortable and wd. be delighted to have you with us as long as you can stay.

Yours very truly,
F. Stringfellow

Jefferson Davis to the Reverend Mr. Frank Stringfellow

P.O. Beauvoir, Harrison Co. Miss.
4th June 1878

My dear Sir,

Your very welcome letter of the 22nd ult. has been received. Few things could be more agreeable to me than to accept your invitation to visit you and to make the acquaintance of your Wife and the young hope of your house, but circumstances do not permit me at this time to enjoy that pleasure.

It is very gratifying to me to know that you, who were so severely tried and never found wanting, should give a general and special approval of my course as the President of the Confederacy. It might have been better as you suggest had I taken the field. It was contemplated when Johnston retreated from Yorktown, but the duties of the Executive office were many & important, and to whom could they have been entrusted? The vagaries on Military matters of the Vice President, and the lethargy & timidity of the President of the

Senate, rendered each utterly unfit for the duty. At a late period of the war both were so despondent as to be willing to abandon the effort for independence and then I could not conscientiously have entrusted them with the powers of negotiation. Civil administration was not my preference and it was a disappointment to me when notified of my election by the provisional Congress as it took me from the head of the army of Mississippi and put me in the office of provisional President. A military training gave me some confidence in my ability to command troops, notwithstanding my years of political service I had no fondness for it and felt always a distaste for its belongings. The trial was too great and the result too doubtful to justify one in declining any post to which he was assigned; therefore I accepted.

I have often times combatted the idea of calm, thoughtful men, that the failure of our righteous cause rendered doubtful the government of the world by an overruling providence. My answer has been first a question, has it failed? Then the reminder that He who knows the hearts of men, required not only that the cause should be righteous but also that it should be righteously defended, to be the object of His favor.

The inimitable principles for which we contended must live, or republican government perish from among us. Had we succeeded, how well and wisely would we have used our power, was made questionable by various manifestations in the last twelve months of the war. Perhaps the furnace to which we have been subjected was necessary for our purification. Has it not been shown by the result that we were more right than even our own people generally knew? And the world may now learn how faithless, dishonest, and barbarous our enemies were. From such bad roots good plants may spring, and in the distant future which lies beyond human vision, there may be consequences which will fully compensate for our present losses. The high race of men who sprung from a governing class, and had their noble morals nurtured by care of dependents, can hardly be expected in the changed condition of our section, but more self-reliance and usefulness in the community work may be the sequence.

My labors in preparing reminiscences have been much obstructed by the loss of my books and papers. Our people have been very reluctant to write so that my inquiries have met partial answers generally where I had hoped thus to supply the loss of documents by memoranda of events. It was therefore with much joy that I received your offer of information, and realize the peculiar character your observations must have had. Please give me as fully as your leisure hours will permit your recollection of matters & things which came under your view. I am, for the time, residing on the Gulf coast about midway between Mobile and New Orleans. A way station is a short distance in the rear of the house, Beauvoir, and it would be a great pleasure to me to receive you here. Genl. Early spent the last Xmas with us. Mrs. Davis joins me in affectionate regard for Mrs. Stringfellow and Miss Ida, with kindest remembrance of yourself.

Ever sincerely
your friend
Jefferson Davis

PESTILENCE, BEREAVEMENT, AND A BLESSED LEGACY

Jefferson Davis to Maggie Hayes

Mrs. Davis had finally joined her husband at Beauvoir in July. Mrs. Dorsey did all in her power to make her comfortable and released to her the job of amanuensis. By mid-September, 1878, Mrs. Davis had decided that she rather liked the Gulf Coast after all. All was going fairly well with the Davises when yellow fever in a most virulent form broke out in New Orleans and began spreading north and east. In answer to a solicitous query, Davis asked the prayers of Bishop William Green, Chancellor of the University of the South. The Hayeses seek refuge in the country outside Memphis.

Beauvoir
Harrison Co. Missi
Sept 25, 1878

My dear Daughter,

Accept my thanks for your full & kind letter. I hope you will be able to find quarters, at least so far removed from the station, as not be endangered by the cars standing there. The disease which has so long surrounded us is gradually removing the circle. We have it now in Missi City, in Biloxi, & one case near Handsboro. Though we avoid intercourse with persons coming from infected places, Dr. Hollingsworth & young Mr. Leacock in their professional visits, necessarily come back after being in contact with diseased persons. We see very little of them, and if we were in our own house would not hesitate to declare a quarantine. As for myself, I have passed unharmed through so many epidemics, that I think I am more than usually exempt. Your Mother, though she hears a great deal of the disease in our neighborhood, is most concerned about our children near to Memphis. I am disappointed that Addison found it unpracticable to remove the Bank office so as to avoid the necessity of going daily to Memphis. Of course, I honor the devotion to duty which has led him to stand to his post as long as it was needful to hold it.

One of the sad features in our case is the impossibility of going to you or of your coming to us, not only because of the danger of passing through infected places, but also because of the obstruction by quarantines on every road leading from or to us. The recent reports show that the disease at Memphis is becoming less fatal, which is the usual course of all epidemics, and we find comfort in the fact, but most of all desire to hear of an early frost which as far north as Memphis may be soon expected. We have had some cool weather here, but it is again quite hot. A ride yesterday to Handsboro proved the sun to be as oppressive as at any time during the summer. I think your Mother is better than for some time past she has been.

Please give my love to Addison & Jeff & take a Benjamin's portion to your dear little self, in all of which your Mother, who writes for me, joins. May God preserve my darling Pollie ever prays her Father

Jefferson Davis

Jefferson Davis to Addison Hayes

Davis has received telegraphic news that Jeff, Jr., has been stricken with yellow fever.

Beauvoir, Missi
12th Oct. 1878

My dear Addison

Your telegram of yesterday was received late in the afternoon and answered by the messenger who brought it. I have sent to the office with the hope of receiving further intelligence about my dear boy. Your Mother would not consent to my going but insisted upon going herself. As it was impossible to go otherwise than through New Orleans, and by that route it was necessary to remain in the

City some twenty hours and then to pass through many infected places, the probability was that she would arrive sick and add to your cares rather than divide them, she at last consented to accept the kind offer of Maj. W. L. Walthall to go instead of either of us, and take charge of our Son. I did and do feel some confidence that I could, as I have done in former times, pass through the contagion unscathed and you can realize how much I desire to be with my child, but reason compels me to admit that Maj. Walthall can do more for him than I could. May God shield him and our other two children is my constant prayer.

I sent an emphatic refusal to the proposition that my little Pollie should attempt to nurse her Brother. Your watchfulness will insure the attention of the professional nurses and that gives assurance that all which can be, will be done for my boy. Your Mother and I have passed a night of painful anxiety about our sick child and our beloved daughter and your dear self. Powerless to aid and fretting under the restraints which keep us from you all, our misery may be imagined, it cannot be described. I recommended the removal of Margaret from the house which is infected, a short distance may suffice. Your Mother, save her mental trouble, is well as usual. I am far from well, but think not of myself, but of our loved ones. The letter from your Mother which is inclosed with this, contains a preventive prescription, it can do no harm to try it.

Please write fully, who is the Doctor, how did the disease reach Jeff, and all other details which afflicted parents desire to learn.

Give my heart's tenderest love to my daughter and son, if he can safely receive a message from his Father, who would willingly die to save him.

My trust is, under providence, in your good sense and fraternal care—

> Ever affectionately
> Your Father
> Jefferson Davis

Jefferson Davis to Addison Hayes

Although Jeff, Jr., rallied on the fifteenth, death came to him on the sixteenth.

Beauvoir, Missi
18th Oct. 1878

Dear Addison,

The sad news came yesterday by telegram of the previous day, from Maj. Walthall. Hope had sustained us to the last though the warning caused us to feel much fear.

The last of my four sons has left me, I am crushed under such heavy and repeated blows. I presume not God to scorn, but the many and humble prayers offered before my boy was taken from me, are hushed in the despair of my bereavement.

Now what of my Daughter, where and how is she?

I thank you from the bottom of my heart for your unfailing efforts to save my boy to me. My own little Pollie is your further charge.

Your Mother is prostrate under a complication of painful diseases, among which neuralgia is chief. She was far from well when we received the first news of our boy's attack, she has grown worse from that time, and now is quite helpless in bed. We are endeavoring to keep her quiet and to obtain for her sleep, the absolutely needed remedy for nerves & brain.

Doctor Hollingsworth has been here twice to-day and has promised to return this evening. He expects the case to be manageable and of brief duration. Should the case develop into the pestilence which surrounds or otherwise prove more serious than is anticipated I will notify you by a telegram. If she is up to morrow or next day, she will give you the best assurance of recovery by a letter, autographic.

If my good friend Maj. Walthall is yet with you, do tell him if words may convey it, how grateful I am to him.

With tenderest love to my darling daughter, and to my son Addison, I am

Jefferson Davis

Jefferson Davis to Maggie Hayes

Mrs. Davis was in bed for a fortnight, apparently with brain fever. Mrs. Dorsey hardly left her bedside during her worst days. Now Varina has gone to help nurse a child relative in a nearby coastal town.

Beauvoir, Miss.
8th Nov. 1878

My darling Pollie,

Your Mother has been for two days at Cousin Anne Smith's helping to nurse little Helen, who is seriously ill with a low continuous fever. The attending Physician *now* says she has typhoid pneumonia. Your Mother and I are very anxious about you and notice the weather prophecies with unusual care.

I think she will be more cheerful with you and near to her friends in Memphis, than she is here or would be elsewhere, and I am consequently desirous to go with her to you as soon as it is safe to do so. The delays and failures to make close connections have been so common of late on the Rail Roads that there is now the twofold danger of exposing her to infection and of overtaxing her patience.

Mrs. Dorsey nursed her with unwearied care and your Mother said no one had ever so nearly approached the skill of your Grandma as did Mrs. Dorsey. "The sick man knows the Physician's step, but when he is well cannot remember his face."

Give my cordial love to Addison, who if it were possible has come nearer and dearer to me by the fond care he lavished on my boy. God bless you, darling. Let me hear from you and of you very often. With devoted love,

Your Father

Jefferson Davis to Varina Davis

This letter contained four bud chrysanthemums, two red, one yellow, one white, which Jeff, Jr., was holding in his hand when he died. They may be seen today, dry and faded but intact, at the Jefferson Davis Shrine, Biloxi, Mississippi.

Beauvoir
Nov. 11th 1878

Dear Wife

Yesterday evening Mrs. Weed came to see us. She had received a despatch, summoning her to a dying grandchild & her departure was thus unexpectedly hastened. After she left me I made the enclosed Memorandum of her statements, for preservation and for your information. The flowers she brought, four in number, are all sent to you, for whom they were entrusted to Mrs. Weed. They are precious as having been held by his hand when he was dying and were still more dear to you for the sentiment with which they are associated.

Mrs. Weed seemed to retain both affection and esteem for our boy. She wept repeatedly when talking to me, and grieved for our loss of one so clearly marked for honorable distinction and to be a support to the declining years of his aged parents.

I am not well this morning; the pain has passed to the right side of my face, but as for myself is rather welcomed for the distraction it creates from less endurable or irremediable ills.

Bishop Green writes affectionately to us, and prayerfully asks for peace and consolation to us both.

With love of many years undimmed by shadows dark as ever fell on man, I am

Your Husband
Jefferson Davis

Jefferson Davis to Winnie Davis

Jeff, Jr., had died on October 16 but the grieving father could not bring himself to write to his little girl in Germany until late November.

Beauvoir. P.O. Mississippi
27th Nov. 1878

My darling Baby

I have long wished to write to you. Sick and sorrowful, the task of writing to you of our sad bereavement has been delayed.

Soon after your Brother was taken from us, I mailed a newspaper to you containing the announcement, and hoped a letter from your Mother which followed it would first reach you. She felt that you would be less shocked by a letter than by the paper notice.

Day after day we received notice that all were well. Margaret and Jefferson were in the country. Mr. Hayes went daily to town but returned before night. As time wore on we gained assurance of the safety—when we were startled by a telegram stating that your Brother had the yellow fever. Your Mother was too ill to go by the only route not under the quarantine, and on which there were long detentions and many infected places. I believed I could go, but all others pronounced me too ill to travel and I realized that my presence was needful to my wife and would probably be useless or worse than useless to my son. So it proved, for my friend Maj. Walthall, who has had a large experience in the yellow fever, urged me to allow him to go in my stead, and started by the first train. Travelling with all practicable speed he arrived after my boy's fate was sealed.

What is unusual in that disease Jeff retained his faculties to the last. In Christian faith he received the comforts of our church, and peacefully his spirit passed from those who loved him here, but may we not hope to a love better worth than ours. I write in the cottage where he and I worked together before he went to take a place in the bank at Memphis; around me are many objects associated with him and dear, very dear, for his sake. I have bowed to the blows, but in vain have sought for consolation. So many considerations, not selfish, plead for his longer stay on earth that I only shut my eyes, to what it is not permitted me to see, and stifling the outward flow, let my wounds bleed inwardly.

Your Mother has been for some days at Cousin Nannie Smith's assisting to nurse little Helen who is dangerously ill. She sent your letter to-day for me to read and noticing your request for a photo. of your Brother, I will send it to you.

Robert, our old servant, has just been in and was much pleased to see your recently taken likenesses. He says he cannot tell you how much he loves you, but hopes you know it.

My dear child, I long for your bright loving face. In my bereavement it seems doubly hard to be separated from you. Yet I remember your stoical heroism when you started from London, or rather when we were deliberating as to your going, and try to feel as you spoke that "the necessity for education had to be met."

Mrs. Dorsey to whom I showed the photographs of you, greatly admired the one in standing posture and wished she had one. It would gratify her very much if you would send her one.

Please give my affectionate regard to the Misses Friedlander.

My darling, my sweet Winanne, may God have you in His holy keeping prays

Your Father

Varina Davis to Maggie Hayes

In February of 1879, while Mrs. Davis was visiting in Memphis, Mrs. Dorsey sold Beauvoir to Davis for $5,500, to be paid in three installments. She felt that he had found his right retirement home, and she desired him to be as peaceful as possible while writing his book and in his last years. She had come to realize that Varina's smoldering attitude toward her would continually present problems. So she was selfless enough to be willing to bow herself out of the picture and out of her favorite home. Temporarily she went to stay in New Orleans and consult a physician. When Mrs. Davis returned to Beauvoir in April, Mrs. Dorsey was gone. In early May, Mrs. Dorsey was operated on for cancer in New Orleans.

Mrs. Cochrane is a cousin of Mrs. Dorsey who had lived with her as a companion when Mr. Davis boarded at Beauvoir. Minnie Howell, Varina's sister-in-law, was with Mrs. Dorsey when she underwent the operation. Mrs. Dorsey planned to live on one of her Louisiana plantations, but was detained by her illness in New Orleans.

May 11th, 1879
Beauvoir, Harrison Co.

My darling:

The weather here is more than charming—cool & fresh as winter & the sea is exquisite. Our garden gives us plenty of vegetables, such as they are—leeks, lettuce, asparagus, and we will have roasting ears before very long. The only fig tree is coming into bearing. The oranges, however, are nearly all dying from the cold of last winter. I am to have a new chicken house next week—the chicken houses go for a stable. The dairy is to be roofed & cleaned. Daisy has a young calf & will be ready to milk next week. Butts gives a good deal of milk & I could make you blancmange every day if you were here. I am the very quietest housekeeper you ever saw. Indeed I am up betimes, give out my dinner & see to my servants all before breakfast. I have a little maid to clean up, fifteen, but no bigger than Winnie was at the first Court Street house. She is a nice child, respectful & willing & she & I do the rooms. I drive the mule when I go out which is not often & drive as well as any body.

Your father and I are going to day to see a very nice family who have recently moved here, Mr. Davidson, a gentlemanly

Englishman who has not been well lately, has had a pretty sharp "attack" of rheumatic gout. I have given him one of my little alterative pills & he is better. Mrs. Cochrane arrived safely last night, I sent the carriage for her to the station. She is very sweet and affectionate to me. Her son is a nice young man.

Minnie Howell was detained in town with Mrs. Dorsey & could not be spared from the St Charles, but came home the day before Mrs Cochrane. Mrs D. is fast recovering from the operation & is said to look well & to be going away the first of June.

Give dearest love to my Addison.

Devotedly, your Mother

Jefferson Davis to Mrs. George Negus

Mrs. Dorsey had died at four o'clock in the morning on July 4, 1879. Jefferson Davis was at her bedside when she received Holy Communion, and at her request he repeated from memory the Beatitudes to her. She asked him to take down certain deathbed bequests to nieces, cousins, and servants, which he did with pad and pencil. She told him that she owed absolutely nothing to her brother and half-brother, that she had given them cash and property in the past, that they had squandered her gifts and proved ungrateful. When her will was read Davis learned that she had left Beauvoir to him, which he had purchased from her, but on which he had made only one payment. In fact, she had bequeathed "all my property, real, personal, and mixed . . . without hindrance or qualification, to my most honored and esteemed friend, Jefferson Davis, ex-President of the Confederate States." She constituted him her sole "heir, executive, and administrator." The will ended, "I do not intend to share in the ingratitude of my country towards the man who is in my eyes the highest and noblest in existence."

The following letter to Mary Eliza Thompson (Mrs. George Negus), a long-time friend of Davis and a cousin of James McNeill Whistler, is self-explanatory. Mrs. Dorsey's half-brother Mortimer Dahlgren had attacked Jefferson Davis in the newspapers.

Beauvoir P.O. Harrison Co. Missi.
August 4th 1879

My dear Mary,

It has been so long since I wrote to you that you would have been excusable if you had stricken me off your lists, instead of which I perceive by a recent St. Louis paper that you have been valiantly defending me against malignant politicians and greedy expectants of legacies. Another paper of your city gives what purports to be the revelations of one Mortimer Dahlgren, a half brother of the late Mrs. Dorsey. His avowal of having come to her with the expectation of being provided for by her, sufficiently accounts for his supposing others might be influenced by like unworthy motives. His statements are a tissue of falsehoods. Instead of his being driven off by me, I prevented him from going away in anger with his sister, and used my best influence with both to promote a reconciliation. Instead of his going away in anger with me, he solicited & obtained a letter of introduction to aid him where he was going.

I feared he would not do as well elsewhere as he might here, and invited him to stay, assuring him that the sale of the place by his sister to me need make no difference to him, as he was welcome to remain with all the privileges he had previously enjoyed, which were freedom of expense for himself & his horse, and the full enjoyment of everything about the place, at which he showed much emotion & expressed great gratitude.

Instead of my having lived here on his sister's bounty as he asserts, he knew that I contributed every month a *full* equivalent of any increase which my presence made in the house expenditure.

Mrs. Dorsey's accts. with her merchants will show that I gave her monthly of never less than fifty dollars, and when any members of my family were with me, which was a large part of the time, the sum was proportionately increased. You will not understand that my friend Mrs. Dorsey exacted or ever desired this, but I only consented to reside here upon those terms.

There has been a vast exaggeration as to the value of the estate, which to a great extent consists of wild & unsaleable land, to pay the taxes on which has been so great a burthen that much of that kind of property has been forfeited. The gross income of all her property is say about $2,500 & I shall be glad if in the next two years this suffices to liquidate the claims against the estate.

As to this place, her former residence, it never was the source of income & it will require a great improvement in the current expenses of maintaining it as a residence. The depreciation of property in the neighborhood has been great for many years. I have been thus full in my explanations for your satisfaction & have marked my letter "private & personal" because of my unwillingness to follow my slanderers into the Newspapers, and feared your zeal in my behalf might induce you to give my letter to some member of the Press.

With kindest remembrance to your Husband & others of your family I am ever

Affectionately your friend,
Jefferson Davis

Winnie Davis to Her Mother

Winnie has heard indirectly about Mrs. Dorsey's bequests.

27 September, 1879
Carlsruhe, Baden

My dear Mother

I was so glad to receive those papers you sent me. The new girls are all very fond of me but I am not so fond of them as I ought to be because I can not agree with their way of thinking. They are so high-church that they make objections to praying in an unconcecrated church and an awful fuss about things that are natural, for instance standing at prayers and sitting to sing.

Motherly, do tell me, I heard from Pin that Mrs. Dorsey had left Father three plantations and also all her money, but I heard the other day that there is still a law suite impending about the will. I see our meeting being pushed away by those old plantations again.

Motherly, I do not want to take the reigns of government into my own hands. I want you and Father to decide how long this life is going to last, although I am quite happy.

Do take a thousand kisses for yourself and the same number for Father, and as much love as would weigh down your own so you may know how much I have for you both. Give love to all, not forgetting Robert.

I am as ever your own child
Winnie

Jefferson Davis to L. B. Northrop

Colonel Northrop was the South Carolina-born Commissary General of the Confederacy, who came under the attack of Joseph E. Johnston and Beauregard.

Beauvoir
1st Nov. 1879

My dear Friend:

I am deeply grieved to hear that you are so lame, and disappointed that you cannot come to winter with us. My wife had looked forward with pleasing anticipation to our reunion, and her joy would be if, instead of leaving dear Mrs. Northrop, you would bring her with you (my heart would be less sore after seeing you both in our house D.V.). Our home has a name less significant than yours, and was given by its former possessor to express a beautiful prospect. The air is soft. In winter especially the sea breeze is invigorating. The oranges are shining golden on the trees, and our pine knot fires soar in the chimneys, in their light I try to bury my unhappiness.

Mrs. Davis joins me in love to you and yours.

As ever, your friend,
Jefferson Davis

Jefferson Davis to Varina Davis

Mrs. Dorsey's brother and half-brother are suing for the property she willed to Jefferson Davis.

New Orleans, 18th Dec., 1879

My dear Wife,

I am not the worse for my travel, no doubt partly because of your care as to the flannel shirt, etc.

I have purchased all the articles asked for by Robert and have sent to the hardware store for those ordered by you.

This morning the Marshall served notice on me as defendant in the suit of Ellis et al.

Cousin Ned Farrar regards the bill as fustian, and says the first step will be to demur to the jurisdiction of the U.S. Court in a probate matter on which the State Court has acted.

It is probably as true now as in Mr. Jefferson's time that the U.S. Judiciary will ever seek to enlarge its jurisdiction, and therefore that the demurrer will fail. If the demurrer prevails it will be fifty pages of useless Mss. which it would be a waste of money to have copied.

Mr. Payne is here, and says he is the better for his trip up Red River. I staid at the St. Charles and propose to leave this evening by rail road.

My dear Wife, do try to look on the best side of life, we have common sorrows and memories, and loves of many years. Let us put afar such things as are discordant and make the best of what is irremediable.

Remember me to Robert. I have tried to give him pleasure in the choice of his clothing, which is quite as good and more plentiful than I would have bought for myself.

Ever with trust and truest love, I am

Your Husband

Jefferson Davis to Varina Davis

Mrs. Dorsey's relatives did not take the case to the Supreme Court. Col. C. S. Fenner is the son-in-law of Jacob Payne. It was in the Payne-Fenner house that Davis was to die.

Payne, Kennedy & Co.
Cotton Factors
New Orleans, 10 March, 1880

My dear Wife,

I have the pleasure to inform you that the Court has decided in favor of the Demurrer not only on the point of jurisdiction but upon all of those presented.

Col. Fenner says he has no intimations as to the future course of the "complainants," but as it will cost little to appeal to the U.S. Sup. Court thinks it probable that will be done.

Mr. Fenner & Mr. Payne regretted that you did not come in with me.

In haste, but not too great for the offering of all the love of my heart, I am

> Your Husband

Varina Davis to Winnie Davis

The first volume of *The Rise and Fall of the Confederate Government* is finished and ready for the publishers.

> Beauvoir, Harrison Co., Missi.
> 25th April 1880

My own precious Darling,

We are about as usual now. Your Father is as well, though of course not so vigorous, as any man of thirty. I have tried everything with him, and think I have now settled on a plan to keep him well. The weary recital of the weary war, to be compiled into a splendid but heartbreaking record of cherished hopes now blasted, brave warriors bleeding and dying, and noble men living, yet dead, in that they are hopeless—this tremendous record is being given to the world, and the while as he writes the graves give up their dead, and they stalk before us all gory and downcast, but for all that a gallant, proud army, ready if they could again put on their fleshly shield to do battle for their rights.

The first volume of the book is to be delivered in a few days— 1st of May.

God bless you my child—more at length tomorrow or next day.

> With devoted love
> Your Mother

PUBLICATION,
LAST TRIP TO EUROPE,
AND THE SHADOW OF J.E.J.

Father Abram J. Ryan to Jefferson Davis

Father Ryan, Catholic priest and soldier-poet of the Confederacy, was a devoted admirer of Jefferson Davis. He asks, as numerous patriotic persons did, to be allowed to give his free service in helping Davis with the burdensome details of his book, the purpose of which, as he eloquently expresses, is "to give to the world of false policies the doctrine of deathless principles."

The publishers, Appleton's, had recently sent down from New York to Beauvoir Judge W. T. Tenney to help speed the work.

St. Mary's Church
Mobile, Ala.
Nov. 5th 1880

My dear & honored President:

Since I saw you last and owing too, in part to a long conversation I had with the Judge, I have been thinking and thinking day and night about *your* work & *our* defense. It ought to be (and I can say it with all reverence) the "Sacred Scripture" of our Confederacy. And you ought to be *almost inspired* to give to the world of false policies the doctrines of deathless Principles. I have written to Bishop Lynch of Charleston for some data; also to Father Hamilton for data of his own and Father Whelan's in regard to Andersonville prison & their summons to Washington City. I will have the documents in a few days. Now, my dear Sir, if I can, (and I can) be of any aid, in any way, in such a work, my services (for it would be a service of love for the cause and reverence for yourself) are at your wish. If you think well of it & would wish my assistance (of course gratis), it is offered before it is asked. If accepted, you

503

could write to Bishop Quinlan of Mobile, who is over me and a great admirer of your personal character, to let me spend a few weeks with yourself and the Judge in the preparation of the work. He would consent. Day and night I would be willing to work for you, because you, in dark days, worked for all, —and among the all, there is no one living that gives you a heart-loyalty and love more sincere than mine.

Believe me to be with love and reverence,

Your humble servant
Abram J. Ryan

Charles O'Conor to Varina Davis

The renowned New York lawyer Charles O'Conor had been chiefly responsible for Davis's release from prison at Fort Monroe. Davis had stayed with O'Conor at his home on the Hudson immediately after he was freed on bail.

The Davises are preparing to go to Europe to fetch Winnie home. Mrs. Davis had written O'Conor her hope of seeing him as they passed through New York.

Nantucket, Mass.
April 7th 1881

My Dear Mrs. Davis

In this my somewhat solitary new abode I was rejoiced to receive your kind favor of the 30th ult. gathering as I did from its silence on the topic that you and Mr. Davis were quite well.

I may be considered so, as for a person of my years I am getting on pretty well. The asperity of my native air is no longer suiting me. I have removed to this place where during the probably short balance of my lease I count upon spending my time except in winter when I may take a trip to the southward. Bermuda will be my probable resort.

This island, Nantucket, is in summer the most delightful climate in the United States. If you and Mr. Davis go to Europe and bring your children home it will cost you little time or trouble to turn in here and I should be delighted to see you. The young folks would find much to amuse them.

I hope Mr. Davis will finish his book leisurely and deliberately.

I wish it to come forth full-armed and capable of resisting all just criticism. On its great subject the whole of our literature is bribed or intimidated. His ability and knowledge are ample and he should take all the time needful to give their results fair play.

Please to present him my best respects and for yourself accept the assurance of my sincere desire for health and happiness.

As ever
Your friend
Ch. O'Conor

Judah P. Benjamin to Varina Davis

Benjamin had been severely injured in a carriage accident the year before.

Temple—London
25 April 1881

My dear Mrs Davis

I have just received your very kind letter of the 7th inst, and must answer it at once although by obeying your wishes I must appear very egotistical— My condition I am happy to say is very much improved but I have not yet entirely recovered from the effects of my severe fall in May last. All fractures are healed and the dislocated arm is quite restored to its former strength, but I *cannot* get over the effects of the general nervous shock, and have at this moment my left side under the action of blisters, in the attempt (hitherto vain) to cure the neuralgic pains which have not left me at peace for one moment for the past seven months— Still in spite of this my general improvement is so marked that it excites the observation of my friends and I live in hopes of perfect recovery.

I am just back from *Toulouse!* My son-in-law was recently ordered there on the Head Quarters' Staff of the Military Division there stationed, and I took advantage of the Easter Vacation to go with my wife on a visit for a week to our only child. On arrival we learned that just two hours before her husband had received orders for instant departure to join the Army in Algeria, and he was compelled to leave the next day; so that we brought Ninette back to Paris a disconsolate Widow, to await the result of the Tunisian Expedition.

I have been expecting for some time to hear of the publication of "the book" but from your letter I begin to think that the prospect of its appearance is still remote. Public interest in our struggle has now quite died out in England though of course military men will read with great interest any account of the Campaigns. But here *political* questions have grown up so numerous and important that in the present feverish action of men in all spheres of life, what happened 15 years ago is regarded as "ancient history."

Your letter holds out some hope, but it is almost too good to be true, that you & Mr Davis may make another visit to this side of the water. I need scarcely say how delighted I will be if your project is realised—I shall enjoy your visit more than formerly, as I have more leisure. I am gradually giving up my practice on the ground that when a man has worked for three-score and ten years, he has a right to repose, and I am acting on that theory.

Good bye, my dear Mrs Davis—a thousand kind memories to yourself and husband. You don't know how much pleasure your letter gave me.

Yrs very faithfully,
J. P. Benjamin

Varina Davis to Winnie Davis

This letter, overflowing with tender sentiments, is full of both worldly and Christian advice.

Margaret Howell Stoess had come with her two children for a six months' stay at Beauvoir, while Jefferson Davis was finishing his book. Mrs. Dorsey had left Mr. Davis her excellent library, to add to what was left of the Davis books.

Beauvoir
May, 1881

My own Wincie, my precious darling—

Listen & believe your Mother. If God spares us to go over, I think we shall go to you in Paris about the middle of July. During the time that you are there Miss Mason will be with you at Miss

Dinne's. I propose to let you have some singing, and painting lessons from a *Master*, and French until we come. You will go out every afternoon with Emily Mason, who will take your heart at once by her elegance and tenderness, and you will receive your Mother's friend with the tenderness due to her. In your place I would give myself over to Miss Mason to advise and dress me. She has an extensive acquaintance with the best people, and has lovely taste. She is an authoress of some note, too. I for one am glad to bear testimony to her noble traits. I know you will love her.

Now dearest, best & tenderest beloved, let us with our arms about each other advise together about the Misses Friedlander. It is offensive to me to hear them talk as they do about the girls going away—but they do not mean it to wound you. *Control your words*, do not speak to any one, not to Miss Mason or any one else except kindly of them. Keep your counsel until I come & then say everything out to me.

I know there are disagreements there—you will find them *everywhere*—except in heaven. Look behind the mask at their souls and recognize their many and high virtues. Leave with God their faults, it is His to judge, not ours, and render them heart homage for their wise care of my little ewe lamb. The rough German manner is offensive to me when fault-finding is necessary, but it *means* less harshness than the French Mademoiselle.

Enjoy every hour you can, my precious, so as to lay up a store of jewelled memories with which to decorate your old age.

Your sister is very well off now, and Addison keeps a horse & phaeton. I think you will both be more than comfortably off, and I can die in peace.

Your poor Aunt Margaret is thinking of going home [to Liverpool] the end of next month. Poor child, the prospect is not bright before her, but I trust that Carl's fortunes may improve. The children have benefitted greatly by their stay here & I think Philip will be much stronger than he has been for his six months of America.

Like you, I prefer to be alone with you and your Father here—and oh such larks! such baths in the sea at our door, such drives, such laughs, such drawings & paintings & jokes & cheer. Such a famous big library as we have—with all the dear little childish books, too, with the marks of your precious hands all over them.

Well, dear love, *the* book is done & coming out—"whoop La."

Your Father is well, thank God, too. Now my sweetest sweet—
Goodbye—Goodbye—With dearest love

Your devoted Mother

Jefferson Davis to Varina Davis

Mr. Davis has gone to Montreal to arrange for publication of his book
in Canada.

Mrs. Howell, Davis's mother-in-law, had died in Montreal on November 24, 1867, and was buried there. A handsome monument marks her
grave today.

St. Lawrence Hall Hotel
Montreal, Canada
29th May 1881

My dear Wife

If I had waited until there was something definite to tell of my
trip, I should not be writing now. It seems that we must wait
until an answer is received from England, it may be tomorrow or
some other day.

Yesterday I went to Ma's grave. It is in the most beautiful part
of the cemetery on the mountain, but is unmarked and unprotected.
Both must be done and I would attend to it now if I had the
money. The leaves enclosed were plucked from the grave. Our
loved ones are widely scattered. They are at peace, for whom we
mourn, though today they are lost to us.

Mr. Derby of Appleton's wrote to me that our book had been
sent to Texas, Savannah, Mobile & Memphis.

Goodbye dearest, I am longing to be with you—

Ever lovingly
Your Husband

In June of 1881 *The Rise and Fall of the Confederate Government* was published by Appleton's in two thick volumes and in
several bindings from elegant to plain. The work was well sub-
scribed for in the South and naturally welcomed and praised. But
the Northern papers generally ignored it; even professedly Democratic periodicals gave it only scant attention or none. The New

York *Herald* printed an adverse criticism by General Longstreet, who had turned Republican and was hated by loyal Southerners. Some highly favorable reviews, however, came from English magazines and papers. Appleton's did virtually nothing to advertise or push the book. The chilly reception of his monumental work in the North was but another of the manifold disappointments Jefferson Davis had endured since the war. Yet he took comfort in the belief that posterity would eventually judge the Southern cause and Confederate administration aright, to realize that secession was not a revolution but the exercise of a Constitutional right. His mail was flooded with personal letters of appreciation, three of which are reproduced here.

L. B. Northrop to Jefferson Davis

Commissary General Northrop had been in a position to appreciate fully the magnitude of Davis's task and the harassments and petty treacheries he had to endure as President.

Minor Orcus (Va.) July 25th, 1881

Dear Davis,

Many thanks for your volumes received from the Appleton house 12 days ago. Though incompetent to estimate such a work, I am sufficiently informed to say, that no man *has ever lived,* who had such a problem as you undertook and had to face. American politicians and their followers being the worst of material—they scrupled not at open opposition and secret machination while the members of Congress speculated in stocks and commodities, and the people generally became speculators.

America has never produced another man who could simultaneously have comprehended the problem of organizing, supplying and directing internally civil and military, while conducting all external relations.

There is a marvellous unity in your character, manifested in this work. Charlemagne managed civil and military affairs but he had unity within, and no secret assailants to his position. No other man could have done what you did and *no man in America could have held your ground for one year.*

May you have health and long life is the prayer of yours ever

L. B. Northrop

Alexander James Beresford-Hope to Jefferson Davis

Davis saw Beresford-Hope in England before he received this letter sent to Mississippi.

> Arklow House
> Connaught Place, W.
> August 7, 1881

My dear Mr. Davis:

Your gift is indeed a generous and most acceptable one and what I shall ever prize for the sake of the donor, for the tale it tells and for the war which it commemorates.

I had already made myself acquainted with it and even dared pride myself as advertising it on this side of the Atlantic.

I have directed a copy of the Saturday Review containing the notice to be forwarded to you.

You may have heard of my irreparable calamity. My wife was called away at Nice on March 18th, just as we were looking forward to years of peace and renewed health. Thank God, however, her last months were not only painless but bright and happy and full of all interest to her about those subjects which always were most interesting to her pure and brilliant mind.

Happiness for me is at an end but duty remains and the hope of the hereafter. I had a short time since published (anonymously) and unknown to her a novel as a surprise. I have now brought out another edition with a commemoratory preface as a memorial of her and I beg your acceptance of a copy of it.

I trust that Mrs. Davis and your family are well. Pray offer my kindest regards and believe me, my dear Mr. Davis,

> Yours very truly,
> A. J. Beresford Hope

William Nelson Pendleton to Jefferson Davis

General Pendleton, though an Episcopal clergyman, had been Lee's famed chief artillerist in the Army of Northern Virginia. He is now Rector of Grace Episcopal Church in Lexington.

Lexington, Virginia.
Sept. 6th, 1881

My Dear and honoured Friend.

Since receiving your valued favour of June 21st—I have not written to you, mainly because of the probability you then indicated of your taking with Mrs. Davis a voyage across the Atlantic. Now I write, taking for granted you have reached home again.

First let me thank you for your two admirable volumes, most kindly sent me by Judge Tenney.

With the deepest interest and with more than full approval, have I read them. Even with wondering thankfulness to the Supreme Guide unto truth, that you were enabled to secure so many documents proving the right, —and that you were granted the wise virtue of *charitable allowance* for dreadful wrongs of all sorts, while faithfully exhibiting the wrongs.

Your great estimate of Genls. A. S. Johnston, R. E. Lee, and Stonewall Jackson, is in full accord with the judgment of Christendom.

The facts brought out by you in the latter half of your 2nd Vol. respecting what they call, "the period of reconstruction," will tell more than all else and stamp upon the conscience of Christendom, horror at Yankee atrocities.

The difficulty is to get any large number really to look into and consider the realities. In Appleton's Review, I have noticed extracts from some English publications justly and highly commendatory of your great contribution to reliable History. But rarely has been published, so far as I know, any mention of your work, even in professedly democratic papers, at the North. They are prejudiced. They are afraid for the actual truth to be known.

A pleasant account of the "Golden wedding" of my wife and self, on the 15th July, was published. I hope it fell under your eyes.

Farewell! Love to you all. And God's blessing be yours forever!

Your affectionate Friend,
W. N. Pendleton

Jefferson Davis to Varina Davis

Mr. and Mrs. Davis had sailed on August 17 to fetch Winnie. Mr. Davis has left Mrs. Davis and Winnie in Paris while he visits Dudley Mann.

Chantilly
13th Sept. 1881

My dear Wife:

I arrived safely and had a cordial welcome. Mr. Mann inquired most affectionately of you and Winnie. I am much better than when we parted, slept well, and move without pain. It rained hard when I reached the station, the first stop after leaving Paris, but now it is bright and I write in the sunshine. God grant it may be bright in Paris and that our richest treasure may be well enough to enjoy it with you. Pray do not fatigue yourself or allow the cares of shopping to prey upon your spirits. Though not rich, we can meet all your requirements without going to the "poor 'ouse."

With all my heart's fondest love for you & my baby

I am,
Your Husband

Mr. Mann sends his kindest regard to you & Winnie with hopes of soon seeing you. J. D.

Varina Davis to Jefferson Davis

Marie is the maid of Dudley Mann who followed Toinette.

Paris
September, 1881

My dear Husband,

Thanks for your kind letter. I am so glad that your cold was not increased by the journey and that you found Mr. Mann well as usual. Was it not a tender thought in him to speak of willing to Winnie a present which pleased her. Marie came in a few hours after you left us and was as she usually is very agreeable. She brought Winnie a lovely basket of her own work. If she were a lady she could not be better mannered or more comme il faut.

Today we went with Miss Durette on the top of a tram to Sèvres & saw glowing china, and the world seemed to me to be the throne of ceramics. As I looked on the angel forms depicted there, the longing of my life to create something that would live after me was greater than ever. A vague kind of awe came over me in looking at a vase of men running foot-races which had been baked 350 years before Christ's coming. We wanted to bring away a little thing, but the prices of ever so small things were above us. We reached home at night to find your letter.

This house is full to the brim tonight & so as you may imagine is our little room with the contents of the two poured into it. Do give to dear Mr. Mann all the love which I can feel for the most stainless of men and the purest patriot, as well as the truest friend. People nowadays do not grow old like him with the faith and tenderness of youth in old age.

Devotedly,
Your Wife

Jefferson Davis to Varina Davis

Winnie, who had been remarkably healthy during her five years in Germany, has now been taken to a Paris physician by her sedulous, anxious mother, and when he can find nothing whatever wrong, his diagnosis is "overwork."

Chantilly, France
September, 1881

My dear Wife,
Your letter was welcome as your letters ever are to me, but I am at a loss to understand what the Doctor means by "overwork." My baby may have been fatigued by going about, but that her mind has not been oppressed appears not only by brightness but still more by the ready comprehension of a new or different phase of a subject.

May not the air of Paris be too stimulating for her? God grant that she may be as soon and as certainly relieved as you hope. I will go to the Hotel here today and see what sort of a place it would be for you. There is much here to be seen out of doors—Race horses, stag hounds, etc.

Mr. Mann is but little changed and we took a long walk over the race course from which neither of us suffered. He does not seem to think of my ever leaving him.

Wm. Mann & Wife are expected in Paris about this time. She is an invalid and requires constant change.

Marie is everything in this establishment and fulfils her varied duties wonderfully, so that Mr. Mann probably could not be as comfortable elsewhere or "elsehow."

With boundless love, my heart's treasures, and kisses for you both. I am your devoted

J. D.

Jefferson Davis to Varina Davis

Varina has paid a visit to Chantilly, and she has begged her husband to be examined and treated by some Paris doctor who claims to rejuvenate the aged. Davis passed his seventy-third birthday in June.

Chantilly
22d Sept. 1881

My dear dear Wife,

After your brief visit I found that I had neglected to give you the key of my valise. It is herein inclosed.

I have put on the the thick socks purchased in Canada and my feet are warmer by the change. If you were in America it would be easy to find patent medicines promising more than a Parisian Medicine, and I have not "the face to be shaved" by either. It is not for me like the Eagle to renew my youth or by the equally silly fiction to find restoration in some spring. Let us "accept the situation" in this the natural and inevitable decay of all earthly things, and by cheerfully yielding to the law, mitigate its device.

It is not that I am obstinate, and so I will promise to come to town say tomorrow if the day is bright and will hear your Doctor;

but whether I will take his prescription is more than doubtful. Plainly I have not force enough to resist much treatment and prefer to die a natural rather than an experimental death. "I am satisfied."

Kiss my baby so lately in her fader's arms.

With all the love of my heart for both, and earnest prayers for your health and happiness, I am ever devotedly,

Your Husband

Jefferson Davis to Varina Davis

In November the Davises sailed from Liverpool for New York on the *Necker*, which docked on December 7. Mr. Davis was very happy to be back on American soil, and told a newspaper reporter that he was looking forward to peaceful retirement at Beauvoir. But a few days later (December 18, 1881), Joseph E. Johnston gave a story to the Philadelphia *Press* that virtually accused Davis of stealing the Confederate treasure, which he exaggeratedly estimated at $2,500,000. The libel poisoned Winnie's homecoming. Johnston's attack on Davis's integrity stirred indignation in the North as well as the South. Hundreds rushed to Davis's defense in newspapers. An enormous amount of mail poured into Beauvoir. Davis kept absolutely silent and let people defend him as they would. Johnston's calumny lost him the respect of many of his former friends and advocates.

Mrs. Davis is visiting Maggie Hayes in Memphis.

Beauvoir, Harrison Co., Miss.
23 Jany 1882

My dear Wife,

I returned from New Orleans sooner than I expected. A heap of letters received about my book keep me very busy. Benjamin I learn has made a full and conclusive exposure of Johnston's slander. It was said to have been published in the *Picayune,* but the paper which I expected to find here seems to have been destroyed, in my absence.

It is quite cold here to day. Tell the baby we have two little lambs & she is wanted to take care of them.

We had a grand meeting and banquet of the La. Division of the Army of Va. on Saturday night. Many flattering demonstrations were made for "meuns" & though I had written excusing myself on the ground of a cough from speaking, I was not permitted to be silent. Your friends in town made many inquiries for you.

Kiss my dear children one & all for their loving Father and grand Father.

Your devoted Husband

Jefferson Davis to Addison Hayes

At seventeen Winnie Davis attends her first Mardi Gras ball.

Addison Hayes has taken over the business management of Brierfield plantation, while retaining his improving position as a bank cashier in Memphis. The Mississippi River flood of 1882 damaged Brierfield severely. And for the rest of his life Davis was to be plagued by overflows which took most of his income to repair levees.

Maggie Hayes now has two baby girls.

New Orleans, 23rd Feb. 1882

Dear Addison,

I came over to attend Winnie on the night of the Mardi Gras, and shall return this afternoon to Beauvoir.

The news from the river above Vicksburg renders me apprehensive for the fate of Brierfield. The cut-off raised the water at Ursino above the former level of flood tide and I fear that the levees adjacent have been neglected so as to be insufficient. I have written to Mr. Cox suggesting to him to see the Ursino and Palmyra people and call their attention to the matter.

Your Mother and Winnie have been here since last week. Winnie proposes to remain some days longer, but your Mother will return with me.

I was disappointed that my daughter Pollie did not with the babies come to us when your Mother returned and often wish they were with us in our soft climate and clean sand. Tell the baby I am lonesome for her and very pleased that she thinks and talks of me. I intend to go to Brierfield soon. Have heard nothing of the hands engaged for you. With tenderest love to my daughters, I am affectionately

Jefferson Davis

Jefferson Davis to Addison Hayes

Vicksburg
20 April 1882

Dear Addison,

I propose to go to the Brierfield to-morrow on the "Headlight" and fear there will be little land to be seen. Mr. Cox wrote to me that he would, if well enough, go on the next day to the plantation, but I do not learn of his passing here as would have been the case if he had gone down.

The anomalous action of the river puts it out of my power to form any opinion of the future, but I hope we may yet make a partial crop of cotton.

With love to my Daughters, I am ever affectionately

Yours
Jefferson Davis

Burgess T. Montgomery to Varina Davis

This letter from a former slave at Brierfield was written more than five years after Jefferson Davis's death in 1889, but it gives an unusual slant on Brierfield plantation life in 1882 and reveals Davis's solicitude for his Negro tenants and their feeling for him.

Treasury Department
Office of the Secretary
Washington, D.C., January 7, 1895

Esteemed and Kind Madam:—

You will please pardon me, your humble servant, for the indulgence assumed in writing you.

I desired very much to see you when you were here at the National City in October, but was denied the pleasure, owing to urgent duties which prevented me at that time.

The writer is Burgess Montgomery, nephew of Ben Montgomery and cousin of Thornton and Isiah, formerly of your plantation at Davis Bend, Miss.

It is now twelve years or more since I saw you, then you were accompanied by the President, your illustrious and dear companion and our devoted friend, who was visiting the plantation just after the overflow of 1882, looking after the interests and distresses of those with whom he, and you, were so long related. In the meantime contributing to the needs of many that were rendered destitute by the floods, who would otherwise have undergone severe hardship and suffering were it not for the generous and immediate aid extended them at the hands of the Deceased. If you remember, about that time the writer was leader of the little Brass Band, and on occasions when you and the President were on a visit to the plantation, it was always for me, a great pleasure to call the Band out for a serenade in honor of your distinguished and welcome presence in our midst.

If you further remember, it was also your humble correspondent (Burgess) who wrote the President on behalf of the Band, asking his kind assistance in procuring uniform suits for the latter, in reference to which, I am proud to say, he promptly responded, as was usual for him in all matters or requests pertaining to the promotion and advancement of his colored friends.

I am often remindful, and shall never forget, the kind and friendly letter in reply, which *he* (the President) addressed to me, containing, in substance, expressions of the warmest sympathy for the members of the Band. In the meantime, your kindly interviewing the writer in relation to same, on leaving the Bend en route to your lower Mississippi home, at the same time requesting that I (your humble servant) should forward you the measures of each member of the Band, which would enable you to select suits to advantage. This I did, and in a very short time the Band was called together to receive their true friends, the Honorable Jefferson Davis and Mrs. Varina Davis.

This was an occasion of thankfulness and rejoicing on the part of the members of the Band, and the community as well, though many of us to whom the Deceased and yourself were so long devoted and cherished were driven from the dear old home by the boundless and destructive floods of the Mississippi.

On hearing the sad news that the monster death, having reached forth a defiant hand, thereby bereaving us of him that was true and dear to us all, laid aside our labors and assembled with offerings of eulogy and homage to his excellent and immortal memory, in the meantime expressing our deepest sympathies and sorrow for the bereaved wife, and the dear ones that survive him.

Since that time, however, many of the dear old friends who were gathered together in commemoration of the departure of that great soldier and statesman, they have also fallen by the wayside. I have just received a letter from Arkansas, about the sudden death of Uncle Granderson Bray, he fell dead in the field, picking cotton, his wife, Aunt Amanda, was with him at the time. They were living at Corner Stone, near Pine Bluff, Arkansas; he died of heart disease. George, Steward, William, Kanagan and old lady Hagar Allen, are the only ones left of the old folks now in that neighborhood.

I have a situation at present in the Treasury Department. Having access to the Library at the Department, I have selected and am reading at present *The Rise and Fall of the Confederate Government,* by the Distinguished Author and Statesman above referred to. I have just finished reading the first volume, commencing with the second volume, and judging from what I have read thus far, I am satisfied to say, there is not, to my mind, a book or volume in existence containing a more truthful, succinct, and impartial, account of the casualties of the late war and its subsequent events.

My dear Mrs. Varina, I shall have to again ask your kindly sympathy and pardon. If in any way, referring to those gone days I have overborne your friendly patience, forgive me, as I feel constrained to admit of some expression of feelings that were so long suppressed.

I enclose herewith a specimen of a circular, with description and drawings of a Ditching Plow, as invented by my Father and myself, which I hope you will be pleased to notice.

With the highest regards and best wishes for you and Miss Winnie, I beg leave to remain, as ever,

Your obedient and humble Servant
Burgess T. Montgomery

Mrs. Varina Davis
Hotel Marlborough, New York

Becket Howell to Jefferson Davis

Becket Howell, Mrs. Davis's brother, who had failed to succeed on a rented farm in Louisiana, has come to Brierfield to act as overseer. O. B.

Cox, who was plantation manager for many years, has withdrawn. Hughes is the storekeeper.

May 25th, 1882

My dear Brother

I arrived here all safe on Monday and found every thing moving along. All the teams are at work breaking up land and planting just at fast as they can. The water is going down and I think if we don't have any more mishaps, we will make a very fair crop. We have nearly all of the land out planted and a good deal of cotton up and chopped out. Mr. Hughes has been sick, he says he will write to you in a few days. We will both meet the steamer on Monday. I will write tomorrow about the place when the water gets so that I can ride over it.

Give love to Sis & Winnie.

Your affec— Brother
B. K. Howell

P.S. I have sent for more hands. We have room now for 8 families.

William Nelson Pendleton to Jefferson Davis

William Preston Johnston had been installed as President of Tulane University.

Lexington, Virginia
July 14th, 1882

My dear & honoured Friend,

Your very gratifying letter of the 2nd inst. in reply to mine of the 24th ult., was duly received. And I now write again under special instructions of the Executive Committee of our Lee Memorial Association, &c, Chairman of said Committee, to convey to you the Committee's cordial thanks for the measure of promise in your letter, respecting the Memorial Address desired of you next summer.

Col. Wm Preston Johnston, so truly valued by us all, is with us just now, on a little excursion from his at least supposed Malarial Scene of Service in Louisiana. And as he is a member of our Committee, we held a meeting today to profit by his presence. Had he been communicated with, as my last to you supposed, he would gladly have visited you, & delivered more urgently in person, our cordial invitation.

As said, it is our united & most earnest request, that, you will deliver the Lee Memorial Address at the Inauguration of the Genl's Mausoleum here, & statue therein, on June 28th, 1883, the Mausoleum being a rear Structure entered from the chapel of Washington & Lee University.

For controlling reasons we judge & feel that, Providence permitting, as we trust & pray, the just tribute to Genl. Lee on the occasion, can be more fitly rendered by yourself than by any other mortal.

Meantime, in the entire view, may I not, as an honouring friend ask you to set about at once preparing the Address desired? So as to have it ready, if granted life & vigour to deliver it. Or to let us have it for other use, should the Lord remove or disable you.

Of course, if we have the happiness of your coming, Mrs. Davis, & any other home mate, must come with you. And while Genl. Custis Lee will press for you, my plain household will, as would several others, longingly open, heart, arms, & doors.

Your attached friend,
W. N. Pendleton

God bless you all!

Jefferson Davis to Maggie Hayes

In a serious "bread riot" in Richmond during the war, President Davis calmed the mob by making them a speech and exhibiting his own empty pockets.

Beauvoir, Harrison Co., Miss.
7th Aug. 1882

My darling Little Pollie,

By letters from your Mother and Husband I have the great satisfaction of hearing that you have so much improved that in a few days will be able to start for Beauvoir. I cannot express the joy it will give me to have you in my arms, with the confident assurance that the sea air will be beneficial to you as well as to the dear children. It has been so difficult to get you back, that I thus early insist upon your coming so fully packed up, as to enable you to stay a long, long time with us.

Winnie and I are quite alone here, and she, I fear, finds it very dull. As for me quiet is most desirable and my correspondence is more occupation than is agreeable. All sorts of people write to me about all supposable matters and if I don't answer they generally write again. Those who fall in debt must think like Prince David, I have a refuge for all such, rather they must think I have the Philosopher's stone with which to turn Yankee maledictions into gold, for they do not ask to join the refugees, but to have money sent to them. It would cost me very little to repeat my action with the so-called "bread rioters," whose clamor I hushed by turning my pockets wrong side out, and telling them to take the contents.

We have had rain almost every day since St. Swithin's Day, and some times it has rained twice in the day, to make up for misses. One old friend of yours arrived to-night, Robert, and he seemed much pleased at the prospect of seeing you.

If your Mother should be with you when this arrives give her much love. With love to Addison and the dear babies, I am with tenderest devotion,

> Your Father,
> Jefferson Davis

Jefferson Davis to Varina Davis

Becket Howell has been taken seriously ill at Brierfield four months after his arrival. Mrs. Davis is frantic, and Mr. Davis has left Beauvoir for New Orleans to go to his brother-in-law's bedside. Becket died after a brief illness.

> New Orleans, 12 Sept. 1882

Dear Wife,

I have waited in vain for a telegram from Vicksburg which I hoped Hughes would send up by the "Cannon." If I do not get news before 5 P.M. I will start for Brierfield, by rail if the little boat does not leave before I can reach Vicksburg, otherwise by the Steam Boat "Cannon." Give my tenderest love to my dear children each and all. I pray you to exercise as much self-control as is possible; it is needful for the preservation of your health.

Whatever is practicable shall be done for Becket and we will be down to Beauvoir without unnecessary delay, D.V.

Ever affectionately,
Your Husband

Jefferson Davis to Maggie Hayes

Maggie with her two baby girls has just made a visit of several weeks to Beauvoir. The elder, christened Varina, is often called Daughter. The younger is named Lucy.

Beauvoir, Harrison Co., Miss.
12th Oct 1882

My darling Pollie,

I miss you every hour and long for my sweet baby more and more as her absence lengthens. It is one of the misfortunes of age that its power to dispense with the presence of the loved one diminishes while its dependence on them increases.

Your Mother went to New Orleans last evening, expects to return to morrow.

Times here are quite as you left them, the most important change being that the oranges are ripening.

Addison has no doubt fuller and later news from Brierfield than I could give him, and they are not so cheering as to warrant being twice told.

Give my love to him and to the babies. Tell "Daughter" the coast is but half the place it was when she was here and that as you have two babies her Bampa thinks he ought to have his, to help him to be happy.

Farewell, my precious child, you have ever been to me a source of joy, and a comfort in saddest hours, when joy was only possible in the sense of relief to sorrow. With a Father's blessing on his child, I send you a thousand and more kisses.

Devotedly
Your Father

Jefferson Davis to Varina Davis

Many Northerners, as well as Southerners, named their sons for Jefferson Davis.

                                        Beauvoir
                                        Monday Night—February
                                        1883

Dear Wife,

We have had a dismal day, the rain drip, drop as described on
the "ghost's walk," & I fear you have had as much trouble as on
the day we spent when last in the city together.

Joe Davis came up today with Mr. Clark, the Atty of the R.R.,
and Mr. Jeff. Davis Bill of Conn., who brought a letter from
his Father stating that he had named his Son for me on the day
of my farewell address to the Senate. The young man is intelligent,
direct and quite satisfactory. Winnie had resolved to be neuralgic,
but as the necessity of effort demanded she came out and if the
visitors did not admire her the defect was in them not in my baby.

All is as you left it, and we are lovingly expectant of your coming,
as ever

                                        Affectionately,
                                        Your Husband

Varina Davis to Jefferson Davis

While Davis is at Brierfield Mrs. Davis is directing the occasional
workers needful to keep the Beauvoir place in condition.

                                        Beauvoir Feb. 26th 1883

My dear Husband,

There is no news here since you left except that the fence in the
vineyard will be done tomorrow, and I thought I had best plant
the corn before William left, after first hoeing & manuring the vines.
I have not seen Aleck to speak to him. After much "looking around"
I think I have found a man in Biloxi who will plow the orchard
on Wednesday next. Tom is getting on fine with the trees, but
Richard is with Robert, so I set William Stone to hoeing, and made
Dan burn the brush which he has finished today.

I think Robert's tastes in hardware are inclined to the "too too
utterly aesthetic" & since you have gone away they have burst
forth in hammers; he sends for two for himself he says, having

broken two today. I found myself reflecting on the very superior manner of building adopted in Solomon's temple when hammers were not needful.

It is very cold here & the North wind is howling round this corner like the voices in "The Tale of Two Cities." It is hoped that the change will prevent the water from covering us out of sight.

As I am more than tired, having been to Biloxi to see the plowman, "Will coil up my rope." Bishop Green has not come yet. Dr. Jones wrote to say he & Genl Fitzhugh Lee would not do so just now as you were absent.

Pray take care of yourself & do not take cold as it is quite too prevalent now to be mild.

With kindest regards to Mr. Hughes & his wife and the baby.

> Affectionately your wife
> **V. Davis**

Jefferson Davis to Custis Lee

The Reverend Mr. Pendleton, who was the chairman in control of the Lee Memorial meeting, had died in January, and without Davis's knowledge the new chairman has invited General Joseph E. Johnston to preside. At the last minute Johnston did not go to the ceremony, but he had prevented the appearance of ex-President Davis.

> Beauvoir, Harrison Co, Miss.
> June 18th 1883

Genl. G. W. C. Lee,

My dear friend,

Though I do not fear that you will misunderstand or ascribe to any want of esteem and affection for your Father's memory the fact of my failing to deliver an address at the inauguration of his statue, it seems proper and due to the close relations which have so long existed between us that I should offer to you a full explanation of the cause which will prevent my attendance. I had declined many invitations to deliver addresses at the inauguration of Confederate monuments, and did so under the sad conviction that I was physically unequal to the task. When the late Genl. Pendleton asked me to deliver an address at the inauguration of the Lee statue, he presented the one ocasion on which I could not decline, D.V., to make the attempt.

The letters which passed between us led me to suppose that he, in every respect so worthy to preside, not the least being his devoted friendship and high admiration of Genl. Lee, was to be the person, who, as Chairman of the executive committee would have control of the meeting. After the death of the lamented Pendleton I received a letter from Mr. J. J. White, informing me that the Executive Committee of the Memorial Association had instructed him to address me giving such information in regard to their work and the ceremonies to be held on the 28th of June next as I might desire to have. He informed me that J. E. Johnston was expected to preside at the inauguration of the monument in June; that my address would be delivered about 11 A.M. and that Maj. Jno. W. Daniel of Virginia would deliver an address expecially on the life of Genl. Lee since the war. To this I replied that among the items so communicated is the statement that Genl. J. E. Johnston is to preside over the meeting. That fact not previously communicated or anticipated caused me promptly to withdraw my consent heretofore given to deliver an address on that occasion.

The persistent hostility of Genl. J. E. Johnston to myself arose from the fact that I would not recognize him as superior in rank to Genl. Lee, culminating in gross misrepresentation in his book published after the war and crowned by his vile slander in regard to Confederate treasure. Confederates generally looked upon this last act as a disgraceful manifestation of a sometime concealed hostility, and I could not with due self-respect appear before a meeting over which he was to preside. But this was not all, he had been the envious detractor of Lee during the war and in the publication referred to had tried to rob Lee of the credit due to him for his successes in the seven days' battle. You will remember his long letter written to me on Sept. 14th 1861, protesting against the relative rank assigned to himself and other Generals.

On the 29th of July, 1861, Genl. J. E. Johnston wrote to Genl. Cooper, Adj. Genl., for which letter I extract the following sentence. "I have received daily, orders purporting to come from the 'Hd. Qrs. of the forces' some of them in relation to the internal affairs of this army. Such orders I cannot regard because they are illegal. Permit me to suggest, that orders to me, should come from your office."

Lee in his generosity, magnanimity and self-abnegation, chose to overlook this insubordination. To him our cause was everything, and questions of rank were by him in comparison with our success, regarded as nothing.

Now, sir, I hope you will appreciate why it was so objectionable to me to see the envious detractor of Lee presiding where honors were to be paid to his memory, and why I could not consent to recognize in that position the man who stained his soul with an inexcusable calumny, which bore not on me only, but was calculated, if not designed, to bring discredit upon the Confederacy. All this I explained to the true soldier, Genl. Early, who was sent to argue with me that I might agree to go to the inauguration, but left me with the conviction that my position was correct. I have written thus fully to you because I wished you to know the motives which governed me and to be satisfied with my decision.

I hope we will be able to place something on the graves of Lee and Jackson on the day of the inauguration which though in itself a small offering, will serve to express how very near and dear their memories are to our household.

My wife joins me in kindest remembrance, and cordial good wishes for you and your sisters and brothers.

I am as ever, yours faithfully,
Jefferson Davis

[*Note on envelope:*]
Genl. Johnston was not present on the occasion in question but even if he had not been invited by those who were not aware of all the circumstances, there was no reason for any one to take exception to Mr. Davis' not being present.

G. W. C. Lee

PLANTATION HARASSMENTS,
VISITORS,
AND A FITTING MEMORIAL

Winnie Davis to Her Father

Jefferson Davis has gone on one of his periodic trips to Brierfield.
Boy, Flora, and Diana were the current family dogs. They enjoyed
morning sea baths with Jefferson Davis. Ned is the horse.

Beauvoir
August 22nd, 1883

My darling Father,

I can't tell you how much I appreciated the sweet note you sent
me from New Orleans, I was just feeling the first pangs of loneliness
after your departure when it came.

Poor *Boy* was taken ill shortly after you left, and although we
did all we could he died this morning; he was buried near his father,
poor fellow. *Flora,* and *Diana* are well and frisk about as usual,
though I see they miss you by the way they scratch the front gallery
in the morning, expecting you to come and take them bathing.

I had the nitre given to Ned, who is now quite well again I believe, as he jumped the fence the other day with great ease.

What shall I do about the grapes as they get ripe? If you will
tell me where to send, I can have them packed and sent to New
Orleans, can I not? I would so like to be able to help some how.

I have not had use for the ten dollars, as yet, so they have answered amply as a reserve fund.

You do not know how all miss you, do come back soon, and take
care that you do not get ill.

With a heart full of love, I am as ever devotedly

Winnanne

Jefferson Davis to Custis Lee

Beauvoir, Miss.
8th Oct. 1883

My dear Sir,

The question has arisen as to what prevented your assignment to command in W. Virginia in 1863–4. It has more than once been represented that your Father declined to approve of your selection for that command, and that my purpose to give it to you was thereby defeated. My recollection is that I offered it to you, and that one or more of your associates on the Staff told me that your repugnance to taking it was so great that I conformed to your wishes. Please tell me as far as your memory serves you what were the facts in regard to this matter.

I was sorry to hear of your ill health and trust that this may find your state normal again. If you find the winter climate of Lexington too severe Mrs. Davis and I would joyously welcome you to our quiet home on the sea shore.

I am as ever, truly your friend,
Jefferson Davis

[*Note on envelope:*]
Mr. Davis is altogether correct in his recollection as above stated.

G. W. C. Lee

Jefferson Davis to Lise Mitchell Hamer

Lise Hamer, Davis's great-niece, is living at Hurricane in the Greek temple library that was not burned during the war.

Brierfield Store, 21st Mch. 1884

My dear Niece,

I have returned late this afternoon from the Brierfield levee. By working night & day we are keeping ahead of the rising water.

The crevasse at Buckner's has caused, I suppose, a check in the rate of the rise, and encourages the hope that we may keep the levee above the river water, but if the water should again commence to rise as fast as reported at Vicksburg, our means will not suffice to prevent it from running over the levee and overflowing the Island. In the pressure of such danger it is deemed due to you to give you this warning.

For our common interest I will do all which is possible, and earnestly hope for your sake, as well as my own, that the threatening evil may be averted.

Affectionately
Your Uncle

Bishop Richard H. Wilmer to Jefferson Davis

Winnie is to be confirmed in Mobile and the Bishop desires the Davises to be his house guests.

Diocese of Alabama
Lock Box 964
Mobile, Ala.
April 9, 1884

My dear & honored Sir

Yrs just received. It gives us all so much pleasure to look forward to the sojourn of yourself & household under our roof. My children & grandchildren are trained in our cherished traditions & your presence will only serve to strengthen & perpetuate their loyalty.

I will meet you at the station & bring you directly to my house. I have said no word about your coming: taking it for granted that you would prefer it so. Otherwise there could be many glad to greet you. I propose that you all come to my house. We have abundance of rooms & it would enhance our pleasure greatly to have you all together. We can ride in, Sunday morning, in time for church. Mrs. Wilmer joins me in kind regards to yourself & the ladies & desires me to express her great gratification at the prospect of having you with us.

Very sincerely & Respectfully
Rich. H. Wilmer

Varina Davis to Maggie Hayes

All sorts of Northern visitors, as well as those from the South, came to call and be entertained at Beauvoir.

Beauvoir, Missi.
11th April, 1884

My own Darling,

I have hardly sat down since you went away trying to get everything in order "for Bessie Landson," who bye-the-bye had "lit out" home. In the midst of it all, when the things were on end, the Illinois Press delegation came & after I had tumbled things all back into the room, they poured over the house. They went, & I made all things turn out again & this time Mrs Miller Owen & two Chicago ladies came—for the day. No butler—that left Ellen waiting like an angel, everybody delighted with her. Roses & lilies & daffydowndillies on the table. Things turned out again with a whoop when a lady & gentleman from N. York, Nellie Grey & Minnie Davis came for the day &,&,&,&.

We were all three to go to Winnie's confirmation tomorrow & stay with the Bishop of Alabama for Sunday & Saturday night, but your father is not well enough to go, and I would stay with him & let the poor child be confirmed alone, but he says he will go if I will not—so I leave with her in the morning.

I packed you a box of flowers today notwithstanding the hurry & poor Mr White went everywhere to get white violets for your Easter. The roses are more splendid now than I ever saw in anybody's garden, and I could pick 500 a day if I wished. The new roses are so splendid they look unnatural—I put one cut short in half bloom & another that looks like pale pink shells—Mme. Françoise Petite. Every thing is redolent with perfume. Oh how we do miss you, my dearest Daughter—my three precious ones & may God give you many joyful Easters, and his grace to enjoy them in holy guise.

Ellen goes home too for good next week as her Mother is laid up with the rheumatism, so behold me ready to teach a new cook when I can find her—green peas plenty here & other "vegebles" coming in.

Your Father says "give abundance of love to my dear Daughters & the sweet little children every one of whom should be on the 'coase' in the big water"—

Devotedly,
Your Mother

Sent flowers this evening, so inquire at Express.

Jefferson Davis to Varina Davis

Mrs. Davis is in Memphis with Margaret Hayes, who has borne a boy child on October first. Always there seemed to be troubles at Brierfield. Cameron is the most recent overseer.

Beauvoir, 22nd Oct., 1884

Dear Wife,

Thanks for your letter which would naturally have more interest than I could give to one from here, so it had logically followed that Winnie's letters keeping you advised of home matters it has seemed to me permissible that the thief of time should be allowed to catch me.

I am in trouble about taking Winnie to Brierfield, Hughes writes that they are all sick there, that the cisterns are dry, and the wells failing. I have written to him dissatisfied with his "way of managing," and have written to Cameron that I would not obstruct a new arrangement he might make elsewhere next year.

I got a horse from Mr. Alba. He is large, gentle, rides well and is warranted to "work any where." Winnie likes his gaits, and if it had not been said he would have to work she would have been satisfied with him. "A man must do something for his bread" and so, maun, poor men's horses do.

With love to my Daughters and Sons. I am affectionately
Your Husband

Jefferson Davis to Varina Davis

Because of weak lungs Addison Hayes has been urged by physicians to move to Colorado Springs. There he later became President of the First National Bank.

Beauvoir, Missi.
25th Oct. 1884

Dear Wife,

I have nothing to tell of home and nothing pleasant of things abroad.

It grieves me to know that the health of Addison required him to leave so directly. God grant the Drs. may be mistaken.

The new horse is quite gentle, rides well, works any where, and is handsome. We have had a general purgation of the chicken house and the maids' quarters.

Winnie and I propose to go to the city on Monday, to return if practicable the same day. She wants to see the Dentist, and I go to meet Hughes, who has notified me of his coming to make harder commercial and fiscal arrangements than I shall approve and so go to check.

With love to each of our children and abounding portion for yourself. I am in lonely desolation, but not in hopelessness, as the hour for your return is near.

Your Husband

Jefferson Davis to Varina Davis

Besides incompetence, storekeepers and overseers were sometimes guilty of drunkenness. The recurring floods had driven the old tenants to seek other abodes.

Brierfield, Missi
9th Dec. 1884

My dear Wife,

Since my arrival one trouble has chased another like waves, each being the herald of one to come, but the hardest to bear has been the disappointment to others from the failure of the new levee.

Lize came to see me, and asked if I would not build a private levee around the front of Brierfield; the survey showed that it would cost about six thousand five hundred dollars, & I had to confess my inability to do it.

Here I am where many of our most peaceful days were passed. Is it that all nature has changed, or is the deterioration in me? It matters little how the inquiry may be answered as both are alike bad and irremediable. We shall make about sixty bales of cotton, some pea vine hay and nothing more. Cameron, to show the island "What we are," has paid the highest wages, wasted and worn the animate and inanimate, with a bill of plantation expenses of say $10,000.

He wants to stay and "work the place out of debt." I looked such surprise at his suggestion that he has not given me any further notice of kind intentions.

Mrs. Hughes has no servant. She has a hard time and looks worn & weak.

There is not one of our old people on the place; reports are current of some on the way, but confirmation is needed, and they may be like Cameron's crowd from Wyoming, "long on the journey."

I hope my darling Pollie and her babies are with you all "safe and sound." When their sweet voices fall upon my ear I shall not weep to the lay, but try to drown dull care and look out for the morrow without fear of the poor house. Hughes came in from a visit to Lovell, just before I turned over the page, and in the condition old Sullivan was when he & Crittenden had taken "a half dozen on the shells," so as the rhetoricians would term it his visit has been an episode; but fear not, as it is not my intention to resume the thread of my Iliad. It would not like that of Penelope do to weave again.

Give my tenderest love to Pollie and the *wee Addison*.

God be with you, ever prays

Your Husband

William F. Howell to Varina Davis

Mrs. Davis's last remaining brother writes from his deathbed in San Francisco. He died two days later. Jefferson Davis had offered his unfortunate brother-in-law a home at Beauvoir.

City and County Hospital
San Francisco, Dec. 12th, 1884

My dearest old Sister

Dear Col. Roach did all that he could to inform you speedily of my illness as soon as he learned it himself, but nobody knew it when I came except two Frenchmen, and I did not expect an invitation home and only expected to die here, so it was three weeks before I, between welcoming death and going into it faster than I then imagined, was enlightened. Sister, my darling, I am coming home. My wife, you can tell, that it makes no matter how often we meet, I shall have nothing to say. With my children it will be different. My whole desire is to see you, and my children—nothing more. This is the first opportunity I have had of answering you, in fact the first I could write, if this may be called writing, but then I thought you would rather have my writing than anybody else's. Thank Brother Jeff for me and God bless his heart and give him my best love.

For my dearest sister the love that rests in my heart may it shield her and watch over her for ever. Sis, if I die, and something makes me think that I will after what Doctor Douglass says to-day, just bear in mind that I take you for my confessor and I die fully in the grace of God, in the mercy of Christ, and the fellowship of the Holy Ghost.

If I can get the money from Roach I will be at our home.

God bless you at your hearth and home, dearest one, and keep you well for Brother Jeff's sake, and don't let me forget poor little sister Maggie. Give her best love and dearest wishes.

Sister, it is awful to say good-by when you know that it may be your last—but good-by, darling and dearest old sister, and we shall meet in the hereinafter to come.

Your only devoted Brother
W. F. Howell

Bishop William M. Green to Jefferson Davis

Sewanee, Tenn.
Oct. 23d, 1885

My dear Friend

Too long an interval has passed since I last heard of you, except an occasional notice in the Papers of the day, which love to fling at you, on the one side, as much as it delights your friends to defend you on the other. How clearly do those malignants seem to forget that hard rubbing is the very way to distinguish the true metal from the counterfeit. I know you too well, to believe that such assailants have the power to disturb your complacency. I am only concerned lest the infirmities of age are pressing too heavily upon you. I want you to live a little longer, that you may see our Country honestly administered, our Union placed on a firm and rational basis, and the rights of every state placed beyond the reach of central domination. I feel sure that the declared principles of our new President [Cleveland] must meet your general approval. His honesty of purpose is really refreshing, after all the "wickednesses in high places" which has blotted our National Record for the last quarter of a century. But away with such a subject.

I want to know the state of your health, and how "the Madam" is, and Winnie, and Maggie, if she is with you, and what is the condition of Mr. Hayes' health also. As to my own, it is as good as that of any one Octogenarian in a thousand. No aches, no pains, with good sleep and good appetite; and yet not enough of strength and nervous command to justify me in attempting any official act of an out-door nature. Ten days ago, in spite of the Protests and Remonstrances of friends, I set out on a six-weeks' visitation; but broke down, after getting a hundred miles, and ignominiously returned home, so amuse myself by sucking my paws through the coming winter, unless I can find some better work to do. During the last twelvemonths I have been engaged in writing a "Memoir of Bishop Otey." It is now in Press. When published it will give me pleasure, if you will accept a copy.

It is a gratification to me to tell you that our University though still unendowed, seems to have a bright prospect before it. Our late Commencement was attended by a much larger number than usual. Our students number, now, 225; and we expect, a year hence, that there will be 300. I hope that you have seen the Letter of Dr. Din in the "Churchmen" of August 22d. Never have we been more thoroughly scrutinized, and never more thoroughly commended. Are we never to see *you* here again? I need not assure you that your presence amongst us would give joy to every heart, and be a healthful stimulus to a noble set of young men.

Much as a good, long friendly letter would delight me I will be content with a few lines, if they only tell me that you are in reasonable health, and all the rest are well. With love to the family, believe me, as ever,

Your strongly attached Friend
W. M. Green

Varina Davis to Winnie Davis

Winnie is in New Orleans visiting the Edgar Farrars. Lucy, the daughter of Mary Stamps, is married to Varina's cousin Edgar (Ned) Farrar. Davis's nephew Hugh Davis, son of his sister Lucinda by her first husband, is visiting at Beauvoir.

Bettie Tillman was a little girl Davis had found destitute on a poor farm near Handsboro in 1879 when she was five years old. He took her home to educate and virtually adopted her. She was a charming, ingratiating child and beloved by every member of the family. For some years Davis sent her to a private school in Louisiana. During her vacations she helped as a maid in the household and captivated the guests. She was to help nurse Davis in his last illness and be at his deathbed. Eventually she married a handsome Indian named Henry Hooks, a noted rodeo performer and trapper, who became a friend of Theodore Roosevelt.

Beauvoir House
My darling child,

Your note was safely received this morning. Hugh and I grumbled at not hearing more. Hugh and I, as I was breathless & swelled up yesterday, went to Biloxi.

I have a cook!!! & a gardener, "bombs bursting in air"—fireworks, Catherine Wheels, et als. The two are married together so the rejoicing is general & sincere.

Mr. Davis is well but torpid this cold day, as would I be but for the impediments that cluster around the devious ways of a sleepy-headed housekeeper, so in the cold I "up, boys, & at them" early & have straightened the house out. Bettie sent you some violets yesterday, I hope you got them safely today. Hugh groans over your absence & says "h a a a, it is lonely."

Give my tender love to dear Lucy & Mary, Ned & the precious little children & believe me as ever devotedly

Your old Mother

H a a a but it is lonely.

Micajah H. Clark to Jefferson Davis

Virginia-born Clark, last acting Treasurer of the Confederacy, now a leaf-tobacco broker in Tennessee, was among those who bought Jefferson Davis's birth site at Fairview, Kentucky, for him to give to the Bethel Baptist Church as an historical memorial.

Clarksville, Tenn. Dec. 19, 1885

My dear Sir:

Enclosed please find deed of your birth-place to you, and deed for you to execute to the Trustees of the Bethel Baptist Church. So the matter is now arranged as I wished it, and the spot where you were born will now have a lasting monument upon it, and the land stands in your name upon the record books of Todd County. It is the intention of the Trustees to place in the Church (which will be a substantial brick edifice) a marble tablet with a suitable inscription recording it as your birth place.

I hope this will find you and Mrs Davis and Miss Varina well. We are all at home now.

Faithfully yours,
M. H. Clark

Jefferson Davis to Varina Davis

Since 1882 there have been many changes of overseers at Brierfield. Now Davis is about to let Hughes, the store manager, go. Crozier is the new plantation manager.

Brierfield, Missi
22nd Dec. 1885

Dear Wife,

I am here in the midst of so much perplexity and annoyance that I cannot wish you a "Merry Xmas" in a cheerful tone.

The weather has been good until today, the field is white and much of the ground covered with cotton, but the pickers are few. Day before yesterday a large squad of pickers came from the bare fields of Ursino to work here. Some who got through at Hurricane came also. Too late, too late. I met at the landing the peregrinating Hughes, he was going to meet the man who never failed and who promised some hands, but the infallible failed for us.

Lize was here yesterday with her children, and inquired affectionately for you and Winnie. Her little one is beautiful and gentle. Lize told me she was trying to sell a part of her land, but that the purchaser wanted a larger tract & thereupon inquired whether I would like to sell a part of Brierfield adjoining Hurricane. I answered in the negative, at least not at present, if ever.

There are many things to be done. Crozier is perhaps too much disposed to electioneer for tenants. The negro is above all things suspicious, and more apt to take alarm at zeal in pursuit of him, than at the absence of promises. They preach on all texts and after their own manner, so my policy has been to leave them alone, like him who was joined to his idols, or to give a few words which might as bread cast upon the waters return after many days. We are in a struggle for success or final failure, we must have a full supply of labor this year and economy in the use of it, how this is to be done, is the difficult problem for our solution.

Mrs. Hughes and her baby are quite well, but there is something undefinable in look and manner as you saw it here, though no want of attention and kindness on the part of every one. Hughes has a notice up in several places, that to close out his business he is offering great bargains at the Brierfield store, but the negroes jestingly tell him they know he is not going away. Crozier wants the change, but thinks he will need the help of Hughes for a month. At the first opportunity, which from no fault of mine has not yet offered, an understanding between Hughes & myself must be reached.

God save me from uncharitable opinions, but it is hard to resist some proofs. Did you ever consider an Irish Yankee? If so, you will know how hard it is to balance the off-hand cordial character of one half against the unscrupulous fleece-shaving character of the other half, and how the sympathies were against the judgement. Having the conclusion that he must go, I can but wish he was gone.

God bless my wife and baby and shield them from all which is painful and injurious.

Affectionately
Your Husband

Jefferson Davis to Varina Davis

Brierfield
1st Jany 1886

Dear Wife

I wish you a happier New Year than you probably have and many happier than this.

The morning is quite cold and wet and everybody looks affected by the order I gave to take stock to-day for the opening of new books. At breakfast this morning Mrs. Hughes and I were alone. The event of a young lamb led her to speak of her regret at having to sell her sheep and she went on to say that she was selling off her furniture as opportunity offered.

Acknowledging my hesitation in speaking to her about our approaching separation, I said that she must not misunderstand me, she replied, in tears, that she never could do so. I pursued by telling her that whether just or unjust, a prejudice existed against Capt Hughes which prevented us from getting tenants. She interrupted me by saying she understood it all. I therefore had no chance to tell her how reluctant I had been to realize the necessity under which I decided.

The mass of blotted, erased and transferred matter would require a patient expert for its unravelling. The most exigent was to transfer the management of field and store, and while the accounts are under revision and in the possible expectation of Addison's being in at the death, I propose to go on Monday to Vicksburg and to return on the *Natchez,* Tuesday night.

Affectionately
Your Husband

Varina Davis to Lise Hamer

The bitterness over the Brierfield lawsuit had long ago subsided and the affectionate relationship was resumed.

Beauvoir,   Missi.
9th July 1886

Dear Lize,

Your Uncle thinks he must go to Brierfield & I write to beg you as you care for me to let me know by telegram if he is at all ill. He is very feeble & cannot stand another severe illness, and he will forbid you to telegraph if you tell him you mean to do it.

With love to each of your household, I am as ever,

Lovingly your Aunt
V. Davis

Micajah H. Clark to Jefferson Davis

In the fall of 1886 Davis goes to Fairview to the dedication of the brick church. Eventually a white obelisk, 351 feet high, was erected as a memorial to Jefferson Davis. The monument dominates the Jefferson Davis Memorial Park and is a tourist attraction.

Clarksville, Tenna. July 11, 1886

My dear Sir:

I thank you for your friendly lines of 9th of June. The object of my present writing is to return to you papers of your deed to the Bethel Baptist Church. The Trustees, having had the deed duly recorded, would like you to keep the deed. The Church is under contract, and they hope to complete it this fall. An engraving was made of the old homestead before being torn down, a copy of which was no doubt sent you, if not, let me know and I will send some to you. The Trustees are studying out a suitable inscription for the tablet in the Church and send below to me for transmission to you for your approval, alteration, or substitution of another—if you will convey your ideas to me I will forward them to Fairview —"Jefferson Davis of Mississippi was born June 3, 1808 on the site of this Church. He made a gift of this lot March 10th 1886 to Bethel Baptist Church as a thank offering to God." Hoping this will find you all well, I am

Faithfully yours
M. H. Clark

THE LAST THREE YEARS

Bishop William M. Green to Jefferson Davis

In April 1886 after much persuasion Jefferson Davis had made public appearances in Montgomery, Atlanta, and Savannah, at dedications of monuments. Special trains, with guards of honor, were sent to fetch him. His "progress" from Beauvoir through the South turned out to be such an astonishing triumph—"one prolonged ovation"—that the correspondent sent by the New York *World* wrote: "All the South is aflame, and where this triumphant march is to stop I cannot predict."

Winnie, now twenty-two, had accompanied her father and witnessed the manifestations of love of the Southern people for him. In Atlanta before a tremendous throng she was given the epithet of "The Daughter of the Confederacy."

Sewanee, Tenn.
August 20, 1886

Hon. Jefferson Davis,

Many thanks to you, my dear friend, for the kind solicitude about me, as proved in your letter received two days ago.

I am thankful in being able to tell you that, for the last nine months, I have had uninterrupted health, and no perceptible decay of strength or spirit. Our mountain has lately been filled with an unusual number of visitors; and our permanent population is rapidly increasing. We are fast adding to our Faculty, and the number of our Students will soon reach three hundred.

I was with you, in spirit, during your late "ovation" in Alabama and Georgia; and no heart among those vast crowds sent up warmer thanksgiving to God, at seeing such just and long-due honors paid to you; insufficient as they were to repay you for what you had

547

done and suffered for them. I was glad to see Winnie was with
you, not only to take care of you, but to see how truly you are
loved by all our people.

Please present me affectionately to Mrs. Davis, and to Winnie,
and to Maggie, also, if she is with you. And believe, as ever,

Your affectionate Friend and Bishop
W. M. Green

Jefferson Davis to Addison Hayes

The boy referred to is Addison Jefferson Hayes, who was born in
Memphis, October 1, 1884, shortly before the Hayes family moved to
Colorado Springs. After his grandfather's death in 1889, because there
were no male Davis heirs, his name was legally changed to Jefferson
Hayes-Davis. Eventually he became Vice-President of the First National
Bank of Colorado Springs, where he now lives retired.

Beauvoir, Miss.
11th Sept. 1886

My dear Addison,

I have been discussing with my Daughter the question of her
return to Colorado. She is anxious to be with you, and you are no
doubt equally desirous for her return. The feeling I can readily
estimate by the reluctance with which I contemplate her departure.
The question as it presents itself to my mind should be decided
outside of sentiment.

The boy is very well—growing in strength and flesh and grace
of many kinds. Walks about the lawn with self-reliant air, and
says a few words distinctly and tries to say many more. The girls
are well.

My dear Daughter is certainly better than when she came to
us. At this season it will be hot and dusty on the R.R. At the close
of this month or in the beginning of the next these conditions will
be modified, and the trip can then be made with comparative
safety and comfort.

If I could mould things to suit myself, it would be to have you
and the rest with me for the short time it may be granted me to
live. I feel sadly enough that this cannot be and, trying to take a
practical view of the case, to take the medicine of self-denial.

The new store keeper at Brierfield has proved a failure and been discharged. He is as dishonest as Hughes, but not so capable in concealment.

Please let me hear from you as often as your convenience will permit, and especially inform me as to your health and any effect realized from office work.

Ever affectionately
Jefferson Davis

Margaret Weber to Jefferson Davis

"The Life of President Davis" referred to was the biography, *The Life of Jefferson Davis,* written by Frank Alfriend, onetime editor of the *Southern Literary Messenger,* and published in 1868.

Sewanee, Tenn.
Feb. 15th, '87

My dear Sir,

At the request of the family, I write you of the decease of our venerable and beloved Bishop Green.

Although his extreme age made us think year by year he must shortly finish his course, his death came so suddenly at last it seemed more like a translation!

The dear Bishop often spoke of you; and the very night before his death, he asked for "The Life of President Davis" and said to his children, "He is a noble man, and every one should read that book that he may know how to live!" Knowing how truly, Sir, you deserved this tribute, and believing it would gratify you, I promised the family to write. We shall all miss his presence, this St. John of the Church, so gracious was he: his life was a benediction.

Believe me, Your friend,
(Mrs.) Margaret J. Weber

Bishop Richard H. Wilmer to Jefferson Davis

This letter is chosen from one of many from high churchmen expressing admiration, love, and even veneration for Davis.

Diocese of Alabama
Mobile, Ala. March 11, 1887

My dear & honored friend

I feel a great pride & joy in feeling myself privileged to address you thus. There is not an honor paid to you that I do not claim the humble privilege of sharing it with you in some small way. There was never an ignominy put upon you that I did not lend myself to share & resent. As I have said in my book—now in press—"The extensive grounds of the 'Fortress of Mourn'—Monroe—are not large enough to hold all your friends who would have loved to share your captivity"—aye, your chains.

This reminds me of the object of this letter—to say to you, that of my book in press, I have *given* but one copy & that to yourself. I have ordered the Publisher to send the first volume to yourself—in token of my love & veneration. I have written "without gloves" but with clean hands—so far as some matters admitted—with many sharp points, but with no venom. The fact is that I have been playing "Old Mortality."

The Book will be much abused, for which I thank God. The crown of thorns from some hands is to me a crown of glory.

Commend to me your good wife and to Winnie.

I love to think of yourself receiving that wonderful ovation at Montgomery—and of your daughter, so surrounded by her well-wishers that I could but press her hand for a brief moment. It gladdened my heart to know that she was privileged to witness the honor paid her dear father. It will illuminate her whole life.

Affectionately & with veneration,
Richd. H. Wilmer

Alexander James Beresford-Hope to Jefferson Davis

Beresford-Hope and Davis have corresponded occasionally since 1868.
The Marquis of Salisbury (Robert Arthur Talbot Gascoyne-Cecil, 1830–1903), brother of Beresford-Hope's wife, was a favorite Prime Minister of Queen Victoria.

Arklow House
Connaught Place
London
10th July 1887

My dear Mr. Davis

Any reminiscences of you, anything that shows that I am still in your friendly recollection is most acceptable and precious. Great therefore was my pleasure in receiving the newspaper which you were so good as to send me. It came at a time when it was very welcome, as I am only recovering from a somewhat serious illness, the troubles and sorrows of the last few years had been imperceptibly accumulating till they culminated this year in a sort of nervous collapse, from which however I am thankful to say I have rallied and though I am excusing myself from Parliament this year, yet I am glad to see that there are members enough and to spare to counterplot that maniac Gladstone. It is a great comfort to see Salisbury doing so very well; he, at least, has not forgotten the tender care with which his sister tended him during their youthful years. The Queen appreciated his services and is personally greatly attached to him. Next year I shall hope again to take my place in Parliament. My constituents are very kind and leave me all the time I want to pick up health. I hope you can give good accounts of Mrs. Davis, to whom pray let me beg to be most kindly remembered.

Believe me, my dear Mr. Davis,

Yrs most Sincerely
A. J. Beresford Hope

Bishop J. N. Galleher to Jefferson Davis

In the last week of October, 1887, Jefferson Davis was prevailed upon to speak in Macon, Georgia, at a grand reunion of the Confederate Veterans. A special train was sent to Beauvoir for him and his family. The enthusiasm along the way was called by numerous correspondents "indescribable." At every stopping place "veterans and sons and daughters of veterans stormed the train and took him by assault." "We seemed to be borne forward upon the crest of some mighty wave in a sea of voices. Flowers covered us, and the train ran under triumphal arches."

Fifty thousand visitors, including five thousand veterans, jammed the town of Macon. It was Atlanta of 1886 over again, but with more excitement and more emotion. The strain proved too great for the old gentleman, who yet made his address, but suffered a heart attack.

Bishop Galleher of Louisiana, reading in the papers that Jefferson Davis was near death in Macon, offered by telegram to go to him. But Davis recovered quickly and went home to Beauvoir.

657 Carondelet St.
New Orleans
3 Nov. '87

My dear Mr. Davis:

I hope my dispatch sent to Macon did not seem to you intrusive and officious. I read in the newspapers that you were desperately ill; and it occurred to me that you might be pleased to have an old soldier of the Confederacy to minister to you & your family on a time of such solemn import. That was all. I thank God that you are still spared to our people, and to your own household.

Very respy. yours
J. N. Galleher

Jefferson Davis to Maggie Hayes

Davis is seriously concerned about his son-in-law's health.

Joseph Pulitzer, owner of the New York *World,* arrived with his wife at Beauvoir on January 18 in their private railroad car. They came to pay their respects to Jefferson Davis and to persuade Winnie to accompany them on their transcontinental tour. Winnie, loath to leave her father in his eightieth year, could not be persuaded.

Beauvoir
17th Jany 1888

My darling Daughter,

For many days I have been returning thanks for your escape from the storm and freeze that has swept over the N. West, but this evening your letter to your Mother has put a severe check to my joy, by the announcement of dear Addison's illness. Is it not well now to review the favorable estimate you both have put on the climate of Colorado? During the many months I was at

Monterey, Mexico there was but one sudden change of temperature, then we had a "norther." At no time was it cold enough, except on that occasion to want a fire, and the whole town there had not a chimney, so you see there is no danger there of being in a heated room. A country Doctor who has probably been seldom quoted for his professional wisdom, remarked that "took cold" was a misnomer, that persons did not take cold but "took heat." The meaning of which no doubt was the injury resulted from becoming heated and then being suddenly chilled. Such I infer is Addison's case. If you would doubt your climate, perhaps the occupation of banking may not be so safely intrenched in his favor.

It was a great happiness to hear about what the children say of those who were left behind them. I am indeed lonely in their absence and pray for the speedy fulfillment of the promise to come back.

Mr. & Mrs. Pulitzer are to be here to-morrow; perhaps Winnie may accept their invitation to go with them to California. A private car offers the two-fold temptation of comfort and economy in seeing a new and interesting country. She says, no.

God grant this may find Addison relieved from his recent attack and resolved to regulate his life so as best may secure him to length of days.

Kiss the beloved and lovely children for their old "papá," who thinks of them constantly and most hopes to see them again.

Good night my sweet Pollie, give much love to Addison & the children.

Your Father
Jefferson Davis

Jefferson Davis to the Reverend Mr. Robert Hinsdale

On June 3, 1888, Jefferson Davis celebrated his eightieth birthday quietly at Beauvoir. Except for family members and a single reporter from the New Orleans *Picayune* who was granted a brief interview, people were kept away. The reporter found the onetime Secretary of War and the President of the Confederacy "immaculately dressed, straight and erect, with traces of his military service still showing in his carriage and with the flush of health on his pale, refined face." He revealed, said the newspaperman, "a keen interest in current topics, political, social, religious." His birthday was cheered with telegrams and letters of felicitation and presents from strangers as well as friends.

Davis himself wrote one note—to the Northern-born Rector of the Church of the Redeemer in Biloxi, of which he was a vestryman. The letter and envelope were marked *Personal*.

Beauvoir
June 3, 1888

Dear Mr. Hinsdale,

Enclosed I send as a contribution a small sum, which you must regard not as a measure of my will, but my ability.

To *you* is made the confession that circumstances have made me poorer than an average fisherman, but other demands are held subordinate to the cause of Him, who died for the redemption of fallen man.

With best wishes, I am

Faithfully,
Jefferson Davis

Wade Hampton to Varina Davis

General Hampton had been United States Senator from South Carolina since 1879. His wife had died while he was Governor (1876–1879). Hampton disliked politics and accepted public office only because of the insistence of his fellow citizens.

Washington, D.C.
June 3rd 1888

My dear friend,

You do not know what pleasure your letter gave me, for while it recalled many sad memories, they were all most tender. More than ten years ago you wrote to me, to comfort me when one of the greatest sorrows of my life had come upon me, and though your letter touched my heart deeply, I had not the courage to reply to it. But your kindness then has never been forgotten and I have often thought of you and of your dear husband.

Every manifestation and respect that he has received has gratified me greatly as showing how dear he still is to those for whom he labored and suffered. This is his birthday, and while he would regard it as an empty compliment to wish him "many happy returns," when he has found like all of us that no happiness is to be looked for here, he will be pleased to know how many heartfelt prayers go up for him on this day. None are more sincere than mine, for I have shared in his sufferings, and I have loved him sincerely.

I am tied down here, having no interest in public life, and only remaining in it because my people insist on my doing so. But the life is harder than when I lived in camp!

I hope to hear from you again and with the most affectionate greeting to you and yours, I am

Sincerely your friend
Wade Hampton

Jefferson Davis to a namesake

The recipient of this letter is not identified, but he was born after the fall of the Confederacy.

Beauvoir, Missi.
30th Oct. 1888

My dear Friend and namesake,

Your Father bestowed upon me a high compliment in giving my name to you, the higher for being done *after* our disaster. I trust that the name you bear may not prove incumbrances to you. The history of our country from 1776 to 1865 furnishes the vindication of the cause for which your Father & I contended.

You ask for a word of advice as to your course in life. There is no certain road to success, but it is possible to deserve it, and what is far better, to preserve one's self-respect. It is a common error to say that man is the creature of circumstances; upon himself depends the development of the talent with which he may have been endowed. It is true that if our revolution had not occurred in the time of Washington he could not have achieved the fame which has made his name the synonym of good and great; but if he had not qualified himself both morally and mentally for the high duties to which he was called, the opportunity would have availed but little. To be prepared for whatever the chances of life may present requires systematic, persistent labor; all useful learning may be expected, sooner or later, to have requisition made upon it. Hence the aphorism that "Knowledge is power."

Let me recommend to you, as worthy of attentive reading, the beautiful poem by Burns, "Epistle to a young friend." There is a large amount of worldly wisdom and good advice attractively presented.

With best wishes for your welfare and happiness, I am,

Faithfully

Jefferson Davis

Jefferson Davis to Maggie Hayes

Mrs. Hayes had brought the children again to Beauvoir to see her father, and is now back at her home in Colorado Springs.

Beauvoir

26th April '89

My darling Pollie,

Your letter made me very happy in the announcement that you had a comfortable trip and found Mr. Hayes quite well.

The loss of your presence and the absence of the joyous voices of the dear children render this less home than it was when you were here to give it the charm which makes a cot all the heart needs.

Your Mother has not been as well as usual for some days past, and speaks with dread of the approaching summer, but is not disposed to adopt any of the plans I can devise for change of climate, because they do not include my going away also.

She would like to be with you in June, but has been informed that the climate is dangerous to those who like herself have heart infirmity. I do not know what will be the final decision either as to herself or Winnie further than that neither are disposed to spend the summer here.

God bless and shield you, my beloved child, is the fervent prayer of him to whom you have been a joy and a comfort from your birth.

Give my true love to Addison and the children.

Ever devotedly

Your Father

Jefferson Davis to Addison Jefferson Hayes

Davis's grandson is now four and a half years old. He has scrawled some marks on a sheet of paper, which his grandfather chooses to consider a letter.

Mr. Hayes-Davis told this editor that "Johnnie Arcoley" was a very simple card game and that his grandfather generally let him win.

> Beauvoir, Missi.
> 26th April, 1889

My darling Son Jeff

Your much prized letter, written in New Orleans, was duly received, and we have since had the good news of your safe arrival at home, and that your dear Mother had not suffered from the trip as we feared she might.

This place seems very dull without the gay voices of my children and the loving embraces you all habitually gave me. I long for the time when you will return and hope your Father may then come with you. There is no one now to play "Johnnie Arcoley" with me, or to put the soldiers in line of battle, so the early evening brings the sad remembrance that my boy has gone away. Your Aunt Winnie has gone to New Orleans, your Cousin Hugh and your Grand Ma play backgammon as usual. With love to your Parents and Sisters and very much to yourself, I am lovingly your "Papa."

> Jefferson Davis

Jefferson Davis to Bettie Tillman

In May, Davis became ill, and, partially to relieve his wife of the strain of nursing, he sent for Bettie, who is at school in Louisiana.

> Beauvoir House
> May, 1889

Dearest Bettie:

Come at once. I have been much unwell and need your loving hands and touch to again restore me.

Show this letter to Miss Monro and to Mr. Alexander and I am sure they will excuse you.

Bring the "makings" for the delicious herbal tea also.

Now for the future don't worry, my dearest little girl. This crisis will pass and your old Banny will show you several new tricks, maybe sooner.

As ever your dutiful
Father
Jefferson Davis

Jefferson Davis to Maggie Hayes

The grandson Jeff had again made some marks on paper, which he called a letter to his grandfather. Maggie now has a second son, born in June and named William.

Beauvoir, Missi
12th Sept. 1889

My dearest Pollie,

With this is enclosed a letter for my dear little man. It was very gratifying to me to hear of his trust that his Papa would understand his letter. What letter could tell more than that I was thought of, wished to be conversed with. I hope Mr. Hayes will have a pleasant time in the hunting field and return all the better for breathing the air of the mountains.

With love to my Daughters and Sons and much, very much to my own Darling Pollie,

Your Father

Jefferson Davis to Addison Jefferson Hayes

Beauvoir, Miss.
12th Sept. 1889

My darling Son,

I was very glad to receive your letter, and you were right in supposing your Papa would understand it. It was a full letter to me, for what more did I wish to know beyond the fact that my dear boy was thinking of me, and wished to talk to me. You are now the big boy of the family and will have to teach your little brother some of the many things you have learned. I look hopefully forward to the time when you will all come to see me. Your Grandma is well. Your Aunt Winnie has been ill for some weeks, is now better. Give my love to your Parents and Sisters and little brother. And take an armful for yourself from your own Papa—

Jefferson Davis, Sr.

Jefferson Davis to A. Dudley Mann

This note to Mann was to be delivered in Paris by Winnie, who was leaving with the Joseph Pulitzers for an extended sojourn in Europe. It was one of the last letters Davis wrote.

Beauvoir Miss.
23d Oct 1889

My dearest Friend,

Varina starts to day for New York to sail thence for Havre, from there she goes to Paris and to have the enviable happiness of seeing you. She can give you all our family news and may shed on them a more rose color than I could give. She will remain abroad until next spring, when I trust she will return in good health and bring back the light which goes out when she goes away.

Give my kindest remembrance to good Marie and accept for yourself the heart-felt devotion of your friend,

Jefferson Davis

[Note on envelope in Winnie's handwriting:]
Mr. Mann was dead before I could deliver the letter. And father had gone before mine could get to him, he died while I was writing to him.
Lord Keep his memory green—
Very Precious

Varina Davis to Maggie Hayes

Winnie is engaged to the "Yankee" Alfred Wilkinson of Syracuse, New York, with her father's consent; but a widespread resentment in the South caused a decline in her health. She is now in Paris with the Joseph Pulitzers. James Redpath, the New York editor and publisher, has spent some weeks at Beauvoir helping Davis with his *Short History of the Confederate States of America* and three magazine articles.

Beauvoir
8 Nov. 1889

My darling Child,

It was just like you to send me the first proofs of the children's photos. The baby boy is the loveliest creature I ever saw except his little Uncle. My dear son Addison tells me you have had no end of trouble getting your servants renewed. It is a dreadful ordeal you are passing through. I had it for five months and I failed visibly under the infliction.

I have heard of Winnie's safe arrival in Paris by an ocean telegram. Mr. Wilkinson also had one sent me from the ship's office. She went away with an immense number of flowers & quantity of fruit, etc. Every wind made me shiver until I heard she was safe. I was in hopes I should then have a little rest, but Hugh Davis & Laura came with their little Hugh Jefferson for a short stay.

Your poor old Father went off on a trip to Brierfield positively refusing to let me go though I urged it very much. I found out just as he started that he wanted to go to Cousin Florida's, who has lost both husband & her preacher Nephew about a month ago within a week of each other, so, as he expected to be only a day or two at Brierfield, I did not so much mind his going alone as he was well.

I am in bed with an intense earache, as my hand in fine will show, though better than yesterday much.

I am somewhat cheered in my "winding way" by Fred Wilkinson's cheery, loving letters. He sends me books & papers too. Mr. Redpath, when he is here, is agreeable. So on the whole, the Xmas work filling in the time is not long as it would seem, but I do not get many minutes for work & none for play. As your Father gets older he takes up all my time pretty much, & my eyes are failing.

Excuse my fist, I am nervous, but always yours, Addison's, & the children's devoted

Mother

Jefferson Davis to Varina Davis

In New Orleans on his way to board the *Laura Lee* for Brierfield, Davis caught a severe cold in a sleety November rain. Grippe seized him and then bronchitis and he arrived at the plantation house seriously ill.

In this last letter Jefferson Davis ever wrote he was so near delirium that he misspelled some words and omitted others.

Brierfield Miss.

12 Nov 1889

My deerst

If I can get to the landing I will go down on the heathers [*Leathers*] to-morrow. Lest you should hear alarming I write say I have suffered much but by the help of the Lord I—

Nothing is as it should be, and I am not able even to look at the place—

With best wishes to all the household

I am as ever

Your Husband

Jefferson Davis to Alice Evelyn Desmaris

The last lines penned by Jefferson Davis were in the album of Alice Evelyn Desmaris, the ten-year-old niece of John C. Trainor, the plantation agent. She was on a visit at Brierfield when Mr. Davis's illness took an alarming turn. Alice had been helping to nurse him, and when he had been dressed to be driven to the steamboat landing to return to New Orleans, the little girl bade him a tearful goodbye and timidly presented her album for his autograph and a sentiment. Weak as he was and only half-conscious, Mr. Davis took a pen and wrote:

Brierfield, 13th Nov. 1889

May all your paths be peaceful and pleasant, charged with the best fruit, the doing good to others.

Jefferson Davis

Winnie Davis to Her Father

Davis had refused to let either daughter be apprised of the seriousness of his illness. Winnie wrote this touching letter to her father unaware that it was only a few hours before his death after midnight on the morning of December 6.

> Dec. 5th 1889
> Rue   Courcelles
> Paris

My darling Father

Today I got Mother's letter saying that you were better, but had been very ill. I am broken-hearted to think that you could have had bronchitis and I have been away off here. Had I known, or had an idea of what was the matter I should have come home immediately, but from the telegrams I concluded it was one of those exaggerated reports so often in the newspapers about prominent men. My dearest, I know now that you were suffering all the time, and I cannot get reconciled to the idea of my having, no matter how unwittingly, left you while you were ill.

I think of you all the time, but every time I eat my breakfast, with a platefull of those little white grapes you used to talk about, I wish, oh how I wish, that any good fairy would lend me his travelling carpet for an hour that I might take them to you.

My constant letters to Mother must have kept you well posted about my doings, as yet we are still in the same, houseless condition as before, although poor Kate spends half her days in the company of the numerous house agents, a kind of leech which has just begun to suck the blood of the Paris house hunter. She has climbed up stairs, and gone poking around stables to no purpose however, as just as she thinks she has a house tight and fast, away it goes again.

Mr. Pulitzer is away in Italy, which makes her feel all this more, and on Monday the two eldest children are going away to St Moritz in the mountains of Switzerland, where there must, from all accounts, be a climate very like that of Colorado Springs. It is becoming quite a winter refuge as well as a summer resort. When they are gone that will leave the three little tots here, Joseph,

Loulou, and Constance, who is a most remarkable fine child, and full of all sorts of funny little ways which are very charming.

The other night Kate and I took Ralph to the opera, and you should have seen the grandeur of that little fellow with his miniature beaver and dress suit! He opened the box with an air, and altogether behaved like the fine little gentleman he is.

I have been thinking for days what I could send you to show you that I have thought about you, and amuse you through Xmas day, which is always I know a heavy trial to people after they are grown, and remembering all the pleasure we got out of a bundle of Illustrated papers that was once sent to me, I have bought you all the Christmas numbers I could find, and hope you will not open them until Xmas, when I hope, dearest, you may be thus enabled to while away a few hours of that day which is sad enough for us all, as we are separated this year.

I have been so anxious about you that during the last two nights I have hardly slept at all, but as I am sure from a telegram I received this morning saying that you were convalescent I hope I may get a good rest tonight.

Dearest darling Father, when as now, I want to tell you how much I love you I grow bewildered; what words to choose which are able to express to you the devoted love and tenderness of which my heart is and always will be full for you, my darling Father. My pen is the mutest thing about me unfortunately and when I am away from you I can only think, and think, and love you for your goodness and tenderness, with which you covered me as with a cloak, all through my little childhood, screening my faults and answering my unreasonable questions with always an honest reply, the rarest thing given to a child in the world. And so, I will end by saying as I began "My darling Father." Good-night.

With all the devotion in the world

Your Winnanne

ACKNOWLEDGMENTS

IN EACH OF the three volumes of my biography I took occasion to thank Mr. Jefferson Hayes-Davis of Colorado Springs, the only living grandson of Jefferson Davis, for access to some thousand heretofore unpublished letters. These were held for my exclusive use until my work on Davis was complete. With the publication of these selected private letters I consider my work on this unique historical figure done, so the hundreds of letters and documents which Mr. Hayes-Davis has since so generously given to the University of Alabama and Transylvania College are now in what is termed "the public domain." But again I am impelled to express my gratitude to Mr. Hayes-Davis for the majority of letters that are reproduced in this volume. I am also grateful to his wife, Ruth Hayes-Davis, who generously helped me decipher difficult handwriting. Among other direct descendants of the Confederate President I offer special thanks for assistance to the only living granddaughter, Mrs. Lucy Hayes Young of Colorado, and to Mrs. John Wolcott Stewart, the eldest living great-granddaughter, of Santa Barbara, California.

First, among collateral relatives who have aided me with information and given me letters to choose from for reproduction, I must thank Mrs. Anna Farrar Goldsborough, great-grandniece, now living in Newark, New York. The late Mrs. Mary Lucy O'Kelly, another great-grandniece, of Pass Christian, Mississippi, was also generous with her store of family letters. Other family members who furnished letters include Mrs. Stamps Farrar and Maude Ellen Farrar of New Orleans, Lucinda Ballard Dietz of Long Island, and Mrs. Ralph Wood of Biloxi, Mississippi.

I appreciate the letters sent me by the Reverend Mr. Randolph Blackford of Florida, by the Hon. B. M. Holtham, Q.C., of Sherbrooke, Canada, by Mrs. Homer Beckwith of Sewickly, Pennsylvania, by Mrs. H. E. Suits of Kirkwood, Missouri, by Mrs. R. E. Wilson of Denver, Colorado, and by Carl Haverlin, President of Broadcast Music, Inc., New York.

I am especially indebted to Matt Tom Green of New Orleans who possesses a sheaf of letters from both Mr. and Mrs. Davis to his grandmother, Bettie Tillman, as well as other Davis letters. Dr. Chester Bradley, Curator of the Jefferson Davis Casemate at Fort Monroe, Virginia, furnished me with photostats of letters from Varina Davis to her husband in prison, which had never been delivered to him. Mrs. Jessie Palfrey Leake, granddaughter of Josiah Gorgas, Confederate Chief of

Ordnance, kindly gave me access to letters from Davis to her grand-parents.

Besides the privately owned letters I have made use of some that are in the Library of Congress and the New York Public Library and several university libraries. I am particularly indebted to Miss Eleanor Brockenbrough of the Confederate Museum in Richmond for helping me select intimate letters for this volume.

Among other librarians or department heads or regents to whom I am indebted for beneficial co-operation are the following: Miss Charlotte Capers and Mrs. James Melton of the Mississippi Department of Archives and History; Mrs. Marguerite Murphy, Regent, and Mrs. Salome Brady of the Jefferson Davis Shrine at Beauvoir; Mrs. Ruth Rowell, Regent, and Mrs. Eltrym Chalker of the First White House of the Confederacy in Montgomery; Dr. Irving Lunger, President, and Miss Romel Henry, Librarian, of Transylvania College; Dr. William Stanley Hoole, Librarian, and Mrs. Catherine Jones, Mrs. Addie Coleman, and Mrs. Joyce Lamont of the University of Alabama; Miss Mattie Russell of Duke University; James W. Patton of the University of North Carolina; Francis L. Berkeley, Jr., Curator of Manuscripts, University of Virginia; Robert W. Hill and Edward R. Morrow of the New York Public Library; Dr. C. D. Powell of the Manuscript Division of the Library of Congress; and John McKenzie of the British Museum.

The Honorable Frank E. Everett, Jr., historian of Vicksburg, Mississippi, was most helpful with legal documents concerning Brierfield and other matters. I conferred with him twice in Vicksburg, and he kindly brought a sheaf of pertinent materials to my home in Tuscaloosa, Alabama.

I am indebted to John M. Finlay, Instructor in English at Alabama College, for valuable assistance in the selecting and discarding of letters. My thanks to Frank Stallworth and Robert Lee Campbell for special services in the mechanics of preparing the manuscript for publication.

Again I express gratitude to Jonathan W. Warner, President of Gulf States Paper Corporation, and to Prewitt Semmes, Jr., great-grandson of Confederate Admiral Raphael Semmes, for foundation grants that greatly facilitated my research travels.

To Ernest Going Williams, member of the Board of Trustees, University of Alabama, I express uncommon appreciation for his encouraging interest in my long-term undertaking from its inception.

And I shall ever be grateful to Count Lennart Bernadotte, only nephew of King Gustaf VI Adolf of Sweden and great-grandson of the Grand Duchess Luise of Baden, who was patroness of the girls' school in Carlsruhe which Winnie Davis attended for five years (1876–1881). I stayed with him at his Castle Mainau on Lake Constance in June, 1962, and June, 1965, and he took me to Carlsruhe to gather research material.

As with all my books, my debt to my wife Thérèse is incalculable and boundless. I am deeply grateful for her perceptive help in the choice of letters and in the editing, for her faithful typing and retyping, and for her extraordinary patience, which has not flagged since the inception of the work on Jefferson Davis in June of 1951.

INDEX

Abbeville, S.C., 152, 161
Abinger, Lord, 305, 311, 330, 331, 341
abolitionism, 114
Advertiser, Boston, 214
Ahern, Mary, 173, 192, 255, 256, 285, 363, 364
Alabama (Confederate warship), 136, 255, 257
Alcorn, J. L., 327
Alfriend, Frank, 396, 397, 549
Anderson, Mary, 426
Anderson, Robert, 119, 120
Appomattox, xix, 151
Atlanta, Ga., 160, 233
Atlanta House, 233
Ayres, Mrs. S. A., 399–400

Bache, Alexander Dallas, 73, 98
Bache, Eliza, 89, 104
Baltimore, Md., 263, 264, 318
Bancroft, George, 189
Beauregard, Pierre de, 139, 142, 156
Beauvoir, 421–22, 445–46, 534; bought by Jefferson Davis, 494
Benedict House, 147
Benjamin, Judah P., xii, xix, 157, 195, 215, 218, 293, 295
    letters to: Davis, Jefferson, 293; Davis, Varina, 170–73, 202–04, 505–06
Beresford-Hope, Alexander James, 293, 304, 510, 550
Bethel Baptist Church, 541, 544

Biloxi, Miss., Jefferson Davis Shrine in, 491
Bishop's College, 282
Black Crook, The, 254, 255
Black Hawk War, 8
Blackwood, John, 305, 306, 307, 310
Blackwood's Magazine, 305
Blair, Francis C., Sr., 103
Blair, Montgomery, 103
Blair House, 103
Bliss, Betty, 58
Bowdoin College, 99
Boyle, Lucy, 348, 351
Bradford, Amanda Davis, 6, 48, 100, 375
Bradford, David, 6, 10, 20, 148
Bradford, Jefferson Davis, 100
Bradford, Mary Jane, 25, 33, 61
Brand, W. F., 263, 265, 325, 344
Brazil, 289; Southerners in, 238
Breckinridge, John Cabell, 148
Brierfield plantation, 17, 20, 24, 42, 44, 48, 87, 92, 101, 104, 107, 108, 120, 254, 283, 354; Jefferson Davis brings lawsuit for, 371, 377–83 *passim*, 401–02, 409, 411–14, 418–19, 422–23; winning of lawsuit for, 455, 456, 479; managed by Addison J. Hayes, 516; and floods, 516, 517, 532–33, 536; overseers of, 519, 535, 541; various troubles at, 535, 536
Brodhead, Charles, 61, 62, 71, 271
Brodhead, Malie, 245, 254

Brown, Granville, 97
Brown, Joseph E., 139, 395
Brown, Robert, 147, 173, 174–75, 186, 203, 332, 446
Buchanan, James, 82, 83, 92, 107, 115
Buchanan, W. Jefferson, 138
Buena Vista, Battle of, 46
Bulloch, James D., 386
Bulwer, Lady, 58, 59
Burns, Robert, 399
Burt, Armistead, 58, 153
Burton, Henry S., 268, 269
Butler, Benjamin F., 119

Calhoun, John C., xiv, 33, 34, 35, 58, 60, 153
Campbell, George, 319, 433
Campbell, John A., 467, 468, 469, 471
Campbell, Lord, 330, 331, 341, 342
Canada: Davis children at school in, 180, 181, 194, 215, 224; William Preston in, 194, 195; refuge in, for Davis family, 281–82, 288
Carlsruhe, Germany, 433–38 *passim*, 448, 462, 480, 513
Carlyle, Thomas, 445
Carolina Life Insurance Co., 323, 325, 362, 365, 366, 367, 369
carpetbaggers, 287, 321, 394
Cary, Constance, see Harrison, Constance Cary
Cary, Hettie, 263, 264, 265
Catholic Universe, 473
Chase, Salmon P., 282, 286
Chesnut, James, Jr., 141, 152
Chesnut, Mary, 301
Choppin, Dr., 380, 381
Civil War, see War Between the States
Clark, Micajah H., 541, 544
Clark's Hotel, 282
Clay, Clement C., Jr., 128, 166, 176, 177, 189, 205, 247
Clay, Henry, 20
Cleveland, Grover, 539

Clyde (steamer), 201, 202
Cobb, Howell, 232, 233, 289
Cobb, Mary Ann, 337
Cochrane, Mrs., 494, 495
Coe, Thomas J., 101
Colorado, 415, 416–17
Communards, in Paris, 392–93, 394
Confederate Memorial Hall, in New Orleans, 121, 472
Confederate Museum, in Richmond, 121, 130, 566
Confederate Naval Academy, 96, 400
Cook, Jane, 5
Cooper, George E., 247, 248, 268
Corelli, Marie, 305
Cox, O. B., 126, 519–20
Craven, John A., xii, 167, 168, 182, 183, 193, 208, 211, 243, 245, 247
Cushing, Caleb, 122
Cutts, Adèle, see Douglas, Adèle Cutts

Dahlgren, John, 136
Dahlgren, Mortimer, 495, 496
Dahlgren, Ulric, 136
Dahlgren Raid, 135
Daily Enquirer, Richmond, 121
Daniel, John W., 526
Danville, Va., 147, 150
Davidson, Julia, 180
Davis, Anna, see Smith, Anna Davis
Davis, Eliza (Mrs. Joseph), 20, 23, 24, 31
Davis, Evan, 5
Davis, George, 209
Davis, Hugh, 13, 138, 320, 540
Davis, Isaac, 7, 191, 355
Davis, Jane, 12, 13
Davis, Jefferson, 5, 17, 20, 41, 119, 120, 126, 147, 157, 158, 165, 170; personality of, xi–xiv, xv–xvi; religious convictions of, xii; and assessment of marriage to Varina, xiv; assessment of letters by, xviii; as Representative, 33, 35; in Mexican War, 38, 39, 40, 42, 43, 44, 46–47; and Senate, first years in, 53, 54, 56, 58; as

Secretary of War, 71, 72, 74; and Senate, later years in, 87, 93, 98, 102; receives honorary Doctor of Laws degree, 99; becomes President of Confederacy, 120–21, 123; capture of, 166; imprisonment of, 166–70, 173, 175–79 *passim*, 185, 187–91, 193, 196, 200, 205–08 *passim*, 211, 213, 214, 217, 226, 230, 241, 242, 247, 263, 266; released on bail, 268, 269; refuge of, in Canada, 281–82, 288; postponements of trial of, 286, 288; and Pres. Johnson's general amnesty proclamation, 288; has accident in Lennoxville, 289, 290; first European trip by, 293–314; returns to America, 318–34; becomes President of Carolina Life Insurance Co., 323, 324, 325; in family reunion, 353; as executor of Joseph Davis's will, 354; and panic of 1873, 363–71 *passim;* resigns as President of Carolina Life Insurance Co., 367; and Brierfield litigation, 371, 377–83 *passim*, 401–02, 409, 411–14, 418–19, 422–23, 479; second European trip by, 382, 384–97; returns to America, 399; as prospector, 407–08, 415–17; welcomed in Texas (1875), 409–10; welcomed in Kentucky (1875), 418; elected President of American Department of Mississippi Valley Society, 424–25; invests in ice-making machine, 426; third European trip by, 428–29, 433–36; disappointed in hopes for Mississippi Valley Society, 433; in Carlsruhe, Germany, 436; Mrs. Dorsey offers haven to, 446–47; writes *Rise and Fall of the Confederate Government*, 450, 451, 456, 494, 500, 503, 506, 508; wins Brierfield lawsuit, 455, 456, 479; buys

Beauvoir, 494; Mrs. Dorsey's bequest to, 495; last trip to Europe, 512; returns to America, 515; calumniated by Johnston (1881), 515; Johnston prevents appearance of, at Lee Memorial meeting, 525; triumphant public appearances of, in South (1886), 547, 551–52; at eighty, 553–54; death of, 559, 562

letter(s) from: Bache, Alexander Dallas, 98; Benjamin, Judah P., 293; Beresford-Hope, Alexander James, 304, 510–11, 550–51; Bradford, David, 9–10; Chesnut, James, Jr., 141–42; Clark, Micajah H., 541, 544; Coe, Thomas J., 101–02; Davis, Jane, 12, 13; Davis, Jefferson, Jr., 402–03; Davis, Joseph, 42–43, 126–27, 262–63, 265–66, 270, 282–83; Davis, Margaret (Maggie), 127–28, 210, 235, 239–40, 286–87, 302–03, 322–23; Davis, Samuel Emory (father), 6–7; Davis, Varina (Winnie) Anne, 364, 448–49, 531, 562–63; Davis, Varina Howell, *see* Davis, Varina Howell, letter(s) to Davis, Jefferson; Galleher, J. N., 551–52; Green, William M., 538–40; 547–48; Hampton, Wade, 154–55; 160–61; Harrison, Burton N., 159–60; Howell, Becket, 519–20; Howell, Jefferson Davis, 289; Howell, Margaret (sister-in-law), 339; Lee, Mary Custis, 249–50; Lee, Robert E., 129–31, 274–75; McCaleb, Florida Davis, 8–9, 13–14; Mann, A. Dudley, 138; Mason, James Murray, 272–73, 284; Minnegerode, Charles, 285–86; Northrop, L. B., 509; Pendleton, William Nelson, 510–11, 520–21; Pierce, Franklin, 113–14; Reagan, John H., 273–74; Reed, William B., 356; Ryan,

Davis, Jefferson (cont.)

  Abram J., 503–04; Slidell, John, 298; Stamps, Lucinda Davis, 91–92; Stamps, Mary Elizabeth Humphreys, 133–35; Stamps, William, 354–55; Stringfellow, Frank, 480–82; Taylor, Zachary, 41; Weber, Margaret J., 549; Wilmer, Richard H., 533, 549–50

  letter(s) to: Ayres, Mrs. S. A., 399–400; Buchanan, James, 92; *Catholic Universe*, 473–74; Cobb, Howell, 289–90; Davis, Hugh, 138–41; Davis, Jefferson, Jr., 142–43; Davis, Sarah Knox Taylor, 10–12; Davis, Susannah, 7; Davis, Varina (Winnie) Anne (daughter), 343–44, 434–35, 450–53, 474–75, 492–93

  letter(s) to Davis, Varina, 18–26, 71–72, 73, 93–94, 270–71, 348–49, 352–53, 357, 376–78, 380–81, 382–86, 419–20, 425–28, 435–37, 471–72, 477–78, 515–16, 522–24, 535–37, 541–43, 561; during first years of marriage, 41–42, 46–47; during Presidency of Confederacy, 122–23, 126, 128–29, 148–49, 152, 155–57; during imprisonment, 168–70, 175–79 *passim*, 187–91, 196–97, 206–09, 211–14, 219–20, 223–32 *passim*, 238–39, 241–43, 247–48; during first European visit, 293–98, 304–07, 309–14; during panic of 1873, 363–64, 365–72 *passim;* upon return to America, 318–19, 323–25, 327–30, 340–41, 344; during second European trip, 386–89, 391–97; on Brierfield litigation, 401–02, 408–09, 411–14, 418–19, 422–23; on trips as prospector, 407–08, 415–17; on welcome in Texas (1875), 409–10; on sinking of *Pacific*, 420–21; on Beauvoir residence, 421–22, 445–46; on being elected President of American Department of Mississippi Valley Society, 424–25; U.S. to Europe (1876–1877), 439–41, 445–47, 449–50, 453–54, 456–59; on death of Jefferson Davis, Jr., 491–92; on lawsuit of Ellis et al. for Dorsey property, 498–500; on visit to his mother-in-law's grave, 508; during last trip to Europe, 512–16

  letter(s) to: Davis, William L., 349–50; Desmaris, Alice Evelyn, 561; Gorgas, Josiah, 143, 333–34; Hamer, Lise Mitchell, 332, 346, 532–33; Hayes, J. Addison, 448, 464, 488–90, 516–17, 548–49; Hayes, Margaret (Maggie) Davis, 284–85, 303, 308, 351, 387, 423–24, 428–29, 446–47, 463, 487–88, 521–23, 552–53, 556, 558; Hayes-Davis, (Addison) Jefferson, 557–59; Hinsdale, Robert, 553–54; Howell, Margaret (mother-in-law), 29–30, 103–04; Howell, William B., 87, 108, 112; Ives, Cora Semmes, 300–02; Lee, Custis, 525–27, 532; Lee, Robert E., 131–33, 151; Mann, A. Dudley, 299–300, 559; namesake (unidentified), 555–56; Northrop, L. B., 498; Pierce, Franklin, 121–22; Stamps, Lucinda Davis, 39–40, 361; Stamps, Mary Elizabeth Humphreys, 321–22, 345, 353–54; Stringfellow, Frank, 482–84; Tillman, Bettie, 557–58; Young, George H., 287–88

Davis, Jefferson, Jr., 81, 83, 88, 89, 94, 97, 100, 104, 105, 106, 109, 111, 209, 246, 256, 353; at Virginia Military Institute, 402, 403; accompanies father on prospecting trip, 415–17; lives with father

at Beauvoir, 449, 450, 451; obtains position in Memphis bank, 472; death of, 489, 490, 492, 493
letter(s) from: Davis, Jefferson, 142–43; Davis, Margaret (Maggie), 141
letter(s) to: Davis, Jefferson, 402–03; Davis, Varina, 362, 454–55
Davis, Joseph (brother of Jefferson Davis), xv, xvi, 17, 20, 24, 42, 48, 56, 78, 80, 110, 121, 126, 227, 244, 254, 262, 265, 270, 282, 283; death of, 346; will of, 354
Davis, Joseph Evan (son of Jefferson and Varina Davis), 110, 216, 414
Davis, Joseph R. (nephew of Jefferson Davis), 191, 235, 323, 376, 381, 382, 383, 471
Davis, Lucinda, see Stamps, Lucinda
Davis, Margaret (Maggie), 79, 83, 87–89, 94–95, 97, 100, 103–06 *passim*, 127, 141, 180, 181, 188, 194, 197, 207–08, 210, 235, 239, 256, 284, 286, 302, 303, 308, 317, 320, 322, 351, 387; marriage, of, 422; see also Hayes, Margaret (Maggie) Davis
Davis, Mary Davis, 12, 354
Davis, Maurice, 433
Davis, Robert, 12, 354, 355
Davis, Samuel Emory (father of Jefferson Davis), 5, 6
Davis, Samuel Emory (son of Jefferson and Varina Davis), 67, 71, 72, 75, 76, 77; death of, 78, 414
Davis, Sarah Knox Taylor, xiv, 10, 12, 17
Davis, Susannah, 7
Davis, Varina (Winnie) Anne (daughter of Jefferson and Varina Davis), xx, 149, 256, 257, 322, 324, 328
letter(s) from: Davis, Jefferson, 343–44, 434–35, 450–53, 474–75, 492–93; Davis, Varina, 500, 506–08, 540
letter(s) to: Davis, Jefferson, 364, 448–49, 531, 562–63; Davis, Varina, 437–38, 479–80, 497
Davis, Varina Howell, 17, 18, 29; assessment of marriage of, xiv; personality of, xiv, xv, xvi; assessment of letters by, xviii, xix; first child of, 67; arrives in Richmond, 123, 124; and imprisonment of husband, 166, 167, 168, 173–75, 185, 193, 200, 206, 217, 224, 230, 241, 248, 250–54, 255, 263, 266; in Savannah, 184–86, 198; receives permission to visit children in Canada, 227; arrives in Canada, 246; receives permission to see husband at Fort Monroe, 248; attempts to secure husband's release, 250, 254, 255, 263, 266, 268; in family reunion, 353; collapses in England (1876), 433; at Carlsruhe, Germany, 433, 434, 435, 436, 438, 448, 462; in guest room of Friedlander School, 448; returns to America, 467; helps husband with book, 467; joins husband at Beauvoir, 487; illness of (1878), 490
letter(s) from: Benjamin, Judah P., 170–73, 202–04, 505–06; Cobb, Mary Ann, 337; Cooper, George E., 248; Davis, Jefferson, see Davis, Jefferson, letter(s) to Davis, Varina; Davis, Jefferson, Jr., 362, 454–55; Davis, Varina (Winnie) Anne, 437–38, 479–80, 497; Hampton, Wade, 554–55; Hayes, Margaret (Maggie) Davis, 455–56; Howell, Jefferson Davis, 397–98, 400–01; Howell, William F., 537–38; Lee, Mary Custis, 357–58; Lytton, Lord, 341–42; Mackay, Charles, 328–29; Mann, A. Dudley, 298–99; Montgomery, Burgess T., 517–19; O'Conor, Charles, 504–05; Preston, William, 194–96; White, Anastasia, 197

Davis, Varina Howell (cont.)
  letter(s) to Davis, Jefferson, 57, 58,
    94–95, 104–07, 111, 114–15,
    124–25, 150–54 *passim*, 158–59,
    161–62, 347–49, 350–51, 375–
    76, 378–80, 414, 472–77 *passim*,
    524–25; during his imprison-
    ment, 173–83 *passim*, 191–93,
    198–202, 204–06, 209, 212, 215–
    19, 224–38 *passim*, 240–41, 243–
    47, 250–51, 254–57, 263–68;
    Europe to U.S. (1869–1870),
    317–20, 325–27, 330–32, 338–
    40, 342–43; sea voyage urged in,
    379, 381–82; U.S. to Europe
    (1874), 389–91; on living in
    Texas, 410–11; Europe to U.S.
    (1877), 449, 457–58; 459–63;
    on Hampton Roads Peace Con-
    ference, 468–71; during last trip
    to Europe (1881), 512–13
  letter(s) to: Davis, Varina (Win-
    nie) Anne, 500, 506–08, 540;
    Greeley, Horace, 251–52, 253–
    54; Griffith, Mrs. Richard, 137–
    38; Hamer, Lise, 543–44; Hayes,
    Margaret (Maggie) Davis, 494–
    95, 534–35, 559–60; Howell, Jef-
    ferson Davis, 135–37; Howell,
    Margaret (mother), 30–33, 35–
    39, 45–49 *passim*, 53–67 *passim*,
    72–78, 82, 87–91, 96–102, 108–
    11, 123–24, 252–53; Howell,
    William B. (father), 82, 83, 93,
    95; Howell, William F. (broth-
    er), 125–26; parents, 62–64, 79–
    81; Stamps, Mary Elizabeth
    Humphreys, 261–62
Davis, William Howell, 126, 256;
    death of, 357, 361, 386, 414
Davis, William L., 349
Democratic National Convention
    (1860), 119
Dent, Louis, 327
Derby, Lord, 386
Desmaris, Alice Evelyn, 561
Diamond Place, 8, 411, 412

Dispatch, Richmond, xxi
Disraeli, Benjamin, 386
Dorsey, Sarah Anne Ellis, 421, 422,
    445, 446, 447, 450, 451, 458,
    487; letter to A. Dudley Mann,
    478–79; sells Beauvoir to Jeffer-
    son Davis, 494; death of, 495
Douglas, Adèle Cutts, 80, 97
Douglas, Stephen A., 80, 81, 119

Eardly, Lady, 342
Edinburgh, Scotland, 304, 305
Ellis, Mary, 450
Emory, William H., 37
England, 293–95, 299, 312, 386–89,
    391–92, 396, 433
Erlanger, Matilde, 393

Fairview, Ky., Jefferson Davis's birth
    site at, 541, 544
Farish, William, 128
Farish, William Stamps, 128
Farrar, Edgar, 376, 499, 540
Farrar, Thomas, 371
Fenian Society, 215
Fenner, C. S., 499
Foot, Solomon, 97
Foote, Henry, 54, 62
Fort Gibson, 9, 10, 12
Fort Monroe, 128, 147, 166, 167, 168,
    201, 205, 245, 248, 250, 255, 268
Fort Moultrie, 119
Fort Sumter, 103, 120
Fort Warren, 213, 218
France, 295, 296, 297, 298, 392–95,
    399
Franklin, Benjamin, 37, 73, 196
Fredericksburg, Va., 128
Freedmen's Bureau, 244
Friedlander School, 433, 434, 436,
    448, 460, 462

Galleher, J. N., 551–52
Garnett, Dr., 126
Garrett, John W., 266, 268
Georgia, 337

Germany, 433–38 *passim,* 448, 462, 480, 513

Gettysburg, Battle of, xviii, 129, 133

Gittings, Charlotte, 254, 263

Gittings, John, 263

Gladstone, William E., 386, 551

Glasgow, Scotland, 305, 306, 307, 308, 309, 310

Glenn, Wilkins, 416

Gorgas, Josiah, 143, 333

Grant, Ulysses S., xix, 143, 151, 152, 158, 198, 299, 327

Greeley, Horace, 119, 176, 268; letters from Varina Davis, 251–52, 253–54; urges Jefferson Davis's release from prison, 253

Green, George, 244

Green, Henry, 329, 352

Green, William M., 487, 538, 547

Greenhow, Rose, 80

Griffith, Richard, 137

Griffith, Mrs. Richard, 137

Gwin, William M., 33, 295; wife of, 96

Hagar, 32, 419

Hamer, Lise Mitchell, 231, 244, 332, 346, 401, 413, 532, 543

Hamer, M. E., 375, 418

Hampton, Wade, 154, 160, 324, 371, 554

Hampton Roads Peace Conference (1865), 468

Harrison, Burton N., 143, 165, 166, 230, 232, 233, 234, 238, 241, 268, 270, 464

  letters to: Cary, Constance, 269–70; Davis, Jefferson, 159–60

Harrison, Constance Cary, 269, 467

Hartington, Lord, 339, 340

Hatchard, Miss, 319

Hayes, J. Addison, 422, 446, 463, 472, 535; letters from Jefferson Davis, 448, 464, 488–90, 516–17, 548–49

Hayes, Lucy, 523

Hayes, Margaret (Maggie) Davis, 423, 428, 446, 455, 463, 467, 487, 490, 494, 521, 534, 552, 556, 558, 559; children of, 452, 455, 458, 459, 516, 523, 535, 558; *see also* Davis, Margaret (Maggie)

Hayes, Rutherford B., 439

Hayes, Varina, 523

Hayes, William, 558

Hayes-Davis, (Addison) Jefferson, 548, 557–59

Herald, New York, 167, 509

Hill, Benjamin, 395, 396

Hinsdale, Robert, 553

Holley, Horace, 41

Hood, John Bell, 139

Hooks, Henry, 540

Howell, Becket, xvi, 136, 137, 255, 256–57, 377, 519; death of, 522

Howell, Jefferson Davis, xvi, 55, 96, 100, 135, 153, 218, 246, 257, 377; dismissed from position, 400–01; lost at sea, 420

  letters to: Davis, Jefferson, 289; Davis, Varina, 397–98, 400–01

Howell, Jinny, 30, 31, 73

Howell, Joseph B., 37, 72

Howell, Joseph Davis, 32, 33, 43

Howell, Margaret (mother of Varina Davis), 29, 67, 79, 176, 255, 281; death of, 508

  letters from: Davis, Jefferson, 29–30, 103–04; Davis, Varina, 30–33, 35–39, 45–49 *passim,* 53–67 *passim,* 72–78, 82, 87–91, 96–102, 108–11, 123–24, 252–53; Howell, Joseph Davis, 33–35, 43–44; Wood, Robert C., 81

Howell, Margaret (sister of Varina Davis), *see* Stoess, Margaret Howell

Howell, Minnie Leacock, 377, 445, 494

Howell, Richard (grandfather of Varina Davis), 71

Howell, Richard (uncle of Varina Davis), 37

Howell, Varina, *see* Davis, Varina Howell

Howell, William B. (father of Varina Davis), 17, 24, 82, 83, 87, 93, 95, 108, 112

Howell, William F. (brother of Varina Davis), xvi, 12, 32, 44, 125, 377, 537

Humphreys, Benjamin Grubb, 133, 261, 321

Hunter, R. M. T., 467, 468, 469, 470, 471, 481

Hurricane plantation, 17, 19, 20, 24, 65, 89, 254, 283, 541, 542

Huse, Caleb, 385

Illustrated News, London, 165, 304

International Chamber of Commerce and Mississippi Valley Society, 415, 427, 428, 433

Inverlochy Castle, 305, 311, 330

Irvin, Agnes, 73

Irwinville, Ga., 147, 165, 166

Ives, Cora Semmes, 300

Ives, Joseph, 300, 301

Jackson, Miss., 137

Jackson, Stonewall, 511

Janauschek, Fanny, 470

Jefferson, Thomas, 5

Jefferson Davis: Confederate President (Strode), 121

Jefferson Davis: Constitutionalist (Rowland), xvii, 121

Jefferson Davis Memorial Park, 544

Jefferson Davis Shrine, 491

Jefferson Davis: Tragic Hero (Strode), 121

Jefferson Hayes-Davis Collection, of letters, 121

Jennings, J. B., 312

Jewett, Cornell, 201, 203, 215

Johnson, Andrew, 166, 193, 216, 250, 252, 253, 266; impeachment trial of, 288; general amnesty proclamation by, 288

Johnston, Albert Sidney, 121, 149, 194, 471

Johnston, Joseph E., 147, 153, 156, 158, 160, 378, 395–96, 397, 515, 525

Johnston, William Preston, 129, 149, 151, 165, 179, 180, 194, 201, 214, 234, 245, 362, 468, 520

Jones, James, 143

Kappa Sigma Fraternity, 402

Keary, Helen, 127, 381, 420

Kemble, Fanny, 102, 426

Kenner, D. F., 202

Kentucky, 541; Jefferson Davis welcomed in (1875), 418

Knox, John, 307

Lady of the Lake, The, 308, 309

Lamar, L. Q. C., 235, 238

Lamon, Ward, 356

Leacock, Minnie, *see* Howell, Minnie Leacock

Lee, Custis, 124, 353, 362, 471, 525, 532

Lee, Fitzhugh, xxi

Lee, Mary (daughter of Robert E. Lee), 393

Lee, Mary Custis (wife of Robert E. Lee), xi, 147; death of, 371
letters to: Davis, Jefferson, 249–50; Davis, Varina, 357–58

Lee, Robert E., 124, 137, 143, 147, 148, 156, 158, 282, 300, 396, 397, 469; corresponds with Jefferson Davis, 129–33, 151, 274–75; surrenders to Grant, 151, 152

Lee, Robert E., Jr., 357

Lee Memorial Address, 521

Lee Memorial Association, 520

Lennoxville, Que., 282, 288

Leonard, Caroline, 110

Library of Congress, Manuscript Division of, 147

Life of Jefferson Davis, The (Alfriend), 549

Limber, Jim, 141, 143

Lincoln, Abraham, 80, 103, 115, 122, 356, 468, 469; becomes President, 119; sends "relief" ships to Fort Sumter, 120

Locust Grove plantation, 348

London, England, 293, 294, 299, 312, 391–92, 396

Longstreet, James, 153, 240, 509

Lothian, Lord, 342

Louisiana, 439, 520

Lovell, John A., 281

Lubbock, Frank R., 165, 234, 392, 393, 471

Lyons, James, xiii

Lyons, Lord Richard B. P., 104, 105, 106

Lytton, Lord, 341, 342

McAlpin, Mrs. Henry, 198

McCaleb, David, 8

McCaleb, Florida Davis, 8, 13, 411, 412

Mackay, Charles, 304, 305, 311, 314, 328, 331

McRae, C. J., 170, 171, 194, 202, 281, 375

Maginnis, Frederick, 228, 248, 256

Magruder, Ella, 330, 331

Magruder, John B., 311, 330

Mallory, Stephen R., 209

Mann, A. Dudley, 295, 296, 393, 394, 435, 472, 512, 514; death of, 559
letters from: Davis, Jefferson, 299–300, 559; Dorsey, Sarah A., 478–79
letters to: Davis, Jefferson, 138; Davis, Varina, 298–99

Martin, Bessie, 473

Mason, Emily, 295, 297, 299, 393, 472, 507

Mason, James Murray, xiii, 272, 281, 282, 284, 288

Maury, Dabney, xxi, 241, 244

Meredith, Pinnie, 428, 433

Mexican War, 38, 40, 42, 43, 44, 46–47

Mexico, Southerners in, 238

Miles, Nelson A., xv, 167, 168, 173, 176, 182, 191, 211, 247

Minnegerode, Charles, 149, 151, 216, 247, 268, 285

Mississippi, 368; secession of, 120, 121, 122; destruction in, by Federal troops, 286; carpetbaggers in, 287; radicals win election in (1869), 327; Jefferson Davis Shrine in, 491

Mississippi Valley Society, 415, 424, 427, 439

Mississippi Volunteers, in Mexican War, 38, 40, 41, 43, 47

Mitchel, John, 189, 205

Mitchell, Charles, 42, 48

Mitchell, Joe, 128, 375, 401

Mitchell, Lise, *see* Hamer, Lise Mitchell

Monterey, Battle of, 42

Montgomery, Ala., 120, 121, 213

Montgomery, Ben, 244, 254, 265, 266, 282, 375, 419, 517
letters to: Davis, Joseph E., 283; Davis, Varina, 517–19

Montreal, Que., 281

Morgan, James, 143

Morse, M., 415

Napier, Lady, 97, 106

Napier, Lord, 96, 97, 100, 104, 105

National Intelligencer, 58

National Republican ticket, in Mississippi (1869), 327

Negus, Mrs. George, 495

New Orleans, La., 25, 29, 47, 112, 121, 125, 238, 261, 321, 376, 383, 433, 472; yellow fever in (1875), 487

North Carolina, 143, 158

Northrop, L. B., 498, 509

Northumberland, Duke of, 342

nullification, 33

O'Conor, Charles, 250, 254, 255, 267, 269, 270, 272, 288, 356, 504
Official Records, Jefferson Davis letters reproduced in, xviii, 121
Onsely, William Gore, 97
Oregon territory, 36, 37
Ould, Mattie, 403

Pacific, sinking of, 420
Page, Walter Hines, xvii
Paine, Thomas, 387
panic of 1873, 363–71 *passim,* 384
Paris, France, 295, 296, 297, 298, 392–95, 399
Payne, J. U., 425, 427, 499
Pegram, John, 263
Pemberton, James, 5, 9–10, 17, 42, 355
Pendleton, William Nelson, 510, 520, 525
Perkins, John, 64, 411
Petersburg, Va., 143
Picayune, New Orleans, 515, 553
Pierce, Franklin, xi, xiii, 67, 71, 72, 75, 76, 79, 87, 107
 letters to: Davis, Jefferson, 113–14; Davis, Varina, 271–72
Pittman, W. B., 381, 402, 411, 428, 479
Pius IX, Pope, 138; death of, 472, 473
Polk, James Knox, 20, 22, 35, 38, 53
Porter, Mrs. Gerald, 307
Pratt, Gov., 254, 255, 264, 265
Press, Philadelphia, 515
Preston, John, 204
Preston, William, 194, 204, 245
Prison Life of Jefferson Davis, The (Craven), 168
Pritchard, B. D., 166, 183, 478
Pulitzer, Joseph, xvii, xix, 552, 553, 559, 560, 562

Randolph, John, 370
Randolph-Macon College, 288
Reagan, John H., 165, 166, 209, 213, 273
Reconstruction, 286, 325, 422

Redpath, James, 560
Reed, William B., 267, 356
Republican, Savannah, 185
Richmond, Va., 121, 130, 136, 150, 268, 288, 521, 566; siege of, 138; evacuation of, 147; Lee questioned in trial at (Nov., 1867), 286
Rise and Fall of the Confederate Government (Davis), 500, 519; publication of, 508; letters of appreciation for, 509–11
Rob Roy, 309
Roosevelt, Theodore, 540
Rosemont, 10, 91, 372
Ross, Edmund G., 288
Rowland, Dunbar, xvii, 121
Royal Insurance Co., 388, 391
Ryan, Abram J., 503

St. Romain, Rossine, 393
Salisbury, Marquis, 550, 551
Santa Anna, Antonio López de, 44
Savannah, Ga., 184, 185, 192, 198, 201
scalawags, 321
Scotland, 304–12 *passim,* 328, 329, 330, 341, 399, 454
Scott, Walter, 306, 308, 309
Seaton, William W., 58, 59, 64
secession, 115, 119, 120
Seddon, James, 209
Semmes, Raphael, 136, 301, 377
Sewanee, University of the South at, 329, 330, 333, 351
Seward, William H., 97, 468, 469
Seymour, Thomas H., 113
Sherman, William T., 139, 140, 153, 155, 156, 158, 160, 192
Short History of the Confederate States of America (Davis), 560
Shrewsbury, Lord, 293, 294, 341
Slidell, John, 295, 298
Smith, Anna Davis, 12, 320, 321
Smith, Gerrit, 268
Smith, James, 305, 309, 387, 399
Smith, Joe, 191, 192, 401

Smith, Kirby, 195
Smithsonian Institution, 77, 78
South: conditions in, after War Between the States, 179, 199, 200, 205, 206–07, 218, 228; under martial law, 261, 262; Reconstruction in, 286, 325, 422; Jefferson Davis's triumphal tour through (1886), 547, 551–52
South Carolina, 120; secession of, 119
Southern Historical Society Papers, 468
Southern Life Insurance Co. of Memphis, 366
Southern Literary Messenger, 396, 549
Southern Pacific Railroad, 318
Speed, James, 174, 204, 212, 225, 227
Speight, Jesse, 44, 46, 53
Spotswood Hotel, 268, 269, 285
Stamps, Isaac Davis, 133, 254
Stamps, Lucinda Davis, 13, 138, 261, 320, 321; corresponds with Jefferson Davis, 39–40, 91–92, 361; death of, 372
Stamps, Mary Elizabeth Humphreys, 133, 254, 255, 256, 261, 332, 376, 383; corresponds with Jefferson Davis, 133–35; 321–22, 345, 353–54; financial difficulties of, 347, 348, 350
Stamps, William, 13, 354
Stanbery, Henry, 250
Stanton, Edwin, 167, 266, 268
Stedman, Gen., 173, 187, 192
Stephens, Alexander H., 139, 214, 237, 395, 468, 469, 481
Stewart, Mrs. John Wolcott, 56
Stirling Castle, 308
Stoess, Karl, 338, 339, 340, 386, 387
Stoess, Margaret Howell, 29, 30, 60, 80, 136, 194, 262, 338, 339, 341, 390, 437, 457, 506
Stringfellow, Frank, 480–84
Sutherland, Duke of, 342
Sutherlin, W. T., 147
Switzerland, 295, 296, 299

Tate, Allen, xiii
Taylor, Dick, 241, 245, 265, 267
Taylor, Margaret, 58, 61, 62
Taylor, Sarah Knox, see Davis, Sarah Knox Taylor
Taylor, Zachary, xi, xviii, 8, 10, 12, 46, 47, 58, 59, 62; letter to Jefferson Davis, 41; death of, 62–63
Tennessee, 324
Tenney, W. T., 503
Texas, 155, 158; Jefferson Davis welcomed in (1875), 409–10
Thompson, Jacob, 37, 115
Tilden, Samuel, 439
Tillman, Bettie, xvi, 540, 557
Times, London, 170
Times, New York, 415
Trainor, John C., 561
Trenholm, W. L., 149, 151
Tribune, New York, 119, 251, 253
Trigler, George, 54
Tulane University, 520; Howard Tilton Library at, 130
Tyler, John, 30

Van Benthuysen, Jefferson, 55
Van Benthuysen, William, 20, 21
Vicksburg, Miss., 90, 120, 129, 244, 410
Victoria, Queen, 550, 551
Vienna, Ga., 170
Virginia Military Institute, 362, 402, 403
Vizetelly, Frank, 165

Walker, Norman Stewart, 385, 386, 387, 388
Walthall, W. L., 446, 450, 451, 489, 490
War Between the States, 80, 81, 96, 103, 120
Washington, Ga., 152, 160, 165
Washington and Lee University, 362
Weber, Margaret J., 549
West Point, 8, 20, 73
Westminster, Marquess of, 342
Westminster Abbey, 295

Wheeler, Joseph, 140, 160, 240–41
White, Anastasia, 197
White, J. J., 526
White, Spillman, 10
Wilde, Oscar, xvii
Wilhelm I, of Germany, 479
Wilkinson, Alfred, 559, 560
Wilmer, Richard H., 533, 549
Wilson, Charles, 287
Wilson, J. H., 166
Wilson, Woodrow, 166
Winchester, George, 17
Wood, John Taylor, 81, 165–66, 171, 180

Wood, Nina, 76
Wood, Robert C., 81, 89
Wood, Sarah, 393
Woodville, Miss., 8, 9, 10, 91, 261, 320, 372
World, New York, 547, 552
Wright, Crafts J., 477, 478
Wright, J. S., 217

Yancey, William, 120
yellow fever epidemic, in South (1878), 487–90
Young, George H., 287, 327
Yulee, Mrs., 263, 264

Other titles of interest

**DESTRUCTION AND
RECONSTRUCTION**
Personal Experiences of the Civil War
General Richard Taylor
New introd. by T. Michael Parrish
288 pp. 80624-X $14.95

ABRAHAM LINCOLN
His Speeches and Writings
Edited by Roy P. Basler
Preface by Carl Sandburg
888 pp., 6 illus. 80404-2 $19.95

THE ANNALS OF THE CIVIL WAR
Written by Leading Participants
North and South
New introd. by Gary W. Gallagher
808 pp., 56 illus. 80606-1 $19.95

THE CIVIL WAR DAY BY DAY
An Almanac 1861-1865
E. B. Long with Barbara Long
1,135 pp., 8 pages of maps
80255-4 $19.95

THE RISE AND FALL OF THE
CONFEDERATE GOVERNMENT
Jefferson Davis
New foreword by James M. McPherson
Vol. I: 636 pp., 10 illus.
80418-2 $16.95
Vol. II: 696 pp., 26 illus.
80419-0 $16.95

THE STORY OF THE CONFEDERACY
Robert Selph Henry
526 pp. 80370-4 $14.95

THE WARTIME PAPERS OF
ROBERT E. LEE
Edited by Clifford Dowdey and
Louis H. Manarin
1,012 pp. 80282-1 $19.95

NARRATIVE OF MILITARY
OPERATIONS DURING
THE CIVIL WAR
General Joseph E. Johnston
644 pp., 21 illus.
80393-3 $17.95

PERSONAL MEMOIRS OF
U.S. GRANT
New introduction by
William S. McFeely
Critical Notes by E. B. Long
xxxi + 608 pp.
80172-8 $15.95

THE LINCOLN READER
Edited by Paul M. Angle
608 pp., 40 photos
80398-4 $16.95

Available at your bookstore

OR ORDER DIRECTLY FROM

DA CAPO PRESS

1-800-321-0050